MW00774089

The World Ahead

MARGARET MEAD: The Study of Contemporary Western Culture
Published in association with the Institute for Intercultural Studies
General Editor: William O. Beeman, Brown University

Volume 1
The Study of Culture at a Distance
Edited by Margaret Mead and Rhoda Métraux
With an Introduction by William O. Beeman

Volume 2
And Keep Your Powder Dry: An Anthropologist Looks at America
Margaret Mead
With an Introduction by Hervé Varenne

Volume 3
Russian Culture
Margaret Mead and Geoffrey Gorer
With an Introduction by Sergei Arutiunov

Volume 4
Themes in French Culture: A Preface to a Study of French Community
Margaret Mead and Rhoda Métraux
With an Introduction by Kathryn M. Anderson-Levitt

Volume 5
Studying Contemporary Western Society: Method and Theory
Margaret Mead
Edited and with an Introduction by William O. Beeman

Volume 6
The World Ahead: An Anthropologist Anticipates the Future
Margaret Mead
Edited, with an Introduction and Commentaries by Robert B. Textor

THE WORLD AHEAD

An Anthropologist Anticipates the Future

Edited, with an Introduction and Commentaries by
Robert B. Textor

Berghahn Books
NEW YORK • OXFORD

"Forethought is the basis of civilization."
Bertrand Russell

Published in 2005 by
Berghahn Books
www.berghahnbooks.com

© 2005 The Estate of Margaret Mead

Library of Congress Cataloging-in-Publication Data

Mead, Margaret, 1901-1978.
   The world ahead : an anthropologist anticipates the future / Margaret Mead ; edited by Robert B. Textor.
      p. cm. -- (Margaret Mead--researching Western contemporary cultures ; v. 6)
      Includes bibliographical references and index.
      ISBN 1-57181-817-0 (hardback : acid-free paper)
      1. Anthropology--Philosophy. 2. Anthropology--Forecasting. 3. Forecasting--Study and teaching. 4. Mead, Margaret, 1901-1978--Criticism and interpretation. I. Textor, Robert B. II. Title. III. Series

GN33.M43 2004
301'.01--dc22   2004055432

British Library Cataloguing in Publication Data

A catalogue record for this book is available
from the British Library.

Printed in the United States on acid-free paper.

CONTENTS

TWENTY-FIVE WRITINGS AND LECTURES
BY MARGARET MEAD

DEDICATION

This volume is dedicated to the memory of

EDWARD ARMAND FRIEND

Attorney and humanitarian

1921-2003

SERIES PREFACE

To celebrate the one-hundredth anniversary of the birth of Margaret Mead, Berghahn Books and the Institute for Intercultural Studies are proud to reissue a series of classic works. Written or inspired by Dr. Mead, the materials in these seven volumes investigate the study of contemporary Western cultures.

Most of the world today knows Margaret Mead through her earliest publications, *Coming of Age in Samoa, Growing Up in New Guinea, Sex and Temperament,* and numerous others that examine the peoples of the South Pacific, New Guinea, and Indonesia. Two decades after these pioneering works appeared, Dr. Mead had significantly turned to the study of the contemporary societies of Europe and the United States. Through this later work she gained her widest public audience and arguably became the best-known cultural anthropologist who has ever lived. All of these works on contemporary culture, a number of which were originally issued in limited editions, have long been out of print.

The volumes in this series are being issued under the general title Margaret Mead: The Study of Contemporary Western Cultures. It is thought that this will provide a clear identification for the series. However, a more accurate title for the series might be Margaret Mead and Friends. Mead was a great collaborator; in the seven volumes that compose the series, dozens of her contemporaries are represented. One volume, *Themes in French Culture:A Preface to a Study of French Culture* for example, has as its primary author Mead's close collaborator, the eminent anthropologist Rhoda Métraux, with Mead as second author. Another volume combines Mead's study *Soviet Attitudes toward Authority* with Geoffrey Gorer and John Rickman's *The People of Great Russia,* upon which Mead's study heavily draws.

Mead as solo author is represented in her pioneering critique of American life, *And Keep Your Powder Dry.* The last three volumes in the series, likewise compilations of Mead's solo writings, examine the methodology of studying contemporary cultures, the study of the future, and visual culture—all of which have lasting relevance for today's researchers.

The first volume, *The Study of Culture at a Distance,* is in many ways a key to the entire series. This book, edited by Mead and Metraux, is a "manual" showing the research methodologies of the group of scholars that surrounded them in New York during the 1940s and 1950s. It could be argued that Mead—along with Metraux, Ruth Benedict, Gregory Bateson, and Geoffrey Gorer, among others— was instrumental in founding a true school of anthropological research at that time. More than 120 scholars were associated with this group during its five-year formal existence from 1947-52 as the Columbia University Research in Contemporary Cultures (RCC) project. The number is even larger when one considers that the impetus for the research began in a more informal manner in 1940. Organized by Ruth Benedict, efforts were made to contribute to cultural understanding in order to meet the crisis of World War II. The Institute for Intercultural Studies was founded in 1944 to serve as a home for this research. Aside from Mead, Bateson, Benedict, Métraux, and Gorer, those whose names will be most familiar to anthropologists today are Conrad Arensberg, Alex Bavelas, Jane Belo, Ruth Bunzel, Erik Erikson, Paul Garvin, Ruth Landes, Eleanor Leacock, Vera Schwarz, Y. C. Wang, Eric Wolf, Martha Wolfenstein, and Mark Zborowski. Volumes two through seven of this series all derive in one way or another from the work of this research group. Had the McCarthy era not intervened in the 1950s to spread suspicion and doubt about the virtues of trying to understand foreign cultures on their own terms, this group might still be active today.

One of the most exciting aspects of bringing these works to life again has been to realize the remarkably modern quality of the methodologies developed by Mead and her associates during and immediately following World War II. This group was the first to adopt many of the now commonplace analytic tools of scholars who today identify themselves with cultural studies and media studies. The analysis of film, literature, and public imagery in particular was thoroughly and exhaustively explored in this early research. Although the theoretical goals of Mead and her contemporaries often differed from those of many current students of culture, their methodologies and clear analytic vision could be emulated with much profit by today's researchers.

In fact, their contributions have inspired three generations of intellectuals, though often those who have been influenced by their work are unaware of the source of that influence. Whereas Mead and her colleagues are recognized as public celebrities of the past, among anthropologists today there is a vaguely patronizing attitude toward their work. In short, their intellectual achievements do not receive the attention they richly deserve. Why this is so is a poignant question. It is hoped that the reissue of these important works will help to remedy this oversight.

Acknowledgments and Dedication

I am pleased to acknowledge the help of the following people in making this series possible: Matilde Andrade, Mary Catherine Bateson, Shannon Carson, Wilton Dillon, Frank Farris, Shirley Gordon, Richard Gould, Katherine Grimaldi, Karen Iny, Philip Leis, Anne Brownell Sloane, and Mary Wolfskill and the staff of the Library of Congress Documents Division where the Margaret Mead Archives are currently housed. I would like to dedicate this series to my mother, Florence Lucille O'Kieffe Beeman, who, as a highly successful professional sociologist and social worker, led me to the works of Margaret Mead and her contemporaries, and ultimately to my own profession as an anthropologist.

William O. Beeman

INTRODUCTION
Robert B. Textor

Margaret Mead, during her long and fruitful career, made persistent efforts to anticipate the future and to alert leaders and citizens of the need to make preparations in the short term, so that they might realize desired outcomes, and avert undesired ones, in the longer term. Although Mead practiced anthropology in many modes, her work in the mode that has, since her death, come to be termed "Anticipatory Anthropology" is of special interest because of her pioneering role from a remarkably early date. It is an honor to edit and provide commentary for this volume, which presents, here for the first time, a collection of Margaret Mead's truly Anticipatory Anthropology.

Out of Mead's prodigious output of writings and lectures, which numbered in the thousands, this volume presents a selection of twenty-five items judged to be most directly relevant to Anticipatory Anthropology. The major selection was made by the overall editor of this Mead Centennial Series, William O. Beeman, who selected some thirty-odd items, which the two of us then further winnowed to twenty-five. Our selection procedure gave priority to those of Mead's writings and lectures that treated the future systematically—that is, explicitly, comprehensively and coherently. Beyond this criterion, our procedure sought to do credit to the wide variety of problems she addressed, and to minimize redundancy.

The items we selected date from 1943 to 1977—from long before most social scientists showed any serious interest in the systematic study of the longer-range sociocultural future, until one year before Mead's death. Of these twenty-five items, twelve appeared originally in published form, and thirteen were lectures, symposium presentations, or, in one case, a testimony to the United States Congress. The twenty-five items are arrayed chronologically, so that readers may more readily understand and appreciate both the historical context in which each item appears, and the general pattern of Margaret Mead's evolution as a scholar, thinker, and public anthropologist. I have written a separate commentary for each item, in which I have tried to make my remarks appropriately appreciative, yet fair and rigorous.

Notes for this section begin on page 29.

If Mead were alive today, I am quite sure she would enjoy the former and demand the latter.

Anticipatory Anthropology is seen here not as a special subfield of anthropology, but rather as a mode of gathering and using available data, information and knowledge to assess future possibilities. Cultural anthropologists have long had expertise in analyzing the past career and present status of Culture X. Anticipatory Anthropology calls for them to use available knowledge of Culture X, plus ethnographic inquiry as appropriate, to anticipate or visualize possible alternative future paths for that same culture. To put it in simplest possible terms, Anticipatory Anthropology is a disciplined effort to discover what members of a society want and fear—as well as the sacrifices they are willing to make, and the initiatives they are prepared to take, toward realizing the outcomes they want, and preventing the ones they fear. Put another way, Anticipatory Anthropology (like the general interdisciplinary field of Futures Studies) is about the possible, the probable, and the preferable. The "possible" refers to what could happen. The "probable" refers to (among other things) what would likely happen under appropriate circumstances subject to human control—such as political will, leadership skill, resource allocation, regulation, and education. The "preferable" is a normative judgment as to what should happen—by the values of an interviewee, a panel of citizens, or the like.

Anticipation is here seen as a kind of "soft" prediction: broad, approximate, conditional, corrigible, and usually focused on the middle range of the future—say, the next five to twenty-five or so years. It is thus distinct from the more precise and shorter-ranged "hard" prediction of the economist with respect to the future price of a stock, or of the political scientist with respect to voting behavior in an upcoming election. It is also distinct from sheer wish-fulfilling speculation, magical thinking, science fiction, or romantic fantasizing.[1]

MARGARET MEAD'S HISTORIC CONTRIBUTION

Mead's contributions to anthropology and the social sciences were enormous and varied. Since there are others much more qualified than I to assess the variety and totality of her contributions, in this volume I shall limit my comments rather narrowly to her contributions to Anticipatory Anthropology.

Mead's Ameliorative Drive

Margaret Mead's anticipatory efforts were deeply rooted in her drive to ameliorate the ills of society, a drive that seems to date back to her early adolescence, and that, as her career progressed, harnessed more and more of her energy and expertise as an anthropologist. In Volume One of the present Mead Centennial Series, the editor, William O. Beeman, puts it this way: "Mead believed in the amelioration of human life through increased understanding between groups....Thus, discovering and reporting central truths about different societies was not just an intellectual exercise. It was something that would ultimately make the world better" (Mead and Métraux 2000: xxx).

Mead was, of course, hardly alone among anthropologists in harboring an ameliorative drive. Throughout the twentieth century many other cultural anthropologists also felt a sense of urgency to use their expertise to protect many of the tribal and peasant cultures that had become endangered—all too often because of mistreatment or exploitation by members of more powerful societies. Sometimes these protective efforts were successful, but often they were not. When they were not, it was often because such efforts sought to minimize or even prevent contact between the local culture and outside systems—rather than to work out ways to confront those systems effectively.

Such a "keep out" attitude, often verging on sentimentality, was not shared by Mead. Though she certainly respected the integrity of individual cultures, she also recognized that change was inevitable and not always bad. She did not flinch from the challenge of working with local people, when so invited, to help them map out coping strategies to defend themselves against negative outside influences, while also selectively and adaptively borrowing those aspects of outside cultures that would be genuinely beneficial. Mead's strong ameliorative drive led her, in 1941, to become a founding member of the Society for Applied Anthropology, an organization that thrives to this day. In 1949 she was elected President of that organization, the first woman to be so honored.

World War II Experiences

The onset of World War II saw an important evolution of Mead's interests and influence. Like many other Americans, she felt a strong need to defeat the Axis powers, and offered her expert services to the U.S. government, where they were eagerly welcomed. Numerous other anthropologists did the same, including Mead's mentor and friend, Ruth Benedict.

Those were hectic times. The government constantly found itself in urgent need of anthropological advice as to how to deal effectively not just with small non-literate cultures in battle areas (e.g. in Oceania or New Guinea) but also with large national cultures. This need for advice often involved the cultures of peoples living in enemy-occupied lands—whether enemies (e.g. Japan), friends (e.g. France), or neutrals (e.g. Thailand). Such lands were of course not available for fieldwork, so Benedict, Mead, and their associates had to rely either on existing published knowledge, or on a new genre that came to be termed "the study of culture at a distance." Thus the first systematic effort to think anthropologically about the cultures of large modern nation states coincided with the effort to carry out such studies at a distance. This new genre was based on a variety of non-conventional data sources then available in the U.S., such as interviews with natives of Culture X then resident in the U.S., or literature and films about Culture X.[2]

Ruth Benedict, Margaret Mead, and their associates began work in this new genre at Columbia University in 1940, more than a year before Pearl Harbor, in a program that came to be known as the "Research in Contemporary Cultures" (RCC) program. Original funding came from the U.S. Navy Department's Office of Naval Research. In 1944 these efforts at studying culture at a distance, which eventually evolved to include much non-war-related research, were integrated into a new "Institute for Intercultural Studies" (IIS). After the war, in the period from 1947 to 1952, the RCC program was formalized and greatly expanded, eventually involving the input of as many as 120 social scientists of various disciplines. It thus stands as the largest anthropologically-inspired and -led interdisciplinary research effort ever undertaken anywhere, before or since.[3]

From their earliest days, the RCC and the IIS, by the very nature of their assignments, were seriously concerned with anticipating alternative futures. William O. Beeman, for example, notes that this research effort "resulted in a number of significant governmental policy decisions, including the decision not to execute the Emperor of Japan at the end of the war" (Mead and Métraux 2000: xvi).[4]

Another wartime example of Mead's concern with amelioration, application and anticipation is seen in Volume Two of this Mead Centennial Series (Mead 2000). This book is not as rigorous as Mead's other works, since she produced it in just six weeks, out of a sense of great urgency. As is made clear in the commentary by Volume Two's editor, the French-born scholar of American society Hervé Varenne, this book was certainly no ordinary ethnography. It was as much about what Mead wanted the American sociocultural system to become, as it was about the existing realities of that system (2000: xii, xvi). Mead's purpose was not just to inform Americans about an anthropologist's analysis of her own culture, but also to motivate her American readers to make the sacrifices necessary to win the war, by suggesting a better future—an inspiring national "optimistic scenario"—that would be realizable once the war was won. The ensuing events of that war—and especially the atomic bomb and its catastrophic effects on Hiroshima and Nagasaki—changed the world forever. All this stimulated, even more, Mead's ameliorative urge to "win the peace" and build a better and safer future for the entire world.

Manus and "New Lives For Old"

As influential as the war and the atomic bomb were in stimulating Mead's development as an applied and public anthropologist, it must be noted that these experiences were, after all, shared by all the other anthropologists of her generation—even though few of them may have responded as vigorously as she did to the vast new challenges presented. In addition, Mead possessed one powerful experience that was utterly unique to her, and sprang from her next to last major fieldwork effort, summarized in her book, *New Lives for Old* (Mead 1956). This fieldwork took place in 1953 among the 4,000 or so Manus people of Great Admiralty Island in the Bismarck Archipelago, now part of the Republic of Papua New Guinea. The 1953 fieldwork was a re-study of the same people she had first gotten to know twenty-five years earlier, when she and her then husband, Reo Fortune, had done fieldwork there. Since the end of the war in 1945, she had been hearing rumors of significant changes in the intervening years, and was eager to see these changes for herself. On this second trip she would be getting re-acquainted with her Manus friends, many of whom she had known as children during the earlier study. This time she was joined by two younger anthropological colleagues, Theodore and Lenore Schwartz.

Upon her return, it was immediately obvious to Mead that in the intervening twenty-five years Manus culture had changed almost beyond recognition as a consequence of the island having been used during the war as a major staging base by Allied, principally American, troops. During 1944 and 1945, as many as one million American servicemen had passed through Manus. They had created airfields, set up organizations, hired local labor, and built barracks, mess halls, and hospitals. They had thus demonstrated to the local people, day after day, a completely different way of life. Here had been a "culture contact" situation so powerful and all-encompassing as to have brought about previously-unimaginable changes in Manus behavior and aspirations.

However, as anthropologists are well aware, externally-induced changes in behavior and aspirations do not always eventuate into stable and positive changes in the local sociocultural system. Often the opposite is true. Sometimes the result is cultural decay and disastrous social anomie. However, this was not so with the Manus. There, a mere eight years after the war, Mead found vast and apparently stable changes in basic Manus social organization and cultural value patterns. The explanation for these changes lay not just in the American stimulus. It also lay, as Mead is at pains to explain, in the nature of the pre-existing Manus sociocultural system—plus, extremely fortuitously, a gifted charismatic local individual, Mr. Paliau, to lead the change process. The specifics are complex, but Mead's own summary will suffice here: "This book—the record of a people who have moved faster than any people of whom we have records, a people who have moved in fifty years from darkest savagery to the twentieth century, men who have skipped over thousands of years of history in just the last twenty-five years—is offered as food for the imagination of Americans...." (1956: 21).

The Manus experience, unique to history, and unique to Mead among all the world's social scientists, was clearly a powerful stimulus to her ameliorative thinking. It exposed her to a radical, "all at once" model for sociocultural change, in contrast to the more conventional models calling for "step by step" incremental change. It gave her a wider angle of vision than most of her colleagues, and a deeper appreciation of the possibility that positive sociocultural change could, in some circumstances, occur more rapidly than previously supposed. This is evident in many of the writings and lectures presented in this book.

Mead's Anticipatory Drive

Amelioration and anticipation are close partners. When one desires amelioration as ardently as Mead did, one quite naturally finds oneself developing some kind of vision, or "optimistic scenario," about how life could and should be made better in the future. An ameliorator, to be effective, must also be an anticipator.

What makes Mead's early emergence as an anticipator especially notable is that it ran counter to the prevailing spirit of anthropology during the 1920s and 1930s, when Mead came of age as an anthropologist. Most anthropologists of that day were far more interested in the past, the "ethnographic present," or the actual present—than in the future. Anthropology, as the great Alfred L. Kroeber used to say as late as the 1950s, was essentially a historical discipline. Mead shared this interest in history—but she was also interested in the future.

Mead was, of course, not the only anthropologist of her generation to engage in anticipation. Others also did, especially a number of those who defined themselves as "applied" anthropologists. However, most applied anthropologists of that period seem to have been content with relatively circumscribed anticipatory efforts—often limited in scope primarily to the particular innovation they were attempting to promote. Efforts at broad-scale systematic anticipation addressing alternative futures for whole sociocultural systems, and spelling out complex processes of change, were rare. In this more ambitious style of anticipation, Mead was outstanding.

Final Decades

In the final two or three decades of her life Mead's ameliorative, applied and anticipatory activities increased exponentially. Her personal networks with people from many different nationalities and disciplines expanded dramatically. As carefully chronicled by Dillon (1980), the reach, scope, and ambition of her attempts to better the human condition through politics and government were impressive, and certainly unique in the history of American anthropology. By the 1960s Mead had become one of the most famous women in the world—perhaps *the* most famous. She clearly saw her fame as a gateway to her influence, and her influence as a gateway to her service to society. This service was recognized shortly after her death, when President Jimmy Carter awarded her the Presidential Medal of Freedom, America's highest civilian award.

It seems clear that Margaret Mead's strong interest in improving the human condition sprang in part from her early religious enculturation. At the age of eleven, against the wishes of her atheist parents, she volunteered for instruction and confirmation in the Episcopal Church, an organization in which she remained active throughout her life. When the World Council of Churches sought her advice, she gave it. Upon her death, she received the equivalent of a state funeral at the National Cathedral in Washington and was buried in the Pennsylvania parish where she was confirmed.[5]

MEAD AND FUTURES STUDIES

This volume takes the position that almost any anthropologist who wishes to work in the anticipatory mode, could do so if he or she wished. At the same time, an anthropologist such as Mead, who becomes seriously involved in such anticipatory work, sooner or later

comes to be regarded as also being a "futurist," that is, a serious specialist in the interdisciplinary field of Futures Studies.

Emergence of the Future Studies Movement

The last ten years of Mead's life were the years when the Futures
Studies movement, as we know it today, took flight. Although precursors to Futures Studies date back at least to the nineteenth century in Europe and America, today many futurists date the launch-
ing of this hybrid field and movement to the 1960s. For example,
the World Future Society was established in the U.S. in 1967, and
during the ensuing twelve years its membership grew from a few
hundred to nearly 60,000. This movement, and its social, scientific,
and philosophical foundations, are comprehensively and accessibly
summarized in Bell (1997: 1–72). I strongly recommend this two-vol-
ume work as the best single introduction to Futures Studies for the
serious scholar.

Although Mead was, as far as I know, not visibly active in the
affairs of the World Future Society, she clearly was a part of this general movement, and in some ways ahead of it. For example, according
to her associate and friend Wilton Dillon, as early as the mid-1950s
she was publicly advocating that universities ought to have a Chair of
the Future, just as they might have one for the Middle Ages or Classical Greece (personal communication, 2003). It is no accident that, of
the twenty-five items that appear in this book, five date from 1968
alone, and another eleven between 1969 and 1977.

Mead's Recognition as a Futurist

While it is easy, with the benefit of hindsight, to criticize some of
Mead's anticipatory work, I believe we should credit her for being a
full generation ahead of almost all of her contemporaries. In her pre-
science, her wisdom, and her willingness to risk ridicule in order to
proactively serve the broad needs of society, she exemplified a true
humane commitment. Most of the issues she raised remain relevant
today as we continue to look ahead.

This positive judgment is shared by one of Futures Studies' most
respected intellectual leaders, Alvin Toffler, who has written many
influential books on the future. In 1972 he edited a volume entitled,
The Futurists (Toffler 1972). In it he described the activities and successes of the world's most respected futurists, and in each case
included excerpts from their publications. Toffler identified twenty-
three such individuals. He emphasized that these futurists, being
unusually creative thinkers with unusually broad interests, were difficult to categorize, except under very broad rubrics, of which he pro-

vided three, as follows. First, there were eight "scientists," namely Arthur C. Clarke, Olaf Helmer, Herman Kahn with Anthony J. Wiener, Theodore J. Gordon, M. S. Iyengar, I. Bestuzhev-Lada, and Erich Jantsch. Second, there were eight "philosophers and planners": Kenneth E. Boulding, Yujiro Hayashi, Daniel Bell, Ossip Flechtheim, Bertrand deJouvenel, Fred L. Polak, John Wren-Lewis, and R. Buckminster Fuller. And finally, there were seven "social critics," in which category Toffler places himself and Margaret Mead, along with Paul Ehrlich, John McHale, Marshall McLuhan, Robert Jungk, and Arthur I. Waskow.

On this list, Mead is the only female and the only anthropologist. Toffler estimated the mean age of these twenty-three individuals to be about fifty-five. Mead at the time was 70, and had by then been doing futures-type work for thirty years. In summarizing Mead's contribution, Toffler states:

> In this striking chapter from her book *Culture and Commitment*, the famed anthropologist argues that we have shifted from a culture that is "post-figurative" (one in which the young learn from the old) to one that is "cofigurative" (one in which both children and adults learn chiefly from their peers). She appealed for a "prefigurative" culture in which, as the future explodes into the present, the old learn to learn from the young. Her voice, crossing generational and academic lines, has been influential in preparing the soil for the futurists (Toffler 1972: 27).

MEAD'S INTELLECTUAL APPROACH AND EXPRESSIVE STYLE

Many of my comments on Mead's approach to, and style of, the art of anticipation are to be found in the commentaries I provide for the twenty-five items in this book. Here, however, are a few general comments.

With respect to her intellectual approach, one notes that some of Mead's items are systematically analytical, and organized into sections. Other items, even long ones, lack any sectioning whatsoever. A number of her items—especially those based on oral presentations—have a spontaneous and "notional" spirit about them—supplying (and even overstating) powerful ideas and suggestions, though sometimes not tracing out all their major implications.

With respect to expressive style, one should bear in mind, first of all, that Margaret Mead valued the English language as a thing of beauty. She was a serious and published poet, and some of her anthropological writings—the more "humanistic" ones—have an almost poetic ring. While some of her items are clearly the result of careful, deliberate writing and re-writing, others seem hurriedly produced, doubtless under the pressure of a heavy schedule of other commitments. But always, she tried hard to communicate not only to fellow scientists, but also accessibly to the interested general public.

Holistic, Non-Quantitative Approach

Like most cultural anthropologists, Mead looked at cultures as whole entities. For example, her Manus report, *New Lives for Old* (Mead 1956), deals with overall changes in every major aspect of the Manus sociocultural system. As she turned her analytical and anticipatory attention increasingly to the entire world, this holistic approach quite naturally evolved into a general systems approach, an interest that led her to become one of the founders of the Society for General Systems Research, and eventually its President.

As indicated in my commentary on Item 1974a, Mead's work in general systems theory brought her into collaboration with a variety of renowned scientists, many of whom were highly quantitative in orientation. In this respect, Mead is the exception. She limits her anticipatory work to qualitative analyses, and refrains from quantitative analyses even in those situations where it would obviously be useful—e.g., in dealing with the world's demographic growth.

Since Mead was known to be familiar with quantitative approaches, a reader of today might wonder why she avoided using them. Part of the explanation lies in the nature of the fieldwork that she—like most other cultural anthropologists educated before World War II—carried out. Typically, the anthropologist journeyed to a small non-literate sociocultural group, often one that had had limited contact with the wider world. Ordinarily, there was no local quantitative data base to build upon—no reliable local census figures, no systematic health statistics, no cadastral record of land use rights. And what is more, the fieldwork period was short, perhaps less than a year, and almost always less than two years. Much of this valuable time was necessarily devoted to settling in, getting organized, developing rapport, and so on and so forth. In addition, the anthropologist, ideally, would make a concerted effort to develop some facility with the local language. For all such pragmatic reasons, it is not surprising that Mead, most of whose fieldwork was carried out in a half dozen such non-literate cultures (the single major exception being that of Bali), does not use a quantitative approach in her anticipatory work.

In addition to the above pragmatic reasons, there is the more basic intellectual reason that anthropologists of the day were more interested in variation between the cultural population under study, and other such populations—than in variation within the population under study. So, the anthropologist would tend to concentrate his or her efforts on developing a good overall understanding of the local culture as a whole, which tends to be a largely qualitative undertaking.

Non-Use of the Scenario Method

I find it regrettable that, with just one partial exception (Item 1968c), Mead did not use the scenario method—doubtless because this method did not come into widespread use, outside of the community of Futures Studies specialists, until after her death. Thus Mead missed the opportunity to take full advantage of a method of basic importance, as explained by futures scholar and sociologist Wendell Bell:

> The end product of all the methods of futures research is basically the same: a scenario, a story about the future, usually including a story about the past and present. Often, it is a story about alternative possibilities for the future, each having different probabilities of occurring under different conditions. Also, it often includes goals and values, evaluating alternative futures as to their desirability or undesirability" (1997: 317).

Use of the scenario method would have greatly enriched the comprehensiveness, and enhanced the coherence, of many of Mead's anticipatory statements. It would have led her to be more explicit in fleshing out processes of change, and more concrete in identifying key driving forces, and specifying how these forces would interact. If she had lived a few years longer, it is highly plausible that she would have started using scenarios and—given her rich background, brilliant imagination, and powerful writing skills—that she would thus have made an even greater contribution to Anticipatory Anthropology.[6]

The Meadian "We"

Through the years, Mead's writings reveal an unusual and remarkable penchant for using "we," "us," and "our." This usage merits some exploration. To begin with, it must be emphasized that the Meadian "we" is not the polite editorial "we" invoked to express a personal opinion in mock-modest fashion. Rather, her "we" seems to mean, essentially, "Margaret Mead plus other concerned, informed, and humanely inclined citizens of both the society concerned, and of the world." This concept of the "we" is consistent with her career-long preference for working with teams of people from various disciplines and cultural origins, as a way of harnessing their energies toward a common purpose, and learning from them which of her own ideas they deemed valid or invalid, and why.

Psychologically, Mead's "we" is seen by her daughter, Mary Catherine Bateson, as relating to the tradition of the religious sermon. It is an inclusive and persuasive "we" – we who are here united. It seeks to persuade the listener by projecting the probability of agreement (personal communication, 2003). Sociologically, Mead's "we" seems generally to refer to, and address, people who were quite well educated and financially stable. Though her ethical and emotional concerns were certainly with the less fortunate people of the world, her immediate operative "we" tends to apply primarily to those among her likely audience who possess the knowledge and sociopolitical power needed to effectuate change.

The sum total of all of Mead's "we-s" is truly impressive, as is suggested by the size of the Margaret Mead Collection in the Library of Congress, created in connection with the Mead Centennial. Remarkably, this Collection is the largest of all the numerous collections to be found in that great national repository, memorializing so many important historical figures. The Mead Collection contains more than half a million individual items: publications, speeches, fieldnotes, data files, memos, and letters written by Mead, often jointly with one or another of her numerous "we" cohorts.

The spirit of the Meadian "we" is also found in the arrangements made to celebrate her Centennial, in which a Margaret Mead Awards Program was established, with the following Meadian quotation as leitmotif: "Never doubt that a small group of thoughtful, committed individuals can change the world, indeed it's the only thing that ever has." The Margaret Mead web site describes these awards as follows:

As part of the Margaret Mead Centennial celebration, the Institute for Intercultural Studies and *Whole Earth* magazine joined together to honor small groups of thoughtful, committed citizens who have changed the world. The first awards were given in mid-1999, ...and continued through the Centennial. These awards honor organizations that reflect Mead's broad sense of the relevance of anthropology to social action: groups that have demonstrated effective, imaginative, and compassionate actions on race, gender, culture, environmental justice, child rearing, and self-empowerment within communities. Mary Catherine Bateson, president of the IIS and Mead's daughter, says: "We recognized groups of committed citizens who have created a level of community awareness that did not exist previously, and who have invented new social forms that can teach and inform other communities. We found organizations that have done things that can be replicated, that have wide resonance, and demonstrate the choices we have in shaping cultures for the future. My mother would have appreciated that." [7]

Limited Use of a "Political Economy" Approach

The above sentiments are, in my view, highly appropriate. At the same time, I would be even more satisfied with Mead's approach to Anticipatory Anthropology if she had devoted as much attention to the macro-political and -economic variables, as she did to the psychological and micro-sociological. Although she was clearly opposed to the exploitation of peoples without power—by their colonial rulers or anyone else—in her publications she paid less attention to such matters than would many other anthropologists, especially those professionally educated subsequent to World War II. My personal bias would favor a considerably greater emphasis on a "political economy" approach, and a considerably stronger focus on such phenomena as the exploitation of nation by nation, race by race, gender by gender, and class by class.

The twenty-five items in this book, beginning on page 35, will enable you to come to your own judgments about Mead's intellectual approach and expressive style. In these items you will meet the disciplined scientist Margaret Mead, who became only the third woman to be elected President of the American Anthropological Association in its first 60 years, and who later crowned her career by serving as President of the American Association for the Advancement of Science. You will also meet the humane, imaginative Margaret Mead, who was regarded as one of the world's pioneer futurists.

EDITOR'S PERSONAL CONTACTS WITH DR. MEAD

In this section I will briefly describe my contacts with Margaret Mead, both to shed light on the energetic, fascinating, and generous person I found her to be, and to provide you with a basis to judge whether I am being adequately fair and objective in my commentaries. I do this in the spirit of Mead's consistent advocacy, to her students and colleagues, of what she called "disciplined subjectivity."

My personal contacts with Margaret Mead were in fact very few. I was never her student and never worked for or with her on any project. Our relationship was based simply on her interest in, and willingness to help, my professional work. I was thus just one of many younger scholars whom she reached out to encourage.

Contacts Concerning Cross-Cultural Statistical Analysis

The summer of 1964 found Mead, myself, and hundreds of other anthropologists from many countries, in Moscow to attend the quadrennial meeting of the International Union of Anthropological and Ethnological Sciences. I was on the program to present briefly the rationale and methodology of a book then in preparation, entitled *A Cross-Cultural Summary* (Textor 1967).[8] My presentation was scheduled for 8:00 AM, and I wondered whether anybody would bother to attend, given the early hour and the conference's myriad other papers, attractions, and distractions. Suddenly, to my shock, a few minutes before 8:00, in walked Margaret Mead and her friend, the late Rhoda Métraux. I felt flattered that anyone so senior would take the trouble to come to hear my presentation—but also a bit unnerved, since it was common gossip that "Margaret doesn't like statistics and doesn't approve of the Human Relations Area Files system." Anyway, I went ahead and gave my paper. At the end of the session, Margaret Mead came up to me and proceeded to shock me once again. She informed me that she highly approved of what I was doing, and that my method allowed her, and people of her persuasion, to make good sense out of the Human Relations Area Files' cross-cultural statistical approach.

The *Cross-Cultural Summary* could not have been produced without the computer. In 1964 there were many anthropologists who viewed this new device with suspicion, and some, even with hostility. But not Mead. Despite the fact that she had never used a computer—and, as it turned out, never did—she saw merit in this particular use of that new tool, and offered her support. Not only was I grateful; I was highly impressed and remain so today, four decades later. [9]

In conjunction with the Moscow conference, the Soviet tourist agency, Intourist, arranged bargain tours for the foreign anthropologists to visit Leningrad, and also Uzbekistan. Many of us took advantage of these bargains, including Mead and myself. I thus had a chance to become better acquainted with her. Two impressions remain deep in my memory. First, there was her immense physical and intellectual energy. She was then 62 years of age, but threw herself into these tours with vigor, despite a weak and bandaged ankle. On several occasions she assumed a sort of "school-marm" stance toward me, pushing me to learn as much as possible about Russia while I had the chance, and to "develop plausible hypotheses" about Russian society and culture. At first I found this a bit gratuitously intrusive and vaguely annoying, but I soon began to enjoy it. Margaret had, after all, made a serious study (at a distance) of Russian culture and personality, and it was soon clear that she really did have a lot to teach me.[10]

My second recollection is of Margaret's pragmatic commitment to liberal political goals. It so happened that our visit to the Soviet Union coincided with the now-infamous Tonkin Gulf Incident, which President Lyndon B. Johnson promptly proceeded to use as grounds for his escalating the American military involvement in Vietnam. When the news broke in the Moscow media, I was outraged (as were many other anthropologists specialized on Southeast Asia) and I mentioned to Margaret that I was considering "going public" with my criticism right then and there. Once again she assumed the school-marm stance, saying something like: "Bob, you will do no such thing. My God, do you realize who the alternative to Johnson is?"—meaning, of course, that year's Republican presidential nominee, Senator Barry Goldwater. There followed a heated discussion, I taking the position that "Look, character does count; this man is not to be trusted; and he is going to cause great loss of life," and Margaret taking the position "Yes, but—under Goldwater it would only be worse." In the end, I decided to wait until I returned to the U.S. to vent my wrath, feeling that for an American to do so in a foreign country, especially the Soviet Union, would not be appropriate. Clearly, she influenced my decision.

Contacts Concerning the Peace Corps

I had only one other significant contact with Margaret, and that concerned a book I wrote and edited, *Cultural Frontiers of the Peace Corps* (Textor et al. 1966). This was a collection of reports on early Peace Corps experiences in thirteen host countries located in Asia, Africa, or Latin America, each written by a social scientist or historian with special knowledge of that country. Knowing of Margaret's long-standing interest in applied anthropology, I sent her a copy of our manuscript and requested that she consider writing the Foreword. I then waited some while for an answer. Finally it came—from Aghios Nikolaos, Crete, where she was vacationing and writing. It was a cablegram that said simply, "Will write foreword. Mead."

Some time later the manuscript came back by airmail. To my amazement, Margaret had gone over every page of that bulky manuscript, and written in her suggestions and corrections on perhaps one page out of every three or four. Then, just to make sure I did not overlook any of her suggestions, she had placed a paper clip on every one of those marked pages! At this point, though I did not quite realize it at the time, my contributors and I had become part of a Meadian "we."

In writing her Foreword, Margaret correctly but modestly identifies herself as "an anthropologist who has been concerned with the development of the theory and practice of applied anthropology since its beginning efforts just before World War II" (Textor et al 1966: ix). She then offers an endorsement of our work which also reveals something of her own self-concept as a public anthropologist:

> The aim of writing so that what is said will be exact, meaningful and acceptable to everyone, everywhere, is one that anthropologists have tried to fulfill only in the last twenty-five years. The necessary skills are exceedingly difficult to acquire, and as yet we do not wholly understand them. But in this book, the editor and the authors have made a mighty effort in the direction of the purposeful inclusion of the whole potential audience in order that, in the end, each reader will appreciate the achievements and wish to correct the defects in the still developing program of the Peace Corps (Textor et al 1966: vii).[11]

Thereafter, until the end of her life, I would see Margaret at annual meetings, and we would have an occasional exchange of letters about routine professional matters. That was the extent of my subsequent contact with her.[12]

This concludes my Introduction. For the reader anxious to get to the heart of this book, I recommend turning immediately to Margaret Mead's twenty-five writings and lectures, starting on page 35. For those interested in the rationale of Anticipatory Anthropology, as it has evolved in the twenty-five years since Margaret Mead's death, as well as in her legacy for the future of this emerging mode of inquiry, I recommend first reading the Appendix to this Introduction, and then turning to her writings and lectures.

APPENDIX: THE RATIONALE AND FUTURE OF ANTICIPATORY ANTHROPOLOGY

Margaret Mead died in 1978, and in the quarter century since then the interdisciplinary field of Futures Studies has matured greatly, as have certain related aspects of anthropology. This Appendix examines a few of these changes that I consider most relevant to gaining a better appreciation of the Mead legacy, as well as a deeper understanding of the rationale of Anticipatory Anthropology and its potential for serving society in an era of ever more rapid global change.

Ethnocentrism and Tempocentrism

As background for appreciating the value of Mead's contributions, it is helpful to start by briefly examining two "centrisms": ethnocentrism and what is here termed "tempocentrism." As used here, ethnocentrism refers to one's being excessively centered in one's own culture, and tempocentrism to one's being excessively centered in one's own timeframe. Most humans are subject, most of the time, to both centrisms. Both have the advantage of providing considerable short-run psychological comfort—although sometimes, as I will discuss, at a huge long-run personal or social price.

Ethno- and tempocentrism are close psychological cousins. One of the first things the anthropologist notices about the people he or she studies in the field, is how automatically they take for granted—and invoke—the premises and values of their own culture. Similarly, one of the first things the professional futurist notices about a group of people he or she studies, is how automatically they take for granted the situation, premises, expectations and values of their own timeframe—even when that timeframe is inappropriate for the purpose at hand. Tempocentrism makes it harder to pay critical yet imaginative attention to future possibilities and probabilities, and hence harder for individuals, communities or societies to realize future opportunities and avoid future dangers.

Both centrisms are frequently characterized by "secondary ignorance," that is, ignorance of the very existence (and importance) of one's own ignorance. Futurists frequently find people whom they judge to be not only tempocentric, but also unaware of their own tempocentrism. Likewise, cultural anthropologists frequently find people whom they judge to be both ethnocentric and unaware of their own ethnocentrism. When such "secondarily ignorant" people hold positions of political or economic power, they can do great harm.

In today's and tomorrow's dangerous world, it is essential to find ways to transcend both of these centrisms. But the task is daunting, because both types of mis-centeredness do in fact function to promote a sense of psychological security by providing the individual with a firm, taken-for-granted framework for perceiving, thinking, feeling, believing and evaluating. Indeed, a person might be highly intelligent and generally rational, and yet so prize this sense of security that they will strongly resist—consciously or subconsciously—any efforts to suggest that they might be mis-centered.

A costly example of ethnocentrism in action is the Vietnam War, during which much official American policy was based on historical ignorance, which in turn was deeply rooted in racial biases toward Asians, as well as a variety of ethnocentric assumptions about the Vietnamese. An understanding of (primary and secondary) ignorance and ethnocentrism helps explain the disastrous American political and military policies that resulted in the loss of two million or more Vietnamese and over 58,000 American lives—not to mention a dangerous erosion of the fabric of American democracy.[13]

Costly examples of tempocentrism in action also abound—especially in the realm of environmental policy. Today, some American
leaders take comfort in a psychological "denial" of the very notion
that current unrestrained urban growth policies in the southwestern
U.S. will result in unsustainable demands on available water supplies
in the future. Such policies have already led to a serious desiccation of
a number of waterways and a substantial depletion of numerous
aquifers. The future will prove these tempocentric policies disas-
trously wrong. Posterity will pay a punishing price.

For decades, cultural anthropologists have been deeply aware of
the problem of ethnocentrism. They have pioneered in efforts to de-
ethnocentrize not only themselves, but all of the social sciences. The
result is that if an anthropologist were today to challenge an economist, political scientist, sociologist or psychologist as being "ethnocentric," there is a good chance that the latter social scientist would
actually take such criticism to heart, and revise some of his or her
premises. Overall, anthropology's contribution toward discouraging
ethnocentrism and building cultural awareness and sensitivity—a
massive undertaking in which Margaret Mead herself eventually
became one of the world's most articulate and effective spokesper-
sons—ranks as one of the major social science-based educational
achievements of the entire twentieth century. If anthropologists can
similarly develop self-awareness with respect to the phenomenon of
tempocentrism, they will substantially leverage their ability to contribute to the well-being of society.

The Value of Anticipation Despite its Fallibility

All sane humans anticipate. All goal-directed behavior is by definition
anticipatory in some sense. We behave in a certain way because we
anticipate that this will enhance our chances for a more desirable
future situation, or reduce our chances for an undesirable one. This
capacity to anticipate in a reasoned, conditional, corrigible, strategiz-
ing manner is disproportionately developed in the human species. It
is part of being sapient, and has conferred enormous evolutionary
advantages upon *homo sapiens*.

This human capacity is, however, much more effective at the
level of the individual, family, or small community—than at the level
of whole societies, let alone complex inter-societal or global relationships, where our ability to anticipate is much more limited. Given
these limitations, many of us fall back upon simple platitudes or
aphorisms, or magical beliefs of one kind or another. What makes
Margaret Mead special is that she had the ability to transcend many
such limitations, and address alternative futures for large population

groups or whole nations, or for the whole of the world's people. This is an ability that is crucially important in today's world, where global demographic, techno-economic, political and sociocultural changes are occurring at an ever-accelerating rate, and where major populations could face annihilation by weapons of mass destruction, or ecological catastrophe. Indeed, it was the emergence and proliferation of such weapons, and an awareness of such ecological dangers, that spurred Margaret Mead to become a " futurist before her time."

When Mead, or anyone else, engages in any kind of prediction or anticipation concerning the future of a sociocultural system, this is, of course, clearly different from describing (or speculating about) that system's past or present—for the very fundamental ontological and epistemological reason that there are no future facts. There are only facts about the past or present that a researcher (or an expert, a leader, or an interviewee) regards as *relevant* to the future—for example, facts concerning such extant "driving forces" as high technology, global electronically mediated commerce, rapid population growth, resource depletion, or environmental despolation.

Nonetheless, some people, including some leaders who are otherwise intelligent, take a very different position, and simply refuse to engage in any kind of systematic anticipation, citing the fact that there are no future facts, and contending that all anticipation is hence fallible. I disagree with that position. I believe that despite this inherent fallibility, there is an important, indeed necessary, place for broad systematic anticipation in modern life. Further, having devoted much of my research effort over the past quarter century to Anticipatory Anthropology, I consider it plausible that the anthropologists who do take the time and trouble to engage in systematic anticipation are at least as aware as those who do not, that such anticipations could prove wrong.

More specifically, I base my argument in favor of Anticipatory Anthropology on the following seven-point line of reasoning.

1. Our anticipations of the future do, after all, often turn out to be essentially correct.
2. The best kind of anticipation is usually the kind that is repeated through time. To be most effective, anticipation— whether in anthropology or any other social science— should be an iterative process, not a "one shot" operation. This makes anticipations corrigible. For example, if an anticipation framework requires iterations to occur every five years over a twenty-year period, then at Year 5 the anticipator can take cognizance of the changes in reality that have occurred, and make needed corrections in

deciding what to project for Years 10 or 15 or 20, etc. Thus, I personally favor a research strategy that is focused primarily on the intermediate rather than remote future, and is repeated at intervals, with projections systematically updated each time.

3. If one engages in systematic anticipation using a holistic approach of the type that has long been the hallmark of cultural anthropology, one soon finds oneself dealing not just with the possible and the probable, but also with the preferable. Such systematic anticipation can thus serve as a powerful means for clarifying and prioritizing the values held by an individual, a community or a society. These values apply not just with respect to what people want their future reality to be, but also with respect to the price they are willing to pay, and the initiatives they are willing to undertake, in order to realize that preferred future.

4. The best way to realize a preferred future is first to visualize it—in concrete enough terms to provide the motivational basis for appropriate action needed for its realization. An individual, community or society that fails to visualize its preferred future, risks being seriously dissatisfied with what it gets when the erstwhile future becomes the present.

5. An act of anticipation or visioning can sometimes eventuate into a socially useful "self-fulfilling prophecy." For example, in 1961, shortly after his inauguration, President John F. Kennedy announced a vision that seemed highly fallible to many at the time, namely that the U.S. would send a man to the moon and bring him safely back to earth by the end of that decade. In 1969, to the excitement of the world, that vision was realized. Kennedy's vision was itself a crucial factor in the creation of a specific program, which ultimately led to a changed reality. Of course, it is for each of us to decide whether we regard the U.S. space program as being, on balance, desirable or undesirable. As of the year of the first moon landing, at least, Margaret Mead regarded it as desirable. (See Item 1969, below.)

6. Just as there can be self-fulfilling prophesies, so there can be socially useful "self-negating prophesies." The act of anticipating a negative outcome can be correct as of the time of anticipation, yet lead to subsequent action designed to prevent the anticipated outcome from becoming reality. For example, the U.S. government's publicly articulated anticipation that at current rates of smoking, X percentage

of American smokers will die prematurely, can have the direct or indirect effect of helping to cause many individuals to quit, and many others never to start.

7. Finally, much useful Anticipatory Anthropology can be practiced using quite conservative, or "soft" predictions. For instance, if the ethnographer uses a "scenarios elicitation" method, he will probably choose to elicit from an interviewee both her "optimistic" and "pessimistic" scenarios. In such a case, all that is logically required is that the interviewee consider these two scenarios to be simply "possible"—having a probability of realization that is judged to be greater than zero. Even if the interviewee sees a scenario as having a low probability—say, .05 or .10—such a scenario can still be heuristically useful. A case in point would be an ecologist interviewee's Pessimistic Scenario, which might project a major ecological breakdown. Even if the ecologist assigns to it a low probability, such a projection, dealing with a matter of such fundamental importance to the long-range survival of an entire society, deserves our serious attention.

    A similar logic applies to an interviewee's Optimistic Scenario. The mere fact that such a scenario is regarded by some as being of low probability is not in itself sufficient grounds for refusing to take it seriously. President Kennedy's optimistic vision of sending a man to the moon during the Sixties was seen by many as having a very low probability. Yet it became reality. Indeed, it is in the very nature of an Optimistic Scenario that it is typically seen as having a lower probability than numerous other plausible (and less preferable) scenarios.

To recapitulate: Anticipatory Anthropology and Futures Studies are generally more about designing the future, through articulating alternative future scenarios, than about predicting a particular future. That said, logically there is no escaping the fact that all anticipation does embody some kind of prediction. But the key point is that this need not be "hard" prediction. At a minimum, a given vision or scenario need only be deemed possible, rather than impossible. Logically, to say that a scenario is "possible" requires only that one assign to it a probability greater than zero—an extremely "soft" requirement. Only if the ethnographer were to ask an interviewee to provide a scenario designated as "most" probable, or "highly" probable, would "hard" prediction be involved (Textor in Sippanondha 1990:

135–152). Taking into account all of the above seven points, I believe that fallibility should not be seen as a sufficient reason to shrink from engaging in serious anticipation. If Margaret Mead were alive today, I believe she would essentially agree with the above line of reasoning.

A Personal Example

Because Anticipatory Anthropology will be new to some readers, it might be helpful at this point to report briefly on why and how I developed my commitment to doing some of my research in the anticipatory mode. In so reporting, I will be following the advice that Margaret Mead constantly urged upon her students: "Use yourself as data."

My report begins in 1958, when I returned to Cornell University to write my dissertation, after five years of fieldwork in Thailand. I brought home with me an enormous corpus of field notes, including systematic data on certain cultural subsystems that, I discovered, could best be analyzed using the university's new computation center (a facility that had not even existed when I left Cornell for Thailand in 1952). I started by using IBM cards and simple counter-sorter and tabulating equipment, but soon realized that use of a computer would be much more effective. I thus "got onto the computer" at a very early point in the Age of the Computer, from 1959 to 1964, first at Yale and then at Harvard. I did this simply out of perceived necessity, despite little background in statistics, and despite the need to rely on others to do my programming.

In 1958, computers were so new that few people had a clear or confident idea as to what would be this strange device's longer-run impact on society. It is well known that as late as the mid-1950s, even the head of the International Business Machines Company (IBM) projected only an extremely limited market for this new device. And within the anthropological community, the great majority knew very little about the computer, let alone about its potential.

Let us imagine that it is 1958 and you are interviewing me ethnographically about my anticipations regarding the future use of the computer by the Thai people between that year and a twenty-five-year horizon date of 1983. To your introductory questions, I might have replied: "Well, it seems likely that computers will become more numerous in Thailand, and have an appreciable sociocultural impact, but I am not sure how." You are not satisfied with such a vague answer, so you probe further: "Could you just relax a bit, speculate a bit, and flesh out that picture?" To that probe, I might have hesitantly replied that maybe the Thai census bureau and some other large governmental organizations, and perhaps also some large banks and businesses, would use the computer and find it cost-effective.

Even this projection would have been a hesitant one, however, because I was mindful that just a few years earlier the Thai census bureau itself had been hesitant in making use of business machines – not computers, but just elementary IBM punch-card counting-sorting and tabulating machines. However, the bureau had had so little faith in this new equipment, that it was spot-checking these machine-produced results by using a centuries-old instrument that it truly trusted, namely the abacus.

At this point you still suspect that I have other ideas to share, so you decide to probe more aggressively. You try to open up my imaginative resources, by asking me a wild, "off the edge" question: "Do you anticipate that, in the middle run—say, 1963 to 1978—many middle-class Thai families will be using computers in the home?" Although this is indeed true today, I would then certainly have answered No. The very question would have seemed utterly preposterous to me, since the reality in 1958—at the Cornell Computation Center and elsewhere—was that a computer was an enormous and mysterious device that had to be kept in a large air-conditioned room, and manned by a crew of professional technicians who would not let anyone else go near "their" machine. To make any kind of use of this machine, one had to have, or hire, programming skills. How could such a machine ever be installable and useable in an ordinary person's home? In 1958, I could not possibly have anticipated the advent of microelectronic miniaturization, the breakthrough that ultimately made the personal computer possible. Nor could most electrical engineers of that day. After all, it was not until about 1973 that the microchip emerged, and not until about 1978 that the prototype personal computer became available.

Let us fast forward to 1978. You are interviewing me again about the future of computers in Thailand in the near or middle term. By that year, microelectronics had evolved to the point where I could and soon did produce visions and scenarios of considerable specificity, with enough lead-time to be of possible value to policy-makers, planners or citizens.[14]

I confess that I find it a little embarrassing to relate this personal example, since one of the main reasons I entered anthropology in the first place was to discover creative ways to use modern technology humanely and effectively in improving living conditions in economically less developed nations such as Thailand. I certainly would have done a better job as a development anthropologist if Margaret Mead or someone had offered me a course in Anticipatory Anthropology before I left for the field in 1952. Unfortunately, however, to my knowledge no university at that time offered such a course.

What If Margaret Mead Had Used a Scenarios Elicitation Method?

Today, interviewing people by eliciting their scenarios for the future, and helping them build visions of their own, is a key method in Futures Studies—and one that fits remarkably well into the holistic ethnographic tradition of anthropology (Textor in Sippanondha 1990: 146–150). There is general agreement that this method produces its richest results when multiple and contrastive scenarios are elicited, because almost all futurists today construe the future as embodying a multiplicity of possibilities, rather than a single inevitability.

All of us, as we pass through life, have our own special "retro scenarios," visions of what we might have done if circumstances had been different. Here, with respect to Margaret Mead, is mine. Though it might seem implausible to some readers, it seems quite plausible to me.

During the Seventies I decided to enter the futures field. I started in 1976/1977, when I took sabbatical leave one year early and began reading the futures literature. I did this primarily because I had become convinced that the rapidity and complexity of on-going global sociocultural change had made it necessary for some of us in anthropology to engage in systematic anticipation, if our discipline as a whole was to have its best chance of remaining robustly relevant to the needs of society. In particular, I felt that there was a need for systematic anticipation by those anthropologists heavily involved in Development Studies, as was true of both Mead and myself.

Browsing the futures literature, I was impressed by the broad array of methodologies that futurists had invented, or borrowed and adapted, for use in Futures Studies (Bell 1997: 228-317). Some of these methodologies were impressively sophisticated and creative. However, I was disheartened to discover how extremely limited the impact of my discipline had been on Futures Studies. I felt that anthropology, for all its limitations, had something special to offer. It was clear to me that anthropology's emphasis on understanding whole sociocultural systems was needed in Futures Studies, where most research was more narrowly focused often on just one or another subsystem. I reasoned that ordinary people everywhere do, after all, aspire to live desirable and worthwhile future lives in the context of a whole sociocultural system—not just a business subsystem, a political subsystem, a communication subsystem, etc.

Moreover, I saw a great opportunity for anthropologists to enhance and improve research on alternative futures for peoples indigenous to the non-Western world. Although the great majority of social scientists in the world, of whatever discipline, are Westerners, cultural anthropology is unique among disciplines in virtually requiring that its members at least try to develop sophisticated and empathic understanding of non-Western peoples. For this reason, also, I felt that anthropology ought to become involved in Futures Studies.

I therefore began searching for a methodology that would allow anthropology to make a useful contribution—one that would be seen as useful not just by anthropologists, but by social scientists and futurists in general. Why not, I thought, find a way to adapt ethnography, the classic methodology of cultural anthropology, to the needs and constraints of Futures Studies? Why not ask people questions directly about their future? Why not develop a way to elicit from an interviewee their visions of possible, probable, and preferable futures for their sociocultural system? So, I proceeded to do just that, in a spirit later encapsulated by Bohannan and van der Elst: "What people hope will happen and what they fear will happen can easily be made part of every ethnographic study—all you have to do is ask and listen. Doing that can open windows on the future as people work to bring about their hopes and avoid their fears (1998: 100)."

The method I developed, known as Ethnographic Futures Research (EFR), builds upon one's ethnographic knowledge, but systematically asks questions about the future. The EFR interview has much in common with the conventional ethnographic interview. It is confidential, interactive, semi-structured, flexible, open-ended, and focused on patterns and systems. In an EFR interview, three contrasting scenarios are elicited: an Optimistic, a Pessimistic, and a Most Probable Scenario. The ethnographer probes non-directively, seeking to free the interviewee from their tempocentrism, and to achieve a high degree of clarity, comprehensiveness, contextualization, and coherence. An interview might take as little as an hour, or as long as ten or more hours in several sittings. The interview is tape-recorded, and then written up in summary protocol form, for editing and approval by the interviewee. The quality of the final product depends on the robustness of the interviewee's knowledge and imagination, and on the skill of the interviewer.[15]

EFR was still in the early stages of its development in 1978, the year Margaret Mead died. If she had lived a few years longer, or if I had developed EFR a few years earlier, I would almost certainly have made an effort to interview her using this new method.[16] To minimize bias and enhance robustness, I would have involved perhaps three other scholars as co-interviewers. For example, suppose that Mead chose to deal with alternative middle-range futures for the U.S. in the context of a rapidly evolving global system. In that case I would have involved, say, a political economist, a development-oriented social scientist from an economically less developed country, and a respected futurist or systems scientist with global interests. For gender balance, at least one of these three co-interviewers would be female, and at least one, male. I think there is a good chance that Mead would have accepted our invitation, in part because of its subject matter, and in part because she loved to work with teams of colleagues from a variety of disciplinary and cultural backgrounds.

The EFR procedure seeks to achieve comprehensiveness and coherence by requiring the interviewer to probe using an agreed-upon list of broad domains. Possible domains could include demography, technology-economy, energy, environment-ecology, transportation, tourism, information-communication, politics-law-government, social structure, education, religion, and cultural identity. In my opinion, a book of this sort, authored by Margaret Mead, would have made her visions of possible, probable and preferable futures accessible to the worldwide social science and general audience in an eloquent, memorable and quotable fashion.[17]

Anticipatory Anthropology in Practical Service to Twenty-First Century Society

My personal "Optimistic Scenario" is that anthropologists and futurists will work together with increasing closeness over the next ten to twenty years and beyond, to their mutual advantage and that of society. In many ways, it would be a natural partnership (Riner 1987). Futurists, after all, have just as strong a professional "vested interest" in identifying and counteracting tempocentrism, as anthropologists have with respect to ethnocentrism. Futurists can help anthropologists to "de-tempocentrize" their thinking and methodology. Similarly, anthropologists can help futurists to "de-ethnocentrize" their thinking and methodology.

Developing a certain amount of anthropological sophistication would be useful to futurists, the majority of whom are upper- or middle-class urban residents of economically advanced Western industrial nations, and are hence not likely to possess adequate knowledge of, or empathy with, ordinary people from economically underdeveloped non-Western nations. These are the very kinds of ordinary people that many cultural anthropologists seek to understand through intensive fieldwork.

If Margaret Mead were alive today, I believe she would be urging her anthropological colleagues to devote their attention—descriptive, analytical, and anticipatory—to the world crisis in population, resources, and environment. I believe she would also point to the potential, for good or ill, of such profound global "driving forces" as the Information, Biotechnical, Materials Science and Energy Revolutions, as well as the ever more pervasive digital "global marketplace." Today it is not just small isolated sociocultural groups that are being impacted by these powerful, all-pervasive forces, but virtually every society across the globe.

Listed below are several kinds of anthropological research in the anticipatory mode that I believe Mead would be encouraging today:

- Working with governmental or civic leaders to visualize alternative *demographic* futures, assessing the main sociocultural and human well-being implications of each, and formulating culturally grounded policy recommendations. This is an absolutely vital problem area given the enormous demographic momentum throughout much of the world today, especially in its poorest and ecologically most fragile areas.

- Assessing possible, probable, and preferable futures for a given human group as a consequence of the *Information* Revolution and its vast potential for bringing about broad sociocultural change. Such research might, for example, take the form of a fieldwork-based technological forecast of the impact of the Internet on a given community or culture, with recommendations as to public policies needed to ensure democratic access, personal privacy, and the preservation and enrichment of cultural identity.

- Assessing possible, probable, and preferable effects of the *Biotechnical* Revolution on local peoples. This Revolution provides the scientific and technical basis for previously unimaginable medical treatments, or for the design of new food plants that can grow in forbidding climates and inhospitable soils, or for ecologically sound means of pest control. At the same time, this Revolution carries profound ethical implications in such areas as human cloning, organ transplants, and the substantial extension of the human life span.

- Assessing the potential, for a given society, of the *Materials Science* Revolution, which generates completely new materials, not found in nature, that will possess the particular properties needed to relieve pressure on natural raw materials that are non-renewable, or that would be better used for purposes of greater social value.

- Analyzing the *energy* needs and resources of a given population, and its readiness to develop and utilize

alternative, often non-traditional, energy sources that would
be sustainable and non-polluting.

- Doing a *cultural-ecological* analysis and projection of resource
use and renewal for a given region, with appropriate policy
recommendations.

- Assessing the *readiness* of a given community for a new type
of productive tool, technique, or educational input, while
also assessing possible adverse consequences for the local
people.

- Working with land use and transportation *planners* to
develop culturally grounded alternative scenarios concerning
problems of urban crowding, traffic congestion, and air and
water pollution.

- Using field and library / electronic research to develop
alternative scenarios concerning the possible, probable and
preferable effects of the emerging *global* economy on local
productivity, employment, cultural continuity, ecological
sustainability, or the equitable distribution of the benefits of
techno-economic innovation.

- Conducting deeply contextual fieldwork on *ethnic tensions* in
areas such as Israel / Palestine, Serbia / Kosovo, or Indonesia /
Aceh, to produce grounded yet imaginative visions and
policy recommendations aimed at preventing future
genocide.

These are some of the daunting challenges that lie ahead. They are
challenges that I believe Margaret Mead, if she were alive today,
would lead in addressing. If other anthropologists rise to meet these
challenges, they will be serving society and anthropology well, and in
the process, honoring her memory.

ACKNOWLEDGEMENTS

I gratefully acknowledge the help of the following persons in cri-
tiquing the manuscript for my part of this book: Mary Catherine Bateson of George Mason University, William O. Beeman of Brown
University, Wendell Bell of Yale University, Wilton S. Dillon of the
Smithsonian Institution, and Reed D. Riner of Northern Arizona University. I am indebted to photographer Ken Heyman, who worked
with Margaret Mead for some years, both in the U.S. and overseas, for
his remarkable generosity in contributing all but one of the photographs in this book. For contributing the remaining photo (show-

ing Mead at a microphone) my thanks go to photographer Rick Stafford of the Harvard News Office. For the task of digitizing and otherwise preparing these photographs for publication, I am indebted to Michael Seric Thompson and Robert K. Costello, both of the Smithsonian Institution. Finally, I wish to thank Ms. Vivian K. Berghahn for her very helpful and professional editorial assistance and, similarly, Mr. Mike Dempsey for production assistance. Responsibility for any errors is of course mine alone.

EDITOR'S NOTES

1. For more on the rationale of Anticipatory Anthropology, please see the Appendix to this Introduction, p. 16.

2. For an example, see *Themes in French Culture*, Volume Four of this Mead Centennial Series (Margaret Mead with Rhoda Métraux, 2001 [originally 1954]). See also the appraisal of that effort by the editor, Kathryn M. Anderson-Levitt, a specialist on French culture (2001: vii-xxii).

3. For more information, see Volume One of this Mead Centennial Series (Margaret Mead and Rhoda Métraux, eds. 2000 [originally 1953]). In his Introduction to that volume, William O. Beeman provides a comprehensive account of the history of the RCC and IIS and of their significance to the social sciences, and to society. The IIS remains active to this day serving as Mead's literary executor and home to the activities of the Margaret Mead Centennial. For further information, visit http://www.interculturalstudies.org/aboutus.html. On this site, one can find a mission statement that is highly relevant to the present volume: "The IIS is committed to celebrating Mead's Centennial by emphasizing the human capacity to imagine and work toward a positive future."

4. The U.S. government's decision not to try the Japanese emperor as a war criminal was highly controversial at the time. But today, most serious scholars agree that retaining the emperor (or at least the imperial institution) was the correct decision. It enabled the Allied Occupation to promote democratic change in collaboration with liberal Japanese elements, with no need to worry about military, paramilitary or physical resistance—and ultimately with impressive success (Textor 1992). Today, two generations later, the Japanese political culture has changed profoundly, and Japan is a stable, functioning and peaceful democracy.

5. For the reader desiring background on Mead's career, personality, and ameliorative drive, there are several good sources. One might start with the memorial issue of the *American Anthropologist* (1980), where several of

her colleagues report on various aspects of her life. I also recommend Mead's autobiography (Mead 1972), and the various biographies and memoirs by Bateson (1984), Dillon (2001), Grinager (1999), Howard (1984), and Lapsley (1999). Additional such studies are now being written and a continuously updated listing will be available from the web site of the Institute for Intercultural Studies: http://www.interculturalstudies.org

6. This matter is further discussed in the Appendix to this Introduction, p. 24.

7. Accessible through http://www.interculturalstudies.org

8. The goal of this book was to bring together the entire coded cross-cultural literature (from the Human Relations Area Files and thirty-seven other sources) into one volume in accessible form. To do this, I used a then-novel device, the computer, and developed a "Pattern Search and Table Translation Technique" to render each of the book's more than 18,000 statistically significant two-by-two tables into a single declarative English (or, if desired, Russian, French or German) sentence that expressed the essential meaning of that table. The book would thus present a comprehensive array of statistically-based cross-cultural information in both quantitative and qualitative terms, with a high degree of transparency.

9. Three years later, when I was preparing to publish the *Summary*, I asked Margaret Mead for an endorsement, and she obliged with the following: "A real forward step....goes a long way towards making the Human Relations Area Files more significant." The jacket for this book also contained endorsements by six other scholars: George Peter Murdock and Irvin L. Child of Yale University, Harold E. Driver of Indiana, Philip E. Slater of Brandeis, Raoul Narroll of the State University of New York, and John M. Roberts of Cornell. All six had long been committed to, and productive in, statistical cross-cultural analysis. Mead was the only exception. In my view, this episode illustrates an important aspect of her personality, namely her empathy for the new and her ability to imagine middle and long-run human consequences of this or that innovation.

10. For an account of her contributions to the anthropological understanding of Russian culture and to the ongoing tradition of Russian anthropological research, see Mead 2001 [1955 and 1962]), and especially the comments of its editor, Sergei Aruitnov, on pages xiv-xx.

11. *Cultural Frontiers* was well reviewed. And it sold well, which gratified all of us who participated in its writing. (We donated our proceeds to the Peace Corps.) Today, thirty-eight years later, the book is apparently still widely available in public libraries around the U.S. Unquestionably, a key reason for the book's success, and especially its longevity, has been that it bears a stamp of approval from Margaret Mead.

12. There is, however, one exception. In March 1970 my son Alex was born, and his mother and I sent out the usual routine birth notices to many of our friends, including Margaret. A few weeks later a silver cup arrived in the mail, inscribed "from Margaret Mead." It became, of course, an instant heirloom.

13. In my view, there should not have been a Vietnam War, and, if American leaders had had their ethnocentrism under better control, I believe major conflict there could have been avoided.
14. See Textor et al. 1983, 1985 and Textor 1986.
15. For specifics, see Textor in Sippanondha (1990: 135-152), or Bell (1997: 312-15).
16. I would have proposed that the protocols generated by the interview be written up in book form — either by her, or else drafted by me for her editing and approval. She would make that decision, and in any case, she would be the sole author, since the ideas in the book would be solely hers.
17. If you find the above idea too fanciful I would refer you to a book that was actually produced using a closely similar research plan, so that you can judge for yourself how well such an approach might have worked with Mead. In 1988 three collaborators and I used EFR to elicit alternative middle-range future scenarios for Thailand by interviewing a single highly qualified individual, namely the Thai scientist and national leader Sippanondha Ketudat. Sippanondha was a Harvard-educated nuclear physicist and university professor, who at various times had been Minister of Education, a major figure in Thailand's premier national planning agency, and head of that nation's national science foundation. At the time we interviewed him, he was serving as founding President of Thailand's National Petrochemical Corporation, a public-private company. He was, in short, a man of great learning and experience, comparable in many ways to Margaret Mead. Hence, taking a look at his book, which is available electronically, will give you a rough idea of what a similar book by Mead might have looked like (see Sippanondha 1990).

EDITOR'S REFERENCES

NOTE: This list of references includes only a few works by Mead herself. For a listing of all her works, see *Margaret Mead: The Complete Bibliography, 1925-1975*, edited by Joan Gordan, 1976, The Hague: Mouton. In addition, many of her publications are searchable on-line at http://www.interculturalstudies.org. For those readers able to visit Washington DC, I strongly recommend visiting the vast collection of Meadianna available at the permanent Margaret Mead Collection at the Library of Congress.

American Anthropologist. 1980. "In Memoriam: Margaret Mead (1901-1978)", Vol. 82, No. 2 (June). Pages 267-372 contain two articles about Mead's life and career by Rhoda Métraux, and one each by Mary Catherine Bateson, Nancy McDowell, Lola Romanucci-Ross, Wilton S. Dillon, Peggy Reeves Sanday, Francis L. K. Hsu, and David Hurst Thomas.

Bateson, Mary Catherine. 1984. *With a Daughter's Eye: A Memoir of Margaret Mead and Gregory Bateson.* New York: William Morrow.

Bell, Wendell. 1997. *Foundations of Futures Studies.* Two volumes. New Brunswick NJ: Transaction Press.

Bohannan, Paul, and Dirk van der Elst. 1998. *Asking and Listening: Ethnography as Personal Communication.* Prospect Heights IL: Waveland Press.

Coates, Joseph F., John B. Mahaffie, and Andy Hines. 1997. *2025: Scenarios of US and Global Society Reshaped by Science and Technology.* Greensboro NC: Oakhill Press. Also available electronically at www.josephcoates.com.

Dillon, Wilton S. 1980. "Margaret Mead and Government." *American Anthropologist,* Vol. 82, No. 2 (June): 319-339.

———. 2001. "Margaret Mead (1901-1978)." *Prospects,* Vol. XXXI, No. 3 (September). Available electronically at www.ibe.unesco.org/International/Publications/Prospects/ProspectsTablesOfContent/pr119tc.htm - 8k

Grinager, Patricia. 1999. *Uncommon Lives: My Lifelong Friendship with Margaret Mead.* Lanham MD: Rowman and Littlefield.

Howard, Jane. 1984. *Margaret Mead: A Life.* New York: Simon and Schuster.

Lapsley, Hilary. 1999. *Margaret Mead and Ruth Benedict: The Kinship of Women.* Amherst: University of Massachusetts Press.

Mead, Margaret. 1956. *New Lives for Old: Cultural Transformation—Manus, 1928-1951.* New York: William Morrow.

———. 1964. *Continuities in Cultural Evolution*. New Haven and London: Yale University Press.

———. 1970. *Culture and Commitment: A Study of the Generation Gap*. Garden City, NY: Natural History Press / Doubleday and Company.

———. 1972. *Blackberry Winter: My Earlier Years*. New York: William Morrow.

———. 1975. *World Enough: Rethinking the Future*, Boston MA: Little, Brown. With photographs by Ken Heyman.

———. 2000 [1942]. *And Keep Your Powder Dry: An Anthropologist Looks at America*. New York: Berghahn Books. Volume Two of the present Mead Centennial Series on the Study of Contemporary Western Cultures. Introduction by Hervé Varenne.

Mead, Margaret, and Rhoda Métraux, eds. 2000 [1953]. *The Study of Culture at a Distance*. New York: Berghahn Books. Volume One of the present Mead Centennial Series on the Study of Contemporary Western Cultures. Introduction by William O. Beeman.

Mead, Margaret, with Rhoda Métraux. 2001 [1954]. *Themes in French Culture*. New York: Berghahn Books. Volume Four of the present Mead Centennial Series on the Study of Contemporary Western Cultures. Introduction by Kathryn M. Anderson-Levitt.

Mead, Margaret, Geoffrey Gorer, and John Rickman. 2001 [1955 and 1962]. *Russian Culture*. New York: Berghahn Books. Volume Three of the present Mead Centennial Series on the Study of Contemporary Western Cultures. Introduction by Sergei Aruitnov.

Riner, Reed D. 1987. "Doing Futures Research—Anthropologically." *Futures: The Journal of Forecasting and Planning,* Vol. 19, No. 3 (June): 311-328.

Sippanondha Ketudat. 1990. *Thaang Saaj Klaang khaung Sangkhom Thaj naj Anaakhod: Thegnooloojii Saudkhlaung kab Wadthanatham lae Singwaedlaum*. English edition: *The Middle Path for the Future of Thailand: Technology in Harmony with Culture and Environment*. Honolulu: Institute of Culture and Communication, East-West Center and Chiang Mai, Thailand: Chiang Mai University Faculty of the Social Sciences. English version available electronically at http://www.stanford.edu/~rbtextor/.

Textor, Robert B. 1967. *A Cross-Cultural Summary*. New Haven CT: Human Relations Area Files Press.

———. 1986. "Shaping the Telemicroelectronic Revolution to Serve True Development." In Mohan Munasinghe, Michael Dow, and Jack Fritz, eds., *Microcomputers for Development*. (Co-keynote

address to a conference sponsored by the Computer and
Information Technology Council of Sri Lanka and the U.S.
National Academy of Sciences. Colombo: Sri Lanka Department
of Government Printing, 1985. Library of Congress Catalogue
No. 85 – 71396). Also in *Microcomputers and Their Applications for
Developing Countries*. Boulder CO: Westview Press, 1986.

———. 1992. "Success in Japan—Despite Some Human Foibles and
Cultural Problems." Pp. 151-72 in *The Occupation of Japan: The
Grass Roots: The Proceedings of a Symposium, 7-8 November 1991*,
ed. William F. Nimmo. Norfolk VA: The General Douglas
MacArthur Foundation. Reprinted in William Leary, ed.,
MacArthur and the American Century. Lincoln NE.: University of
Nebraska Press, 2001, 257-286.

———. 1995. "The Ethnographic Futures Research Method: An
Application to Thailand." *Futures: The Journal of Forecasting,
Planning and Policy*, Vol. 27, No. 4 (May): 461-471.

———. 1999. "Why Anticipatory Anthropology?" *General
Anthropology, Bulletin of the General Anthropology Division,
American Anthropological Association*, Vol. 6, No. 1, (Fall): 1-4.

———. 2003. "Honoring Excellence in Anticipatory Anthropology,"
Futures: The Journal of Forecasting, Planning and Policy, Vol. 35, No.
4 (May): 521-527.

Textor, Robert B., et al. 1966. *Cultural Frontiers of the Peace Corps*.
Cambridge MA: M.I.T. Press.

———. 1983. *Österreich 2005: Einflüsse der mikro-elektronischen
Revolution / Austria 2005: Projected Sociocultural Effects of the
Microelectronic Revolution*. Foreword by State Secretary Ernst Eugen
Veselsky. Published in joint English-German version under the
sponsorship of the Austrian Association for Future Policies.
Vienna: Verlag Orac. Available electronically at
http://www.stanford.edu/~rbtextor/.

———. 1985. "Anticipatory Anthropology and the
Telemicroelectronic Revolution: A Preliminary Report from
Silicon Valley." *Anthropology and Education Quarterly*, Vol. XVI,
No. 1: pp. 3-30.

Toffler, Alvin. 1972. *The Futurists*, New York: Random House.

Margaret Mead's remarkable ethnographic career took her to a half dozen cultures in the South and Southwest Pacific, culminating in Bali (the only one of her fieldwork sites here depicted). Mead did her first stint of fieldwork in that fascinating culture in the late 1930s. She then returned for a second stint in "her" village of Bayung Gede in the late 1950s, where photographer Ken Heyman captured her with students in front of the village school.

Here Mead revisits and interviews an old Balinese friend in his house, probing for instances of continuity and change since her original fieldwork two decades earlier.

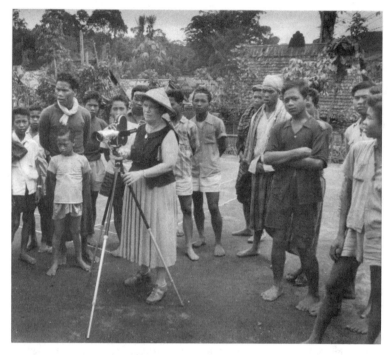

During the Thirties Mead and her then-husband, Dr. Gregory Bateson, working in Bali, pioneered in the use of motion pictures in ethnographic fieldwork. Here, during the Fifties, she gets behind the camera again.

Mead was fascinated by Balinese dance and trance, and is here being ceremonially honored by a young girl dancer.

Photographer Heyman reports that Mead loved this photograph of herself holding a Balinese infant, and used it as her Christmas card. The white spot on the infant's head is a charm to offer protection against evil, in accordance with the local form of Hinduism.

In January 1958, Mead addresses a class of secondary school boys in Den Pasar, the largest city in Bali. They are discussing the Russian satellite Sputnik, which had just recently orbited the earth. Mead took the opportunity to do a bit of ethnography in the anticipatory mode, asking the boys to prepare drawings of their concepts of that portentous event, which she then collected and analyzed.

Although Mead was for many years an Adjunct Professor at Columbia University, her career-long "home base" was the American Museum of Natural History. The forked "thumbstick" she is holding here gave her support in walking with a weak ankle. In due course it became an integral part of her public image.

Here, during the Sixties, Mead is organizing some of her endless stock of ethnographic photographs.

Typing up notes in a quiet corner of the Museum.

Working with an assistant, organizing museum artifacts.

Visiting a fossil display.

Examining a diorama of a New Guinea village, including a replica of the house on stilts she lived in while doing fieldwork in 1929 among the Manus, a sociocultural group located in the Bismarck Archipelago in what is now the Republic of Papua-New Guinea. Mead's fieldwork in Manus is discussed on page 5. The diorama is part of the Museum's "Margaret Mead Hall," established during the Sixties.

Mead loved to teach, and here seizes the opportunity to explain an Easter Island statue to some young museum visitors.

Here, in 1960, Mead conducts a seminar at the International House at Columbia University.

Part of the "Meadian we" (page 11) were the numerous organizational boards on which she tirelessly served.

In the final decades of her life, Margaret Mead, public anthropologist (page 7), had become one of the most famous women in the world, in demand everywhere as a lecturer. Here, in 1976, she is giving a distinguished visitor's lecture at Harvard. Unlike the other photos in this collection, all of which are by Ken Heyman, this one is by Rick Stafford of the Harvard Public Affairs office.

A happy moment with daughter Mary Catherine and son-in-law Barkev Kassarjian.

Mead loved to spend time during the hot summer months at a lakeside cottage in New Hampshire. Here, in 1960, she and her daughter, Mary Catherine Bateson, join the grandchildren of Mead's friend Prof. Lawrence K. Frank for a hike along the shore.

At the lake, with her friends' grandchildren. Photographer Heyman has observed that "whenever she could, she would get down on the level of the children she was observing, perhaps having them play with a cup and a spoon."

The light of Mead's life was her granddaughter, Vanni Sevanne, pictured here in 1971 in this three-generation photo.

This portrait of Margaret Mead, taken in 1976, is Ken Heyman's last and favorite photograph of his friend and mentor.

1943

THE FAMILY IN THE FUTURE*

Editor's Commentary

Out of Margaret Mead's prodigious array of publications from the 1920s to the 1970s, this is the earliest one that is essentially antic-ipatory in approach. Remarkably, it dates all the way back to 1943 and World War II. It deals with a subject dear to her heart, the family, and contains many useful insights unlikely to have been provided by anyone other than an anthropologist.

During the U.S. involvement in that global conflict, thousands of American scholars, including numerous anthropologists, took leave from their regular jobs and went to work for the American government or military "for the duration," dedicating their efforts to the task of defeating the Axis powers. However, only a tiny fraction of these thousands were also devoting serious effort toward envisioning and planning post-war reconstruction on a macro or societal scale. The redoubtable and hyper-energetic Margaret Mead was one of the rare few who undertook both chal-lenges: winning the war and winning the peace.

Another one of those few scholars who took a serious interest in postwar reconstruction was the respected social theorist Ruth Nanda Anshen, who here edits a collection of essays about "the world that could be"—beyond Allied victory. Among anthropolo-gists of the day whom Anshen might have invited to contribute an article, it is hard to imagine a better choice than Margaret Mead.

In this article Mead reveals an imaginative willingness to enter-tain the possibility of technological breakthroughs that might open up a wide range of possible changes in family forms. For example, she anticipates the birth control pill by some twenty years: "It is possible to imagine—at not too far distant date— complete control of her own fertility in the hands of a woman, so that ... childbirth is no longer the inevitable or even the possible concomitant of voluntary sex relations."

Indeed, this article contains an abundance of interesting and audacious propositions about the future, including some that anticipate, for America and other industrialized nations, such phenomena as a decline in national birth rates, changing notions

---

* In: *Beyond Victory*, ed. Ruth Nanda Anshen. (New York: Harcourt, Brace and Co., 1943), 66-87.

of the "traditional" family, and an increase in illegitimate births
and single-parent households.

Here Mead is adopting a stance that is common among futurists: imagine a technological breakthrough—and then project its
alternative possible, probable, and preferable sociocultural consequences, including especially the unintended or unforeseen
ones. Even though some readers might find some of her propositions shaky in their grounding, it is difficult not to appreciate the
courage and creativity of Margaret Mead, sixty years ago.

*   *   *

THE contribution of the anthropologist to a subject such as the one,
which this book embraces, lies primarily in the diversity and variety
of cultural forms, which form the anthropological stock in thinking.
Findings on cultures of different types provide us with a knowledge of
limitations and potentialities, indicate various sorts of incompatibili-
ties in social planning and provide clues to types of social invention
which may be consciously made in the future.

We may ask: "What has been constant" in the interrelationships
between a male, a female and their children—which is what we locally
mean by the term "the family." It is possible to argue that these con-
stants which have endured through changes in technology, size of
group, degree of political integration and the rise and fall of great religious systems have become so much a part of our human inheritance
that, like language or the use of fire, the family, in this basic form, is
virtually indestructible. Such an argument would not assume that
there was some necessary connection between human beings—seen
biologically—and a family form, but only that there was a necessary
connection between human culture, as it has developed, the human
beings which now develop within it, and some family form. It would
claim that as it is impossible to rear human beings without the mediation of other human beings, themselves shaped by the family, it is
therefore impossible to rear human beings who will not, as adults,
desire and recreate family forms. Without subscribing wholly to this
argument, it is worthwhile to inspect what is known of "the family"
all over the world, at different levels of cultural integration, and to
identify and classify the constant elements. From such a survey we
find that in every known culture, some formal relationships between
a woman and a designated male mate, serves to establish the status of
the children for whom they are held responsible. Furthermore, while
neither social parent need be the biological parent of the child, the
relationship to the woman in all cases, and to the man in a majority
of cases, is modeled upon physiological parenthood. So, even in those
societies where a great number of the children are adopted, the forms

of the mother-child relationship derive from and are continually referred back to biological motherhood. In the case of the male parent, it may be said that the primary terms of reference are: permanent—at least not merely temporary—and publicly recognized sex partner of the woman, economically responsible sex partner of the woman, and finally, with less universality, the physiological father of the child.

From this point of view if we considered whether there is a possibility of some invention for rearing and giving status to children, superseding the family, we would have to ask whether the ties between mother, child and mother and male partner could be finally disallowed and made non-significant. When this question is asked it becomes immediately apparent that it is the father's position, which is weakest, least bolstered by biology, and most in need of legal sanctions. Seen from this point of view, it is clear why discussions of the abolition of the family usually start with the abolition of the father, and plan to substitute some surrogate—the community, the state—for the father's socio-economic role, and so minimize completely his physiological role as the begetter of the child. As in primitive society it is, in most cases, the male partner who provides the protection and food for the pregnant and lactating woman, who decides whether and how the child is to be reared; so the state which would supersede the father, would also thereby gain the right to decide upon the strength of the mother-child tie, and to determine for how long it should endure. The state might decree, for example, whether labor pains were to be awaited or whether some new method of precipitating them so that the child could be born on a certain date is to be substituted, whether the mother is ever to see her child, whether the child is to be breast-fed or bottle fed from the start. In fact, inventions now exist for bringing up a child entirely unaided by the mother from the moment that the unborn child has reached maturity; the co-operation of the mother is no longer needed for delivery, lactation, or the sort of continuous care, which was once provided by the human arm, but is now provided by crib and baby carriage. It is important to note also that the parallel inventions which would make it possible for the mother to refuse to have the child are very much less completely developed; but it is possible to imagine—at no too far distant date—complete control of her own fertility in the hands of a woman, so that while she is no longer necessary to her child's life, once it is born, childbirth is no longer the inevitable or even the possible concomitant of voluntary sex relations. But when we examine the father's role further, we find that it has been extended primarily by the degree to which it guaranteed to the father care and continuity in his relationship to his children. If the state should find that, owing to the perfection of abortive and contraceptive devices, women were unwilling to bear children unless guaranteed a continuing and personal relationship to them, it might find that it was again underwriting also woman's continuing and personal relationship to a single male mate, in which the family would be psychologically reconstituted even though the support of the child were no longer the father's responsibility.

But in order to consider the probabilities of this continuing male mate, we have to consider another universal function of marriage, and that is the reduction of competition among males for females and among females for males. Whether this competition be for the exclusive sexual favors of a woman, or a man, or for some other value more difficult to obtain such as a woman to chew one's frozen boots—as among some Eskimos—or a man to weave one's wedding clothes—as among the Hopi—or merely for a woman to ignore all evening while one reads the newspaper—in every known society marriage does solve the competitive problem which will exist as long as men and women have something to offer each other which individuals of the same sex do not. While a large number of culturally created sex differences have intensified this intrasex competition for the services of the opposite sex, even if all these were eliminated so that each individual man or woman was a socially autonomous being—as the berdache, the man who dresses like and follows the vocations of women, among the Navajo, is enviously said to be—the exclusiveness and complementary character of the heterosexual act would continue to make the problem of intrasex competition a serious one. There are some societies, which have attempted to solve it by giving all the men access to all the women, either symbolically, or actually, but this has been done against a sharply defined background of who the actual spouse is who submits to the wider distribution of sexual favors. It is possible that we might develop individuals who were uninterested in this competitive problem, as we know we have developed people who fail to compete over other obvious limitations in supplies, but it seems unlikely. It would be necessary, if some social power were to take over the protection and economic care role of the father, for a simultaneous diminution to take place in men and women's desire for socially recognized stakes in each other's continuing sexual favors and personal attention. As they stand today, however, it may be said that a woman's need for socio-economic protection while she is carrying and if she is to care for a young child is only one factor in the determination of marriage forms. The elimination of this need would only partially reduce women's competition for sexual partners, and might actually enhance men's competition for women who would be less of a socio-economic responsibility than they are today. So while the most direct attack upon the family comes with the elimination of the father's services to the mother, the type of social change, which eliminates the father, would not guarantee the disappearance of the family if the children were left with the mother after birth.

There is a third function of the family, which is also universal in that it serves as the individualizing agency in society. The family has been glibly called "the transfer point of civilization" and a great deal of emphasis has been laid upon the function of the family in rearing the young as accurate replicas of the culture of their parents. If that culture is viewed atomistically, and we say that the growing child has to learn: to feed himself and to choose among those things, which are food and those which are not, to walk, to speak the language, to respect property, to control his sphincters, to distinguish among persons in terms of status, etc., then as we look over the cultures of the world, we can find each of these various culturally defined acts taught by someone other than the parents, by older children, servants, slaves, elders, teachers, etc. With the development of artificial feeding, there seems to be no single rearing act which the parents necessarily perform, and even here our ignorance has caused us to overestimate the essentiality of the mother's role, as it is quite possible for women who have not been pregnant or who have not borne a child recently, to produce milk to nourish some other woman's baby. In fact, it may be said that the very emphasis upon the family as a transfer point of civilization has been the background against which much of the lugubrious prophesying about the shrinking role of the family has come. Because in the pioneer American home, women wove their own children's clothes and today the same aged child can shop for his own with the assistance of an expert clerk, or because religious instruction was given in the pioneer American home, or letters and numbers learned there, the change in agencies which fulfill these services is alarming. Yet it is not any single teaching or rearing function of the family, which is actually crucial or universal. It has never been demonstrated that children reared by nurses, whose fathers and mothers perform the roles assigned to them for their status in that society, have weaker parental images, or show less impact of the parental personalities, than is the case for children whose parents spend much more time performing rearing services for them. But every society, of which we have any knowledge, depends upon a personal relationship between the growing child and a male and a female who are socially assigned to it as models, as clue-giving, path finding guides to its emerging role as a human being.

This role of parents as models may be diluted, as in Samoa where the child lives in a great family where several adult males and several adult females treat it in very much the same way; it may be shared between father and maternal uncle, as in the Trobriands, or between the father and the head of a clan, or a chief, etc., or between the mother and her co-wives, or her sisters-in-law, or grandmothers. Furthermore, when the parental role is shared among others, e.g., a mother and her sisters, the individuality of the child is correspondingly diluted, individual differences are blurred, the socially defined personality supersedes in definiteness the manifestations of idiosyncratically organized behavior. Upon the basis of the evidence, which we have at present, we can say that the family, the male and female parents as points of reference, is exceedingly significant in the process of individuation. In a society like our own, postulated upon the small biological family, the orphan, the child of broken home, manifests characteristic phantasies of one or both parents, and these phantasies then become potent determinants of personality development.

It is with this aspect of the family, in shaping individuals who differ one from another and who are conscious of the difference that the totalitarian state is at variance. To produce marching rows of identically healthy young people, with faces all stamped with the same attitudes and emotions, it is a logical step to try to minimize the importance of the family, not because the parents remain ideological heretics, but because parents who have too much influence, interfere with the rubber-stamping process. There is not sufficient data to make detailed and reliable comparisons, but it is interesting to note the difference in the fate of the ideological attack on the family in the early Soviet Union and in Nazi Germany. In the Soviet Union, the purely theoretical objections to the family seem to have been overcome by the incompatibility, within the personality, of no personal ties and responsible public behavior. In a socialist state, founded upon a belief in the ultimate potentialities of the individual, the emphasis has to be more upon social responsibility than upon rubber stamped docility. Put in the simplest terms, it looks as if the Soviet Union modified its early theoretical derogation of the family, because Russians reared in families made more responsible citizens if they founded them and more or less stuck to them. The early socialist dislike of the family as an institution was based upon the degree to which it fostered the peculiar competitive and acquisitive character structure of an individualistic capitalist society, and was identified with that type of society, but the more the Russian socialist experiment became integrated with the Russian national character, the more it seemed that the type of personality, fostered by the family, was desirable in the State. Probably nowhere else so much as in attitudes toward the family is the contrast more striking between a form of totalitarianism which avowedly develops the individual, and a form of totalitarianism devoted to the aggrandizement of the State, in which the individual becomes mere devisor.

In Nazi Germany we have a wholly different set-up, although superficially the relationship is similar. The Nazi opposition to the family appears to be grounded in a contradiction in the German character structure, an ambivalence toward the assumption of family ties, toward identification with the lower—the heterosexual and civilian side of the father's personality. This contradiction may be assumed to be established in the child personality owing to the special form, which husband and wife relationships take in traditional German culture. So the present attack on the family, perhaps the most complete attack in history, is nevertheless rooted in a personality structure itself dependent upon the family. To the extent that the Nazis change the form of marriage, relegate the woman to a husbandless home in which she bears children to Hitler, and permit the man complete sexual satisfaction, including the exercise of his duty to his country by producing children without having to settle down as a husband and father, they are actually altering the very mechanism which now gives dynamic force to the creation of a permanently adolescent army which is willing to march on and on to death. The course of the experiment will be so interrupted by the conclusion of the war that it may never be possible to assay the outcome. Nevertheless, something of the complications, which ensue when even an all-powerful state attacks the family may be guessed from these two instances: the Russian, lacking any such psychological spring board as the typical German adolescent day dream, simply evaporated, and the German, utilizing the force of a day dream destroyed the institution which created the psychological mechanism upon which its dynamics depended.

THE FAMILY AND THE IDEALS OF DEMOCRACY

Among the divergent definitions of democracy, that which insists upon the individual as an end for whom social institutions exist, and not as a means for their perpetuation, is a common platform today. It may therefore be a fair question to ask, if one accepts the individual as a value, where does that place one in regard to the acceptance of the family as an institution? Were it possible to eliminate the family entirely, would such a program fit into a culture dedicated to the development of the individual?

Here we may examine various levels at which the family functions to develop the individual. At the simplest level, the family, by providing a child with a male and a female model, defined as his father and his mother, two parents of opposite sex, gives the child his basic equipment for the psycho-sexual role which he is to play later in life. With our present data on the development of human instinctive drives, we have no way of telling how completely dependent a child is upon such models for even the most rudimentary later discharge of a "normal" sexual role. It is possible to say, however, that the type of sexual role, which a child will play, is, within homogeneous cultures, set up by the type of relationships, which he has with parents and parent figures. Highly generalized relationships to adults, as in Samoa, produce a type of sexuality, which responds with ease to whole categories of men or women. Intense, walled-in, exclusive family life will produce individuals who in turn are capable of forming intense, exclusive relationships, so that we get the odd contrasts which exist in cultures in which premarital relationships are casual, but married relationships are exclusive and possessive. If one aspect of complete human individuality is the exercise of choice and discretion in sexual responsiveness, it would seem clear that the mechanisms for developing such differential responses lie in the individual family; that the larger the number of parental surrogates, the easier, the less personal and discriminating, sexual choices are likely to become. It may, however, also be argued that the integration of sexual responsiveness with choice and discretion in other areas, is actually a handicap to the development of full individuality; that we would have freer individuals if they could rely upon their unquestioned ability to respond sexually to any member of the opposite sex and so could base their choices on other considerations. Against this may be argued that one of the necessary steps in the development of a free individual is the reduction in irrelevant and uncontrollable bodily impulses, and that just as the reduction of hunger to appetite three times a day, of weariness to sleepiness late in the evening, so also the reduction of sexuality from an insistent and perhaps rhythmic phenomenon to a response to a given individual valued for other reasons, is also a step in this direction. It has yet to be demonstrated that we can produce an individual with easy, undifferentiated sexuality who will not find the very unpatterned quality of his sexuality an interference with his choices in personal relationships. The difference between men and women's ability to channel their lives in terms of persons rather than urges, culturally attributed to differences in sexual drives, may actually be due to a differentially personalizing education in early childhood when the young child realizes that mother's attention is focused on father and father's attention is not so exclusively focused on mother. (It is probably quite possible for a child of three or four to learn something of this sort without any data on his father's actual or phantasied sex relationships.)

Under the learning of one's sexual role, as a child, should be placed of course also the way in which a child learns what membership in a sex means, for him or for her, and whether this learning is vague and general, or highly colored by the individuality of the parents who, in a limited, small family world, are the surrogates of maleness and femaleness. With our characteristic dependence upon the small biological family, young children take the most diverse clues from their own parents, deciding that maleness is related to gentleness or brutality, accuracy or bluntness, ability to handle machinery or inability to carve a roast, punctuality or lateness, vanity or disregard of personal appearance, etc. Where these individual conclusions run directly counter to the culture, they provide one false clue to later identification of the self as a sexual deviant. Conversely, where individuals differ so strikingly from each other, in personality and gifts, a boy who resembles his mother, in his preferences or his talents, may be led, in our close family situation, to make a false psychosexual identification of himself, and this again may lay the psychological basis for psychosexual deviation. Again, especially if reinforced by the large number of extra family contacts, a child concludes that it is more important to be a member of his own sex than to follow any other trend in his personality, following a parental model may make a child disallow some precious personal gift; for example, the mother may be a singer and the child also have a beautiful voice. If his father and the prevailing emphasis of the culture both tell him that men don't sing, his singing may be left undeveloped. If a boy is reared in a woman-dominated home, and later comes to feel that a man should be dominant in his own house, he may never be able to marry because the only women he is attracted to are dominating; but his desire to remain indubitably male has become tied up with his belief in a husband role which his choice of a wife would make impossible for him to play. Those who concentrate upon the hazards, which the family presents to the development of personality would stress conditions like these, and hope that we might find some less highly individualized method of developing children who would nonetheless have individualities.

A second way in which the individual family shapes personality is through all the varieties of sibling relationships. These may be considered in terms of the situational factors, which obtain in any family in which there is more than one child, and the cultural standardizations, which tend to override the significance of these special situations. Under the heading of situational factors we may place: whether the child came too soon or after a long wait, sex in relation to the sex desired, relative sickness and health of the mother during pregnancy, looks of the child, looks of the child as compared with the looks of the siblings, resemblance to parents, resemblance to affinal relatives, health of the child and ways in which its illness or lack of illness articulates with health of siblings, order of birth in terms of sex, age, of parents at birth, relative state of the parental relationship at different ages, life histories of all of the siblings, etc. In senses such as these, each family situation is different and each child's personality will bear the imprint of the situation, of having been a plain child in a family of beauties, a beautiful child in a family of plain children, the youngest daughter of a mother who has herself been a much-imposed-upon eldest, the one child who most closely resembled a tyrannical grandfather, or an aunt who had gone mad. The less homogeneous the culture, the less such matters as age and sex and order of birth have been made the subject of articulate social stereotyping, the greater will be the impact upon the child of the accidents of the composition of his own family.

Against this tremendous impact of situational factors, which is characteristic of our own society, we may place the effects of social stereotyping in which the eldest son, for instance, occupies a position entirely different from that of all the younger siblings. Such an institution as primogeniture is a social device for the creation of individuality by the superimposition upon both constitutional and situational factors of a fixed social expectation. So whether the first-born be healthy or puny, handsome or ill favored, relatively the brightest or relatively the stupidest among his siblings, he will be singled out, valued, specially trained to fill his role. Interaction between his natural and acquired fitness for that role, and the definition of the role, will further differentiate his personality. In the end product, first-born sons will have a type of individuality, which would not have occurred without the presence of the social stereotype. Although order of birth and sex preference—whether for boys or girls—are the commonest of such devices, other institutions like the American Indian device of a "Favorite Child" can be found which are designed to alter radically the development of some personalities in each generation. It will be readily seen that all institutions of this sort are analogous, within the family, to caste and class differentiations in the society at large. Through social expectation, differential rearing, and the presentation of social ideals, personalities are differentiated without regard to the natural endowment of the individual, and often in direct opposition to it.

A third way in which the form of the family shapes individuality is through the cultural standardization of ordinal position from the youngest living member of the family, rather than order of birth. Order of birth and the variants of order of birth standardizations have received so little attention that we actually lack a scientific vocabulary, and in order to describe—even for purposes of communication—the phenomena which I mean, I have to turn to the folk terminology of the south and speak of a "lap baby," a "knee baby" and a "yard child" which is one of the variants of these terms by which a mother describes the state in which her child is, in relation to its position from the bottom of the family. So a southern countrywoman may say, "Jimmy was my lap baby, Jill was the knee baby, and Jack was my yard child, when my mother died." In societies which have sharply defined attitudes toward the youngest, the next to the youngest, etc., and in which the distance between children tends to be stereotyped so that it is expected that a second child will come along when the present youngest is about two, each child goes through a series of well-defined stages in the behavior which is expected of it, and the way in which it is treated. Unlike the rigid conditions enforced by order of birth, each child in turn is "lap baby," "knee baby" and "yard child" in a society, which recognizes all three distinct positions. Even if later births do not follow to intensify the position, the adults will shift their behavior and treat a two-year-old as if he or she had a new baby brother, and treat a four-year-old as if there were two younger children to take up the mother's attention.

Because this aspect of cultural patterning of personality has been hitherto unrecognized we have very few usable records for other societies. On the basis of those that we have, it is possible to venture the following hypothesis: Differentiation of only two positions, that of youngest and next to youngest, seems associated with the development of a competitive personality in which either the expression or the suppression of aggression will be of primary importance and in which there will be a correspondingly low development of what has sometimes been called a "rich culture," that is, a culture replete with symbolic forms. The Arapesh and the Manus of New Guinea and our own Northern and Western American culture are examples of this first form. The child "whose nose is out of joint" is recognized as different from the baby; he is still primarily dependent upon and oriented to adults in behavior, and the relationship to the baby and the baby's relationship to him, are highly charged, subject to articulate comment and folk lore. He learns that he has been dispossessed, and the next younger child learns that he is a dispossessor, and this struggle becomes an important theme in later interpersonal relationships. As the child in the third position is not differentiated out, but is lumped with "children," "older children," etc., and so carries the rivalry directly from the face-to-face struggle of the nursery into the nursery school, the kindergarten, or the street playground, no new theme of greater psychic significance is introduced.

When we compare the patterning of age and position in the family among the Balinese and the Iatmul of New Guinea, we find a situation, which contrasts with this simple, two-position competitive set-up. In both these cultures—so divergent in other ways—we find a patterning of the family into groups of four. Among the Balinese there are four ordinal terms: eldest, second born, third born, and the little one, and these terms are used over again when a fifth child is born, with the expectation that there will be little conflict, that the four of the first set are separate from the four of the second set. Among the Iatmul, the saying is, the first child and the third are friends against the second and the fourth. When you ask about the fifth, you are told, "He would be too little." In both societies, the [third] from the youngest, the "yard child" of the American south, is still oriented to the parents, and not a member of the large diffuse children's group. Twice dispossessed, charged with a good deal of care of the infant, able to re-establish, through the infant, some of the relationship to the mother, which was rudely shattered when the present "knee baby" was born, the "yard child" is given a sort of pause in its social development, and does not carry an unresolved fresh rivalry out into the larger group. Although Bali is a static culture in which the arts alone have plot and movement, and Iatmul is a dynamic struggling culture in which the arts alone have form and stillness, in both one finds this extra "richness" as over against those cultures which define only two positions in the family. This is even more definite when they are compared with cultures like Samoa, the Lepchas, and the Kaingang, which define only one, that of the youngest, and then absorb the next child into a diffuse wider group.

In discussing family forms of the future it may be worthwhile to consider such cultural processes for the creation of more levels within the personality, levels, which in turn may provide the dynamics for a greater development of cultural creativity. In doing so it is important to distinguish between this mechanism and age grading which, especially if begun early enough, seems to be a de-individualizing process working in exactly the opposite direction. Age grading, by orienting a child's behavior to individuals of the same degree of maturity, tends to iron out individual differences, to introduce shame—fear of the disapproval of individuals for whom no great respect is felt but who are conceived of as the same and even inferior to the self—as a sanction for behavior, and so by reducing the complexity of the conscience structure to merely a desire for conformity, also to reduce the complexity of the personality. The contrast in the effects of differentiating levels of development—within the family setting by modeling the differentiating levels of development upon position from the youngest—and without the family setting, by age grading in which absolute size or age or level or maturity provides the clue—is due to the different role of adults, primarily of parents. Within the family, the child is primarily oriented to the parents and the siblings are significant as part of the relationship to the adults—who themselves have fully developed personalities; in the age grade situation the child is not oriented to adults but to contemporaries. It is probably worth mentioning here also the contrast between upbringing by parents, or parent surrogates of the same age and status, and upbringing by child nurses or servants or grandparents, which produces quite a difference in character structure. The present role of the nursery school teacher might easily develop into the role played by these non-parental figures with a consequent effect upon the child's personality comparable to the effect of being reared by a nurse of different social status from the parents. The relative position of the teacher and the immigrant parent, or the parent whose status in the child's eyes is lower than that of the teacher would again produce important alteration in the personality. Where the person who shares the child rearing with the parent is voted less exacting or of lower status than the parent, there is less tendency for the child to develop a conscience and more tendency for behavior to be referred to his own status as defined by parents. Where the persons who share the child rearing are of superior status or more exacting than the parents, it is possible to develop a most violent sensitivity, a kind of bitter shame, which is grounded in the continuing relationship to the parents who are despised but cannot be actually removed from consciousness.

However, the exponent of the future development of the individual, while recognizing the family as the mechanism through which individuality is developed, internal sanctions built up, levels of personality differentiated, may still say, "the price is too high." Family life, because of the way in which it delivers over plastic sensitive infants to the almost absolute power of single pairs of adults, wrecks too many lives, provides too many individuals with a life history so distorting, so limiting that they never can realize their full potentialities as human beings. We must make some inventions, which will preserve the values now developed by the family and prevent the hazards. Such a cry, against what the family offers the individual, is likely to come most vigorously from our present unpatterned world in which no one individual's experience can be adequately matched with another's, in which a poem at best may only evoke an answering

ring in some twenty other breasts. A minimum of patterning of human relations brings out all of the arbitrary features of the role of the family and throws into the background the more deeply valuable ones. For every individual whose personality, whole and complex, can be seen to present the orderly representation of a masculine father and a feminine mother, who loved each other, and treated each child according to his age and sex and degree of maturity, giving that intensity of attention which is compatible with the very narrowness of the family circle, we see a plethora of individuals whose lives have been marred by the relative strength or beauty of a sibling, by reversed roles between their parents, by the fact that they were unwanted or born the year the father lost his job for good. From a scrutiny of the heavy toll which family life as at present organized takes of human potentialities, it is possible to make several suggestions.

We may say, the family is under too much strain today, and the individual tragedies among the children are a result of this too great strain. Let us create in society social mechanisms to take off the strain, to provide for prenatal care, for the children when the mother is ill, for periods when the father is unemployed, for the education of the gifted and the special care needed by the crippled or defective, for the vacation which may be all a mother needs to keep her from breaking up the family entirely, for expert guidance when children or spouses show deep disturbance, for nursery schools to take the strain off the city home, or off the lonely child, or off a pair of siblings who don't get on, for vocational guidance to replace the parents' special ambitions, and for summer camps to provide a gradual weaning. Let us, in fact, examine the points at which the family breaks down, and provide social mechanisms to bolster it, supplement it, complement it, or if necessary take over at these particular points. Such a course of action would do a great deal to produce improved human beings. But such a course is actually necessary, not so much because the family as an institution is inadequate, but because the individual should not be asked to function under conditions which are impossible. It is not the father of a family, but the breadwinner, even if he only wins bread for himself, who should not be asked to cope with a society organized as ours is today. It is not the mother of children who needs advice on nutritional cooking; it is any cook who can no longer depend upon a reliable tradition to balance her meal of over-processed foods. It is not only the son of ambitious parents who needs vocational advice, but any boy trying to find a vocation in a world about which only a specialist can know enough to help him. In fact a great proportion of the weaknesses which we now attribute to the family, are merely the weaknesses of a social system, which has not caught up with itself.[1]

If we assume that this will be remedied, that we will build a society, which gives the individual security and expert help at every turn, could we then rely upon the family, without further inventions, making the largest possible contribution to the development of human personality? I do not think we can. I think it is necessary to begin to plan, to begin to develop a background, for further inventions to meet three conditions: [2] (1) that there are more women than men in the world and we are assuming, with quite deep reason, that monogamy will remain the primary form; (2) that the more complex the culture and the more highly differentiated the individuals within it, the longer will be the period of maturation, and the more chance there will be of couples getting out of step; and (3) the fact that children are very often temperamentally different from both parents or from parent of own sex.

If we are to have full development for every human being, girls as well as boys, we cannot continue to countenance a set-up in which a proportion of the girls will be branded as failures, by themselves as well as by others, because they have not married. If this is to be avoided, not only must there be roles for unmarried women which are equal in dignity with that of marriage, but devices must be found for presenting such a role to the growing girls and boys at the age when their ideals of sex roles are developed. The old suggestion that any woman who wishes should be allowed to have a child is out of key with all our findings on the importance of parents of both sexes in the child's development. It could only be reconciled by the development of some form of social fatherhood, in which a man would be willing to play the role of social father to his own children and say to his wife's sister's child, that child having been produced, for example, by artificial impregnation. Both boys and girls reared in such a home would be psychologically prepared for the acceptance of such a role; again, the girl, in the absence of a husband, to arrange for an impersonal pregnancy with the plan of rearing her child co-operatively with some couple who were willing to have her share their lives; the boy to play the role of social father to some child who was not his own and whose mother was not his sexual partner. Another solution of the extra number of women is the "office wife," the woman who finds sharing a man's work sufficiently interesting to compensate for not sharing some different man's bed and bearing him children. If such a position is to be dignified, however, and so made into a possible choice for a growing girl, then as a child she must be exposed, if not to her own father's "office wife," at least to such situations in other homes, in the movies, in literature, until choosing one kind of relationship to one man, as over against another kind of relationship to another man, comes to seem a dignified solution. With the greater differentiation of personality, we cannot tell which result we will finally obtain, a greater desire on the part of every individual for physical reproductivity, or a greatly lessened desire in many. Almost inevitably, however, during the next few decades while our cultural processes of developing personality remain as confused as they are at present, there will be many individuals whose desire for reproductivity, or for permanently sharing the lives of others, is low. At present these individuals, especially when they are women, often act like dogs in the manger, marrying not because they want any of those things which can only be obtained in marriage, but because marriage is status giving. We will probably only dare to take status giving away from marriage and give equal respect and free movement to the unmarried woman, if we cease to be interested in the increase of population. Once, however, the world is organized so that one nation is not pitted against another, the advantages of a rising population should fall in favor of the advantages of developing fewer people into better persons, and at that point it will be no longer necessary to reward marriage and child bearing. Possibly at the same time, inventions which control the sex of conceptions, medical inventions which can preserve a larger number of babies born and minimize the greater risks to the male sex, the abolition of war, and reduction in the size of families, may level out the birthrate so that great discrepancies in the sex ratio will no longer occur. Meanwhile, stabilizing the role of the unmarried woman is one necessary precaution for protecting the family from the instabilities, which come from greater individual complexity and resultant failure of husbands and wives to stay in step.

If, because we want families in which to rear children, we continue to give status only to married women, refuse to make the necessary inventions so that unmarried women can have children and find social fathers for them, and to deny guilt-free sex relationships to those who have no intention of having children, we are likely to end up with increasingly brittle family situations in which the psychic development of the children is jeopardized rather than promoted. Very strong compensatory social forms of this sort must be developed to take the strain off the family in which the parents no longer find each other the single interesting choice for sex, or social or intellectual companionship. Otherwise, every family must face the continual insecurity, which comes from shifts in interest and personality as each parent develops in ways which were not anticipated at the age of twenty-one when they married. Alternatively, especially with a decreased premium on population increase, we might seek to establish a pattern of late childbearing marriages, prefacing these by socially sanctioned, childless contracts. Such planning, however, must wait upon better medical knowledge of whether late child bearing handicaps the child in any way. If it were found not to do so, emphasis upon final late marriages, entered into in maturity, after the instabilities of early experimentation were past, might be an effective way of guaranteeing to children a home which would give them a real chance at complete personality development. Such a social pattern would also reduce one other inequality between the sexes and a potential threat to the monogamous marriage, the fact that the man of forty who had children at twenty-one is far younger, physically and psychologically, than his wife of the same age whose children are now grown. With children as the principal common interest in marriage, the late child bearing marriage is ensured against the instabilities of this dangerous age, and the difference in the period of reproductivity between man and woman is minimized.

However, there will still be a further invention to make somehow to adjust the difference in temperament, in inherited constitution, between parents and children. It may be, although it seems hardly likely at present, that constitution may be found to be inherited in some reckonable way, so that at least the potentialities of one's children's inheritance can be calculated as can be the chances for fraternal twins, or color blindness, now. Even if this were found to be so, this would only permit parents to protect themselves against a marriage which might give them a kind of child they didn't want. It would not permit them to select the temperament of their children, nor would it help the children. Meanwhile, we have a form of society, which, because all types of human beings are cross fertile, subjects a large proportion of the human race to having their personalities irrevocably shaped by persons who are profoundly alien to them. In homogenous cultures, such as primitive societies, where the cultural forms are so uniform that the basic character structure of all adults is tremendously alike, the child is ensured a large amount of coherent treatment, which will guarantee that he will turn out very much like the children next door, no matter how different from himself, temperamentally, his parents may be. But as these cultural uniformities break down and the individual parents are given more and more latitude in the ways in which they treat their children, the outrage of having children of one type of sensitivity reared by parents with a quite different type becomes steadily greater, and the casualties, not only in loss of potentialities but also in neuroses and psychoses, become greater. We do not know what the differences are between being reared by parent of own temperament, of own sex and own temperament, of opposite sex, of growing in a family where both parents are own temperament, or whether neither is, of having siblings whose temperaments are like the parents when one's own is not, of being reared by a parent whose temperament closely approximates the cultural expectation for personality as over against one whose temperament is very divergent to that expectation when one is, or is not, oneself the temperament which the culture assumes for one's sex or class. There are a staggering number of possibilities even if one only assumed an improbable small number of basic temperaments, such as four or eight. Yet this condition must be reckoned with. At present the culture, through the family, bullies each developing individual into some final character which for thirty [or] eighty per cent of those born into it, is a poor fit, and adds, wherever the family is important, the extra complication of the distortion of a culturally determined character structure A, transmitted to female child B, by a mother who is actually C, and has married a man who is B, but was brought up by a C father. Therefore, we cannot know whether what we call human personality is the valuable complication contributed by such a series of deviant interpretations of the culture, or merely the thinnest and feeblest approximation to what a human being could be, brought up by a man and a woman of own temperament, and provided with cultural forms congruent with that temperament. In thinking about the future of the family as the primary agent for the development of the individual, one matter, which deserves study, will be—as our knowledge of temperament, of the relationship of original temperament to culturally imposed character develops—to decide whether we may someday want to substitute foster parents of own temperament for parents of own blood, or at least provide highly stylized mechanisms by which they—equipped with cultural forms to offer the child—can share in its upbringing.

NOTES

1. As a corollary of all the suggestions and inventions, which may be loosely lumped together under the heading of social security, it is worthwhile mentioning the modern trend toward developing agencies of society which treat the family as a unit, and in whose vocabulary the word *family* has become a pronoun. These new developments come from two sources, as a logical development of the application of modern social adjustment techniques to farm families whose family life still embraces their entire way of getting a living, and as a corrective to the fractionating tendencies of urban agencies of amelioration which have often failed to take into account the only unity left to urban families, their personal interdependence.

2. Some exception may be taken here to my failure to discuss whether women are or are not to remain inside the home. It seems, however, sufficiently obvious that if women are individuals, a society devoted to the development of individuals will allow women as much opportunity as men, allowing also for the special aspect of their sex, producing and rearing children. If we are discussing the preservation of the individualizing aspects of the family, the preservation of the essentials of family life, patterned, continuing and close relationships between children and both parents are essential. The circumstances that at present such relationships are tied up with the endless waste of effort involved in individual cook stoves, and individual washing machines, is not the sort of situation over which it is necessary to linger long here. Furthermore, employment of women outside the home for a large part of their adult lives is inextricably tied up with the type of economy which we develop. In the development of an economy of abundance they will be badly needed; in the enjoyment of an economy of abundance hours of labor would be so reduced that both parents would be able to work and to have ample leisure for personal relationships.

1945

HUMAN DIFFERENCES AND WORLD ORDER*

Editor's Commentary

This second of the twenty-five selctions in this book dates from the year World War II came to an end. In it Mead addresses a religiously concerned audience, in somewhat impromptu fashion, and deals with a question that suddenly became salient in 1945: How to construct a new, humane and sustainable world order? Mead, who was a lifelong member of the Episcopal church and often active in church affairs, seeks to bring religious thinking together with anthropological thinking, so that each may nourish the other. She argues strongly that a successful new world order must be founded upon a respect for each culture, thereby capturing from each its own special excellence, for the benefit of all humanity.

*   *   *

I am going to talk today within the Judeo-Christian tradition but without prejudice to my right to talk with wider reference, because I feel that if we are going finally to build a world order, we must have an ethic that will use the best of all the great religions. But the problem that we have to tackle first is how to deal, within the framework of our own religious backgrounds, with the moral problems raised by human differences. I am going to discuss particularly the relationship between the religious valuation put upon every human soul regardless of any attributes, including intelligence, color, or status—a basic religious tenet—and each problem of difference as it comes up. The minute you start discriminating between the feeble-minded and the dull, the normal and the brilliant or the genius, you face a religious problem if you are going to construct a society, which favors one and does not favor the other. So that if we take as a demonstrated fact, demonstrated over and over again, that some

---

* In: *World Order: It's Intellectual and Cultural Foundations*, ed. F. Ernest Johnson. (Institute of Religious Studies, New York: Harper & Brothers, 1945), 40-51.

people are better at some things than others, the minute that is made into any sort of policy, we come up against the religious valuation of each human being. This problem has taken a great many forms at different times. However, I do not want to discuss today specifically the problem of human differences within one culture because that is not within my competence.

I want to talk about human differences, potential human differences, as they have been institutionalized in different cultures. If we look either at the great cultures of the world or at the very small ones—which anthropologists usually look at—we find in either case that they have picked up one type of human being as ideal or as natural. Some people say if anything is natural, that makes it ideal. Others say if it is ideal, it is unnatural. However, each civilization that we know anything about has accepted one or more clues to the ideal. Sometimes they took one type of human being for men and one for women, sometimes they took one for the aristocrat and one for ordinary people, sometimes they took one for priests and one for laymen. But they have taken one or more special types and exalted their possibilities—exalt is probably too heavily charged a word—but at least, they have said, "This is the way people ought to be," or "the way they are," and then have developed, unconsciously in most cases, consciously in a few, such as the great military states, a method of pulling all the people who were born to be something else into a closer and closer approximation of the norm or type adopted.

We can see that process very clearly in primitive societies, much more clearly than in big diversified societies like our own. Among the American Indians, for instance, you find tribes where male bravery is of tremendous importance. To fail to be brave is to fail to be male, and is to disgrace your parents. The minute the baby is born such societies begin to teach it not to fear the scorpion or the tarantula. They exaggerate the merit of physical bravery. Grandfathers make up booby traps for small boys. They will send one down to the spring where something falls on his head or jumps out from behind a rock. In a good many tribes the training is too extreme. They have picked a type of behavior to which ten per cent of the human race can measure up very easily, and fifty per cent can do it without much effort, but the rest cannot.

Various phenomena result among American Indian tribes. Some boys give up and say, "I can't do this and I am not going to try." Then the tribe says, "You dress like a woman," and so he dresses like a woman. They push the standardization so far over to one type of human potentiality that they automatically throw out some people at the other end who just cannot achieve it.

We also have done that in a good many cases. Whenever our standardization of women in one way and the men in another has been too extreme, a certain number of men decided they preferred to act as women and, vice versa, a certain number of women decided that to act as women was too difficult.

The standardized sex position is the most striking, but the same sort of extreme demands obtain in tribes where they do not make a sex distinction in personality expectation and where both men and women are expected to be bold, cruel, and ruthless; or gentle, warm, and friendly. If the expectation is too extreme, individuals born in that tribe who have no capacity for boldness, cruelty, or ruthlessness, but who have the capacity to be mild and gentle, will be dealt with in various ways. Sometimes they will be called artists. Sometimes the society will call them shameful names, sometimes kill them, and sometimes they give them to an enemy. All sorts of treatment have occurred.

On the primitive-tribe level, the culture is obviously a system of traditional behavior, which emphasizes certain aspects of human potentialities and neglects others. Now, at this period of history, we have several hundred—nobody knows exactly how many—such versions of human behavior on this earth recorded in living people; that is, recorded in flesh and blood, in people's muscles, in their whole style of behavior and expectation of other people's behavior. A good many more versions of ancient civilizations exist on paper of which we have a good enough record to show that no people like them live today, that they were a definable type of human being, with literature, religion, and art of their own.

We have these different cultures in the world: they are identifiable and describable and to an extent we have the tools now for describing or identifying one as over against the others. There are many different ways of doing it, but the method I myself use, and therefore can talk about with the most competence, is to look at the newborn baby as potentially a member of any culture. Now he is not potentially bright if he is stupid, of course; but potentially he is the best-placed person in a group that has picked up his type of temperament, or the worst-placed person in a group that has not, or an average-placed person in a group where his temperament does not interest people one way or the other. Then you watch and see what happens to that child as he is made irrevocably into a member of his own culture and less and less able to be a member of another culture. If you do that, you have a method of describing the differences between societies within the same scientific frame of reference. As long as we explain our great civilizations in terms of their past, we make statements such as this, "The Germans are behaving the way they are now because they had the industrial revolution late." But you cannot describe primitive societies in terms of their past.

In a sense, cultural anthropology has one very important democratic tenet and it is related to the Judeo-Christian tenet of the value of human souls. Our units are cultures and we treat them all alike. We regard each culture, whether it is that of a group of Eskimos or a group of Zulus, the culture of ancient Egypt, of modern China, or of the United States, as a unit, a complete way of life for the people who live it. A culture, if it is a functioning culture, enables those who are reared within it to grow up to have a view of the world, to bring up their children, to feed them and to keep them alive so that they will be able to take over when the parents die. When a culture fails to do those things, it disappears, and in the case of a primitive society, it may disappear without leaving any record.

If, then, we look at the problem of the world order, we may decide that we like our own contemporary culture so well that the thing to do is to turn all these other people to it. That is quite a common American solution; I am not being fantastic in suggesting it. To do that, however, we would need pretty extensive help from scientists, even if we were dealing with 300 cultures—which is probably much too few, but will do as a simplification. We probably would shoot all the people in some cultures because it would be too difficult to bring those 300 into line and the rates at which we would bring them into our cultural picture would differ. By the time the 299th was molded to our values, something pretty extreme might have happened to number one, brought in a long time earlier. Science would be needed to implement even such cultural imperialism. The time factor would be so serious that, even if we had the knowledge to say, "All right, this is what these people are and we want to destroy what they are and turn them into people like us in the shortest possible time, keeping enough people alive while we do it," it would still be an exceedingly complicated process.

I am not discussing ethics at all but simply the science of the situation. It has been done occasionally. One very striking illustration was the action of a group of German missionaries in New Guinea, who studied anthropology very carefully so that they could exactly figure out what the natives were up to. They went, not as missionaries, not bringing any gospel of the Lord to start with, but simply as anthropologists. They found out everything they could about the natives and proceeded to destroy the native culture quickly. In ten years they produced a tribe that had given up everything they had ever lived for. They started gradually pouring something into that vacuum. How satisfactory this could be is another question, but such rapid changes can be produced.

Culture wrecking is possible. Whether what you have left is valuable, whether a human being who has been brought up in one whole series of behaviors and has had all of them taken from him, is valuable in the sight of God, or has been in many, many instances dehumanized by the experience, is another question. But I am assuming in this group that knowledge of that type of procedure is not what you want, that you do not want to know how we can destroy the existing fabric of life in other societies and build a feeble copy of our own, but how to take what is there and build toward something good for the world.

One of the principal differences between anthropology and religion, and it is true of any religion, including in some cases ordinary, garden-variety, ethical philosophers who have none, is the belief that has grown up in the past twenty-five years that anthropologists are ethical relativists, that they say to their students, "You see over there they eat their grandmothers and over here they do not. So obviously it doesn't make much difference whether you eat your grandmother or not." Anthropologists do not do this. Practices that are repugnant to our ethical system, often also to the natives who practice them, tend to disappear on encountering expectation of the reverse. It is very interesting to see the way these practices which are most repugnant to humans disappear quickly when primitive people are given a chance at something else. The invocation of these various barbarous practices in the interest of ethical relativism has come from destructive people from other disciplines who wanted illustrations to prove that nothing matters, not from anthropologists. Anthropologists themselves—maybe somebody will come forward with some dreadful exception—on the whole have realized that these things are part of a system, and that it is not a question of whether killing your grandmother is a virtue in one society and a vice in another, and therefore it does not matter whether you kill your old people or not. Rather, in a given system, in a given set of circumstances, for those people who have grown up in that system, there is a certain code of right and wrong, which always applies to themselves. You cannot pick one practice here and one practice there and arrange them in a row and say that nothing matters. Anthropological material can be used to prove that everything is relative, but the anthropologist who has respect for the material knows this is not so. It is only when you pull single customs out from dozens of cultures and arrange the examples in sequence that you get a natural relativity. When you look at a whole culture, you do not get any relativity at all, but you realize that each society has its own system of ethics. I think that it is an impor-

tant point to get straight if people who are interested in religious values are going to use anthropological material. As long as they feel that
the anthropologist is simply destructive, because they have heard
anthropological material used destructively, we will not get anywhere
because we have not agreed on any sort of common tenet and it is not
possible to go much further.

The next facet of this question I want to bring up is the way in
which a respect for each culture, as something that man has developed over a long period of time, fits into the whole relationship
between science and religion. I have just come back from England,
and if one takes part in ordinary discussions with English people, or
with mixed English and American groups who have been up against
a similar problem, one is very conscious of one great distinction. The
English still think of man as the junior partner of God. Sometimes
they think of England specifically as a junior partner of God, but
always as a junior partner. They have a picture of the world in which
what man can do is very subordinate to that which is already given.
And so the figures of speech that they employ most in human relations are horticultural. In England you have to talk about *growth, cultivation,* and *process.* You can *plant,* you can *pray* and you can *water* the
seed, but you cannot be sure how the plant is going to grow. In talking to any audience you have to use these horticultural figures of
speech all the time to get any sort of response.

With an American audience one uses such figures of speech as
these: we *build,* we *construct,* we *draw blueprints,* we *engineer.* We talk
about human engineering and we give a picture, on the whole, of a
people who are not the junior partner of God but just do not need
God, a people who have a great big open country and who can fix it in
any way they like. One feels this difference very sharply in any sort of
discussion, and it keeps recurring. That contrast is all the more peculiar
because our country has the greater number of church members.

In fact, such an attitude is still very strong in Britain. Some people state it explicitly in religious terms, and some refer to the power
of history or tradition, but what they mean is that something in the
universe is greater than man and the only thing man can do is to find
out what this is and work with it.

Now the American genius has been different. The American did
not have to work within history. He cut off his European history with
an ax when he came over here. He came to a continent virtually unpatterned except by a few Indians. All he saw were a few wigwams
and a scratch on a birch tree. He did not have to respect history. He
did not have to respect the fallow meadow that had been a fallow
meadow for 300 or 1000 years. There was not anything about that

primeval forest that he had to respect and his one idea was to cut it down. There was nothing given in the situation, and the peculiar version of Christianity that he brought with him was one that exalted the individual human being who needed little except his own soul and his own industry and his own virtue to get on in the world. His relationship to God was exceedingly individual and personal so that he had no history, only the ax and the primeval forest and the belief that the Lord prospered the just man, and, since he prospered, the Lord must approve of him.

This very striking picture has been accentuated by a large-scale culture. Because we build such big buildings that we must get our blueprints right, we get a tremendous sense that our blueprints are very powerful. A few years ago a mistake was made in a single benchmark. It was a very small mistake but it cost a large Eastern railroad something like two million dollars because it meant that the blueprints were wrong. From that sort of thing we got this great sense of the importance of our blueprints, and we tend to identify science on the whole with the American blueprint, and to identify respect for the old established way of doing things and for a universe greater than man with the old-fashioned European point of view.

This seems to me to pose a very difficult problem because if one looks as a scientist at men today—and I am looking as a scientist, but as a social scientist, not as a technologist—we can see that a sense of absolute power is not very good for men. You may think this is speaking in too simple ethical terms, but we have not yet developed the type of man who can stand a sense of absolute power. I do not say we could not, but we have not, and on the whole every time that we have built a civilization where man had an enormous sense of power we have not been able to develop the checks and balances that go with it, to keep it in abeyance. Looking at the situation religiously one may say that man becomes arrogant and lacking in humility if he thinks he can have everything his own way. If we look at it scientifically, we say we have not yet developed a civilization which can give man his sense of absolute power to do as he likes and still develop human beings who can live with dignity, making continuingly developing contributions to the world.

The problem is in a sense the same problem whether posed by the religious or by the scientist looking at different societies. What are the implications of the American's belief in man's absolute power to alter and change the environment unchecked by anything? He does not see why he cannot build a temperate city in the tropics; he will just have air conditioning inside every building. Climate means nothing to him. Weather means nothing to him. No conditions are insurmountable. In the same way he will rear the kind of human beings he likes.

Now it would seem to me that one of the clues, if we are going to use social science in a society in accord with our religious ethics, is that the religious ethic demands a sense of humility in man. Technology, especially the engineering type of technology, tends to breed a sense of power and certainty: "Draw the blueprint and we will make it."

How are we going to reconcile those two attitudes, especially in this particular field that I am talking about? We may consider three conceivable courses that might be taken with this great diversity of culturally defined human differences, differences that are due to the fact that one group of people were born under one set of historically developed institutions, and people of another group were born under another set. We have cultural differences in the world, what can we do with them?

First, we might refuse to associate with people of other cultures, but this has ceased to be a practicable method. It is a logical possibility, but it is out.

Secondly, we might destroy all others except our own. But in so doing in all probability we would destroy our own. And I am not saying that simply in religious terms, but in scientific terms. Finally, we might use what there is. We might try to find out what is the special contribution and special gift of each of these cultures. But if we are going to do that, there still remains the question of what tone of voice we are going to use. Are we going to accept the Chinese, the Mohammedans, and the Indians, if we go outside our own religious borders, or, if we stay inside, are we going to try to combine the kind of culture one finds in the Mediterranean with the kind one finds in the British Isles and Scandinavia, because we cannot help it—every other course of action being more expensive and more destructive— or shall we elect to do so because there are definite values there?

The question whether there are definite values in such a course takes us back to the idea of humility. If we could draw blueprints for the kind of society we want, if we knew enough to say, "All right, if we want a diversified world, let's have ten kinds of cultures, one that emphasizes the scientist, one that emphasizes the artist, and one that emphasizes religion. Let's have one group that likes being industrious and one that likes mopping up floors and doing other uninteresting things, and so on. Let's plot new cultures. We can find out how to do that. All we have to do is study human psychology and study existing civilizations, write a blueprint, and capture babies and bring them up and we will produce these societies."

To a degree that is the tone of voice of Nazism and it was earlier to some extent the tone of voice of Russian Communism. I think the shift back to the family in Russia is an interesting thing and an example of alteration in the tone of voice. I think they found they could not get the formula to produce responsible individuals without going back to a very hoary institution. Whether they went back to it in humility, I do not know.

On the one hand, we might say, "We can build the kind of diversified culture we want by taking the cultures of the present world. As long as we have some anyway, let's use them." That would still be a point of view lacking in any humility that is religiously acceptable. But, on the other hand, we might say, "We do not know enough and in all probability will never know enough to build human cultures synthetically; so the experience of countless generations, interacting in a way so complicated that to get it down on paper is exceedingly difficult, is greatly better than anything we can conceivably plan and execute. We could not, acting like a group of engineers, write out the specifications and produce the sort of human beings that we wanted. Therefore, we take what history has provided for us, the infinitely diverse expressions of the human spirit, the ones that have survived— and only a few have survived. We have no idea how many other possibilities there might have been, how many other forms of art, how many other languages, how many other ways of putting the baby to sleep there might have been in the world besides the ones we know of. We take this heritage realizing that we do not know enough, that if we attempted to build a culture synthetically we would fail because this whole process is more complex than we are able to understand, and that, once one of these cultures disappears completely, we cannot replace it. We are working with a set of irreplaceable things. New ones may develop but the ones that are destroyed will probably never appear again. And each of these cultures, because it has concentrated on one possibility, one potentiality of man, or two or three only, to the neglect of others, has within it implicit inventions that we would not be able to make."

This seems to me a possible ethical platform for a meeting of those who believe that man thinking of himself as a junior partner of God develops reasonably respectable character, but feeling himself to be a senior partner to date has developed a very bad character, and those who feel that to the extent that science says, "We know everything, we can make and we can fix everything, and we do not need religion and we do not need anything else," science itself is missing the truth. There seems to me to be a possible common platform where scientists say, "We can study, we can identify, and we can tell you what these cultures are, and we can tell you how they may be able to blend and combine, but we could not make them. They have been made over a long, long period of time and we have not the omnipotence to reproduce them or to produce anything that is half so good."

Thus one gets an approach to world order in which scientists and those whose major orientation is religious, can work side by side instead of against each other, in which respect for each culture becomes a tenet of man's humility, in which we build a world that is richer because there are all these experiences of the human spirit in it and that would be poorer if it lost any one of them. In practice, this means that as we start planning any sort of world order we must believe that each of the great civilizations has a contribution to make, and that within our own Judeo-Christian group each of the great religious orientations has its particular contribution to make, and that if any one is left out—and by left out I mean not only not given a seat at the peace table, but not allowed to participate in all the planning, policy making, implementation and reconstruction at every step—we will be just so much poorer. Not only will we lack the thread in our planning that would appeal to millions of people who are unrepresented because their own particular faith has not contributed, but also because the solution itself will be poorer. No single culture can produce so good a solution as can a group of cultures working together.

In every single culture only a few people have been developed to their best. But because each culture has one emphasis at the expense of another, if America developed one kind of person, England another, France another, Italy another—until we put them together we could not tap the potentialities of the human race. The only way those full potentialities of the human race can be tapped is by making use of the various ways in which these different potentialities have been picked out and institutionally developed over a long period of time until each particular kind of personality is given the fullest implementation, having a language that suits him, an art that suits him, the method of conducting interpersonal relations that suits him, and a marriage system that suits him. Each culture gives some people, some members of that society, a special chance. If we want to tap the whole range, we must tap it through the different cultural expressions of human differences, which have been built up for several hundred thousand years.

1950

UNIQUE POSSIBILITIES OF THE MELTING POT*

Editor's Commentary

In this lecture Mead proclaims a theme that will undergird much
of her subsequent career as a public anthropologist, namely that
sociocultural life in the U.S. had become so complex, and sociocultural change so rapid, that people were being called upon to
handle their lives in numerous new ways for which their personal enculturation had not prepared them. People were
being forced to deal with problems so new to them, that the culturally transmitted standards and guidelines they had learned as
children and adolescents—from their parents, grandparents, and
other early role models—were often useless or worse. Parents
were being forced to raise children in unfamiliar ways, and their
children were emerging as persons very different from what the
parents had been like at a similar age.

Since past guidelines were no longer adequate, people had a
greater need to adapt. And, although Mead does not explicitly
say so, a logical extension of her message is that since change had
now become so rapid, success in adapting to new situations
clearly called for skills in anticipating future change.

These themes of rapid change and accelerating complexity
gave birth to a related theme that Mead continued to proclaim
until the end of her life, namely that the present era, and the
next generation or so, would probably prove to be the most crucial period that the human species had ever known.

In explicating these two fundamental themes of her emerging
role as a public anthropologist—as here, in addressing an audience
of social workers—Mead anticipates some of the key points of a
book she published twenty years later, which gained the respect of
futurists as a fore-runner to the Futures Studies movement.[1]

* * *

I WANT TO DISCUSS what is necessary for us as Americans to know
about ourselves if we are going to be able to judge accurately what we
can do in the world, if we are going to be able to tell where we stand

* In: *Proceedings of the National Conference of Social Work*, 79-89.

in the whole world picture and what inventions we are better able to make than other people because world trends have gone farther in this country than in other countries. If we know these things accurately we must know where we are ahead, where we are coping with something that other people may not have to cope with for twenty years, maybe for forty, when we ourselves will be somewhere else. Only if we are quite clear about the relationship between our problems and the world's will we be able to make a good contribution to the world. On the other hand, if we are awfully impressed with the fact that we eat three meals a day and go about the world trying to get everybody else to eat three meals also, we can do a great deal of harm. Perhaps social work is one of the fields in which it is most crucial that Americans should understand who they are and where they are; because social work is so much more advanced in this country than in most parts of the world, inevitably it will make a large contribution to any sort of international development in social work.

There are a great many things that could be said about our position, but I shall choose just a few. We are further along than any other country in the experiment of mingling all the races of the world. We are the only sizable country that has large contingents of all three races, all living together, all being educated the same way. We are perfecting an enormous number of inventions every day that will make these people look more alike, we are curling the straight hair and straightening the curly, using cosmetics to "widen" the narrow cheek bones and "narrow" the wide ones.

What have we learned in the course of our experiments in ignoring—or at least beginning to ignore—physical differences that have no psychological or social meaning except what we give them? First, we have perfected some inventions for the rest of the human race; for in this country, now that everybody is trying to look like the national stereotype, beauty has become what one makes it oneself instead of that with which one was born. We say less often, "What a beautiful girl." We say, "She makes the most of her possibilities." (And social casework records are filled with descriptions of how the little client puts on cosmetics. The first time I read a case record that approved of the client's beginning to use rouge I knew that something momentous had happened.) We have done a great deal with the experiment of taking people of enormously different physiques, washing them all with special soap, putting them all in well-ventilated rooms, after they have slept in laundered and sterilized sheets—building sanitation to a level that it has never reached in the world before. Most peoples in the world like smelling the better class of their own people, they do not like smelling any other class or any other people. And so

Americans have had to cease to smell like any class or any nationality. And we have done it; that is, we are on our way to doing it, we are moving in that general direction. No other country has tried any comparable experiment. It is difficult and it is worth realizing that it is difficult.

In the second place, we have gone farther in social design organization, in taking people away from every kind of kin and neighborhood and locality, away from the place where their ancestors were buried to live in a place where they themselves probably will not be buried, or even cremated—moving them, moving them, moving them, from one place to another, from flat 26C at number 1125 39th Avenue to flat 31F at number 2147 37th Avenue in a different city, so that even if they had had years of experience in keeping records for the FBI they could hardly remember their addresses. People move from one anonymous flat to another anonymous flat, and someday in the psychiatrist's office they try in vain to remember where that picture was that once hung over the bed. We have gone further in moving people away from everyone they have formerly known than any culture has ever done. However, we can expect that in Europe and in Asia more and more people will live the kinds of lives that people live in America, moving and moving again, making new ties and breaking them, all through their lives. Experience that we gain in learning what it is like to move, how to live in new places, and how to leave without too great heartbreak will be useful to the rest of the world.

Then, thirdly, there is another change, which I think is exceedingly important, especially for social workers. We have moved from marriage for life to terminable marriage except for those who live within an orthodox religious fold. Everything that went with life-long, guaranteed monogamy, in which even a couple who did not speak to each other for twenty years stayed married, has vanished. We now have to set to work to devise courtship institutions, marital behavior, rearing of children, to fit the fact that marriage is a terminable institution.

Another drastic change has occurred in the bringing up of children. In old, stable societies you brought up the child that, so to speak, you yourself once were. Now, if you stop to consider, you realize that the only kind of child one knows anything about from personal experience is the child which one was. In a homogeneous society one is a child and then grows up and brings up a child of the same kind, then becomes a grandmother. In the course of being a mother and a grandmother she was taught what it would be like to be the same kind of mother and grandmother. So the children learned in

their grandmother's arms what it was going to be like to be a grandmother, and that they would end their lives as they began them, and
grandmothers were enabled to be grandmothers because the baby
behaved like a grandchild. We are just beginning to realize that this
continuity has disappeared in this country, that we are bringing up
completely unknown little creatures that nobody ever was before,
that nobody knows anything about, harder to study than Hottentots
(and harder on the sofa). We simply have to treat them as something
new in the world. This is true of parents and their children, and of
caseworkers and their clients. It is even truer of the older caseworkers
and their clients. They are dealing with something that is completely
disorienting. We have talked a great deal about how hard it is on children to have old-fashioned parents or old-fashioned teachers—or old-
fashioned caseworkers.

We are just learning how hard it is on parents to have new-fash-
ioned children. We had assumed that people were finished when they
grew up, that you grew up and you knew how to be a mother or a
teacher or a caseworker by the time you were twenty-five and then
could just go on being it for life. We have not realized acutely enough
that the whole aging process—I do not mean by this what occurs
after fifty, but maturing, getting older decently and dignifiedly and
without a nervous breakdown—is dependent upon dealing with a
world, which is in some way understandable and predictable. Today
you have to move in a world where everyone younger than yourself
is fantastically different, where the arguments you use do not work,
where the language spoken is unintelligible—although you can learn
that, even if you have to learn a new vocabulary every year or so—
where everything is so different that it is almost impossible to be a
good grownup because you are being a grownup in a world that is so
undefined. If you, as social workers, start following this single thread
of un-understood expectations as you think over your cases, in the
problems that mothers bring you, problems that teachers bring you,
and the problems of the children and young adolescents themselves,
you will find that you will have to stop saying, "When I was sixteen
my mother said …" or "When I was sixteen I felt like this," or "When
I was sixteen, and engaged in World War I and went to the railroad
station to bid him good-by, I felt …" It is not World War I, and they
will not feel that way when they go to the railroad station—maybe
they do not even say farewells in railroad stations any more.

Recently I discussed with a group of adolescent girls in a Mid-
Western college what the etiquette was about the letters and photographs when an engagement was broken. In my day you returned
them; now they say that they keep the photographs for souvenirs

and the letters they throw away. Some of you will remember the beautiful etiquette of insisting upon the return of that piece of your personality, which you had entrusted to the one man or the one girl in the world. Now a girl often has lots of pieces of lots of personalities—she puts them in different bureau drawers. If we say that we must bring up children of a sort we never were, to live through a childhood we know nothing about, and grow into adults that no one has ever been, this gives us some measure of the complexity that we face and of the sort of new social inventions that are necessary.

Fourthly, we still act on the assumption that people ought to grow up around the age of twenty. We know all about teen-age adolescence and we expect the worst. We know that adolescence is very hard on American young people. We recognize that they are forced to make too many choices at once. We recognize the results of the postponement of the sex impulse—or its nonpostponement. Altogether, we can talk very learnedly about what happens in adolescence. But around twenty to twenty-five we expect people to grow up: they are through adolescence, they are supposed to be ready to get married and settle down and go on to be mothers, and senators and bank presidents. But we are beginning to notice that quite a lot of people do not seem to have grown up at twenty-five. Twenty years ago we just called them "immature." People old enough will remember that in the twenties there was a fashion of calling everything "immature"—motorcars, biscuits, everything. There are still social workers who use the adjective "mature" with approval. (There are lots of supervisors who use it!)

We are going to have to realize that "mature" is no longer a good word. That is a terribly hard thing to do. One of the hardest things you can ask people to do is to take a word that was a good word, a word they bled and died and came home at 10 o'clock for, and say it is not a good word anymore. But what we meant to imply by the word "mature" was that a person had come to terms with life, had chosen a wife or husband, or a job, or both, and had settled down and faced just about how far he was going to get, how many houses he was going to be able to build, or how many automobiles he might expect to buy, whether he was or was not going to be a bank president or an agency head. We called "mature" those who had accurately and soberly evaluated themselves, modulated their ambitions on a reality level. There is nothing the world has less use for today than people of twenty-five who have modulated their ambitions on a reality level. If you look at the whole question in the terms that have become so very popular in social work in the last twenty years—in psychiatric terms—you will notice that some very significant things are happening. You will see how many men are breaking down between the ages of forty and forty-five, either when their daughters marry or when they have their first grandchild. The day a daughter has her first child is a very hard moment for middle-aged, middle-class men in America. It stresses the fact that they themselves must give up their adolescent dreams—their own eighteen-year-old has become a mother. Their whole occupational emphasis has been upon going up, going up. They still have all the sense of wanting to move up, they are faced in this society with a belief that the minute one cannot move up one is finished; if they cannot get a higher position, if they cannot get another raise, they do not know what else to do, because success has been phrased as a gradient, and a single-scale gradient. You do not become wiser or better at your work, you get a raise or a higher position. You do not acquire more skill or a lot of different skills, or a wider range of greater scope; you go from the "state" to the "national level."

The major conflicts did once come at adolescence, and then a good proportion of the population did settle down, but actually we have a society that is so complex today that the major conflicts are not over at adolescence. The center of conflict is probably going to hit somewhere in the late twenties with another good breakdown period in the forties, and another when one retires, and among the really gifted more and more will die immaturely. The degree to which people accept and settle down in a rut that is not there is not going to be a measure of adjustment to reality.

There will be a new measure of the capacity to survive, the capacity to remain tentative, the capacity to change. This is going to be very important to social workers; it is going to be very important in the way they handle counseling, the need for counseling, agencies for the middle aged, for parents whose children are leaving home, for post-menopausal women who are beginning a new life under their husbands' anxious eye. (There are a lot of middle-aged men in this country who are worrying about what their wives are going to do with themselves; and they well may, because if their wives do do something with themselves, they will take a fresh start just at the time that the husbands are feeling discouraged.) It is going to make a lot of difference with what we do with old age counseling and how we set up old age, and whether we are going to try to help very elderly people to keep moving in a moving world, so that what they can teach their grandchildren and their children will be that you can keep developing until you die. That is not what we wanted from grandparents a hundred years ago. We wanted grandparents to sit there quietly and say that the end of life is like the beginning, "the last of life for which the first was made." We do not want them to say that anymore. Instead, we need to have them demonstrate that they can conquer race prejudice at eighty—and they can. You would be surprised at what some grandparents can do; they can even begin to believe in socialized medicine at seventy-nine. Our whole conception of people's capacity to move on, to change, and to grow has to be altered.

And finally, we must alter our whole picture of the pressure under which people are living. We must realize that every statesman, every newspaper editor, every chairman of a board, every head of an agency, all the people in this country who carry responsibilities—people who know what is happening in the world, people who read the newspapers, people who pay attention to straws in the wind—all of them are living under a load of anxiety and responsibility that no generation has ever had to live under before, living with the recognition that the next twenty-five years will probably be the most crucial period the human race has yet known. It is not easy to live under those circumstances; it is not easy to continue the routine work of administration or teaching or writing, carrying this load of anxieties that no one has ever carried before. There is no precedent for it, there are no angels to guide us, the necessary prayers have not been written, and as yet there are no rituals. We have to learn to conduct agency life, board life, academic life, public life, with the recognition that people are living under all the stress of war without the excitement of war; under all the tension of war without the sense that the war will end someday; living instead with the knowledge that this will not end in our time, and that the best we can do is to help take the very first steps in developing a pattern which will keep alive mankind's most valuable learnings.

These are some of the changes we have to face. We have to recognize that we are dealing with an experiment of interminglings of people that we have never tried before, with an experiment of people living far from home, far from relatives, in ever changing situations where one cannot depend upon anybody to support anybody else—except parents with minor children and currently married spouses—and in which the friends who do most of the helping have no legal status at all. We are living in a world where the children are new and different and strange. We are living in a world in which people do not grow up when they are eight, as they do among the Eskimos; or when they are eighteen, as they did in our own past history; or when they are twenty-eight, as they even did in Greenwich Village twenty-five years ago, but in which—in a sense—they are not going to grow up at all but are going to go on making new decisions and changing their plans and changing their orientations toward life all their lives.

Finally, we are going to live in a world where the responsible people are under an unprecedently greater strain. In the light of these conditions what specific inventions can casework particularly, but all social work as a profession, make? How can we match the whole magnitude of the changes in the world that we have to face for ourselves in this country and for the world? Social work was invented in a more stable world by the fortunate for the unfortunate, by the rich for the poor, by the people who spoke English for the people who did not, by the people with good jobs for the people without jobs, by the well, stable, steady, mature, realistic people for flibbertigibbety, neurotic, sick, handicapped, maladjusted people. Services passed from those who had to those that had not.

What comes next? We had a lot of talk in the war years about what a pity it is that only the most disadvantaged group in our society can get good casework, and isn't it a pity that some busy and valuable woman, no matter what she pays, cannot have as good casework as some bedridden, epileptic woman in a tenement somewhere who has never been anywhere in her life, who may not even speak good English—and yet when she is in need, casework comes along. There has been a lot of talk of that sort, and the general idea was to ask the better-off people to pay a fee. But giving fee services to the better-off is not the answer, even if there were not all the problems that agencies organized to serve the poor must face if they are to do anything for the middle class and the rich. But it is not a question of taking the case of a lady who lives on Long Island, or Park Avenue, or Hyde Park, or the Main Line, when she is in trouble of some sort. In working with those on the economically underprivileged levels a caseworker may spend all day finding somebody a cook, but that is not what they call it, of course: they are helping to meet the needs of a family in which the mother has been removed by illness and the father is unable to cope with the problems without interfering with his work and possibly losing his job, and the children are psychologically disturbed, and so forth.

But need arises in all classes. The father may be handling a matter internationally important. In the higher income levels the solution is called finding a cook or a nurse. We all know this situation and we all know that it has not been thought out yet. We know that the privileged very often need casework as much as or even more than the underprivileged. But that is not what I want to discuss. I am just saying this much about it to make clear that it is not what I am discussing. I am discussing something quite different, that we have to stop dividing people into the people that need help and the people who give it. We have to stop dividing this world into the haves and the have-nots. We have to stop acting as if the inability to find a cook or a housekeeper or move a bedridden old mother from one part of the country to another or find a school for a psychologically disturbed child or figure out how to rehabilitate somebody who has a bad accident or prepare a child for its parents' divorce separated those with these needs from the professions and the group who then look after them. We must change our conception from one of the people without trouble looking after the people in trouble—if rich, for a fee; if poor, without one—to the recognition that this is not a world in which the mature, well-adjusted, normal, realistic people do not get into trouble too. We live, all of us, in a world we did not make, in a world we were not reared in, in a world which no one taught us how to live in, in a world in which the social inventions for caring for the sick, for meeting any kind of emergency or change, are woefully inadequate, as inadequate for the gifted as for the ungifted, as inadequate, in many instances, for the rich as for the poor. Social work has done a magnificent job, and I think that it deserves more credit, certainly, than any other profession in the country for changing conceptions about relief, for changing the position of a man who is out of work in an industrial society from that of a failure and an object of charity to that of a dignified citizen quietly claiming a right that is his as a member of his community. Social work has transmuted the whole attitude toward unemployment, from the days of the Irish famine, when they put the soup kitchens miles out of town so that the hungry would have to at least walk two miles to get their food, to the present status in which the unemployed receive help as a right. And it is an enormous achievement.

Now we have to do for social and psychological difficulties the same thing that has been done for economic difficulties. We must get rid of the idea that people must admit that they need help—which means, you see, putting the caseworker and the social agency in the position of the psychiatrist. A psychiatric patient can be defined as one who asks for help—that is diagnostic of the need for psychiatric care, because nobody who is not sick could bear it. We have done a good deal of the same thing in casework. We have said that people must admit need, a pressing need, before they could be helped. This is a form of moral arrogance, a form of wanting to define those who need help as lower or lesser or weaker than those who give it. As a matter of fact, most caseworkers need help with their bedridden mothers just as much as their clients do, only they have no place to go for it. Bedridden older people and little children that have to be put somewhere during an emergency, and broken marriages where people have to be adjusted to their new lives, newcomers in a new town, and the people who are leaving the place where they have been all their lives—all of these are common problems, part of the way in which modern life affects all of us. Casework, the whole of social work, must become a profession whose job is to orient all those who need orientation, both those who are doing better than most people and therefore need more help, and those who are doing less well and so need help. Help is needed at least as much by an important newspaper editor on whose editorial, perhaps, negotiations of an international conference will turn, as by a family all of whom are feeble-minded and epileptic. I want to say again what I am *not* saying. I am not saying that we should stop caring for the feeble-minded and the epileptics. I do not think that we can be a good society unless we look after our unhappy, our grievously troubled, our defective, and our diseased. We must care for them and keep them in as good condition as possible all their lives. But I also do not think that we can be a good society until the profession that knows more than any other profession about getting an ambulance, or finding a place to put somebody for twenty-four hours, is working for everyone in society, the gifted and the fortunate as well as the defective or unfortunate and working for everyone with the knowledge that all of us are in the same boat, all living in a world we never dreamt of, all sometimes losing our way, as we try to keep the world going until we have reared a generation who know better how to live in it.

EDITOR'S NOTE

1. See Margaret Mead, *Culture and Commitment: A Study of the Generaton Gap.* Garden City, NY: Natural History Press/Doubleday and Company, 1970. For background information on the Futures Studies movement, please refer to page 7.

1962

THE PSYCHOLOGY OF WARLESS MAN

Editor's Commentary

This article was written at a time when fear of a nuclear holocaust was widespread. American families were building bomb shelters. Elementary schools were teaching children what to do in case of a nuclear attack.

After the Americans used two atomic bombs in 1945, it took the Russians only until 1949 to explode their first such bomb. They were followed by the British in 1957 and the French in 1960. In 1962, the media were reporting rumors of a similar nuclear weapons program in China, which actually produced its first bomb just two years later. In this atmosphere of imagined Armageddon, it makes sense that Arthur Larson would involve Margaret Mead in a book that earnestly, urgently looked for rays of hope that some day, some way, a warless world could be created.

In this selection Mead is at her best in bringing the phenomenon of omnipresent fear down to the level of the community, the family, and the individual—worldwide. She stresses that the existing social organization had not evolved to handle the dangers and fears generated by a new and ever more powerful military technology. She also stresses that even if war between nation states is abolished, there will still be conflict and violence—and here she refers in broad terms to the kind of asymmetrical conflict that, in ensuing reality, has characterized the world since September 11, 2001.

Mead also, in the spirit of the late William James, calls for cultures to change in such a way as to provide a moral equivalent of war, hence giving males the opportunity to keep identifying as males—a proposition that some might challenge today.

Although Mead had an abundance of ideas about the broad concrete political steps that would be needed to bring a warless world into reality, here she limits herself primarily to a presentation of relevant anthropological knowledge concerning the psychology of potentially warless human beings.

* * *

* In: *A Warless World*, ed. Arthur Larson (New York: McGraw-Hill Book Company, 1962), 131-142.

The establishment of a warless world must be viewed in a strict contemporary light. Whatever can be said now, after the development of
totally destructive thermonuclear, biological, and chemical warfare,
differs profoundly from anything that was or might have been said
in any earlier period of history either about the beauties of peace or
about the horrors of war and its positive by-products-patriotism,
bravery, and radical innovation. We must realize clearly how the
total context has changed from that envisaged as recently as the
beginning of World War II, if we are to appreciate fully our present
situation and the rewards that can be reaped by the abolishment of
war. Poets and prophets have longed for peace and have extolled it.
Religious groups have been formed to work for peace. But these past
activities are now essentially peripheral. Even the warlike have
always recognized periods without war as desirable. The exhausted
have sought for truces, and those who have preferred a quiet life
have welcomed them. But once man had invented the idea of warfare, it was certain that there would be new wars as long as some people, some of the time, could benefit by them. Warfare is a system in
which the unwilling and the unready are just as firmly enmeshed as
are the willing and the ready.

But now, for the first time in human history, war profits no man.
There can be no victor and no vanquished. And now, for the first time,
we have a genuine opportunity to establish a worldwide rule of law
and order. In the past, when men spoke of peace, what they meant in
fact was a truce. The Pax Romanum, the Pax Britannica were no more
than a condition within a single system. As long as it was not to every
nation's benefit to belong within one system, we could not effectively
conceive of such a system and we could not really speak of peace. But
even now, when a warless world is within our reach—because the
alternative is, potentially, complete destruction—peace remains a
vague and too inclusive word.

I shall address myself to the kinds of moral and psychological
change, which we may reasonably expect in the post-Hiroshima
period as a result of steps taken to bring about a war-less world. By
this I mean a world in which resort to force is no longer an acceptable
method of resolving disagreements between groups organized as
nations, liberation movements, separatist movements, and so on.
Such a change does not carry with it, necessarily, any reduction in
other forms of violence. Nor will the existence of a warless world, as
such, protect men and the human race from other dangers, particularly from the uncontrolled, irresponsible application of science to
man's environment, or the relations of man and man, or the relations
of human group and human group.

Given a world in which there was effective disarmament and an effective political organization, which made resort to warfare impossible, what would the moral and psychological consequences be?

The first great outcome would be a restoration of faith in the continuity of human life in all its rich and manifold forms, of faith in man, his civilizations, and his power to grow and change. Faith in continuity has been essential to the existence of all known societies. Men must believe that the sun will rise tomorrow, that summer follows winter, that the Pleiades and other constellations follow fixed paths across the sky, that the moon waxes and wanes and the tides respond, that where game has been found or fruit has grown it will be found again, that a seed planted in the ground will grow into a plant, which will in turn yield a seed, that a pregnant woman will in due time bear a child, that a child will grow into a man, and that all men and women age and die.

In other species, the behavior, which is necessary for maintaining life—for guiding a group to food, for rearing and protecting the young—combines instinct and learning. Each small cue, a change in temperature or wind or light or form, sets off the next behavior. The hibernating bear is not asked to believe, "If Winter comes, can Spring be far behind?" It depends, instead, upon the cues given by the regularities in nature.

But man long ago shifted from an instinctive, day-by-day dependence on light and temperature and humidity to a dependence on his power to imagine, and describe in words, whatever was absent—the unborn babe, the flowering plant, the coming winter. For other creatures, continuity is provided by the complex ecological setting, in which their fate is determined by the balance of their own and other species and the long-term effects of climactic periodicity. But man has made his own world. He learned, and taught his children, that seed must be planted, gardens tended, and the harvest brought in; he learned when the fish would appear, when the herds of buffalo would sweep across the plains. No single part of the complex equipment which a human being needs in order to believe in and anticipate his own growth and to deal with the world, natural and man-made, is left to nature alone. All man's protective knowledge has become cultural—man-made and man-taught—and it is correspondingly fragile.

And men have always had difficulty in trusting their culturally built up beliefs in the future, their confidence in the dependable regularities of the world they were slowly learning to understand. From the young mother who tiptoes in to assure herself that her newborn baby is real, to the peoples who beat drums and make sacrifices, for fear the sun might disappear, when the sky darkens in an eclipse, men have had recurrent doubts. And recurrently, men's doubts have been fed by accidents, by ignorance, by false assumptions about the sequence of events.

But as men have gained mastery over nature through their ability to calculate distances in time and space, to understand natural sequences, and to invent the means of conquering hazards, from the earliest astrolabes to our modern warning systems that protect hundreds of thousands of lives in a severe hurricane, men's faith in the regularity of the natural world also has increased. In the modern world, wherever science was an integral part of experience, there was a tremendous upsweep of faith in the future. Ships could churn across the seas, airplanes could be guided to their destinations by instruments, blueprints could be drawn up for huge dams, a calendar of the moon's rising and setting could be printed for centuries ahead, drugs could give frail children the gift of life. Men's sense of continuity rose to a high point, and the need for magical or religious intervention in the routines of daily life dropped precipitously. Men still prayed for grace. But the desert blossomed as the rose, and soon it might not be necessary to pray for rain but only to resolve the conflicts between the farmer who wanted a real downpour and the baseball team that did not.

Then with staggering impact came the atom bomb, the hydrogen bomb, the intercontinental missile, the manned space ship, the implications of fallout for this and every future generation. From the very source from which man's faith in the continuity of human life had come, it was taken away. Within a single decade, human beings were asked to learn that all the assurance, which was based on scientific knowledge, had been shattered by the very knowledge in which they trusted. They had now to learn that there is no assurance of continuity, not even the fragile, hard-to-believe-in continuity of a single Eskimo family following wind marks in the snow.

This new crisis which mankind faces collectively, as all men now live in an intercommunicating world, is comparable only with the crisis which, over and over, small groups of men have had to face as each group has approached some understanding that death is natural—that individual death is neither an accident nor a punishment nor the outcome of a hostile act by some living being, but only a natural event. For millennia men have struggled to come to grips with this knowledge; most recently, as they have talked about the possibility of curing all disease, they have had to struggle with the implicit, irrational hope that death itself might be conquered.

At the very point in time when, whatever faith or hope men might have in immortality, in an afterlife or a reincarnation, the fact of death was fully accepted and the future was seen in the light of a disciplined reliance on science, man was suddenly faced with a threat far more terrible than that of individual death. Long ago, men learned to place their hopes in the children of their lineage or tribe or nation, in the enduring products of creative imagination—their buildings, their poems and paintings, and the faiths they initiated—and in the paeans of praise raised by those whose life and well-being their acts had made possible.

But now all hope, and with it all certainty, is placed in jeopardy. The threat is not that of individual death or the heroic sacrifice of a whole army or even the destruction of a civilian population, heroically patient under bombing; it is not the loss of country or the destruction of a civilization or even the annihilation of all the art and beauty man has made. It is *all* these things, together. In the past, the end of individual human life was made tolerable by the faith that some part at least of what a man valued would endure. But now this faith is threatened with extinction. Without a future for anyone, anywhere, human life loses its meaning. There is no rationale for the simplest act, no reason to save or to plan or to build; no reason to vote or to sit in committees; no reason to plant or to pray. As men see it, this new possibility of total destruction is not an act of God's vengeance turned against a particular unfaithful people but instead an act which is the outcome of man's fullest development as man.

A disarmed and ordered world would lift this fear, in its most acute form, from the hearts and minds of men. It would restore their full humanity by restoring, in a new form, their belief and trust in the future and so also their capacity to exercise their imagination. In a warless world, men would have time to come to grips with the terrible responsibilities of their new estate.

The one thing we cannot do is restore the past; the change brought about by our capacity to destroy ourselves is permanent. Monitoring for tests, destroying the actual bombs, ceasing to manufacture fissionable materials for the purposes of war—these are only absolutely essential steps to prevent immediate catastrophe. But the bomb, in the sense that it stands for man's newly acquired powers of destruction, is here to stay. The need for vigilance against the exercise of this power to destroy-to destroy the earth's food supply, to contaminate the atmosphere, to make the earth uninhabitable, to distort every infant born, to paralyze men's wills-this will be no less present in a warless world. In the foreseeable future, the tapping of virtually inexhaustible supplies of physical energy can make it unnecessary for men to earn their bread by the sweat of their brow, This will not alter the necessity, in the foreseeable future, of protecting all living things from the human species' own scientifically acquired and based powers of destruction. But in a world from which the pall of fear has been lifted, men's minds will be freed to meet this new requirement. Beside the tremendous consequences of restoring to mankind a trust in the continuity of life, the other by-products of the abolition of war pale to insignificance.

The abolition of war would resolve the age-long conflict between the admonition that it is wrong to kill another human being and the belief that it is right to kill an enemy. As long as warfare was little more than a running feud between two small groups, gratification of the desire for prestige and satisfaction of the impulse of revenge through fighting and killing could be safely enough built into the character of the headhunter, the warrior, the loyal member of a family or a band. But as the scale of civilization increased, warfare necessarily became increasingly impersonal. Organized invocations of their imagination bound men to fellow subjects or fellow citizens whom they had never met. Impersonal symbolic ideas defined not only those who were their enemies and might be killed by sword or spear, by Greek fire or battering ram, by swift attack or slow relentless siege. And in a world in which one's fellows and one's enemies must be numbered in the hundreds of millions, there can be no real relationship between man's individual aggressive response to the threatening posture of another male (whatever this may once have been) and the requirement of killing an enemy, personally unknown and unseen, located perhaps a hundred or a thousand miles away. Nevertheless, man still retains his ability to translate into deeply meaningful symbols his primitive impulse to protect his women and his children as well as to symbolize the threat which men, unknown to him as persons, present to his women and his children, his home, his country, his religion, his highest values.

It would seem that the intractable element in human nature, which has been involved through the ages in organized warfare is just this blind, sacrificial willingness to defend what one values—at any cost. Large, modern states have more or less effectively disciplined the human impulse to settle individual differences and disputes and to right individual wrongs, by fist fighting or knifing or dueling or shooting. But far from curbing man's impulse to fight for whatever he holds dear, modern states have gone to great lengths to create sets of symbols, which will be dependably effective in rousing the willingness to defend one's own. This means that warfare, especially warfare in which the total population is involved, is based not on man's impulse to destroy but on his desire to protect. This makes the problem of how to establish psychological equivalences for war a much easier one. For every society—and a worldwide society more than any other—depends for its continued existence on the active vigilance and the cherishing care of its citizens.

In fact, the new powers which science has put into men's hands require new and more difficult forms of vigilance—more complex, more organized, more exacting. A Manus man who wanted to protect his pregnant wife from eating food cooked on a fire made of wood, which was taboo to her, had an easy task in comparison with that of the modern man who is trying to protect his wife and unborn child from the unknown dangers of some new and as yet little-tried drug. The Manus man had only to watch over his fire and his own wife's coming and going. But to protect his wife and child, the modern man must involve himself in activities that concern the welfare of all the women not only of his country but also of the whole inter-communicating world.

This will require an even greater use of symbolization. But since we have already been able to educate human beings to regard hundreds of millions of persons, few of whom they will ever see, as fellow citizens or as enemies, we have reason to believe it will be possible to extend our symbolic loyalties to include the whole human race. Research has shown that individuals differ enormously in the number of actual persons with whom they can maintain close contact. This does not mean, however, that symbolic interaction—among fellow Americans, among fellow citizens of the Soviet Union, among all the members of the British Commonwealth—does not take place and cannot be expanded indefinitely. But there is, of course, the danger that symbolic hostility, based on no physical reality of personal experience, can just as readily be enlarged to include ever-larger segments of mankind.

One probable predictable effect of the removal of the ever-present threat of war may be an increase in other kinds of organized aggression. For war not only used violence as its sanction, it also served as a sanction against violence. This specter of external attack has frequently served to muffle sectional disputes, just as a quarrel between two members of a group is muted in the face of some attack upon the group as a whole. As yet, it is impossible to estimate the extent to which the idea of a common, shared anger acts to support group solidarity. Group solidarity is, of course, not entirely dependent on a belief in its effectiveness in averting threats of war, but the threat of war is one element in averting the outbreak of internal conflict. It is important to recognize, therefore, that the creation of an international police force, whose duty it will be to prevent the kind of conflict that once was settled by war, may have very little effect in muting the kinds of conflict that far from leading to war actually were prevented by war or a continuing fear of war. Within national states—and today even within larger regions—the clash of interests between management and labor or agriculture, between rival trade unions or rival producer organizations, between rival fishing fleets or rival air lines can lead to conflicts which governments have held down quite effectively in wartime and less effectively in peacetime; and, unless measures are taken to control them, such conflicts may well increase rather than abate with the abolition of war between states.

This is not because human beings have a given quantum of aggression and hostility, which must find an outlet in some form. It is rather because, as nations have been built up, the national interest, expressed in terms of the dangers from external enemies to which all members of the nation are exposed, has been included as one important element in local peacekeeping structures. In particular, the abolition of war will give men no protection against such dissident organizations as the Irish Republican Army or the Organization de l'Armee Secrete nor will it protect citizen groups against the violence of certain types of government action. The very success of efforts to bring about a warless world will necessitate innovations in internal, local peacekeeping structures.

It is also quite possible that there may be an increase in individual acts of violence. This is particularly likely in the period immediately after disarmament when it will be necessary to cope with a generation who were reared to respond with extreme partisanship and unconcealed hostility to special symbols standing for friend and foe, our values and their values. The years since World War II have been marked by a sharply mounting number of small, dangerous acts of anarchy—terrorist bombings and bombs hidden in civilian planes, the formation of secret subversive organizations, the piratical seizure of ships and planes, "invasions" by fleets of ten motor launches, etc. In part it has been difficult to bring such activities under control because, in the precarious state of nuclear armaments and competition among power blocs, it is believed that active intervention by any of the great powers might trigger a nuclear war. The state of nuclear blackmail encouraged small-scale anarchy.

It is equally probable that the administrators of a warless world, preoccupied by the problems of putting into effect the controls designed to maintain world peace, may be relatively impotent to control acts of individual or small group violence directed to minor political and criminal ends. Most countries have resorted to one or another form of internal military action to keep such activities in check. But dissident factions in a nation's armed forces sometimes have initiated or supported anarchical activities, and others have been kept under control by an overriding *esprit de corps*. The dangers of individual violence may be increased by the dissimilarities in experience among the member nation-states. Some will have in their populations many men who know of no life other than that of arms; some will be less than a generation away from tribal raiding or border war-fare; some will include minority groups who are just beginning to assert their rights.

It may well be that this increase in local, intranational, and intraregional violence and disorganization will constitute a major hazard to the commitment to law which will be necessary for the maintenance of a warless world. Just as many people rejoiced because Mussolini made the trains run on time, so a demand for local order may run counter to the demand for world order.

The abolition of the use of armed force will by no means lead to the abolition of other types of competition and conflict or attempts to resolve these through the application of various kinds of pressure. This prospect often is viewed simply as the reappearance of the old Adam—the expression of hostility and aggression in new, substitute forms. However, such conflicts are better viewed as the formal concomitants of whatever institutional arrangements in regard to trade, migration, recruitment and proselytizing, the use of natural resources, and the world-wide management of the world-relevant environment—the atmosphere, outer space, the deep seas—which we succeed in establishing. Here again, conflict does not represent some new outbreak of innate hostility, which must find expression. Rather, it represents the existence of social institutions and various kinds of social situations, which, because of their style, generate opposition and aggression against opponents instead of generating cooperation.

Furthermore, unless continuous precautions are taken, men in one part of the world may seek to alter the common environment without regard for the rest of the planet's people. The absence of military force may also tempt the enterprising into a subtler warfare of control of the minds and souls of their fellow men. New opportunities provided by the application of science—new drugs, subliminal television, the infrared post effect camera—all such things as these will provide new temptations to exploit other men within one nation and between nations. Certain new discoveries, especially those which make it possible to preserve life in grossly distorted or deteriorating forms, present moral problems that have barely been glimpsed by the ingenious constructors of utopias and counter utopias.

In a warless world a great mass of unsolved problems will suddenly stand out in high relief. Old and new, they represent a challenge and a guarantee that men will not be able to sink into overdomestication and dull security. On the contrary, it is the threat of nuclear catastrophe and annihilation, which is today producing apathy and withdrawal. In wartime people breed heedlessly; under nuclear threat they are walling themselves into small suburban refuges against dread and despair. Only a restored faith in the future, a renewed sense of continuity can give men the strength and the will to commit themselves to the hard work of making a viable world community.

The development of nation-states with enormous urban populations underwrote science and, having made modern warfare possible, in the end made it intolerable. At the same time, men were further and further removed from those qualities of strength and skill and endurance, which for millennia had stood them in good stead. Nevertheless, however much the small boy was rebuked for fighting and for cruelty, however much he was enjoined to cooperate with his classmates, to drive carefully, to keep his feet dry, however much he was hemmed in and made to sit still, the mere knowledge that he might one day be called on to expend every ounce of his physical strength and skill and even lay down his life for his country, gave some symbolic support to his masculinity. For many men this possibility served in some measure as a surrogate for hardships and dangers that were never faced; the dangers of the jungle and the sea and the windy heights of mountains; wild beasts; hunger and thirst; and the challenge of his own equals, unflinchingly faced, man-to-man. The extraordinary bravery of city-bred, poorly exercised, inexpert draft armies testifies to the partial effectiveness of this surrogate.

In a warless world, this will be gone. It will be necessary then to give all boys, healthier and more robustly grown than any earlier generation, new ways and much greater chances to test their mettle and the extent to which they can expect their bodies to stand up to trials of strength, skill, poise, and personal danger. It will be necessary, in effect, to establish a different kind of physical life. In taking away war, which had been transformed into wholesale annihilation for which men could only wait passively, we may, indeed we must, give human beings a much closer relationship to their own bodies.

As long as man's need to contend with and match his strength against his fellow men was epitomized by his behavior in war, we saw it majorly as based on hostility. Detached from exploitation in warfare and given freer play, we can see this contending behavior for what it actually is: a measure of and a symbol for a young male's delight in growth. What we need most are political equivalents for the functions which war has served in promoting the interests of human groups and man's pride in their relationships to a group of their fellow men. Given these, then, man's psychological need to display skill and courage, to protect and contend for all he values and loves can be channeled in new directions. Free from the threat of war, exploration of outer space and the depth of the seas await his efforts.

1963a

BEYOND THE NUCLEAR FAMILY*

Editor's Commentary

In this address to the Child Study Association of America, Mead examines two phenomena: the nature of the family worldwide, and the special nature of the family in America, a land that is quintessentially a nation of immigrants.

Mead points to rapid techno-economic change as having forced American society (and other industrial societies) to move from the three-generation to the two-generation residential family model, the latter being more flexible and adaptable in an ever more complex economy and society. She asserts that grandparents, especially if foreign-born and -reared, often lack the knowledge necessary to teach their American grandchildren the specifics of how to function in the future. Their grandchildren, who were born in the U.S., and whose native language is English, are being reared in terms of contemporary American culture. For this reason, they already know more about many of the specifics of the future technology, economy and society they will need to live in, than do the grandparents.

Nonetheless, Mead does see a vital role for grandparents as general and ethical mentors for the young. The grandparents can still provide guidance and wisdom in dealing with problems of survival in the context of rapid change—for the very reason that they themselves have survived many such changes.

* * *

You at the Child Study Association have been pioneers in change, pioneers in helping young mothers, and then young grandmothers to understand more about children and about the family. Now, in your seventy-fifth anniversary year, I think it may be worthwhile for you to consider what is going to happen to the family in the *next* twenty-five years—between now and your hundredth anniversary.

* In: *The Future of the American Family: Dream and Reality* (New York: Better Homes & Gardens for Child Study Association of America, 1963), 13-17.

It is not generally recognized that we are moving towards a new kind of family form, still vague in outline and as yet unnamed. We don't now know what this new kind of family will be like, although the power to shape it lies in our own hands.

Organizations like yours will be partly responsible for the kind of family we have because we live in a society that believes that voluntary action and responsible social scientists can often create what we want. So I am going to limit myself to discussing the conditions that are making it necessary for us to develop a new kind of family to replace the two-generation—or nuclear—family that is going around the industrializing world now at such amazing speed.

Let us go back for a moment to the old three-generation family. Being three generations, it also included aunts and uncles and cousins and it formed a different kind of pyramid. It was extraordinarily suitable for a slow-changing society: young adults could be supported and guided by the experience of their elders because their own experience was essentially the same. The wisdom and first-hand knowledge of grandparents was a steadying force for young parents—and for grandchildren.

Culture for culture, with other things held constant, the old societies that gave grandparents the greatest role were the most successful. Children learned while they were very small what it was going to be like to be old in that society. One of the safeguards, of course, was that there weren't very many grandparents. In the old days, grandparents died quite young and very small groups of "old" people—aged forty-five, perhaps—carried the burden of authority within the culture.

As the world experienced rapid social change, the three-generation family no longer fit. It especially didn't fit in the United States where so many people came to this country as young adults and never fully learned to live here. By the time they were grandparents, and had that delightful attack of remembering everything before they were twenty, they were remembering Poland or Italy or Ireland or Japan and were just a nuisance on the local scene. Americans actually had to forbid memories and daydreaming almost entirely because grandmother sitting and chatting and thinking out loud could not keep oriented in the modern world.

And so the two-generation family was invented—and not only in America. People in Europe, in Asia, in Latin America have been discovering that as they moved to the city, as they tried to adjust to changes in social class and to a more socialized life, grandparents couldn't move fast enough. As a result, all over the world—the old traditional world and the new emerging, world—the three-generation family is breaking down and the two-generation family is taking its place.

The two-generation family is a fine family for a particular moment in a society's history. It is a most flexible and suitable form through which the old traditional ways of life can be abandoned and children reared just to the age at which they are ready to go out and involve themselves in a changing world. But now we are reaching for another kind of change. Social forces are pushing us to develop a new kind of family life.

One of these forces is the changed role of grandparents. Grandparents no longer represent the traditional past that must be evaluated. Today they are vitally needed specialists in how to withstand change. They have changed more than anybody else except great-grandparents. Far from being the most rigid people in our society, if they have survived sane, they are the most flexible; they have moved all the way from the horse and buggy stage to now. Where we used to depend on grandparents for a fixed experience that could be passed on, we now depend on them to give young people a sense of perspective, a sense that you can get from there to here and from here to somewhere else. This means that the whole expectation from grandparents has to be altered. It is not their experience of old tried ways, but instead their experience of the arduous and trying process of continuous adaptation to new ways that is now needed.

This does not necessarily mean that we will go back to the old three-generation household. We have new kinds of transportation, new kinds of buildings. Grandparents may live around the block or several blocks away; they may even have a trailer and travel to see their grandchildren—there are many possibilities.

But even if the family of the future is not necessarily going to be the biological family of the past, the reincorporation of the grandparental generation is absolutely necessary. It is one of the things that's going to happen. We are going to need grandparents who are experienced in change and who can communicate confidence in the possibilities of further change. We need their help in breaking down the appalling fixation on the present—the despair about man and lack of ability to think about the future—that is one of the difficulties of the very young parents in today's two-generation family.

A second condition that is forcing us to devise a new kind of family, one with new relations to the past generation and to community life, is the terrible burden we are putting on our brave young parents. How great this burden is has become very clear in some recent studies showing the relationship between the breakdown of young mothers after the birth of their first babies and the absence of loving, concerned female relatives and friends. The very large number of one-parent families faced with an even greater isolation constitutes

another demand for a changed family style. And the need is accentuated by the number of young mothers who are working in full or part-
time jobs, adding a second responsibility to a first, which is already
too much for them.

It is not yet certain how we are going to solve the problem of the
unsupported nuclear family, how we are going to alter the isolated,
exposed position of two very young parents attempting to rear several
children all by themselves with no one to advise and comfort, no one
to take over in emergencies, no one to rely on in the small day-by-day
details of living. But it is perfectly plain that we are going to have to
solve this problem, somehow.

We may solve it by a change in the extreme American individualistic style of homemaking, which has produced so many women
incapable of sharing a kitchen with another woman. We may solve it
by demanding a greater participation in and control over the marriage of young people still in their teens; by providing real or substitute relatives; or by asking our educational institutions to exchange
regulation of individual students' lives for responsibilities for their
students' children. We may even solve it by being willing to pay our
students for studying, by giving up our fantastic notion that it is only
young people who drop out of school: who do not become educated
or develop their potentialities, who are adult human beings with the
right to wages and unemployment insurance. We may begin to see to
it that educated young men who wish further education do not have
to face almost insoluble economic problems and are not kept from
becoming men in their dependence on parents, their wives' parents
or their wives. Whatever our solution, one must be found, for the present situation is intolerable. We can afford no longer to place so great
a burden on young parents in a period when the complexities of life
are greater than they have ever been before.

A third condition demanding a changed family style is the loss by
parents of their moral authority. This loss stems partly from the
recent transition period when parents were overly permissive and
stopped insisting on their divine right as parents to give any order
they wanted. It also is very much related to the period of rapid social
change when parents, no longer knowing what was right, vacillated
and were unable to give clear ethical directions to their children.
Finally, it is related to the growth of the mass media.

When printing came in, parents gave up some of their moral
authority. The minute a child could read a book it became possible for
him to get hold of a book you didn't want him to read. This has been
going on for a good long time.

But parents could control books, they could throw them out of the local library, they could censor them or burn them. Parents possessed a certain amount of moral authority, however dubious, so long as a child only felt the impact of the outside world in an occasional book.

When radio came in, parents lost more authority, and when TV came in they lost more still down to the age where the child can turn the knob on the TV set.

Parents might manage to win back some of the their authority by refusing to have a radio or TV. But we know that this is not a viable way of life for children today; if we throw out TV, we hamper their adjustment to the modern world.

We must face the fact that this means that the old type of complete mediation between parent and young child and community values is gone, and the only way we can get it back is by new inventions that allow the community to provide what the individual parent can no longer provide alone—ethical direction and content to children's lives. We urgently need new devices that will allow parents and teachers and citizens to take responsibility for all the children in the community, in the nation and in the world.

Only by protecting all children can we now protect our own. Sometimes we're going to have to protect the children from the local movie house or the local TV station. Sometimes we're going to have to protect all the children in the nation in order to protect any children. When it comes to the danger of war, we are the only people who can protect the children of our enemies, and they are the only people who can protect our children. For the first time in history, unless we protect all of the children, we can protect none.

Finally, but not ultimately, there has been a shift in the role of experience. In the past it was assumed that parents and grandparents and adults in general were the sources of the greatest understanding, wisdom and insight. It was they who determined what was right and what was wrong, they who decided what was important or trivial, correct or incorrect.

In the past, parents knew more than children—although this was never quite true for the United States. One reason that we are especially suited to deal with a change in parents' role is that we are a country built of immigrants. The young parents who came here never knew what it was like to grow up here. You had to be born here to have a full membership in the culture, and as more and more immigrants came here from all parts of the world, it became increasingly true that children knew things their parents didn't know.

This has never been truer than it is today. Today, we have in a sense changed places with our children: everybody over 20 is an immigrant in 1963. We grew up before the development of nuclear energy, before the first satellite, before our nation was important, before we were communicating with anybody in the world. We're immigrants—as new as the peasant girls from the Carpathian mountains who had never worn shoes, but put on high heels and in two weeks looked as if they belonged here, as long as they kept their mouths shut. All of us give a fairly good imitation of looking as if we belonged here because we, too, keep our mouths shut.

For the first time we're in a position where our children are the real inhabitants, and we have to learn from them. We still have to give them the sense that some things are more valuable than others; but they know things by birthright that we adults have to learn laboriously and industriously. This again will change the structure of the family. It is going to have to be reorganized so that adults can absorb the children's growing knowledge of the present age of space, of satellites, of the new mathematics, of the oneness of this small planet called Earth on which we live.

The needs that I have outlined here are developing in every part of the industrializing world. We cannot expect India, for example, to reach the nuclear family in the way that we reached it, for our nuclear family style developed before the days of women working and mass media and such very accelerated change. However, the most acute pressures for change from a nuclear family style probably exist in the United States, with Western Europe, the rest of the English speaking world, and Japan, coming next.

Pressures of this sort are felt first in the United States and fortunately the United States is also the country most receptive to the application of the human sciences to changes in family life. As we succeed in designing a new type of family life, so also will, to a great degree, the world, which takes so many cues from the United States.

Fortunately, as a nation of immigrants, we have already been somewhat accustomed to learning from our children—who were born here, spoke American as a mother tongue and lived here, as their immigrant parents never could. We can put this experience to work to develop ways in which we can tap the increasing knowledge of the children while correcting it with the grandparents' experience of change, and with the moral responsibility of the parents—not just as parents but as *experienced persons*,—a phrase that covers a great many important things. What children need is *experienced persons* to care for them, and if you put these all together it will result in a new style of family relationship to the community and to the world.

1963b

PATTERNS OF WORLDWIDE CULTURAL CHANGE IN THE 1960s*

Editor's Commentary

This compendium of practical wisdom illustrates Mead's skills as a public anthropologist urging a general audience—in non-technical, concrete terms—to become less ethnocentric and less tempocentric.[1] Here Mead—who had been one of the key founders of the subfield of "applied anthropology" in America twenty-odd years earlier—provides a comprehensive catalog of experience-based examples to demonstrate why both centrisms are inappropriate. Note, for example, how she resists tempocentrism in urging the widespread use of the computer as a tool for development planning—even though she herself did not use this new device at that time—or, as it turned out, ever.

In this long inventory of ideas, Mead shares much knowledge of good and bad practices in the planning and execution of so-called "scientific and technical assistance," especially by the UN or by national government donors. It should be noted, however, that the "scientific and technical assistance" paradigm has since come to be seen by most developmentists as a necessary but not sufficient approach. Today this paradigm is widely regarded as having been too narrow and as having often sought to maintain, rather than change, the status quo of the economic and political hegemony enjoyed by the advanced industrial "donor" nations, both capitalist and communist, as well as the hegemony of particular classes or groups within an economically less developed recipient nation.[2]

* * *

1. The idea of purposive, controlled cultural change, in which industrialized countries use the methods of modern science and technology to help less advanced countries, is less than 20 years old. There had, of course, been purposive cultural change in the past—change initiated by monarchs, conquerors, reformers, colonists, busi-

---

* In: *Social Problems of Development and Urbanization* (Washington: U.S. Government Printing Office, Prepared for the United Nations, 1963). Volume VII.

nessmen or missionaries seeking to mold some situation to their particular needs. But the theory of change developed after World War II is unique in the demands it makes on the sciences concerned with man's relationship to his environment, including his manmade environment, his relationship to himself, and to his fellow men.

2. Equally new is the style of teamwork, which has developed during the last 17 years, as specialists from foreign cultures and recently trained members of industrializing cultures, working together under the auspices of international, national, and voluntary agencies, have experimented with many kinds of tasks leading to change. In different parts of the world, these teams have been asked to redesign the economy of a country, or to persuade some small group of perhaps 200 people to change their whole way of living, or to design basic kits of simple tools adapted to a changing form of agriculture or building, or to plan the building of a whole city, and so on.

3. Essentially, these extraordinarily diverse activities remain unchronicled. Since each new experience alters what is already known, every attempt to assay current knowledge is likely to be out of date before the printer's ink is dry. Principles of change have been derived from a wide range of situations covering a period of a hundred years or more, many of which are poorly documented and few of which are wholly relevant to the present. But as yet no one of the disciplines concerned with contemporary programs—anthropology, economics, geography, history, political science, or the applied disciplines of administration, agriculture, architecture, engineering, and public health—has developed a full rationale for the whole range of problems of cultural change.

4. This Conference is pointed toward developing a scientifically based and empirically tested applied science of technical change. A first requirement is to divest our thinking of obsolescent ideas inherited from earlier periods when both local and world conditions were different, and to place this developing applied science firmly in the 1960's. Crucial to this task is the definition of premises in terms of the contemporary world. Traditionally, anthropologists have worked in small societies, each of which could be comprehended as a living whole. When, therefore, they are asked to grapple with large-scale problems, their trained ability to maintain a sense of the whole should be one of their unique contributions. That is, anthropologists should be able to place the process of change as it takes place on a small Caribbean island, a remote Greek village, and an African village deep in the bush within the context of the entire interdependent and intercommunicative world. They should be able to work out continuities and discontinuities in the process of change with all the necessary shifts in scale.

5. Initially, therefore, I shall attempt to sketch out the political ethic in terms of which change is conceptualized. Today, this ethic is applied everywhere in the world, from the plans made for the mountain tribes of New Guinea to the designs coming off the drawing boards of architects who operate on an international scale. It is applied equally to attempts made to bring about change in one's own country and in other countries.

6. This new ethic has two major premises. First, any group of people who share a common territory may elect to become a self-determining political unit. Second, each self-determining political unit, regardless of size, recourses, or previous history, may rightfully demand whatever help is necessary to attain all the benefits of the modern world.

7. Acceptance of this ethic has come so fast that the various assumptions which underlie its major premises have gone largely unexamined. It is assumed, for example, that the size of a particular population, its racial composition, past history, and present level of technological advancement are matters which are fundamentally irrelevant to the rapid attainment of a modern style and standard of living or to the attainment of full nationhood and membership in the United Nations. Where a time interval has been assigned to the process of attaining membership in the United Nations, this is phrased not as unreadiness on the part of the population to become involved in international activities but as a necessary stage of organizational transition from colonial status to nationhood. This phasing is related to strongly held beliefs about the role of colonialism in perpetuating a low level of technical advancement. In a contemporary version of these beliefs, lack of change in any part of the world is attributed to the policies of the technically advanced countries. By implication, the kinds of change taking place today are represented as having also been possible in the past. But this widely shared picture of a whole world ready to march ahead obscures recognition of how new, in fact, the idea of worldwide technological change is.

8. Our current ethic of change assumes, secondly, a situation of world affluence, defined partly in terms of natural resources and capital goods, which are available and can be shared, and partly in terms of technical skills and inventions, which can surmount local shortages. It is assumed that as the unindustrialized countries of the world become industrialized, the rest of the world will become richer, not poorer. Clear thinking about these problems is hampered by out-of-date attitudes—odious comparisons of the rich and the poor, ideas about exclusive rights of control over markets, and so on. In general, however, both national and international aid-giving bodies take it for

granted that the poor nations have the right to receive and that the richer nations are able to give the necessary help and will benefit rather than lose by doing so.

9. Implicit in this assumption is the expectation that we are working toward the development of a single world market. In practice, however, we have not gone beyond the idea of limited and bounded ventures, such as the European Common Market or the Little Common Market in Asia. We can continue to arrange for newly industrialized peoples to have atomic reactors, large airlines, complete medical schools and research institutions, and so on, only on the basis of the larger expectation. But the divergence of expectation and practice is obscured, on the one hand, by the fragmentation of disciplines and, on the other, by ethical and ideological polemics. One set of theorists appeal to the heart or the conscience of mankind; others appeal to enlightened self-interest. And the two seldom meet.

10. It is assumed, thirdly, that all desirable changes should take place at once, simultaneously. Arguments as to the relative advantages of fast and slow change have given way in face of the recognition that rapid change is taking place and that efforts to prevent or obstruct change will fail. It is assumed, in fact, that rapid change is a right. The cultural anthropologist may warn that it is disastrous not to take cultural differences into account. The psychiatrist may point out that some types of rapid acculturation may endanger the well being of individuals. The technician may report that a certain kind of complex equipment is unsuitable for a particular local labor force. Despite such warnings, rapid change continues to be highly valued for all peoples everywhere. Lip service may be given to the idea that change should follow specified sequences. For example, it may be said that an elementary school system should be established before a university system is introduced. One difficulty is that there is no complete rationale for such sequences. In any event, the attempt is usually made to tackle all stages at once.

11. It is assumed, fourth, that the people of every country, large and small, whatever their cultural background and whatever their present major occupations may be—farmers, fishermen, or sailors—actively want a type of civilization which in its technical aspects is like the present-day civilizations of Western Europe, the Soviet Union, North America, and Japan. It is taken for granted, for example, that all peoples want all modern communication facilities (airplanes, telephones, radios, television, etc.), a full money economy, and the forms of secularization that have accompanied these institutions in industrialized countries.

12. Deep ideological differences separate countries, which accept a Marxist rationale, countries, which do not do so, and countries,

which are seeking some middle path. In practice, however, all of them agree on a set of technical and economic forms whose acceptance demonstrates successful change. Both those who see capitalism as a transition phase and those who see socialism as a transition phase envisage the less-advanced countries as struggling toward or beginning to achieve known forms of economic organization, fully developed elsewhere. Both visualize the future as substantially similar to the present, based on a technology, which will provide an enormous global population with plenty in already developed ways. The descriptive phrases used by each are different. One group of theorists uses such phrases as "overtake and surpass," "catch up," or "come of age"; others speak of "closing the steadily widening gap." But in both cases, the picture of the future is incomplete. Missing from it are the new forms, which may be expected to develop out of changes taking place within contemporary industrialized countries.

13. In planning for advancing countries, for example, we persist in using concepts of employment appropriate to a country without social services. Or we plan for education as if the idea of "finishing" education in late adolescence, characteristic of earlier stages of education in Europe, had any relevance to a society in which change, which elsewhere took centuries to achieve, will be compressed within the decades of an individual's mature working life.

14. It is assumed, fifth, that governments will be the major agents of change. Up to the present, a tremendous role in technical change has been played by intergovernmental organizations, functioning bilaterally, within groups of military and political allies, and within the framework of the United Nations. However, the emphasis on government obscures the possibilities of private enterprise. Even though, by implication, it will be possible to develop a commercially viable worldwide market, there has been relatively little effort to encourage private initiative in bringing about change. Not only in socialist countries but also in those with capitalist and mixed economies, the only organizations which are regarded as capable of and appropriate for tackling the problems of technical assistance are governments, large philanthropic enterprises, such as the Ford Foundation, aggregations of governments, and the United Nations and its specialized agencies. The enormous, far-flung private enterprises associated with oil, minerals, and other types of raw materials are regarded as in some way ephemeral, replaceable in some unspecified way by new forms of governmental enterprise. It is a common belief, sometimes stated explicitly and sometimes left implicit, that private innovation in an unindustrialized country will inevitably be exploitive. The only alternative to exploitive profit making is, by implication, state-inspired development, sup-

ported by direct and indirect levies on the productivity of the more advanced countries. Yet there is relatively little discussion of how this productivity is to be maintained, once the various incentives operating in competitive industrialized countries are withdrawn.

15. There is, however, one very significant difference between the government inspired and administered technical assistance typical of the late 1940's and early 1950's and that of the 1960's. This results from the reemergence of private initiative. New appraisals indicate that even in countries with very low per capita income, mass markets may become of very great economic interest. Under present conditions, earlier fears of expropriation and of economic exploitations are beginning to give way. Instead, new issues are being raised and new questions asked. For example, in areas where it is necessary to introduce modern transport, alternative questions may be asked: Shall we develop a type of road buil... .ng machinery which is so inclusively efficient that it can replace all the older methods, including the organization of labor by village or tribal groups, by one operation from jungle clearing to surfacing? If this is done, it will be possible to use the same types of trucks now used in temperate zones, with minimal adaptation. Or would it be better to invoke the inventive skills of large enterprises to develop new forms of transport, which will deal with jungle conditions in other ways—by air transport close to the ground or surface transport in new types of tractors?

16. Actually, most official thinking about technical assistance has lacked boldness, and the enormous speed of change, which is desired by and for the industrializing countries, has not been matched by a comparable upsweep of imagination among the planners in the industrialized nations. Models of change, which were appropriate in the United States or the Soviet Union 30 years ago, are still in use. It is possible that the context for a worldwide type of innovation may be provided, within a network of countries with contrasting politico-economic systems, by the recognized need to develop a world market. This in itself will call for the invention of new devices.

17. The most immediate need is for accurate measures of types of change, their rate and direction, in industrialized countries in such matters as automation, redistributions of population, redesign of urban areas, reorganization of transport, and the use of computers for complex predictive activities. No less important is an assessment of new man-machine relationships, which make necessary lifetime education and a quite different use of the human components in industrial operations.

18. With a better understanding of change in industrialized countries, it would be possible to plan for a quite different future

world. Instead of making the future static, as we do when we plan ways for the industrializing countries to enter the present world, it would become possible to deal with their problems in terms of a changing scene. It would be recognized that the peoples of already industrialized countries must transcend their own past, especially the past based on the 19th-century use of the machine as a monster or a slave, and that the peoples of industrializing countries must respond to new, not old, possibilities for speed. In these countries, the absence of limiting and obsolescent habits of thought can be transformed into an asset. If the whole changing scene is taken into account, the peoples of one group of countries have a fresh and uncluttered ability to think about the new, while the peoples of the other group have the benefit of living in situations in which every item—the shape of a room, the contours of a road, the presence of motors—expresses a long-term application of science.

19. The problems of attempting to organize a world in which technical advancement has made the historic sanction of warfare obsolete have divided the energies of mankind and have separated the thinking of one part of the world from another. The result is a kind of world parochialism in which each country thinks of its own version of contemporary industrialized culture as final rather than as part of a newly emerging whole. At the same time, the peoples of the world are seen as one by one taking their places somewhere behind the advanced countries in time, although they are now next to them in space. This picture transposes the future into the past. In order to take cognizance of the future, it is necessary to recognize that all societies are changing and that all peoples, industrialized and unindustrialized, are moving—at different rates and through different kinds of change—toward a future in which their relative positions may be very different from the present.

20. For the most part, earlier theories of change depended on essentially very simple models. One was the sequential model: sequences that had occurred in the past were assumed to be necessary, and the best planner could only hasten passage through them. A second model included the idea of cultural lag: technical change was inevitably disruptive, and it was necessary to develop institutions to deal with the resulting maladjustments. There has also been a persistent attempt to work with simple, implicit taxonomies, in accordance with which countries were grouped together, and techniques developed in one setting were applied in another. Or countries have implicitly been placed on a developmental scale which differentiated, for example, between traditional societies with a high culture, members of the Great Tradition, which could absorb modern

technical ideas in abstract form, and societies so primitive in culture that they had first to be completely transformed, following foreign models of the family, economic structure, education, and so on. None of these classifications has been complete. All of them have defined whole societies in terms of a few variables—literacy, education, type of subsistence economy, type of family structure, per capita income, and so on.

21. Meanwhile, we have accumulated a wide experience of cultural change. Furthermore, we are accumulating experience with a new type of analytical tool—the computer. Putting this experience to work on cultural data, we should be able to include many more variables and to design a much more refined type of analysis. Using our experience of change, we can build an open-ended list of relevant variables, each much simpler than those used in the past (because many more can be explicitly included). Each new situation—a village, a city, a country, a migrant group, etc.—can then be examined in terms of all the relevant variables as well as the elements unique to that situation. There is no reason, today, why we cannot treat each situation of change on a worldwide scale both on its own merits and in the light of our full, recorded experience.

22. This paper will now address itself to some of the more detailed technical problems with which anthropology is specially qualified to deal.

INTERRELATIONSHIPS AMONG TYPES OF CHANGE

23. Given the tools and the basic techniques at our disposal, we can now go on to ask about *clusters of change,* which, if they occur together, will produce one kind of result while, if they occur separately or sequentially, different results will occur. We can no longer assume, as was done in the past, that there is any single optimum sequence of change; nor is it necessary to follow through single strands of change.

24. Instead, for any society or any group of culturally related societies, we can plot out the clusters of change that will be associated with migration, or the importation of new agricultural or extractive machinery, or the use of a written language, or the concentration of dispersed populations in urban centers, or political secularization, and so on. Then, as the next step, we can consider what other elements in the total situation must simultaneously be taken into account to bring about an optimal transformation.

25. Where migration is under consideration, for example, what would be the consequences if the grandparental generation did not

accompany the migrating group? For the migrating group it would mean a break with the particular lineal past, the loss of one kind of supporting manpower, and the need for new devices for saving money and sending funds back to the villages, but also the possibility of sending the chronically ill and the mentally retarded back to the apparent asylum provided by the village as well as of returning to the village in a time of famine or political disturbance in the cities. We have enough technical information about migration under a wide variety of circumstances to systematize the problem and to work out alternative sets of answers.

26. In the past 15 years, it has become customary to transplant successful plans from one part of the world to another with only the most minimal adaptation to new sets of circumstances. But a plan for rapid urbanization, or the mobilization of an underemployed population, or the training of middle-level personnel, or the inauguration of a health service usually has succeeded precisely because it was well adapted to the particular society for which it was conceived and in which it was carried out. Innovations by local nationals may have played an important part in its successful execution. When, therefore, such a plan is transplanted whole to another cultural setting, unexamined and implicit elements may make it unworkable in this new setting. The attempt fails, and nobody knows why.

27. Today, with our ability to use computers to code and simulate alternative plans of action, it is not necessary, even under the pressure of time, to transplant whole plans or, on the contrary, to start anew in each different situation. Instead, we can break the problem down into a large number of segments and, in each case, using a standard set of known variables as our core, build up a plan, which will be viable in the specific locality. By cross-cultural comparison, we can learn which are, in fact, the variables to look for, for example, in a migration which does not involve the grandparental generation, which will involve moving from a rural to an urban setting; living not in old slums but new houses; speaking a familiar dialect or, on the contrary, a new language; and beginning a new work rhythm. In the same way, a shift from a subsistence to a cash economy—with or without the destruction of the traditional ceremonial calendar, with or without a change in the style of family living—can be examined and a plan can be made for appropriate accompanying institutions of credit, savings, retail trade.

28. In a situation of change, the splitting of old clusters of activities and the failure to create new clusters greatly aggravate the difficulties of moving from one kind of economy or style of living to another. Yet, all too often, planning has failed to consider this question of the linkages of change. People who have a well-developed sys-

tem of cooperation in a subsistence economy are suddenly introduced to money wages without the necessary protections of a bank, retail stores, or a developed set of habits for handling their earnings. Women who have lived all their lives in large joint families suddenly find themselves stranded without help or resources in a large urban slum. Manufactured objects, such as furniture, are introduced without reference to the housing, which receives them—inviting the scorn instead of the respect of more industrialized peoples or the more educated segments of the local population.

TRANSFORMATIONAL SEQUENCES

29. Once we have given up the idea of absolute developmental sequences, it is possible to give fresh consideration to the whole problem of practical transformation sequences from, for example, nomadism to sedentary life, from dependence on an oral tradition to literacy, from swidden agriculture to crop rotation on permanent fields or from agriculture that is dependent on irrigation to dry agriculture.

30. One of the serious consequences of our present linear, one-directional mode of thinking about progress is the tendency to ignore situations, which involve reversal or regression. So, for example, when the highly skilled and specialized English farm laborer, trained as a hedger or a cowman, became a farmer in colonial North America, he had to become a Jack-of-all-trades. Or when the breakup of large estates based on a commercial crop—sugar or cotton or tobacco—is followed by the development of small-scale subsistence farming, this is a movement from a more complex to a less complex commercial economy. Similarly, there is a change in the direction of less complexity when individuals who have lived in a culture with intricate, highly patterned relationships among kin move to an urban environment in which associations are much more casual, or when men move from positions of high status in a small remote village to low status positions as casual laborers in a large shifting migrant labor force.

31. In general, we recognize that life in a remote jungle tribe is in many ways a poor preparation for life in a modern city. But we have failed to realize that life in a modern city or in areas with advanced methods of land conservation or health regulation and with a complex organization of labor may be an equally poor preparation for life in a pioneering environment. With the kinds of change that are going on in the world today, planning must take into account both kinds of disability. So, for example, when a nomadic group fails to settle down to agriculture or concentrated village life, this failure may be in part a

function of the inability of officials and experts from the city or from another country to adapt themselves to an environment, which they find too rigorous and demanding. Wherever those who are carrying the burden of leadership and teaching are moving away (in their own estimation) from all the amenities of life, they may provide poor models for those whom they are attempting to assist—unless they can work with a full consciousness of the effects of change on both groups.

32. In the overall planning for transformational sequences, it is important to recognize, first, that they may move in the direction of either greater or less complexity, and, second, that where several groups are involved (including those who will direct the operation) the changes necessary for success may be multidirectional. In establishing sets of generalizations for transitions, therefore, it will be necessary to take into account these several possibilities. Where experts are concerned, there is a further problem resulting from the fragmentation of disciplines and professions. So, for example, agronomists, soil conservationists, and geologists are not accustomed to thinking about the relationship between family form and nomadism, or possible tensions between religious sects, or conflicts between large-scale farmers and herders, and so on. However, if the known and predictable hazards can be codified, much waste motion and many probable failures can be avoided.

33. With full codification, it is possible to work out a long transformation sequence, such as that involved in the acquisition of full literacy in a world language. For a people who speak a local language which has never had a script, a series of steps can be planned: elementary instruction in a phonetic version of the mother tongue; oral participation in a second language; the learning of script in this second language, etc. Overlapping this sequence would be the sequence followed by those participating as teachers. If the known sequences are fully discriminated and their consequences noted it will be possible to map out alternative lines of development and their relative costs.

34. Scrutiny of cases where, for example, great effort has gone into the development of textbooks in a local language, which are almost immediately rejected because their users are already anxious to participate in a wider culture, should make it possible to build the future aspirations of a changing society more securely into its educational planning. But it should also be possible to anticipate and prevent the impasse, which occurs when one link in a chain is broken—when, for example, bilingual European teachers withdraw from the system. In a situation in which the new nation intends to retain and improve the level of use of the European language, the absence of models can result in a deteriorated rendering of the language. In

Indonesia, the established sequence of language learning had been the vernacular, then Indonesian, Dutch, and, finally, English. The removal of Dutch, without correction for the change, made English teaching and learning much more difficult. Today, techniques developed for use on radio and television can be used to bridge these gaps. Furthermore, just as national broadcasting has reduced dialectical differences in countries like England, France, and Germany, so it can be used elsewhere to prevent extreme dialectical divergence and the creolization of languages.

THE CHANGING SCALE OF PARTICIPATION

35. Since, as the world is now organized, every people aspire to full nationhood, education at all levels is a matter of vital concern. Every effort must be made to bring a certain proportion of the members of every industrializing country to a level of political sophistication and social skill, which will insure full participation in political and economic interchange, nationally, regionally, and internationally.

36. The relevant questions can be asked, and the variables can be charted. Under what circumstances will a member of a new nation who speaks a world language poorly but his own language with great eloquence function better than one who speaks the world language well but lacks eloquence? What shifts in the customary patterns of industrialized nations—in factory management, in the management of technical services, in the customary hierarchies of professional training, in attitudes toward intellectual leadership, industrial leadership, political leadership—must be made to permit the small number of individuals in advancing nations, who combine experience, language, education, and individual qualities of intellectual and moral leadership, to make their largest contribution in a rapidly changing world? What are the circumstances in which presence and dignity or eloquence in a language for which there is no simultaneous interpretation can be safely substituted for experience in the industrialized world? When can lack of knowledge of a world language serve to protect a leader because it makes possible more skillful staff work by his associates, who do command the language but do not have his high status? How best can roles for younger men and women, with a different background of education and training, be built into developing activities so as to insure the long-term continuity of responsible experience? An assessment of the roles that must be carried out to insure continuing participation at different levels—attendance at regional conferences, participation in regional planning, visits to other coun-

tries under programs for visiting experts, membership on international teams, service as consuls and ambassadors, etc.—should be combined, in each instance, with an assessment of training opportunities and a roster of presently available personnel.

37. At the same time, it is necessary to calculate the minimal level of literacy, which the entire population must immediately achieve in order to meet the rising demand on literacy as an essential form of communication. For example, how much will effective action depend on the accurate transmission of written communications in regard to taxes, recruitment, health or land use or labor regulations? What kinds of changes will affect the need for written communication between individuals? Between those who are engaging in new kinds of business enterprise? Failure to provide adequately for a whole range of written communications can mean isolation, on the one hand, and the mushrooming of power among inappropriate local intermediaries, on the other. Radio transmission may reach a whole community and prevent certain of these developments, but not all of them.

38. During the past 100 years, many countries have failed to make the full transition from a type of society in which loyalty to kin or local group is a major virtue to a type of society with impersonal contractual relations. In situations of this kind (as well as in others which are structurally parallel), it is not literacy, as such, but the absence of a stable and generalized communications structure in which all groups participate, which has been crucial. The failure of such a generalized, shared system to develop in a changing society has been a factor in producing confusion, dissidence, censure from abroad, and internal social disorganization. Early attention to the establishment of a communications structure, in which all the modern communications media can contribute to its inclusiveness, will also contribute to the development of power structures appropriate to the changing conditions in newer countries.

39. A related problem concerns priorities in the education of different age groups. In societies whose members have a long tradition of written communication but very little experience with modern technology, different results will follow if mature men of influence and experience or, on the contrary, very young men are the target group for new technical ideas. In such a society students educated only in modern schools may be too young to make their influence felt; in addition, they may lack the very mastery of the old culture most necessary to adapt its resources to new technical knowledge. Older members of such a society may actually learn and adapt new techniques more flexibly. If the relative advantages and disadvantages of different methods are clearly charted, better choices can be made

in terms of particular local cultures and specific attitudes toward age and generation, toward continuity or a total break with the past, toward innovation and mastery of ideas and skills, and so on.

40. Similarly, it is important to keep open the question of priorities in establishing elementary and secondary schools and a university system. With a limited number of teachers available, it may be most desirable to concentrate, initially, on the rapid training of late adolescents as teachers for an expanding system of elementary schools. However, the value of such a plan must be balanced against the fact that knowledge of the general Western style of education is now so widely diffused among the educated segments of the industrializing countries that any failure to follow the usual Western pattern will be construed as a deprivation. New departures will, therefore, have to be carefully interpreted not only in terms of local priorities but also in the light of changes in educational style and content occurring in countries with long established systems of education.

41. The problem of women's education is one which requires special scrutiny. Of particular importance is the question of whether women are to be trained as teachers and, if so, which women and at what ages. All these questions must be faced simultaneously. Otherwise, the fact that girls are expected to attend village schools taught by men teachers or that, through an accident of training, women teachers or nurses come from a segment of society which is held in high (or low) esteem may give a direction to the educational system which later can be altered only with great difficulty.

42. It is assumed, in general, that there is a close interrelationship between industrialization, higher levels of education, and, particularly, the social status of women. Yet this is by no means always the case. With industrialization, literacy can decrease as well as increase. Participation in worldwide historic traditions may decrease where local patriotism and the use of a local language are emphasized. Religious orders formerly charged with educational responsibilities may lose their function. Furthermore, the position of women in unindustrialized countries is not necessarily low; but high positions of influence, power, and responsibility for women may be expressed in ways, which are unrecognizable to those who are guiding change. It is important, therefore, that increased education and freedom for women of different ages should be carefully related to particular cultural traditions rather than that they should conform to any stereotyped picture of progress.

EFFECTS OF PAST EXPERIENCE OF CHANGE

43. In conceptualizing problems of change, one source of serious misunderstanding is the indiscriminate mixing of data on primitive peoples, peasant peoples, urban proletariats, migrants, and segregated or unsegregated minority groups. Records of successful attempts—to change health or agricultural practices, to stimulate interest in education, or to evoke political participation and responsibility come from work with one kind of population, and the recommendation about successful methods, based on these results, are then applied to an entirely different kind of group.

44. Work with a self-selected, highly motivated group of migrants to a new country in which there are ample resources and vast opportunities for economic success and for social mobility encourages a belief in the ease of culture change. In contrast, the difficulties of changing the outlook and habits of a subsistence-farming population who remain in their own environment engenders considerable pessimism about what can be accomplished. So, also, the enthusiastic adoption of new ideas and techniques by a people who have spontaneously initiated a program of change contrasts sharply with the obstinate resistance to measures, which may improve their lot, which is characteristic of depressed, crime-ridden, miserable urban populations.

45. Too often, in facing a new situation, an estimate of the difficulties involved in bringing about change is arrived at by striking a balance between these different kinds of experience. Instead, it should be recognized that these several situations are incomparable and that the data collected on one type of situation—and the methods successfully or unsuccessfully applied—are not applicable in a totally disparate situation.

46. For effective planning, we need a classificatory taxonomy of earlier experiences of change. For any given group of people, it is important to be able to chart the past experience of change in order to plan for future change. What has the experience of a people been as individuals, in their own persons? What has their experience been as members of a culture or a subcultural group whose institutions reflect earlier enslavement, indenture, feudalism, colonialism, sharecropping, seasonal migration, submergence by a superior immigrant group, displacement by an inferior immigrant group, double migration, episodes of economic hope followed by stagnation and depression, coercive changes in nationality, occupation by foreign armies, the effects of civil and religious wars, years of ghetto life, social status which combines disability and special privilege?

47. The institutions of all societies carry traces of their historic development, and the past experience of denigration colors the present capacity of a group to confront new conditions with hope or to raise the level of its aspirations. Most crippling of all, perhaps, is the effect of a period of great hope and spontaneous participation in economic and social change, which, in the end, failed to materialize. Nativistic cults or religious and political movements, which are primarily reactive to defeat, may spring up, and a group which has lived through this kind of experience may well be far more resistant to new possibilities of change than is a group which is, for the first time, in contact with the contemporary world.

48. It is important, therefore, in assaying potential resistance, to identify the history of a people's contacts with new cultural forms and the ways in which these have led to advances or retreats and have widened or narrowed their perspective. It may then be possible, in the light of this knowledge, to work with groups in a specific population, who because they are relatively free of the most debilitating effects of past experience, can assume leadership with some optimism and hope.

PATTERNS OF PROGRESS: USE OF MODELS

49. One contemporary effect of attempts to bring about change is the worldwide diffusion of a variety of models of the good society. A changing society may take as a model some aspect of its own colonial past, or the style of living of a particular age or class group, or the style of living of some distant and only partially known society, and so on. In a period of transition from one political status to another, particularly when a country has been disrupted by war or revolution, leadership groups may be split into factions, each of which is oriented to a different model of change. Or the same leaders may select different—possibly incompatible—models for different aspects of their own lives. But these discrepancies may become apparent only if the total modeling situation is fully delineated.

50. In principle, an industrializing country can adopt as its goal the contemporary style of organization and the standard of living of some existing country. However, in practice, there is the double difficulty that the most highly industrialized countries are themselves faced with problems of obsolescence and with the need to generate new styles for which models do not as yet exist. It is easy, even if it is not altogether desirable, to help a newly industrializing country to build in exact imitation of existing styles in the United Kingdom, the

United States, or the Soviet Union. But if it is assumed that current styles, even in the most advanced countries, will soon be outmoded and that it would be preferable for the new country to build in a style, which is not yet articulated, both the advisers and the recipients of the advice are in great difficulties.

51. The solution to problems of this kind seems to lie, for example, in architectural planning which embodies the struggles of members of new professions in new countries to design institutions in new forms, appropriate both to their own cultures and to emerging ideas in the human sciences and emerging technological possibilities by which all countries, everywhere, will eventually be affected.

52. The stages of economic and industrial development through which contemporary advanced countries have gone also provide sets of models for sequential change. But the insistence that new countries adopt one or another of these actual models, even in compressed form, overlooks the worldwide effects of the mass media on thinking, and it ignores the speed with which new methods and new materials are being developed and the possibility that, with present methods of research, new and simple introductory versions of the most complex forms of technology can be developed.

53. The introduction of the more complex contemporary types of farm machinery, or construction tools, or factory methods to a people who have little or no experience of mechanization may well be unwise. But the introduction of the older, outmoded equipment of an advanced country, the use of which is predicated on already obsolescent skills and outmoded forms of organization, is also inappropriate. For to do this is to encourage the formation of work habits and styles of organization, which must be discarded within the lifetime of those who first learn them. What is needed, instead, is a recognition of the value of developmental sequences and fresh thinking about precursor types, which are appropriate to the contemporary world.

54. What is true of technical processes and materials is equally true of social and political forms and the economic arrangements by which they are implemented. Because industry and political forms of one type developed together in Western Europe and the United States and rapid industrialization and political forms of another type occurred together in the Soviet Union, this does not mean that these sequences and combinations provide adequate models for countries with a different historical past which are now becoming industrialized.

55. Scale is a particularly important aspect of transition forms. A scale of operations, which may in the past have been economical and appropriate to a stage of development in one country, may be wholly inappropriate and prohibitively expensive in another coun-

try today. So, for example, the perpetuation of the small-scale, intimate relationship of a peasant to a small piece of land and a few
animals may have been an appropriate transition form in the development of a large farm—or, more generally, large-scale commercial
dairying and stock raising—in one country, but elsewhere it may
actually obstruct the development both of modern agriculture and
of a wider frame of social reference. So also, the interim development of cottage industries, as in the contemporary mainland Chinese effort to increase iron production, not only may hinder the
development of a modern industry but also may contribute to a very
limited understanding of the scale of industrial life and of the necessity for world marketing arrangements.

56. The creation of living conditions, which replicate an older
pattern, can introduce dangerous and unnecessary difficulties into a
new system. This happened when, for example, the 19th century type
of British mining town was inappropriately perpetuated in the United
States. Mining today requires none of the conditions of isolation—the
industry-built houses, the industry-maintained stores, and the caste
like expectations about hereditary occupations and interpersonal relationships—by which it was characterized in the past. But neither is it
necessary to build new mining towns, which incorporate the special
arrangements, made to remedy past failures.

57. In fact, an appropriate use of models combined with careful,
detailed cross-cultural analyses of total situations, past and present,
will lead to a recognition of the essentially detrimental effects of sheer
replication. Planning for change must be undertaken with the knowledge that there are, today, no actual models for the future of any
country, as all of them—old and new—are moving from different
positions toward new forms.

DIVERSIFICATION OF THE UNITS OF CHANGE

58. Finally, it is clear that national governments are suitable
units for the channeling of technical assistance and the implementation of cultural change in some circumstances, at some times, and
for some types of change, but not for all. In some cases, smaller
groups (not whole nations) may need assistance in ways that would
embarrass a national government because giving it would imply
favoritism for one part of a country, or one ethnic subdivision, or
one social stratum. Or, on the contrary, the national group may be
too small a unit for the most effective organization of an experimental agricultural, industrial, or public health program, or the

preparation of suitable text books, or the deployment of highly specialized personnel.

59. In large countries, which include states, provinces, municipalities, and other local units, the organization of complex technology (e.g., in transportation, communications, fuel supplies, etc.) has necessitated the establishment of new authorities with wider, sometimes overlapping, responsibilities. In much the same way, in the new states, whose area and population size are due to a series of unique historical accidents, it may be desirable to establish a variety of units, smaller than and also larger than any single national government, for the implementation of change.

60. In the 1960's planners must be able to dissect a problem into a set of relevant variables and to assemble their total data in such a way as to include, in each case, that which is unique and peculiar to the specific situation. Where it is necessary to do so, ways must be found to channel special forms of aid to small groups within national units as well as to groups, which, for some particular purpose, are composed of more than one nation. Aid so given must fully respect the dignity, the authority, and the motive force for change lodged in each national government.

61. Planning of this kind necessarily involves further exploration of forms of cooperation, appropriate in given cultures and culture areas, through which governments of sovereign states, regional organizations, and international governmental and voluntary bodies can act. At this stage, the roles, which private enterprise and different types of voluntary agencies might play in implementing change, should also be taken into consideration. In the United Kingdom, for example, it is possible to set up organizations in which government functions as a junior partner; in the United States this form of organization is less acceptable. But all planning should include systematic exploration of the various possible forms of cooperation, so that optimum efficiency can be achieved in the immediate use of experience and scarce personnel. If cultural change toward protective standards of living is to be a worldwide concern in which all peoples are asked to play a part, it must be conceived as a flexible, worldwide process.

EDITOR'S NOTES

1. For an explanation of the term "tempocentric" please refer to page 16.
2. This 1963 essay has little to say about such issues in the developing areas as social justice, human rights, the unfair exploitation of cheap and non-unionized labor, the export of pollution, or the despoliation of local environments. Most of these issues came to the fore only in the late Sixties, Seventies or Eighties. If Mead had written this essay ten years later, under non-official sponsorship, it is likely that she would have focused more centrally on these "political economy" issues.

1966a

ONE WORLD—BUT WHICH LANGUAGE?*

Editor's Commentary

In this article, written for the general public, Mead and her close colleague, the late Rhoda Métraux, argue for the desirability of finding a living language that could successfully serve as a *lingua franca* for all the world's peoples. They explain why artificially concocted languages (such as Esperanto) have always failed, despite decades of devoted effort to make them succeed—principally because they are languages that are not embedded in a true, living culture. Hence, Mead believes that if the goal of a global *lingua franca* is ever to be realized, it would be necessary to find a non-artificial, "natural" language to use for this purpose—a language that ordinary people speak in the home, and that is stably embedded in a larger surround of cultural understandings.

In this quest, Mead rules out the languages of large and powerful nations, because she does not want their already-existing cultural hegemony to be further magnified. Instead, she recommends choosing "the natural language of a small, politically unimportant, non-European literate people." However, she stops short of specifying which language should be chosen as the vehicle for achieving this highly desirable end.

Mead's linguist-anthropologist daughter Mary Catherine Bateson reports, however, that Mead had an abundance of ideas about which language would be most appropriate:

> I listened to her in many contexts discussing a world language, perhaps because my training was in linguistics, and she went into greater detail about the differences between languages than would make sense with a popular audience. She was quite specific that an unusual phonology that most adults had difficulty with would not do—indeed she preferred a language with only one liquid (i.e. no distinction between "l" and "r"). This was one reason why one of her two examples was Bahasa Indonesia—being a Malayo-Polynesian language, it has relatively few consonants, most, if

* First published in April 1966. Available in: by Margaret Mead and Rhoda Métraux, *A Way of Seeing* (New York: McCall Publishing Company, 1970).

not all, universal, and not clustered—with no unusual features like tone or glottalization. The other example she sometimes used was Armenian (which in its Western pronunciation lacks glottalization), because it is both eastern and western. She also assumed that the language adopted would be written alphabetically in a widespread alphabet, presumably Latin, and that it would be sacrificed to common use, would lose many of its cultural nuances, etc.

Bateson adds:

> She probably would have agreed that the window of opportunity for a world language has now passed, but this would have saddened her. [Her chief objection was] the fact that native speakers of other languages are at a perpetual (though sometimes slight) disadvantage—second class citizens in interaction (personal communication, 2003).

Though I am no expert, I have studied the Indonesian language, and I concur with Mead's judgment that Indonesian would be relatively easy for most people to learn. However, one must consider not just the language itself, but also the possible limitations inherent in the broader Indonesian culture(s) in which that language is embedded. These are of two types: (1) limitations imposed by what the culture contains; and (2) limitations imposed by what it does not contain. With regard to the first consideration: natural spoken or written Indonesian is rooted in numerous cognitive, perceptual and affective "taken-for-granted" understandings and conventions that are unique or special to Indonesian culture(s), and not widely shared among the world's other cultures. With regard to the second consideration: much of the content of the languages / cultures of the major industrial nations is not a part of Indonesian culture—or if it is, not in a comprehensive way. Consequently, users of this new *lingua franca*, in discussing matters of natural and social science, technology, business, law, etc., would constantly need to refer to the major nations' languages for all sorts of important terminology, documentation, and background.[1]

* * *

How shall we begin to talk with one another all around the globe? What language shall we use? Must we forever be dependent on interpreters? Will the speakers of a few major languages—Chinese, English, Russian, Spanish and French—dominate the earth? Must we lose the "little" languages? Or can we make a choice that will include all the world's peoples?

We are in the process of creating a new civilization in which, for the first time, people everywhere are beginning to take part in the events that are shaping our common future. The realization of the dream of worldwide communication and the growing belief that men *can* plan for change are opening new potentialities for human relationships. But there is a paradox. For although our ability to see and hear has been vastly expanded, we still cannot talk with one another easily or on an equal basis. With every door of communication opening wide, we are held back by the barrier of language.

It has been estimated that there are some three thousand "known" languages. But this does not include a very large number of living languages spoken by people whose voices are just beginning to be heard in the modern world. And looking ahead, we must think in terms of all the languages there are, not only of the few we are familiar with—even if we do not speak any but our own and perhaps one more. But we must also ask whether the idea of protecting the dignity of all languages is compatible with the hope of giving all men the chance to talk with one another.

In the past, when only a few travelers made their way to far-of places, they translated their experiences of new landscapes and new peoples, strange sights and sounds and smells, as best they could into their own tongue. Often, of course, they introduced new words along with the exotic things they brought back home. Commonplace English words like *coffee, tea, chocolate, tomato, tapioca, tobacco* and *cola* all carry distant echoes of adventurous travel, modified to fit the sound patterns of English. And when people went abroad as conquerors, traders or colonists, two things were very likely to happen. Those who were dominant imposed their own language as the high-level mode of communication; and very often they made use of a trade language or "pidgin" as a low-level mode of communication. Both practices accentuated the differences of those who came into contact with one another.

Today all this is changing, and perhaps the necessity of making a new choice presents to us a unique opportunity. We can, if we will, do away with the inevitable inequalities existing between native and foreign speakers of the major languages. It is not enough to have a few people who can converse comfortably or even many people who can address one another formally and correctly. The very rapid movement of jokes and slang, fashions and fads and slogans from one continent to another suggests that even now people, especially young people, are struggling to create a kind of common idiom in spite of language barriers. This may well be the moment, while worldwide communication is a new phenomenon, to establish a secondary world language that all the world's peoples will learn, in addition to their own, for use around the whole earth.

There are those who believe that the choice is already being made. They point to the number of people everywhere who are using one or another of the major languages for business, science and international politics. If they are right, sooner or later the languages of the most populous and powerful advanced nations will swamp the smaller languages and the world will be more strongly than ever divided into blocs. But I believe the choice is still open. If we can move fast enough, we may arrive at a decision that will bring people everywhere into more meaningful contact.

It is possible that Americans may play a decisive role in what happens. We have had a very special relationship to foreign languages ever since English won out over all the languages of other colonialists and, later, of immigrants who came to this country. However, the kind of choice we make will depend on our contemporary interpretation of our historic linguistic tradition.

From one point of view, the more obvious one, we have rejected every language other than our own in our developing of American English. Our insistence that every child in school must be taught in English and that adults, for the most part, must use English in their work has meant two things. Native speakers of English were freed from the necessity of ever having to learn another language and all others broke their ties to the past by giving up their native tongue. Adequate English became a symbol of full citizenship. Those who did not learn it were cut off from freedom of movement out of their own language group, and even from some kinds of intimacy with their American-educated, English-speaking children. Foreign languages became something you might study—but seldom learned to speak—in school.

Only in World War II, when we discovered that it was very inconvenient to be engaged on a world scale and ignorant on a world scale, did we recognize the wastefulness of this. Then suddenly we found that we could teach—and thousands of young men could learn—the most "difficult" languages fast and well. Fortunately, the spark of interest and the curiosity about languages is still alive.

From another point of view, the less obvious one, our insistence on the primacy of English has had as its basis the deep belief that a common language is crucial for social unity. As one result, even in the period of our greatest linguistic isolationism, a few Americans began to campaign for a world language. Out of the tradition that you could be fully American only if you spoke American English they drew the idea that the beginning of world community depended on the invention of a new, artificial language for worldwide use. Since this would be the language of no nation, it could, without offending anyone, become everyone's language. What these pioneers did not notice, however, was that each of these invented languages, because it was basically a simplification of existing European languages, would still give tremendous advantages to those who spoke any one of them. Conversely, these artificial languages offered little to all those with a different linguistic tradition. So the various candidate languages were tried out—in vain. This, of course, did a great deal of harm; for with each failure the danger increased that more people would treat the idea and the advocates of an auxiliary universal language as silly, boring and cranky.

Why, then, are we coming back to the idea? In fact, we have not "come back" but have moved in a new direction. Recently students of the relationship between language and culture, working together with the new scientists of the cybernetic revolution, have learned a great deal about natural languages—all languages that have been molded by the speech of many people over many generations. Especially important has been the concept of redundancy that has been developed by electronic engineers.

This concept has to do with the patterning of the different aspects of speech and with what happens when the patterning is broken or distorted by some kind of interference or "noise." For example, how much can be left out and how much must be expressed in more than one way for someone to understand what is being said to him in a transatlantic telephone call? Using the concept of redundancy, linguists began to think afresh about the usefulness of all the elements, the different kinds of patterning, that give complexity and richness to natural languages. This in turn gave them the essential clue to the unworkability of artificial languages, except for very special purposes. These languages lack the resources of redundancy that make natural languages such good instruments for the most diverse users.

In the abstract, redundancy is a complicated concept, partly because it involves all the levels of speech. But every child, learning to speak, masters its uses in practice, and all of us are aware of some of the elements. Listening to a United Nations debate without seeing the speakers, anyone can tell when there is a language switch. Though we may not understand a word, our ear informs us that we are now listening to a different combination of sound patterns as well as different patterns of intonation, pitch and rhythm.

In the same way, listening to a group of English speakers whose words we do understand, we can—with a little practice—identify one as an Australian, another as a Scot and a third as a South African by consistent variations not only in sound, intonation and rhythm patterns but also in grammatical usage and the meanings given to words and expressions. As we listen, any one or all of these sets of variations may be (from our point of view) "noise"—something that interferes with our understanding of what is said—and yet, because we share what is basic to the language, usually we do get the message.

We can think of speech (spoken language) as consisting of inter-related sets of patterns, each of which, as it is used, gives us specific information. In English, for example, intonation informs us as to whether a speaker is asking a question, making a statement or issuing a command. As spoken, "Go! " sounds very different from "Go?" or "Go." Even if we do not catch the word itself, we do grasp part of the speaker's intended meaning. And when a German or a Frenchman speaks grammatically correct English but uses the intonations of his own language, we may miss a part of the message but still get the part that is communicated, in this case, by words and grammar.

Redundancy refers to the fact that the same or related or confirm-ing information is given by different means—at different levels, through different sets of patterns and by different elements within the same set—all interlocking in speech. A single sentence can illus-trate how redundancy works. If someone said to you, "Mary had her new hat on yesterday," you would recognize this as English from the sound pattern itself. A drop in the speaker's voice at the end would tell you that this was a statement, not a question; the position of the first two words ("Mary had," not "Had Mary") would suggest the same thing. "Mary" would tell you that this was a girl; "her" would confirm your expectation. The form of the verb would tell you the event was in the past; "yesterday" would confirm this and pinpoint the time. This is, of course, a simplification and only a beginning. And if one adds that gesture and posture play a part in communication, the range within which redundancy operates is widened even further.

The important thing is that each language has its own range and regularities of patterning at all levels—on which the poet and the tone-deaf person and the little child will draw, although with a very different appreciation of the resources of the same language. Yet each can make himself understood. We are learning today that deaf chil-dren who can "hear" language rhythms only when they are magni-fied in special earphones can still in this way get a firm grasp of how their language operates in speech.

A language that works has been shaped by men and women, old people and little children, intelligent people and dunces, people with good memories and people with poor memories, those who pay attention to form and those who pay attention to sound, and people with all the diversity of interests present in their culture over genera-tions. This very multiplicity of speakers creates the redundancy that makes a language flexible and intelligible to all different kinds of peo-ple who are its speakers at any time. A natural language allows for the whole range of human intelligence and responsiveness, and it is far richer and more expressive than are any individual's capacities for using it. This is why the invented languages failed—each in its form presented only a very limited set of possibilities worked out by a few people in only one period.

And this is why, if we are to have a universal language, it must be a natural language. It must have the complex resources on which all the world's people can draw. But it cannot be one of the present-day major languages now in competition. For we need to protect all the languages there are. Soon diversity of language will be the principal remaining evidence of man's extraordinary inventiveness in creating different ways of living, and language will have to carry the sense of intimacy in a way of life and the continuity of long generations. As American English expresses our deepest values and other languages give us insight into the values of other peoples, so also every language carries that which is most significant for its native speakers.

In time, this is also what a universal secondary language must carry for the peoples of the whole world—the significance of worldwide talking with one another within a shared civilization. If we chose as a secondary language the natural language of a small, politically unimportant, non-European literate people, we could accomplish our several purposes.

It can be done now. It may be very difficult to do later.

EDITOR'S NOTE

1. For such cultural reasons, I believe—with the benefit of hindsight—that Mead's suggestion to use the language of a non-Western, non-powerful nation as a *lingua franca* for the entire world, though laudable in intent, was doomed from the start. However, having said that, what we have here is another example of Mead's proclivity toward alert anticipation and humane visualization. She was never shy about advancing bold ideas that she thought would or might prove useful—and in this case she did just that. Moreover, she was certainly right about linguistic and cultural hegemony. In the nearly four decades since she and Métraux penned this piece, global political and techno-economic factors have resulted in a dramatic expansion of the very kind of linguistic and cultural hegemony she wished so ardently to avert—principally at the hands of the English language, which has become, or is becoming, the world's *lingua franca* for

business, technology, computer systems usage, the natural and social sciences, entertainment, and much more. If Mead were alive today, one can well imagine her vigorously campaigning for all of Earth's educational systems to be producing people capable of using at least one truly local language to foster cultural identity and continuity, and at least one world language to help insure political and economic viability in an era of ever more pervasive globalization.

She would also be heeding futurists' projections during the 1990s that, by the year 2010 or so, computers or similar devices will be used worldwide in interlingual communication, and that "in text and—to a lesser extent—in voice-to-voice telecommunication, language translation will be effective for many practically-significant vocabularies" (Coates et al 1997). It is not hard to imagine her being totally *au courant* with the policy issues involved in this new technology, and pressing the powers that be, to insure that such computerized translation capability is made available even to some of the smaller, less advantaged, peoples of the earth.

EDITOR'S REFERENCE

Coates, Joseph F., John B. Mahaffie and Andy Hines, *2025: Scenarios of US and Global Society by Science Reshaped by Science and Technology.* Greensboro NC: Oakhill Press, 1998. See Proposition 60, p. 10, and elsewhere.

1966b

THE UNIVERSITY AND INSTITUTIONAL CHANGE*

Editor's Commentary

Today the notion of "life-long learning" is a commonplace mantra. In 1966 it was much less so. This piece presents a glimpse of how Mead envisioned the life-long learning concept—years before the public, or even many educators, took up its cry. The essay also contains a number of delightfully irreverent and entertaining barbs about the attitudes of some conventional professors toward true creativity and social utility.

In this address Mead looks at goals and challenges faced by Oakland University, which had been established seven years earlier in Rochester, Michigan, 20 miles north of Detroit. The new, experimental university was explicitly and energetically attempting to promote lifelong education by meeting the needs both of young secondary school graduates, and also, on a part-time basis, adults of all ages. In 1959 its enrollment was 570; in 2004, about 16,000.

Mead offers her strong support to Oakland University's educational model. She acknowledges the difficulties involved, but congratulates Oakland on its willingness to confront those difficulties. She sees great merit in Oakland's willingness to take continuing responsibility for the continuing education of its alumni, wherever they may be. By way of encouragement, she points to elements of the overall American culture that are favorable to the notion of lifelong learning.

* * *

* In: *Oakland Papers: Symposium on Social Change and Educational Continuity*, ed. James B. Whipple and Gary A. Woditsch (Notes and Essays on Education for Adults, 51, Center for the Study of Liberal Education for Adults at Boston University, 1966), 52-62.

What we are concerned with today is innovation—innovation of a particularly daring kind. There is a familiar story, told during World War II, about the stranger who asks how to get somewhere. The person he asks tells him briskly, "You see, you go out, you turn to the right and go down two blocks until you get to a garage. ... No, no, that won't do it. You go out, you turn to the left and you walk three blocks until you get to a church. ... No, that's not it. You go out and you walk straight ahead. ..." The story goes on and on, until at last, after all his hesitations and reversals, the person who is giving the directions says with conviction, "You can't get there from here! "

Now, everywhere people are trying hard—and Oakland, I think, is trying harder than most institutions—to figure out how to get somewhere from the wrong place. What it really comes down to is how an institution is to find its way to some new place when it must start in the middle. Oakland, more imaginatively than most institutions I know about, is facing up to the problems involved in trying to start in the middle.

How do you get a beginning if you have only a middle? How do you create a past if you are new? How do you build a future if you are old?

These three questions, all rolled into one, are crucial ones, and the program of continuing education provides one way of attacking the problem as a whole. The task, as I understand it, is this: How to define what must be done if an institution, such as Oakland, recognizes that we must change our ideas of what college and university education are—give up the notion that they represent a terminal state and that degrees are the end (as though people didn't need to think any more) and recognize that education is part of life, part of a process that goes on all the way through life. Then, if we are to establish a new climate of opinion, a set of institutions and a kind of behavior that will allow people to continue learning in systematic ways throughout their lives, what kinds of changes must be made in our traditional modes of operation? And how shall we go about the task? These are the problems with all their multitudinous facets that Oakland is attempting to analyze.

WE MUST START FROM WHERE WE ARE

In the first place, you who are involved in the Oakland experiment are taking the students you have and thinking about how these students can learn something about how to go on learning. They must learn how to go about a continual process of learning without antecedents.

There are no alumni for them to learn from. They are brand new and you must take them as they are. Furthermore, nothing as yet has been done about the high schools where they learned that the only reason for going to college is to get a degree. (Of course, very soon something will have to be done about this high-school picture of why people go to college; it is part of the problem of developing a new state of mind in college.) Secondly, in the same program, you are experimenting with ways of allowing very young alumni—graduates who have just found jobs and roles in the community—to go on learning without stopping. And third, you are facing the complex problems of the drop-outs in the community, whoever they may be—the people who were discouraged by institutions that are not as good as this one, the high-school drop-outs, the people who received a technical education without any humanities, and the people whose education was so humane that they know nothing at all about science and technology. You have all the kinds of people who "left" school and moved "out" into the world before anyone really believed that education is a continuing process—all the kinds of people who happen to live in the area for which this institution is trying to provide some kind of systematic continuing education. You are in fact intervening in—starting in the middle of—a whole series of operations for anyone of which one could write a very nice program if only one could begin in the beginning.

We educators could write a beautiful program *now* for two-year-olds, using everything we know, so as to bring them up to love learning all their lives. We would not punish them and we would not reward them (for this is even more devastating); instead, we would make the process of learning and discovery a self-rewarding experience. Starting with two- or four-year-olds would not be very hard. Starting with six-year-olds would be harder, with twelve-year-olds, harder still. Starting with eighteen-year-olds would be grim. But of course starting with the two-year-olds really means beginning with those who will start them off. Before children can learn the things we want to teach them, we must have the mothers and the teachers.

Today, in our kind of society, people in positions to make changes have really come to face the fact that one always has to start in the middle. This is one of the great differences between the present and the past, when innovators thought—as they still do in some revolutionary societies—that the only way to change whatever existed was to silence or kill off the people they had and to start afresh with some others. But in our kind of society, innovators believe that any person can start where he is. This belief is based on the knowledge that if one brings up children differently, the adults will also change. For while the adults are learning to treat children differently, they themselves are changing. In the same way, where teachers and administrators really have the idea that students should learn differently, the faculty will also change. People are beginning to realize that the middle point is a point of leverage—a point from which to begin to alter the society that we all live in. People are beginning to see that any change made at this point with sufficient vigor will change the rest, also.

As I understand it, those who are developing this program of continuing education have in mind the creation of a network that will extend over the United States, so constituted that each institution, each center in each city or metropolitan area, will be ready to receive on a reciprocal basis the alumni of the other colleges and each, in turn, will be able to direct its own alumni to centers elsewhere. The outcome, eventually, will be a completely reciprocal system in which each university center will have a sense of responsibility for all the postgraduates, all the post-professional people in its area. The different centers will take responsibility for providing what is needed for all those who were not in school yesterday but who may be in school tomorrow, for all those who need new skills, new educational interests or new ways of doing things, and for all those who realize that in a rapidly changing world everyone needs more systematic education—very often. I do not think we shall ever be able to say categorically *how* often people will need to go on with their education. I hope we shall not reorganize the educational world so that, in effect, it's back to school every ten years. We do not want a new static form. Rather, we are thinking about a kind of society in which those who need to learn and those who teach them will share the expectation that people will want to learn new things and believe that they are able to learn new things.

At present there are a great many unreceptive faculties in the United States. Where they are concerned, Oakland must become a kind of goad. There are many institutions in metropolitan areas that would like to isolate themselves from the life of the city and to act as if their halls were set in the midst of green fields. Some no longer want part-time students, and by the simple device of insisting that every graduate student must have the money to be in residence full time, they are keeping part-time students out. Why, under these circumstances, students should want to go to a graduate school in a city is anybody's guess. There are, after all, only two good reasons for deciding to study in a city. First, the student who has to do it that way can get work and study part time. And second, the student, while he is studying, can be part of a living community and related to all the activities that are going on in it.

Now here is a basic difficulty that must be faced. Is a university willing to be receptive to everyone around it and to take responsibility for every person in the wider community who wants to learn something? Or will it draw in its skirts and specialize in producing B.A.'s, M.A.'s and Ph. D. ' s? There is the further difficulty that if every institution wishes to boast about the number of Ph.D.'s that adorn its faculty, this in itself will encourage the kind of university that concentrates on producing very large numbers of Ph.D. candidates at the fastest possible rate. The two attitudes are reciprocal, and the issue must, I think, be considered very seriously. Is the most important thing about an institution the number of Ph.D.'s gathered into its faculty? One striking thing about Ph.D.'s is the number of them who never write anything worthwhile after they have completed their Ph.D. dissertation. In this sense, they represent the most educationally "finished" people one can imagine.

All my life—well, not quite all my life, but ever since I started school and began taking examinations—I've had a very special form of the examination dream. In the dream I'm in absolute agony because I have flunked some examination—and then I remember that I have a higher degree and that resolves the dream. I *have* a Ph.D.—I can't flunk freshman algebra. I can never flunk freshman algebra, nobody can get me in a room and examine me in freshman algebra, and never mind whether I could possibly pass it now or not, I once did. One of the very few irreversibles in our society is the academic degree. It cannot be taken away from anyone. It is like having a child, if you are a woman; once you've had one, no one can ever undo that birth. There are very few irreversibles for men, but getting a degree is one. You can betray your country, you can commit a murder, you can become a drug addict—you can do all sorts of things, but nobody can take away your B.A. This is what we have been building up to in our educational system—getting these irreversible degrees that no longer have to be lived up to, once one has them. From the time one has a degree, one is set for life.

Such a situation has to be looked at very carefully. If our aim as teachers is to teach students that people go on learning and changing and growing and that they can, at any point, move into the system and out again, then we cannot simultaneously teach them that a Ph.D. should be a requirement for everyone who wants to teach. But here we create a conflict for those who are trying to produce a first-class institution, since one of the signs of a first-class institution today is the number of Ph.D.'s on the faculty. Another sign is the number of books in the library. As a result, universities and those who teach in them are trying simultaneously to do things that are basically incompatible.

Here I should like to suggest a mark of a really lively, innovative, mid-twentieth-century institution. How many people without a Ph.D. do you have on your faculty, who are so good that they got on anyway? Some of the liveliest places in this country have very good people of this kind. Why should poets have Ph.D.'s? No one has ever proved that a higher degree does a practicing poet any good, and one reason that the humanities are as dead as they are in some places is that they are represented by people with Ph.D.'s who talk about creativity but who have never created anything themselves. Those who are busy creating things may not have time to work for degrees. Now I mention this only as one aspect of the conflict you at Oakland will find yourselves in as you try to produce a first-class, exciting, modern college with very high standards for undergraduates, who will not expect to be "finished" someday very soon. For the only way one can feel not finished oneself is continually to meet other unfinished people who are moving along.

And now, what about the community? Oakland aims at creating a flexible learning culture in our society that will support adults of all ages in pursuit of their personal goals of understanding. We want a system that simultaneously will serve the very specific needs of the young engineer who badly wants tutoring by a hard-to-corner specialist, the curiosity of the retired army officer who really wants to learn a little philosophy, and the reawakened interest of the middle-aged mother who now wants the excitement of learning the kinds of things that are part of getting the B.A. Oakland envisions a program that will systematically place the best available educational resources at the disposal of the adult at every stage of development. There is a hidden blessing in such an ideal. If systematic education is open to people at every stage in life, those who seek it out will be of different ages. One thing that is lacking on college campuses today (except where there is continuing education) is the opportunity to live with and learn about people of different ages, the opportunity to discover what has happened to them and what might happen to oneself. Even more exciting is the aim of spreading this conception of learning to other institutions all over the country. Here, Oakland is saying to other institutions, in effect, "You must take responsibility for our alumni and we will take responsibility for yours, "and in this way alumni will cease to be people on whom universities depend but for whom they do very little. Instead, universities would be centers for all graduates throughout their lives—each one a vital center for an entire community of developing adults.

HOW CAN WE CREATE A DESIRE TO LEARN?

This is an exciting prospect. But it brings us at this meeting back to the problem of how undergraduates are to learn to like learning enough so they will want to do more of it. In some ways, this is our most serious question. It may also be a question to which a new, young college can give a better answer than an old one, and one good reason for Oakland to make the attempt. Years ago when some of us social scientists did a small piece of research on food habits for the Public Health Committee of the Cup and Container Institute, we discovered that it is easier to have new ideas in a new place. At a time when paper cups were relatively new, we set up a series of experiments to find out whether people were more willing to drink a familiar drink or a new drink in a paper cup. Though it was a simple piece of research, the results were interesting. For it turned out that people are more willing to drink a new kind of beverage in a new kind of cup than they are to drink an old one in a new cup or a new one in an old cup. Coffee was attached to a coffee cup, tea to a teacup, and milk to a glass. Whenever an old drink was put in a non-traditional container, people were upset; but they were more willing to try a new kind of container with a newly invented drink called by a new name. By analogy, you are doing much the same sort of thing in this institution. You are a new college, and fewer people will object to the new ideas you produce.

But how will you get these new ideas over to students who have already had twelve or more years of education? Some of them, in fact, have had practically no life at all outside of school. Looking at the continuing education program from one point of view, it might appear that always keeping children in school is one way of getting them to want to stay in school. It might seem that the children who were hustled off to school at the age of two would be the ones who were really prepared for lifetime devotion to education. But, on the whole, it does not work out this way. College teachers are finding out today that most college students with this experience feel they have had enough school. Quite a lot of them had enough before they came to college.

Other institutions and agencies have their dropout problems, too. The Poverty Program talks about the children who are dropouts from the first day of school. On that first day they decide that they do not understand a word the teacher is saying and that she does not understand them—that she never will understand them and that they never will understand her—and they give up then and there. Nevertheless, these children are shut up for sixteen years in what amounts to a prison where they never learn anything. Some of them make very little headway; others manage somehow to pull through.

Among the students who are well enough "prepared," there are a fair number who would not go on to college if they did not have to. They have been told, "If you don't go to college, you won't get a decent kind of job. If you don't go to college, you won't get anywhere. College today is what high school was once, and you know that no one got anywhere without a high school education." Those who are persuaded by these arguments go to college for utilitarian reasons. It is a way to get somewhere and to get there as quickly as possible. There isn't any reason for enjoying learning or for prolonging the process. The thing is to get it over with, like basic training in the army. It is hard to teach this group how delightful learning can be and how lovely it will be to be learning at thirty-five, at fifty, or at eighty. The prospect is not one for which this group is likely to feel enthusiasm.

One of the most percipient things I have heard today was said by a young interviewer, who exclaimed, "But education is painful, I don't know anyone who would go and get any more of it!" Yet, somehow, if the continuing education program is to take hold, learning—and the desire for learning—must become habitual. I use the word *habitual* because, I suppose, *addictive* has connotations we would reject, even though, in a sense, we really do want to make everyone mildly addicted to learning. One of our aims as educators is to induce in our students a mild form of addiction—a state in which people get so used to something that they don't wish to do without it. What we really want is for people to be addicted to learning something new, to be bored with the state of the knowledge they had yesterday—the knowledge that is already chewed, predigested, memorized for examinations—and to realize that if they are not learning something new, the things they already know will become dead, dry as dust, dusty and dead.

How are we to induce this kind of addiction? In a mild form. Of course, we do not want to encourage the perpetual students who still can be seen occasionally on American university campuses. Typically, the perpetual student is someone with a small income, possibly from a trust fund with a provision for paying for education as long as the recipient continues to study on a campus. There are also a few who are related to the draft in rather complicated ways. They are not our concern here. But if an important part of the continuing education program is to discover the kind of college life that will make students value continued education, one major piece of research has to do with just this question: What must a college do to ensure that students will acquire an addictive attitude toward learning? Whatever it does must not be so extreme that students cannot bear to leave school or that they will all want to become college professors. We in this country need people for many other activities in our society. We want only a limited number of people to become so attached to the academic life that they will stay within it permanently. In fact, one of the problems we must face—a problem that will become more acute in the future—is how to get much more interchange between the campus and the larger community. How can we develop more and better ways of moving people in and out of government, industry, and the academic world, as well as back and forth between activities with a national and with an international scope? We need, and we shall need even more people who can see possibilities for combining academic life with other kinds of activities. We need to encourage the individual who will sit down and think, "Well, I might teach for a few years. Then it would be interesting to take an overseas assignment. And after that I'd like to get into government and use what I've lived through and learned overseas. And after that …"

Implicit in the idea of continuing education is the expectation of doing different things at different periods in one's life. Americans despise getting into a rut, but the expectation of doing the same thing for a lifetime is consistent with the idea of terminal education. Once a person has finished school, he is set for whatever it is he is going to do and he won't ever need any more training because he will stay with what he has. Perhaps a young man or woman has been admitted to the bar, has passed the Boards, or has his or her Ph.D.—and is *it* forever. All that is necessary is to prevent anyone else from becoming more *it* than oneself for the rest of one's life.

Among the very effective stimulants for students who are acquiring new attitudes toward continuing education will be a faculty whose members are pursuing the same educational goal—continuing education—colleges and universities will need faculty who are deeply interested in the whole world around them and concerned with how to rouse interest in others. They will need the teacher who views his students in terms of what these students may become in twenty or thirty years. In looking for teachers of this kind, the university is making a search for the kind of imaginative, open-ended vision that was once required of the good elementary school teacher. She had to see her children going ahead—some to high school, a few to college, and perhaps one into medicine or the law—and this kind of vision was very exciting. This vision in the teacher's eyes makes it possible for the students to learn. But how can teachers maintain any vision of the future when they are faced by students who expect to stay only as long as they must and who are just bearing their educational experience—no more than that.

LET US WELCOME THE DROPOUTS

I think, in the future, colleges will have to welcome dropouts. If I were teaching in an undergraduate college today, I would discuss dropping out as an immediate option. I would begin by saying, "Now some of you may be interested in staying for a semester or a year ..." If we adopted this viewpoint, students would not have to go through the turmoil they now do, refusing to turn in papers for twelve weeks or living through fits of depression, before they succeed in indicating to someone that they do not want to learn anything more now. One of the things that will give students greater zest, that will make them mildly addicted to learning, will be a greater sense of freedom of choice. Sometimes a friend comes to me, very disturbed, and says, "Bill isn't going to stay in college. He doesn't believe in it anymore. He says everything in college is totally divorced from life." And I answer, "Of course, this is what lots of students are saying. He's not unusual." The student I wonder and ask questions about is the one who goes straight through. Then I say, "That's a very unusual student. What happened?" I think that cultivating a student body who are in college at any particular time because this is where they want to be will make a difference for everyone. Most of the students now in college would still be there, but they would be there with different attitudes and with goals more relevant to their lives as whole individuals.

To come back to the beginning, the big problem for Oakland today is, perhaps, starting in the middle. Inevitably, you who are concerned with this new program are starting with students whose earlier experiences with education were far from ideal. You cannot go back and undo those experiences. They are there—too much school, too much dull school, too many years of American history taught by rote, the wrong mathematics. And yet there is no other starting point. And if between you, between the students and the faculty, you can discover how to bring about a desirable state of mild addiction to learning, all educators and students will be a little farther along. Educators will be able, in time, to start with students who have had a different upbringing. For, in the not so distant future, today's students will be the parents of children who can be brought up differently. The process, begun here, will be under way, and the new possibilities will spread throughout our society. The exciting thing, here and now, is that Oakland University is taking the responsibility for innovation in this field and, starting where everyone is now, is proposing to take responsibility, in a sense, for all alumni in this country and in other countries of the world.

1967

CHANGING CULTURAL PATTERNS OF WORK AND LEISURE*

Editor's Commentary

This selection is a speech Mead gave on specifically American cultural premises and patterns concerning work and leisure. It offers a glimpse of her speaking style, reinforced by her robust manner of answering a wide range of questions from an educated lay public. Her speech dates from the era of President Lyndon B. Johnson's "Great Society," a bold domestic initiative to rebuild America through vastly expanded federal programs, including his "war on poverty."

Here we see Mead at her public anthropologist's best in explaining to her lay audience the significance of the Puritan tradition in American history, and some of the reasons why that tradition, with its definitions of work and leisure, constituted an obstacle to the humane resolution of problems faced by the American people during the rapidly changing Sixties. Note, for example, her half-humorous presentation of the distinction that this tradition has imprinted upon American culture, between the disapproved concept of "leisure" and approved concept of "recreation." Indeed, throughout her lecture, she stresses the importance of the role of semantic labels in promoting or obstructing humane cultural change.

Mead also stresses her view that successful sociocultural change need not invariably be slow and gradual—as had been the conventional assumption of many anthropologists. She illustrates her point with data from her fieldwork in Manus.[1]

In this selection we note, once again, Mead's early awareness of the revolutionary significance of the computer, which, she believes, will make it possible to analyze and assess a given social problem with unprecedented speed and accuracy. She points to the computer as laying the essential groundwork for what today would be referred to as Futures Studies.

* * *

* *Seminar on Manpower Policy and Program* (Washington, D.C.: Department of Labor, January 1967), 3-16.

DR. MEAD: Mrs. Peterson, ladies and gentlemen. I think that in spite of the introduction, I will have to take a few words to justify my having something to say to you on the subject. I spend my technical and professional time on the South Sea Islands, whose immediate relationships to this topic you may think are confined to leisure rather than to work. You have heard in the course of these seminars—and particularly in the first seminar last year when Donald Michael spoke about all our possibilities of working with human behavior and human society in terms of computers and simulators—that we now can simulate almost any one of our problems with very large numbers of variables and hope to find useful solutions. But we are a fairly long way from knowing what variables to put into the machine. The machine is capable. I don't think there is any doubt of that. It is capable and it is going to serve us very well. It's a machine in the widest possible sense of the whole cybernetic revolution. But it can only answer questions that we know enough to ask.

I work instead, technically, with what we sometimes call living models. That is, instead of constructing a logical mathematical model, programming it, and putting it into a computer, we find living instances placed in history where the real people are solving real problems in their own way within a spontaneous natural setting. We then attempt to get this living model not only to give us new answers, but to suggest new questions and to suggest things we would not have known enough to ask.

One of our principal problems at present, I feel, is that we don't know all the questions to ask. Running through some of the seminars in this series has been the complaint that we haven't the facts to answer this question or that question or the other question.

That is, of course, true. But I also think we don't quite know all the questions we want to ask. Now, the sort of thing that one does in using a primitive community is to take something that has happened that one does not understand and go there and study it. When I went back in 1953 to a Stone-Age community I had studied in 1928, one of my friends who is very committed to quantitative models said, "You know what people say about anthropologists? They say they find what they went to look for. Can't you construct your hypotheses about what has happened to these people in 25 years, then compare it with actuality?" We knew the community had moved from the Stone Age into the present. It had gone through one of the most extreme changes ever reported, although we did not know anything about it otherwise. My friend, who was looking after my reputation, wanted me to make a set of hypotheses. He offered to have them witnessed, sealed, and put in the bank. Then, when I came back, my reputation would be vindicated and it could be proved—I don't know what exactly could be proved, but something—to which my answer was, "If I knew enough to form the hypotheses, I would not go. I would go somewhere else." Because what we hope for from this kind of situation is genuine new information.

What I actually found in this particular case was contrary to the assumptions we had all been making on the basis of pre-World War II change—that slow change is better than fast change, that you have to creep before you can walk. These assumptions are echoed in some of the seminar reports—that it will take at least a generation for us to do this or that or the other, that we cannot hurry people too far, that the only thing we can do is wait until older people are dead or retired. These assumptions were based on a theory of change that had been developed by anthropologists and other scientists—not economists, I might add. Economists were almost always in favor of very fast change and they were almost always on the opposite side from anthropologists. As a result, we were opponents. We, the anthropologists, insisted that you had to grow into a situation.

You had to grow into it slowly. You had to bring up the next generation to understand it. You had to wait until you got rid of the people who did not understand it, and so forth.

What I actually found in this community I had studied in 1928, again in '53, and '64, and from which I have just come back 3 weeks ago ('65) from a fourth field trip, was that the reason it had been able to do what it had done—skip about 2,000 years—was that it moved very fast. The people changed everything at once and did not leave any pieces lying around to drag the rest back. They involved everybody, to the oldest grandparent, and left nobody on the shelf, gave no permission to anyone to be old-fashioned and just sit. They were a little more lenient to the old than they were to the young. They said, "After all, they do lose their temper worse. But they were not brought up right." But this was the only concession that they made.

Looking at this very rapid change gave us a new set of hypotheses about change. We have had a good many other studies since then. Today, many anthropologists and economists are much closer together in their recognition that one of the things that makes for trouble in society is discrepant rates of change. When we were students, we heard a lot about cultural lag and about adaptive culture in which technical change and economic change were supposed to go racing ahead and human relations change was supposed to come crawling behind and there was to be more and more of a discrepancy. Today it is possible to say, instead, that if we can move fast enough and keep all the parts of society somewhat in pace with one another,

so that one part does not pull down another, and so that the old
don't pull down the young, and so that the badly educated school
teachers don't pull down the better educated children, then fast
change may actually be better than slow change.

Predictions Built for Too Few

Another thing I noticed in some of the reports of the other seminars
that I found stimulating was the recurrent statement that our predictions have always been too slow and built for too few. This has been
going on everywhere in this country. Before we get it built, every airport we build is too small for the planes that are going to come into it.
Every student union in the country is too small for the enrollment,
before the roof goes on. Our continuous inability to predict the rapidity of change, which has gone all the way through the space program,
through all of our predictions of new inventions of every sort, to the
predictions of the need for airports or universities or whatever, is one
of the things that I think we ought to ask some questions about.

So what I want to address myself particularly to today in this
background is a series of discrepant ideas that we have about the
problem of work and leisure that are going to bedevil the planners
attempting to make some solutions to this problem.

Mrs. Peterson said, hopefully, you know, that the notion that
"Satan findeth mischief for idle hands to do" is all gone. I'm afraid it
isn't. Certainly not when it affects the lower classes. If you listen to
any discussion in this country about what is going to happen with
this new leisure, one thing is perfectly clear—"the wrong people are
going to have it." No professional person has it. The elite of the country are going to work terribly hard and they are going to work harder
and harder because there will be less and less commitment to their
jobs by the next technical level. The new leisure goes through all the
imperfectly educated, unmotivated part of the community who are
going to "misuse" it. These are the same people who "have too many
children." The notion that leisure breeds mischief, I would say, has
not disappeared at all in many circles, which, fortunately, you do not
move in. But it is a prevailing attitude over the country. It comes up
in a discussion like that on a guaranteed annual income.

The term "guaranteed annual income " is misleading. Those who
would likely get it don't have "incomes." Incomes are something
"better" people have. An income is something you have when you are
a professional and get paid by the month. If it is called a guaranteed
annual wage, you immediately say it belongs only to wage earners. It

comes under the heading of "welfare," rather than under the heading of responsible citizenship.

It is this kind of edge that is going to be significant, just as the invention of the word "dropout" was. You know, "dropout" was the total invention of an entirely new idiom, actually. We wanted to talk about all the people who had not gone to school, had not wanted to go to school, and most of whom nobody wanted to go to school. They couldn't have wanted anything less, most of them, than to go to school. We now speak as if they dropped out when all of us have been working night and day to keep them in. We treat people who stop school in the fifth grade as if they were third year undergraduates in Harvard. Perhaps the word originally came from Harvard. But by applying it to the entire American community and to people who had never thought of going on to school, and by treating them all as failures in obtaining what we now said we wanted everybody to obtain, we were able to mobilize the kind of attention and interest in back of the idea that we could not have done if we had not made such a shift. We might have made a different shift, of course. But we needed some shift. It was important to shift a whole nation away from the notion that some people ought to have some education, a few more people ought to have a little more, and a few people ought to have a little more still. The word "dropout" gave a picture of this procession upward of every child in the United States, each one of whom was supposed to go right through the school system, a procession from which some were falling out. It galvanized some of our thinking on the subject and many of you know how rapidly the word spread, how rapidly State committees, county committees, municipal committees, and committees of all the women's organizations in the entire country began worrying about dropouts.

Attitude Toward Work New

Now, on this whole question of how we are going to look in the future at the problem of work, leisure, and recreation, how we are going to divide employment, how we are going to define it, it will be, I think, useful to look at the traditional attitudes still around and a part of the whole picture. To begin with, it may be rather useful—and it isn't done very often—to realize that our traditional attitude toward work is actually very, very new. The notion that no human being should eat unless he or she has a job or is a dependent of someone who has a job, prevalent for a couple of hundred years, was a new idea. It's true that in Tudor England if someone came into the community as a pauper, the town fathers used to carry him out into a meadow to die so that the community would not have to bury him. But these were strangers. There was not the assumption that the group to which one belonged should not care for one. The idea that each individual buys his way to food and shelter, education and safety, by holding a job is terribly new and was characteristic of the Industrial Revolution with which we have now more or less finished. It is no longer appropriate. So the brevity of the period when work was a job and paid work was one's only guarantee of belonging in a society is very brief and is not an inalienable part of human nature. It is not a correct description of the way man lived for hundreds of thousands of years. In almost every group we know of where peoples stayed where they were or lived in tribes or in villages, working at a fixed job for pay was not the idea at all.

Many peoples do not even have a dichotomy of any sort between work and play. The Balinese have no category for "tired" but they have one for "too tired." You get too tired from occasional things that require massive effort, like a plowing bee when everybody puts a costume on the oxen and plows from morning until night. Then you get too tired. But otherwise, the word that they use for work is also the word they use for feasting, for festivals, and for gay activity. The notion that something must be done that you don't want to do, in order that you will be rewarded with a little bit of time in which you do what you want to do, is a particular Puritan invention. It's like our general attitude toward food. "If you eat enough food that is not good but is good for you, you can then eat a little food that is good but not good for you." This has been our basic notion about work and recreation.

Leisure Is a Reward

We also, I think, have to add in the various uses of the word "leisure," which we still have to think about leisure, on the whole, is when people are doing what they want to do, doing something that is of no human use to anyone but themselves. It does not apply to contributing to the community. That is not really leisure. Leisure may be well earned. On the other hand, it may be based on the hard efforts of ancestors. But however the idea of leisure is qualified, it essentially means something that people have got somehow, preferably by work. So it's very "bad" for unemployed youths to have it, because they got it by flunking out of school. They are utterly unable to use it. They should not have it at this stage. Or take the theory of the leisure class who are using leisure to promote their own status, or people who say,

"I never have any leisure to think." People who say that are people for whom, on the whole, you would say, thinking is an indulgence. You do not get this statement so much from people whose job it is to think. However we look at it, we don't approve of leisure. The picture of a society in which more people, and mainly the wrong people, are going to have leisure, fills us with apprehension. Of course, all sorts of agencies are trying to get hold of leisure and use it "constructively" to see that people are spending their time right. Of course, it's a great opportunity for education and things of this sort!

Now, the idea of "recreation" was a wonderful invention and is one term, which the Government can use, of course. We have had recreation commissions. We have had conferences on recreation, and the Government can use the term without reproach. I think a Government Commission on Enjoying Leisure would be regarded as a frill by many legislators. But "recreation" is all right, because the major point about recreation is that you get ready to work again. Any kind of recreation that does not get you ready to work, such as staying up too late on Sunday night, is unhealthy. Genuine recreation means you are re-created. You are healthier. You don't get rashes from poison ivy or aren't bitten by too many mosquitoes. You don't drink too much and smoke too much, or even stay up too late. But you are bright eyed and bushy tailed and ready for Monday morning. This is healthy, good recreation. A community that has it can be proud of the state that it's in.

So a struggle is going on in this country. It has been going on now ever since the first hint of automation made us begin to suspect that our future problem was not going to be how to create enough jobs, nor how to increase productivity. We are going to be able to do that to an almost unlimited degree. Our problem is going to be how to devise a system in which every individual's participation in society is such that he has dignity and purpose, and the society has a rationale for distributing the results of its high productivity.

Ever since this has dawned on us, we have had to come to grips with the dichotomy between work and leisure, or work and recreation. Recreation is not going to be any good any more, unless you do enough work. So the idea of recreation is going down. You hear instead, about too much leisure. It is said that people are too uneducated to use their leisure, or that people are going to spend their leisure in front of a television set. There is a continuous worry with a picture of society conjured up in which there are going to be only little pieces of work. Some people think of shorter hours. Some people think of shorter workweeks. Some people think of larger chunks of vacations for high executives. But however the thought is phrased, we are drawing up a picture in which work remains the same, but shrinks. Around these little islands of work, which are still phrased as jobs, there are going to be great wastelands of leisure, in which we think of ourselves as having a terrible problem in developing fitting activities consonant with our general ethical idea—which will remain the idea that people should work, that the only thing that gives dignity to a human being is work, that what people need is useful work. The difficulty, of course, is that this has been true and is still true today, but it soon may not be.

If you find 100,000 boys standing on street corners who have finished school, and have no jobs, what they need is jobs, and they are lacking in dignity if they don't have those jobs, So one of our transitional problems is to continue to meet what is really here, but to use what is really here to prepare for the future.

Need to Combine Old and New

I also encountered, in some of these seminar reports that I read, people who said moderately, "Well, I don't think it's going to happen right away. I agree these things are going to happen, but not right away. Meanwhile, we are in a period of transition and we must work in a period of transition." This has been the policy that has been advanced by many of the people shaping the Great Society. Maybe we will not need to talk about full employment in 20 years, but right now we do. So I think one of our major problems is to devise a way of simultaneously talking about full employment—taking the boys that have finished high school in Detroit and do not have jobs, and finding some way to give them jobs—and at the same time, talking about giving them jobs in a way that is not going to bind the future, in such away that we will be able to think about a different kind of society.

One of the things that was very striking when I looked at my primitive people who had skipped 2,000 years is that they had a model to skip to. That is, they were reaching toward a society, which they had distilled from their experience in World War II. It was not exactly accurate in some respects. Their model was the American Army and this meant a degree of generosity that perhaps does not characterize the entire American public. They had a conception of the value we placed on human life, because they saw the tremendous amount of medical nursing and technical care given every wounded soldier in World War II. They said that Americans think that the only thing that matters in the world is human life, individual human life, and material things don't matter. (The Army was giving material things away on a fairly large scale.) They then added that the reason

Americans think material things don't matter is because they have so many of them—whereas, usually the European comment on America is that because we have so many of them, we must think they matter. Anybody who has two bathrooms must obviously think bathrooms are the most important thing in the world. This is the European judgment on the situation.

As the Manus people I was studying moved toward a different kind of society they may have misconstrued us in many cases, and caught our ideals rather than the actuality. But nevertheless, they thought we had done it and that all they had to do was try. There were only 5,000 of them and 180,000,000 of us. They thought that they were going to have to work pretty hard. But they started right away. They moved awfully fast and they were able to practically skip transitions. They were moving toward a known goal. We don't know anything actually about how to move toward an unknown goal in a known direction, that is, toward a series of events or situations that have never occurred before.

Mr. Conway, when he spoke to this group at a seminar last year, discussed the importance of having an agency to assess our overall direction in the discussion of goals. But if we were to set up a public body or set up public bodies in this country, one of their great tasks would be to look at what we are doing now and see what this means for the future.

I want to take one particular example of the way in which we use these terms "work," "pay," and "jobs;" a discussion of what we should do about students. Should we pay them for going to school? Now that sentence brings out almost every attitude we have about work, leisure, responsibility, and age grading in the whole society. "Going to school is a privilege." You should never pay people for privileges. Going to "good" schools is a privilege. People who have worked hard and whose parents have worked hard can send their children to good schools. Therefore, society should not pay students because their parents have already worked hard. They have earned the right to pay for their children, a right that should not be taken over by society. The implication is that children are not people.

As long as one says children are not people, one is very much in danger of saying old people are not people, women are only people some of the time. Any limitation we place on saying every human being is a full person from the moment he is born is dangerous. I think we are moving more and more to the statement that each is a full person from before he is born, from the moment he is conceived—and we may move back a bit and take on a little supervision of whether he is conceived or not, and so give children the right to be born in a different period. This is one of the rights of unborn infants that really ought to be discussed, the right to be born in a less crowded period. But we are moving toward taking responsibility for the unborn, the only conceived, the just born, all the way up through the oldest person in the community. Possibly, we may go in for hibernation in which the fatally ill are frozen, to await new medical discoveries, and we can then conceive all of those individuals, too, as belonging to the total community. We can stop thinking in terms of segments of people: those of working age or not of working age, those who can be retired, the kinds of people eligible for relief, and those whose childhood can be extended as a way of keeping them out of society. Instead of letting children come in, we can pay them to go to school.

But does this not mean that going to school is work? That challenges our complete notion of what is school. Is it a privilege of the upper classes? You still hear a discussion about the means test. The only people who have a right to be helped are the people who did not get enough help in the society. Or, on the other hand, is school a duty that people should be subjected to without any participation in society? This is the kind of subjection under which we place young people, those who are too young to have had a chance to vote on the war they are fighting in. So we take a large segment of society and put it outside the picture. It belongs neither to work or play, but to some other limbo.

If, on the other hand, we say that anybody in school at any point from 2 to 80 years old is contributing to society, and as a contributor to society has a right to receive maintenance from society, then we would not talk about paying people to go to school. But we would be discussing going to school as well as performing every sort of work as part of involvement in society, and not think of the dichotomy between jobs and non-jobs. Or the other dichotomy which we recognize, that work is something you don't want to do, and you do it in order to enjoy 2 weeks vacation or 4 weeks vacation or 6 weeks vacation, and that the difference between a career and a job is that in a career you would pay other people to let you do it if they did not pay you to do it, and a job is something you only do because you have to in order to enjoy some other sector of life.

Of course, now, one of the possibilities is that we will accept this dichotomy between those who are doing what they want to do and those who are doing what they are forced to do. Some prophets are predicting that professional people and people who are technically competent, people who are gifted, will cease to make any distinction between work and leisure, or work and recreation, because for such people, there is no distinction. If they are doing what they want to and enjoying what they are doing, they just have life, that's all. They don't have recreation and they don't have hobbies and they don't have leisure in the ordinary sense of the word at all, just a piece of time to go into something else.

Mrs. Peterson says she doesn't have any leisure. I believe it, and I don't think you really want it.

MRS. PETERSON: I know I don't want it.

DR. MEAD: Then we might build a society in which there is a series of very deep rifts, or possibly a gradual declension to the people on the edge who have to do something that they don't want to do, or as some people envisage, people who are simply supported and aren't allowed to do anything at all. So we will have a tremendous gap between the people who are doing what they want because they want to do it, and the people who are merely existing and meeting some kind of a demand for some sort of nominal service to society. This is one possibility that we could very easily move toward in our phrasing, if we continue to look at life as filled with uneducable older people, poorly educated middle people, uneducated younger people, who are going to increase and who are going to be steadily less manageable, until we end up, as an economy measure, giving them some kind of guaranteed basic wage—while way up on top somewhere there are a group of people who are so delighted with what they are doing that they do not have time to stop working at all.

Dichotomy Must Go

If we did this, we would have completely defined the relationship between leisure, recreation, and work. But we would have built a society in which there would be vast numbers of people who had no real dignity and no real involvement. So I think one of our central problems at present is to begin to get rid of this dichotomy between work and leisure, between what you are paid to do, the way in which you get hold of a bit of the currency of the country, and your involvement in the country—between the right to experience the benefits, at a certain level of food, medical care, and education, and the possibility of using one's gifts to the limits.

We don't know how to do this at present. We have this loathsome word, subprofessional. We write articles about the fact that we really do need to increase the people in subprofessional tasks. Who in the world wants to be "sub" anything? We keep making these statements, which interfere with a new kind of society. This is not going to be easy to change. The ghosts of the Irish Famine—when people were dying in the streets of the towns and the soup kitchen was put miles out of town so everybody would walk to the soup kitchen, so that they would have performed enough work to be allowed to eat—is still haunting a very large amount of our thinking. The notion that children aren't people, young people aren't people, is pervading a great proportion of our discussion about full employment. Full employment as we are now thinking of it will involve fewer and fewer people. If we put lots of people in special categories and define them as not parts of society, we are carrying over these Puritanical types of distinctions between task and career and job, between working for a living and living, that have haunted industrial society since the beginning—certainly since the Industrial Revolution, and in some instances, even before.

We are going to need a new set of words. We are going to need a conception of what constitutes participation in society, with participation being something like citizenship. Citizenship is a magnificent word because it applies to everybody, regardless of age, sex, intelligence, beauty, or skill, and almost without regard to previous record. There are a few exceptions to this. But with those few exceptions, it applies to all of us.

What we are going to need in order to make such an effort is something that will be like citizenship. There is no word for it. The word will have to come out of the great inventiveness of the American public, a word that means participation in society sufficiently dignified so that the question of how much remunerated activity one engages in is not the relevant point. Instead the relevant point will be how the society is organized so that the work that needs to be done is done through all forms of participation—gaining weight as a baby, learning at school, participating at every level in one's community, and taking part in whatever productive services still require human beings—so that all of these things can in some way be placed on a single scale again. The scale will not deny the differences between the ambitious and the unambitious, or the talented and untalented, but will call for the participation of each individual in no less question than we now call citizenship.

DISCUSSION PERIOD

MRS. PETERSON: Thank you very much, Dr. Mead. It has been said there is nothing as painful as a new idea. If that is true, I'm afraid you have given us a lot of pain today. However, it is the kind of pain we all welcome very much. I think you have made a quite broad interpretation of the future implications of the *Manpower Report.*

There are so many questions. What is the first step you would take, Dr. Mead? You spoke about the possibility of work that is useful, that is what we like that is both work and leisure for fullness of participation. Do you have some practical steps that you want to start us off with?"

DR. MEAD: I think I would start off with education. That's the easiest way, recognizing that children are participating in society and, let's say from 14 on, they need to be underwritten like anyone else who is contributing to society—not paid to go to school, but underwritten—because they are making a contribution to their society that society has asked for.

MRS. PETERSON: You were talking about formal education in our schools. What do you feel about other kinds of education—the education we get from the mass media, the education we get from all of this second force? Are we all motivated by these other kinds of education? Are they really shaping our ideas from different directions?

DR. MEAD: I think they are very much more shaped than shaping. If you have enough discussion going on in the country, it gets into the mass media and the mass media begin using the new words. They suddenly discover a word like *"nationhood."* This is a good word. Everything that ends in "hood" is a good word. You all agree "motherhood," "brotherhood," and "nationhood" are good. The mass media pick up very rapidly. They picked up things like the population explosion and took it right around the world. They picked up the idea of school dropouts and worked on it. I think it's our business to provide the mass media with ideas.

MRS. PETERSON: It comes back frequently to schools. Are there some questions from the audience?

FROM THE FLOOR: I would like to know about the Manus people that you spoke about. First, what was the origin of their determination that change was necessary to make this 2,000 years leap in 25 years, and second, what was the procedure by which the change was accomplished?

DR. MEAD: Could you all hear the question? The question was: How can you establish a sense of direction in change? What was the origin of the Manus people's desire to change, and what was the mechanism?

I will have to really answer it at three levels here. They had a kind of education, not formal education, but a whole method of child rearing somewhat like ours. The children's notion of a good life was somewhat different from that of their parents. When they grew up they discovered what the life considered good by their parents really was. So there was a certain divine dissatisfaction in the children. We also cause this by presenting parents as models of virtue. By the time the children find out they aren't, it's too late for them not to have some belief that the things their parents claim to be are possible. From this, comes our idea of progress. These things are related. That is, there was in the Manus children expectation that life might be different from the life that the parents led. This hope was released by World War II because the young people did not go back, as they would have, to get caught in the treadmill of adult life. They sat around a little longer behind the lines, talking about what they wanted in the future. The spectacle of the American Army (we had over 2,000,000 men who went through Manus) and the glimpse they got of a different way of life—although just a glimpse and somewhat distorted idealistically—gave them the image of what they wanted. I think this means, in concrete terms, we have to give images to people of the place they want to go. Rehabilitation in Philadelphia has been an example of giving the public pictures, that is, models of what the city might look like if it did not look the way it does. This is one of the important things that brought Philadelphia forward.

Finally; the most important mechanism to be used was a very good leader, a man who came from a group of about 700 people and had a mind roughly as good as FDR's. The Manus people did it themselves. It was not done to them. All the other change that we had known about were cases where somebody tried to change somebody else, motivate them, generate motivation. I think the moral for us is that we have got to create conditions under which people can do things themselves. It's going to be harder in a slum than it is on a South Sea Island.

MRS. PETERSON: Do you feel that there is a parallel to this in our effort to have participation in the poverty program?

DR. MEAD: Well, I am not very happy about the definition of something called "the poor." I think "the poor" is in many ways as poor a category as "the leisure class." To call people poor and label them as poor and then try to find somebody who is poor to do something, has a lot of things that aren't very good about it. I would rather use as a model what we did In Civil Defense in World War II, when we simply said every block had a task, and on every block somebody had to be a leader. In miles and miles of deadly dull miserable housing in places like Detroit where everybody knew there was no leadership, we found somebody in every block. But we found them by defining a geographic area, not by defining an economic category—not the poor but the residents of particular blocks.

MRS. PETERSON: Are there more questions?

FROM THE FLOOR: I ran across recent legislation passed by the Swedish Parliament under which university students are actually paid. I was attracted, because we want engineers and so many other highly skilled workers. But is it a good idea to give 18-year-olds complete independence from their families and surroundings by, for example, giving them an income? I would like to ask this question: Is there something in a certain age group of our society or the Swedish one that makes it good to emancipate talented 18-year-olds from their families and authority and give them income for studying?

DR. MEAD: The question is based on some considerations of what is going on in Sweden, where students are paid in some circumstances, and this provides a way of manipulating the number of students who would go into particular professions which might be very convenient for national planners. I am paraphrasing at that point: Whether it is also a good idea for society to prepare to emancipate their 18-year-olds from parental control and give them some degree of autonomy. We do this, of course, to some extent in the GI bill. This was the best example that we have had in this country of a case in which young people felt that they had a right to their education. They did not get an education from their parents. They had a right to it for what they had done for their country. They were the GI students after World War II. They were the best students we have ever had in this country. They stood on their own feet. They were not dependent on their parents. They were not dependent on their wives. Our present system of emancipation of men from their families is to turn their wives into the wage earners.

MRS. PETERSON: That should bring up some questions!

FROM THE FLOOR: You might add Robin Hood to this. Robin Hood to motherhood.

DR. MEAD: After all, he was a good bandit.

FROM THE FLOOR: Seriously though, let me ask a question that is perhaps peculiarly and poignantly pertinent to this gathering, or any such gathering in Washington. The conventional category that you described tends to sustain conventional institutions and organizations, since they reap their reward for such categories. Would you care to say something, particularly in the light of your observations on changing institutions in our culture, of what we are up against and how we would like to proceed to overcome obstructions in institutional change?

DR. MEAD: This is a question about the extent to which those who are in positions of responsibility in Washington may be handicapped in innovating institutional change, and what can one say about the process of changing institutions? Of course, there is one thing in this country: you must not say what you are doing. We share this taboo with the British. The British method of changing an institution is to say that it is a reform that is at least a century overdue. That means that your great-grandfather should have done it. He would have done it if he had been the right person, and you are just carrying out the mandate from your great-grandfather who planted the walnut trees that are now bearing walnuts.

In this country we have a different device, and that is to say we face a crisis. This is the first point. You can't do anything if there isn't a crisis. Some people use this rather lightly. They use the term too often and it gets worn out, like "Wolf! Wolf!" But you have to organize your statistics to show that if you don't do something tomorrow morning, absolute disaster will arrive in 6 months, and no longer time perspective from that is going to help very much either. You have to have these unemployed on the street corners standing on each other's heads before anybody will really pay attention.

MRS. PETERSON: Deaths on the highway.

DR. MEAD: Deaths on the highway and lots of deaths on the highway. There are going to be more deaths on the highway right away. Then you sweep this country. If you can get enough people agitated about one of these dreadful emergencies, it leads to overstatement and sometimes exaggerated interpretation of figures. But at the moment I think we have enough figures to prove almost anything ought to be done. If we use them well, we can prove that the delays in the court are such that the court should be reformed and we should have administrative law, or we should have something else, or we should have compulsory insurance on cars and get them out of the courts. There are 50 institutional changes, which ought to be made, all of which can be justified by the state of the courts.

MRS. PETERSON: Is this where you get two packages?

DR. MEAD: Yes. You take the same bunch of figures and you get some figures well organized on the awful condition of practically anything. There are lots of them, and I think almost everyone in the United States would agree that they are awful. Because one of the curious things about Americans is that the people who are against something and the people who are for something agree on the basic premise. That isn't exactly what one means by consensus, but it's related.

During World War II we made a study about American attitudes toward food aid to the Allies at the end of the war. There, was a nationwide study and when we analyzed the material, we found four categories of answers. One group said, "Yes, feed them." One group said, "Don't feed them." One group said, "We ought to feed them," and the fourth group said, "Well, I suppose we ought to feed them, but." All four groups ended their statements with: "But you can't let them starve." This was the key position.

So if you can build your statement on the conditions that require change, or analyze or organize the whole cluster of attitudes that gather around it, and find the key point at which the most extreme opponents in both political parties, and the extreme right and left, in every part of the country agree, then you can use your bad conditions which you started out with (Europe was starving) and you can build a fire under the effort to create the new institution. Now, I know you would also like a few blueprints as to how this is to be done. I don't think anybody has worked out a relationship between a permanent civil servant and a politician in these cases. I, on the whole, would let the politicians have all the credit. Some credit had also better go to the other party.

FROM THE FLOOR: You have a dislike of the term "poor." Would you comment on what the peak problems of the poverty war would seem to be?

DR. MEAD: I don't mind the word "poverty." Poverty describes a condition. It does not describe individuals. I think poverty is a good word that Americans dodged for about 50 years while we talked about "low-income brackets." In World War II, you did not dare mention the word "poverty" in Washington. I had an Englishman come over here once and make a report to a big committee that had representatives from 22 Government agencies. He used the words "poor" and "poverty" and I was almost run out of town. We have underprivileged groups. We had economically underprivileged groups, professionally underprivileged groups, and we had the low-income brackets. That was a very popular term used by taxi drivers and such people. To face the fact that we had people who were poor, really straightforwardly poor, in terms of what we mean by poor; is an important thing.

There are people who are poor, but I don't like the term "the poor" because "the poor" is made up of identified individuals, men, women, and children, and to lump them together in terms of their condition denigrates their dignity. I am not objecting to the word "poverty." And I am not awfully fond of wars on anything, because I think they tend to spread sometimes, escalate in the wrong directions. I am not very fond of the war on cancer or the war on heart disease. I don't really believe we need this number of wars. Representation from the poor is a different thing from saying participation from the people who live in a particular area. They are real people who live there in houses, on streets. They are not a category. They are not lumped together and they are not denigrated.

FROM THE FLOOR: We seem to have a habit in the United States recently, of suggesting "education" as a prescription for a great many ills. Today you have mentioned this as one phase of life that at certain points might be subsidized. Education is many things, not just a television and the institution of schools. It's managed by thousands of school boards in thousands of communities. I wonder if education as we think of it as an institution in the United States is equipped to do the kind of thing you are talking about today. Would you care to comment on this? It's not one institution, it's many institutions. Some of them are perhaps not as forward looking as one might wish.

DR. MEAD: The question is, that education is far more than just schools or mass media. It's many things and it's embodied in many, many school boards and local institutions allover the country. Are these boards and institutions equipped to carry us into the future I outlined? Well, of course, some are more equipped than others. Nevertheless, in this country there is an enormous tendency to copy the rival institution or community that is just a little bit better than one is oneself. We would succeed if we made sufficient use—as we did in World War II, and haven't made a bit of use of since, really—of the fact that Town A regards Town B as its principal rival. If A's schools are better than B's, A will do nothing ever. So you go to B and tell B that A's schools are better than B's. B will fix its schools, and fix them to a point where you can tell A that B's schools are better than its schools. This works at enormous speed in this country.

It's a case of where disparity is picked up promptly and somebody forms a committee and says, "Isn't this dreadful? Look at what Cleveland is doing and Cincinnati is not doing a thing." This matters. This matters down to towns of 5,000. The model setting group for other groups means that even though we do have thousands of educational local school boards and local colleges, local universities and local technical institutions and what not, all over the country, they are all busy copying each other a mile a minute, collecting statistics on what other colleges of their category do, what other school systems of their category do. Everybody in the country is busy competing within his league. What one needs is to get some information in each league about the best member of it.

MRS. PETERSON: Are there more questions?

FROM THE FLOOR: I have been thinking about getting rid of Puritanism because I don't like the Puritans any better than you do, I guess. If we could get rid of all these vestiges of Puritanism and just have participation in society, we would not need much discipline. This discipline we have is a vestige of Puritanism and makes us all feel uncomfortable unless we feel we are doing our best to contribute and this is not very good for our psyches. We feel compulsions and all that. We have an economy that does come from the Industrial Revolution in which many jobs are very unpleasant, although maybe not as unpleasant as they used to be. People have to contribute many times when they don't feel like it. Mrs. Peterson may not want too much leisure, but she probably didn't like to get out of bed and come to work during the recent snowstorm.

DR. MEAD: I thought nobody came to work during the recent snowstorm.

FROM THE FLOOR: I think what people may be worrying about is getting rid of Puritanism before we get completely through the technological revolution, which is going to make all our jobs pleasant. I think we have to worry about removing monetary incentives too fast. Maybe we can substitute more center participation and social approbation, and so forth. I just wonder if we aren't oversimplifying the solution.

DR. MEAD: I am glad this question was asked. My questioner says she doesn't like Puritanism either. She thinks it would be fine if we were all more relaxed and got rid of these compulsions. But she wonders about a society that has grown up and has been disciplined under the imperatives of the Industrial Revolution, because so many unpleasant jobs are to be done that people have to go and do them when they don't want to. Isn't there a danger in just substituting participation or something of this sort for the discipline of the past? Is that a fair statement, would you say?

FROM THE FLOOR: I guess so. I mean I am just wondering if we are not getting a little too Utopian.

DR. MEAD: When I use the word "participation," I mean an order of membership in the whole economic social order of society. I don't mean we won't have to have sanctions. But there are a variety of sanctions that deal with unpleasant work. One of them is that if you do enough of it, then you can have a little more time to do something different. One of them is used in Australia. The nastier the work is, the better Australians are paid and the less they do of it. This is another possibility. I am not necessarily talking about removing monetary incentives. I don't think we are going to stop using money. It's a marvelous invention. The people who dislike it have never lived without it, and I have. I have lived in societies where people say, "But you see, I don't want a male nautilus shell, I want a female nautilus shell. I won't sell this to you." "Yes, you have money. But what we want is tobacco. If you don't give us tobacco, we won't give you any fish." Then you live on canned tomatoes. To have currency that commands everything that is available in the society at a properly fixed price is an incredible, wonderful invention. I don't think we are going to give it up.

We are probably not going to give up a variety of sorts of incentives. This is not a question of giving up incentives, it's a question of giving a redefinition of the different kinds of participation. Some people may like borderline participation, which means that they do just so much. If they elect borderline participation, they may also do even less by doing something very disagreeable. Their share of the tremendous productivity in the society will be proportional.

But there is also the other point you raised. The opposite of Puritanism is not necessarily anything one wants. It sometimes is just plain lust or others among the seven deadly sins. A good proportion of what is going on in this country, at present, is not eliminating the type of dichotomy that once made Puritanism. It is just the other side of the picture. What we want is not the other side of the coin, not to say everything is fun, you know. We had a program in Washington trying to say that nutrition was fun. Everybody knew it wasn't, but we were told it was. Everything is fun. School is fun. Nutrition is fun. Having a lovely engineering job somewhere, where you have a collie dog and five children and a swimming pool is fun. This is the opposite of Puritanism. It can do more harm.

You know the definition: If you get the pain after the fun, it's vice; if you have the pain before the fun, it's virtue. On the whole, under those circumstances, I prefer the virtue. It is going to be very serious if we try to build a system of incentives that says life is fun, which is just the opposite of saying life isn't fun. What we do need to build is a system of incentives where the activity itself is far more self-rewarding than it was in the past, and not simply the other side of the coin. That's the reason I am suggesting we break down the dichotomy—work-play or work-leisure or work-recreation—and break down the dichotomy completely. If we don't, we just switch from one to the other. It's either work or fun, or fun or work. And nobody is going to be very disciplined, having fun.

FROM THE FLOOR: I realize institutional religion is very split up. Yet, I wonder if you would care to comment on the role of institutional religion, both in its own need to change and the contributions it can make in the changes you desire or point to?

DR. MEAD: Institutional religion, in spite of its degree of "split-upness," and because of the degree of ecumenical understanding that is going on today, of course, is still in a position where either it can contribute enormously to the perpetuation of older and now inappropriate attitudes toward work and leisure or it can contribute to a climate of opinion which will make a different evaluation. I think the great contribution of institutional religion today is the elimination of hell, which has practically vanished in the United States. Something like 93.5 percent of Americans believe in heaven, but only a tiny fraction believe in hell.

This is a beginning contribution, but it's only a beginning, because if everybody goes to heaven, that's not very interesting either. It is the same contribution that was made when we stopped punishment in this country, but then depended on reward alone, instead of on the intrinsic quality of a relationship. Many of our forefathers were good because they were afraid they would go to hell, and a much smaller number, I think, were good because they hoped to go to heaven. I think the concrete fear of hell, in the sense that very few religious leaders would espouse it today, was a very important incentive in the past, and may become one in the future. I hope everybody is clear that we cannot predict the future. Anything may happen, including the return of hell, at any moment. But the fear of hellfire as an active incentive to hard work and to goodness is not an important element today. The element that has replaced it, I think, in modern religion of many denominations; is the intrinsic reward of a relationship to God, not designed to colonize heaven on the one hand and not designed to avoid hell on the other. So the church has taken the first step, or whether it took it or not, the step was taken in this country. When people came over here and worked all their lives, and worked hard—with the hope of reward in heaven—they came to a reward on earth for working so hard. This dealt a rather mortal blow to heaven and hell as incentives.

It seems to me another way of getting rid of the dichotomy once so very important—the backbone of all the development that underlay the Industrial Revolution, the development of Western Europe and much of the development of the world, that other countries have valued us for—but which is no longer appropriate in this period of affluence. In this period we no longer say that some must suffer that others may eat. I think the church's great contribution will be to continue to reduce this dichotomy of reward or punishment and put greater emphasis on the intrinsic reward of a religious relationship to God now in this world, that is in itself inclusive, and whole, and rewarding.

FROM THE FLOOR: This may not be an entirely fair question, but it may run to the purpose of reference. I don't know whether your idea is possible or whether it's premature, in a world, which is rapidly integrating. Aren't you talking in terms of a closed culture?

DR. MEAD: No, at least I am attempting not to talk in terms of a closed culture that can't stay closed. I think the only possible help is to talk in terms of the whole world and to keep the whole world in mind every single moment. But if we, who are testing the new limits of the new technology, fumble them and bumble them and fail to develop them right, what then happens to the rest of the world to whom we are an inevitable testing ground? Now, you may not want to be a model. You may not want to be an ideal. We would if we could very likely shirk the responsibility of taking the whole world on our shoulders. But we are the testing ground. We are the testing ground of what can be done with the new technology. A great deal of new technology can do incredible things for the developing world if we would let it.

For instance, many people recommended at the United Nations Conference on the Importance of Science and Technology for the Developing Countries a couple of years ago that we send developing countries our obsolete equipment. Instead, we should develop and send brand new 1966 simplifications, not obsolete dregs of our own past. If we did this, we could make available to the developing countries very readily many of these most advanced changes. Lots of places won't have to go through all the stages we went through and don't have to use our obsolete, broken down sewing machines. We can, instead, use our resources to keep everybody busy, to give everybody a chance to make a contribution in the society, and a share of our tremendous productivity, and use that productivity in a variety of ways for the developing countries. This is one of the visions that has been developing during the last decade.

So I am not talking about a pretty little closed society where we get so much currency a month, like a data processing card which gets checked off when we buy a lot of luxuries, and liquidated at the end of the month, in a society cut off from the rest of the world. I'm glad you asked the question, if it looked as if I were doing that.

MRS. PETERSON: In the Declaration of Human Rights, doesn't it say we have the right to work and the right to leisure? Will you comment on that?

DR. MEAD: Yes. You know, that's out of the old picture. If you can only be a full member of your society, marry and bring up children or support yourself responsibly, if you have a job, obviously, then, a job becomes a human right. Leisure was thrown in because when the drafters mentioned work they thought they had better mention leisure. Look at the constitutions of the new countries, constitutions written after the war. A lot of these human rights were put into them for the first time. That was a great advance in 1950 or 1948. This is 1966. When the Declaration of Human Rights was drawn up, nobody understood automation. They didn't even know about the population explosion at that time. These things are so new. These declarations were fine in their day, but I think they need a little revision now.

FROM THE FLOOR: In terms of some of your references to education and so on, what do you see as the probability that the American Government and the American people will give any effective recommendation to the United Nation's Declaration of Children's Rights—another of the schemas of rights which we have had in the last 10 or 15 years? These interesting formulations are somewhat Utopian, but

I still think they are necessary. Would you comment as to what extent efforts such as Project Headstart are really effective political embodiments of these higher values?

DR. MEAD: I think Project Headstart was an excellent political embodiment of many of these values. I think the American people are singularly unresponsive to the moral leadership of the United Nations. One of the things hard to make Americans do is ratify any noble sentiment the United Nations thinks up first. We treat it as the opposite of us, as it were. The United Nations is the other team. If it starts it up first, we are not so much in favor of it as we would be otherwise. But the principles embodied in the idea of rights for children are exceedingly important in this country.

But recognition of their importance has been going down since the 1920's. The position of children, the importance of children, the importance of people who study children and work with children have been steadily deteriorating. People have noticed it in this country. Universities treat nursery schools as a liability and libraries as an asset in the child development program. The amount of research has gone way down, and up to the point where the poverty bill began picking things up, children were becoming less and less a focus of our interest and effort. This was perhaps a mark of the fact that we were in a static case of dullness, because in a society like ours, it is the focus on what we can do with the children and for the children that is essential.

I was once very much puzzled by a psychiatrist from India who said to me, "Of course, you know it's all very well what you do in this country. I admire a lot of your psychology and things. The trouble is, you are always thinking about the past." I am used to Indians telling me that they have 4,000 years of civilization and we have none. So I was puzzled with this statement that we are always thinking about the past. He said, "You are always talking about children and childhood."

Now, in a revolutionary situation, childhood lies in the past. But in a developing situation, children lie in the future. Lately we have not been paying enough attention to children. The frequency of the "battered child" syndrome and of children suffering from malnutrition and the number of children who burn to death all over this country are symptoms of such strain in a portion of our population that it can no longer think about children in the future, as it was able to do 40 years ago. So Project Headstart certainly marks one move in the right direction.

MRS. PETERSON: I would like you to follow that with any comments you may have relative to the family—and this relates not only to the breakdown of certain minority group families. There is a good deal of discussion about the role of women today, the difference in the family pattern in a woman's life. I think so much relates to this. Would you comment on that area?

DR. MEAD: Of course we have had some statements recently that have read as if the breakdown of family life was specifically a minority group pattern. Actually, the breakdown of family life is one of the concomitants of very low economic status and an inability on the part of the man to earn steadily, which means an unstable family pattern in a society where we either expect the husband to support his wife or favor the support of the wife by all sorts of public institutions when the husband is absent. So today it is possible for a man to say, "You will be better off by yourself. You will be better off than if I married you." We have an incipient institutional structure in which the recognized function is to care for women and children, but the attempt has also been made to punish men who will not take responsibility.

Although a large proportion of our underprivileged population is poor, white, old American, a fairly large share of this group are Negro Americans who have come from disadvantaged areas in the South. Another section comes from the Caribbean, where different forms of marriage and family life have existed. Within these groups we have a type of life incompatible with our present notion of the responsibility of the head of the household for the wife and children. I think we could equally well say that by our insistence on early marriage we put on the families that are not in this category too much of a burden. It is not only the breakdown of family life at a slum level, or among in-migrants from the country who don't know how to live in the city, that is so serious. There is also the breakdown of family life by forcing young people out into pseudo autonomy too early, before they have had enough education, without any help from any of the institutions in the society. This causes a serious breakdown in family life. It means a high rate of divorce and large number of children who are not living with their parents. This is one of the consequences of the ways in which we are handling young peoples' sense of autonomy—to which my questioner who spoke about Sweden referred. The girls leave home today because it's the only way they can get away from their mothers. Their mothers cannot bear to have them in the same house after they reach puberty. A certain proportion of boys have the alternative of going into the Army. But we are forcing a majority of young people into marriage as the only definition of dignity and autonomy. The minute young people marry and get any kind of a job at all, they are people. But if they are regular students we still treat them as dependents who ought to have handouts. They are treated as non-autonomous and, therefore, we are continually founding families that are non-viable because they are too young.

FROM THE FLOOR: Assuming there has been an overemphasis on employment as a basis for participation in good citizenship, can you comment on the Government programs for the unemployed and give us your suggestions for giving the unemployed some dignity?

DR. MEAD: The question is, assuming too much emphasis has been placed on the importance of employment as giving dignity and citizenship, would I comment on Government programs for the unemployed? I did not say there is too much emphasis today. This is really the crux of the matter, you see. There could not be too much emphasis right now on the fact that lack of employment means lack of dignity. Yet, we still have to keep in mind that this is not going to be the point 10 years from now. How are we going to make the change?

Every time we speak of young people now, we say the first thing they need is to be trained for a job. So we have the Job Corps program and we train people who haven't had a chance to be trained, and we try to give them training for some job in which they will have some dignity, because they are paid something. These programs are fine as far as they go. But they may also mold our notion that the world consists of employed, unemployed, and unemployables, and these are three categories of human beings. They make our major job seem to be to shift the relationships between these categories. These work categories are seen as the definitions of human beings in our society. They perpetuate the idea that paid employment is the only way to get dignity, not only now, but in the future. With so much emphasis on employment, we are not laying the groundwork for the future.

FROM THE FLOOR: You commented on the stress toward training young people for jobs. In recent years, there has been some push toward training older persons for leisure. I wish you would comment on what I consider a forced choice for old persons between work and leisure.

DR. MEAD: I have talked about the program for training young people for jobs. How about training older people for leisure?

FROM THE FLOOR: I am more interested in the forced choice.

DR. MEAD: The forced choice. Well, of course, to begin with, if you are not going to let old people have anything but leisure and they don't know anything about using it, I don't suppose there is any harm in having a club to teach them. The evil is not in doing something for people who have been forced to retire and with whom you now can think of nothing else to do. The evil is in letting thinking of an economy of scarcity when jobs were limited and it was economical to keep children in school and retire people as rapidly as possible, influence us now. This shifts our attention from the recognition that in future planning the most valuable thing we are going to have in society is types of experience. In some cases, this will be highly professional, technical experience, and these technical competences may be outmoded. But the other forms of experience are not.

Donald Michael raised in this talk before the seminar group the need for wisdom and how we are going to attain it. Wisdom, as far as we know, is a concomitant of age and experience. That is really what we mean by wisdom. If we can keep older people participating in society and in active relationship to children and people, turn them into teachers instead of putting them on the shelf, and by teachers, I don't mean schoolteachers, but put them in a continuing relation of teaching something, maybe something they have just learned, to young people, we will have a viable society. But if we put more and more older people into golden ghettos, we are creating a form of what people hoped would be a tumor, but which will probably be a cancer.

FROM THE FLOOR: In the recent "Moynihan Report"[1] the point was made that among the people who belong to specific minority groups, family life is not centered or dominated or focused on the male part of parenthood. It seems that Mr. Gorer wrote a book[2] in which he said that this is characteristic of families in the American Nation, because of their immigrant origin. The male is not the head of the family, and the bent of culture direction is his wife. Is this the case, to your knowledge, of our Nation?

DR. MEAD: This question goes back to the "Moynihan Report" and its description of the characteristics of a large number of American Negro families. My questioner said he believes Mr. Gorer wrote and described the American family as not patriarchal, but rather as dominated by women. So I presume the question is: "Are these urban families that have been discussed as being so unfortunate because the father is not at home any more unfortunate than any other American family?"

You know, we have a prejudice in favor of father being home. He may not have the position that he had in an earlier patriarchal society in Europe or in this country, although these have been somewhat overrated. The division of labor in this country among immigrant groups has always meant that the man had to focus on making a living and the wife had to learn how to live here. This was a tough job for two young adults. So the mother took over the way of life, whereas, in Europe, her husband would have shared the knowledge. In America he may never get it.

It is true that the American family is a more companionate family and that there is a different division of labor from that in Europe. Still, it's completely false, I think, to call this a matriarchal Nation. Women go where their husbands want them to go and they stay where they want them to stay, and they say what they want them to say a good proportion of the time. That's not very matriarchal. The division of labor is different. This does not mean that the dispossessed lowest income groups who are the real poor in the cities are really a matriarchal society because the father plays a lesser role in these families.

It is true that in West Africa the position of women is very high. In a group like the Ashanti in Ghana, one-third of the households were headed by women and they were quite up to the responsibility. Such a group produces the kinds of women that head households.

The dispossession of the father in the United States is the result of his economic position. The extent to which the families of poor American Negroes are less stable is due partly to the earlier condition of slavery and partly to the sheer question of being poor, which they share with all the other people who are poor in our community. It's not an ethnic characteristic. American Negroes don't themselves feel they are sharing in the American pattern. You can see this most sharply the minute Negro Americans get enough education to get a decent job. They form highly conventional, monogamous, stable families with a picture window and a dog and all the other things that go with it and conform to the American ideal, in which there is the usual division of labor between husband and wife.

FROM THE FLOOR: It seems what you are discussing here may be summed up as a question of choice: what we need to do, and what we do. You said you worked with living models rather than with mathematical, logical models. Yet, in the part of the discussion in which you were talking about advanced societies, you said that in order to point us in the direction we need to go, we have all kinds of statistics that we can amass and analyze or interpret as we see fit. Well, I think I would like to know whether there is an advantage that an advanced society has over a less advanced society?

DR. MEAD: I think there is a tremendous advantage that society has at its disposal, devices for collecting information and using it at once. No society has ever had this before.

FROM THE FLOOR: We can't jump 2,000 years.

DR. MEAD: The jumps we are taking are qualitatively comparable to jumping 2,000 years. When I have been watching my Manus people who were in the Stone Age in 1928 and coming back from them to us, I think that the changes we are facing are comparable in scope and demand on us. This is the first time in history we have known where we are, while we are there. You know, people in the Old Stone Age didn't sit around and say, "It's getting tough in the Old Stone Age. I wish we lived in the New." They didn't know there was going to be a New. The Industrial Revolution was named after the fact. But when the first atom bomb went off, the Atomic Age was named within a week, and within 2 weeks there was a wagon labeled the Atomic Laundry running around.

   We are the first period in the whole of history that has ever been able to name itself in terms of technological and economic advances because we realized what was happening. This is primarily due to our capacity to collect information and think about it at the same time. People have been working on the weather ever since man thought about anything. But we could not do anything with weather prediction or weather warnings until we got computers that could work fast enough.

FROM THE FLOOR: We don't know the scale we are measuring something against. A good point is the Russian moon shot, when the British published pictures of it before the Russians did.

DR. MEAD: Mean of them.

FROM THE FLOOR: Consequently, the interpretation was way off.

DR. MEAD: If you don't know the scale, you can't interpret. That's true.

FROM THE FLOOR: I think your remarks started off in the main—

DR. MEAD: No, I wasn't starting with an attack on one method and a defense of another. I was simply saying that one method, and the method I happen to prefer to use, is a living model. This is the one I was trained to use and happen to have the experience to use. This has certain advantages over simulation.

When you are talking about scale, you are talking about a difference between a higher society and a lower society. My village is suffering from urban overcrowding. Another village moved in because my village has a better school. We have our first juvenile delinquency, water pollution, and all of the other problems of the modern world. The village expected 2,000 people for Christmas and wanted to know what resources were available to deal with the 2,000. One resource was pressure lamps. People aren't awfully willing to tell other people when their pressure lamps are working because other people borrow them. So the method of getting a quantitative evaluation of the number of pressure lamps was to say that everyone in the village had to put a mantle on, fill the lamp up with kerosene, light it, and come out and stand behind it. So 40 pressure lamps, all working, were displayed by villagers and we knew how many lights we had for Christmas.

In our present society, we don't have to have everybody get a pressure lamp out to know what our resources are. We have other devices. The scale which my village was working with was small and the method concrete. That is neither the scale nor the method we can work with. I don't think we should underestimate for a minute the fact that we have the information-gathering techniques and the methods for analyzing and interpreting our resources to an extent that no society has ever had before. It is not the difference between a complex and a primitive society. It is not yet the difference between primitive and civilized. The difference between us and people 100 years ago is so striking here. That is the scale difference, the speed of handling large bodies of quantitative material. That is the difference of scale I would emphasize.

FROM THE FLOOR: With the increased pace of automation and education, will a group of educated elite have sufficient to do to maintain its dignity?

DR. MEAD: We have this whole world with an enormously increasing population. Three-quarters of the world is still hungry. The educated elite is going to have enough to do within the next 100 years. After that, I trust it will have experience of activity, working on a planet, and by this time, going into space in decent numbers. I think it will find enough to do. I am not really worrying about work for the educated elite.

MRS. PETERSON: Should I say we need to adjourn so we can get back to leisure? Certainly many thanks to you, Dr. Mead. In parting I would remind you of what Adlai Stevenson said about change. He said that we don't know what is going to be, and anyone who thinks he can stop it had better get out of the way, because he is going to get run over.

Thank you very much.

EDITOR'S NOTE

1. For information on Mead's Manus fieldwork, please see page 5 of this volume, and Margaret Mead, *New Lives for Old: Cultural Transformation: Manus, 1928-1951*. New York: William Morrow, 1956.

NOTES

1. *The Negro family* (Washington: U.S. Department of Labor, Office of Policy Planning and Research, March 1965).
2. Geoffrey Gorer, *The American People* (New York: W. W. Norton and Company, Inc., 1948).

1968a

NEW YEAR'S—A UNIVERSAL BIRTHDAY

Editor's Commentary

In this essay Mead and Métraux seek to give to the lay public an appreciation of the wide range of definitions, categories, and meanings that various cultures use to deal with the phenomenon we call time.

* * *

Just before midnight an expectant hush falls on the party gaiety. Someone throws open a window. In the moment of waiting silence the thoughts of some turn to the past, while others, making a half-serious wish or resolution, look to the future. And some only wait impatiently. Then suddenly the spell is broken as bells ring out, whistles and sirens blow and the holidaymakers join in the din with their horns and shouts of "Happy New Year! "

New Year's is a festival of transition, the point where end meets beginning. It is a celebration of the idea of time, an idea that has captured man's imagination for millenniums. Traditional celebrations, however they varied over the centuries and in different cultures, gave formal and public expression to feelings of awe and wonder, mourning and rejoicing, repentance and hope and purpose, the sense of men's relations to one another and to the whole universe.

But New Year's today has become for most people the mere shell of a celebration, without content or focus. Everywhere there are parties: office parties, parties in homes, country-club dances, crowds in hotels and night spots, pushing and raucous crowds in the streets, moody crowds in bars—and the lonely feel doubly alone. There is incessant talking and noise and almost everywhere there is too much to drink—too often the prelude to louder noise, accidents on the road and hangover headaches on New Year's Day.

* First published in December 1968. Available in: by Margaret Mead and Rhoda Métraux, *A Way of Seeing* (New York: McCall Publishing Company, 1970).

We treat the New Year casually. In our time it has become a wholly secular holiday. Only a few tag ends remain of old beliefs. There is the modern Mummers Parade in Philadelphia, but no one now connects this with the old idea that at New Year the world is turned topsy-turvy. We attribute no magical power to our resolutions and no one treats the events of the day as omens for the year. No one waits to see who will be the first to step over the doorsill (a dark man, good luck; a fair man, bad luck; a woman, death).

Few of us remember that the decrepit Old Year, whom we picture in cartoons as a bowed and bald Father Time with his sickle, is also a figure of death; or that the baby New Year, chubby and smiling as a cupid, is also a symbol of love and light. These two figures survive, often as figures of fun, but we barely acknowledge their older meaning. And almost no one now realizes that in our own tradition the pealing of bells, not only at the New Year but also at births and weddings and on other occasions marking a transition, once was intended to drive out evil and all that might endanger what was so newly begun. Instead, our noisemaking has become a very slightly ritualized salute to the future. But noise is only one way of marking a transition.

In Bali, once every four hundred days quiet descends. On this day nothing stirs on the whole densely populated island. People speak of it as "the Silence," the Balinese New Year. On every other day the roads are crowded with hawkers, people going to and from market, small boys driving oxen or water buffalo and people hurrying lightly under heavy loads. On feast days there also are gaudy processions with their orchestras and theatrical troupes traveling to the villages where they will perform.

The air on every other day is loud with the sound of voices, the shouts of vendors, laughter at jokes, the squalling of babies carried on the hips of their child nurses, the yapping of dogs and the music of practicing orchestras. Even in the deepest night the quiet is broken by shrill cockcrowing, dogs barking and lonely peasants out in the fields playing bamboo xylophones softly to themselves. But on New Year no one moves about and every sound is hushed. Each family, its fires out and offerings arranged in the house temple, stays at home to observe the Silence.

Looking the world over, one very striking thing is the limited number of ways in which men have regarded the progress of time. Many peoples treat time as we do, as a stream that flows forever onward, never passing the same point twice. What is passed cannot come again.

Other peoples, such as the Balinese, think of time as a cyclical process, as if time were a wheel that periodically turned on itself. And some peoples have regarded man's life as part of a cycle—the individual is born and dies and eventually is born again. Very often, just at the turning point—at the end of each year or of a set of years—people have believed that this was potentially a period of great danger when the sun might never rise again or the earth might cease to be fertile or all human life might be destroyed in some great disaster. To avert the danger many peoples have ritually fasted and organized their affairs—paying their debts, ending their quarrels, cleaning their houses, rebuilding their temples and in other ways straightening out their own and the world's affairs. Then, when the new time has come, they have celebrated its arrival with other rituals, some expressing joy at danger overcome, some interpreting omens for the future and others designed to make the new time safe and fruitful.

Our own feeling that the turn of the century has a special quality carries with it something of this sense of precarious balance at the transition from an old to a new cycle. Already, at the end of the 1960's, we are engaged in predicting what life will be like for our children in the year 2000, and we are concerned with preparing the world for the millennial shift to a new thousand-year cycle. But we have no rituals to focus our activities, only a diffuse sense of concern that shapes our discussions of the year 2000, as deeper emotions once gave meaning to ceremonies of transition.

To a certain extent the heightened sense of the meaning of time at New Year is related to the invention of calendars, and peoples who have no script and no calendar for measuring regular intervals over a very long span have a more limited conception of time. For them time stretches back only as far as memory does and forward into the lives of their grandchildren, and it is only the seasons that come and come again. Very indefinitely, also, time goes back to the beginning, when they as a people came into being.

The belief may be that this beginning was only four or five generations ago, just beyond the reach of the memory of living men, as it was for some of the peoples of New Guinea. Or it may have been long, long ago, its extent unmeasured and immeasurable, as the Iatmul people of the Sepik River in New Guinea believed. And memory can be extraordinarily stretched out, as it was among Polynesian islanders who kept track of the names and adventures of important ancestors in strings of genealogies that went back sometimes to mythological beginnings.

Even so, without the idea of a calendar it is impossible to conceptualize great spans of time. In the past hundred years we have stretched out time over millions of years in reading the history of the earth. Today we also have the means of dividing time into milliseconds for fine measurements. All this has depended on complex inventions.

But for primitive peoples, day and night, the shifting patterns of the night sky, seasonal changes in winds and weather, seedtime and harvest time, the waxing and waning of the moon, the changing position of the sun and, of course, the birth, maturation and death of human beings—all these changing and recurrent aspects of the natural world have given men ways of punctuating time and marking transitions.

Some peoples have made very little even of these ways of marking time. When I was working among the Arapesh of New Guinea, I myself began to wonder what the date was. They had names for moons, such as "the moon when we get bananas from the deserted yam gardens." But as each family planted its garden with yams and bananas at a different time, they called the same moon by different terms. They said to me: "You count the moons, but we just know their names." All they really knew was some names that could be appropriately used, and no two families followed the same calendar. They even thought it was odd that anyone should expect a moon to have only one fixed name.

Other peoples had a much more definite sense of cycles. In the past the Manus of the Admiralty Islands spoke of days and nights (measuring the length of journeys, for example) and moons and then of time expressed in terms of the life span. They would place an event in terms of other significant events, saying "when my father was a child" or "when I made the last marriage payment for my daughter." But they had no way of measuring, as we do, the months that become a year and the years that become a decade or a century.

When the Manus moved into the modern world they seized upon the European calendar, learned every detail about how it works and now talk endlessly in calendar time. "Today is Sunday, the thirteenth of November, 1966," they would say to me. "It is just six weeks before Christmas." The Manus write down not only the year and day of the month but even the hour on which a baby is born or a quarrel is ended. At home or away from home they know exactly the date on which their children will be taking final examinations and they plan for the future, setting their goals as we do by dates. With one leap they have taken over the conception of time that moves onward and its modern handling.

Heirs as we are to so many traditions, we have relegated all the solemn beliefs and celebrations connected with the turning of the seasons and the year to our different religious calendars. For a time in Western Europe, this meant that people lived by different calendars and celebrated the New Year at different seasons. In 1582, when Pope Gregory XIII modified the old Julian calendar and decided that the secular New Year should come (as it had for the Romans) on January

1, Catholic countries made the change quickly; but Protestant countries continued to use Old Style dates for a long time and to celebrate the New Year as a spring festival, on March 25, as medieval Christians had. England (and so England's colonies) made the change only in 1752. Few people today think of this, though there is an echo in a New Year's song we have assimilated into Christmas carols:

> "Here we come a-wassailing
> Among the leaves so green."

The Jewish religious calendar, by contrast, has been stable for a much longer period, and the ceremonies ushered in by Rosh Hashanah, which comes at the beginning of the first month of the year (the autumn of the secular year), still carry the symbolism of beginning and ending, repentance and rejoicing, death and life, darkness and light, that is the central expression of our human sense of transition.

In spite of our heritage, we make very little of the turn of the year. All that remains is the vague feeling that it is an occasion to be remarked, the sense that it is a time when people should come together, as families do to celebrate a birthday. And perhaps, just because it is a holiday that once focused men's deep emotions about the past and the future and the continuity of time, the New Year may again become infused with meaning. A world society that must take into account the lingering traditions of all peoples may come to observe it as a day in which humanity can celebrate a common birthday in time.

1968b

ALTERNATIVES TO WAR*

Editor's Commentary

This selection is a chapter in a book edited by three of Mead's fellow anthropologists at Columbia University. In it she systematically reviews a wide range of literature from anthropology, ethology, cybernetics, general systems theory, and political science. She then makes a number of imaginative concrete suggestions for building a global future free of war. The connections between the literature review and these suggestions are not always as clear as one might wish. Yet the piece, taken as a whole, is otherwise important for its thoroughness, and shows Mead at her best in her willingness to cast off old taken-for-granted shibboleths and paradigms that she felt would not be helpful to world society in facing a different, dynamic, and dangerous future.

*   *   *

IN CONSIDERING ALTERNATIVES TO WAR, I shall consider together all forms of warfare in which defined groups engage in purposeful, organized and socially sanctioned combat involving killing each other. I will not introduce any distinctions between primitive warfare and warfare in states organized on the basis of script and other organizational devices of civilization. Nor will I, for purposes of this analysis, distinguish between warfare among sub-units of a society, such as so-called banditry, or vendetta in remote parts of modern states, guerrilla warfare within states in which revolution is being attempted, or gangland warfare between juvenile or adult gangs. Warfare exists if the conflict is organized, and socially sanctioned and the killing is not regarded as murder. The fact that imperfectly superordinate units attempt to suppress it will not be considered relevant. The figurative extension of the term warfare to forms of conflict in which the killing of persons is not sanctioned, as in tariff "wars," "battles" between labor and capital conducted without lethal physical violence to per-

* In: *War: The Anthropology of Armed Conflict and Aggression*, ed. Morton Fried, Marvin Harris and Robert Murphy (Garden City, NY: The Natural History Press, 1968), 215-228.

sons, psychological "warfare," etc., may be treated as one set of "alternatives to war." In these cases the hostility, desire to dominate or destroy which characterizes warfare, may be present but lethal violence directed against members of the other side is not sanctioned by both parties to the conflict. Also political activities in which those in power hunt down, and if necessary kill the individual "traitor" or "outlaw" will not be considered to be warfare if the traitor or outlaw does not belong to an organized group which regards his activities as having legitimacy within the sub-system which he represents. The criteria used will therefore be: organization for the purpose of a combat involving the intention to kill and the willingness to die, social sanction for this behavior, which distinguishes it from murder of members of its own group, and the agreement between the groups involved on the legitimacy of the fighting with intent to kill. Socially sanctioned revenge to the point of inflicting physical injury, or death itself, by one member of a group towards another, as in the case of Eskimo individual murders, cases of men who shoot their wives' lovers and are acquitted under "the unwritten law," fighting which inflicts small injuries but in which killing is interdicted—Iatmul fighting with sticks but not with spears within the language groups and between friendly villages, (Mead, n.d.[1]) clashes between fraternal groups, freshmen and sophomores, representing town and gown—will also be excluded.

Warfare will be regarded as a cultural invention consequent upon group identification, the existence of shared taboos against intra-group killing—comparable to and to some degree related to cultural taboos on incest (Mead 1968; Durkheim 1963)—and the equally culturally defined social sanctioning of killing members of the opposing group. If a people have, as part of their cultural repertoire of behavior, a set of articulated rules, which distinguish intra-group killing from organized extra-group killing, they will be said to have the institution of warfare, whether it occurs frequently or infrequently in practice. Further distinctions may be made between peoples who put a positive or negative value on warfare, as for example when membership in a military caste confers high distinction, or participation in organized killing is a necessary validation of manhood—as in headhunting societies, etc. The development of societies in which resort to warfare is regarded as legitimate only in the face of invasion, while it may be seen as one of the conditions that may lead to the suspension of warfare for long periods in a particular region of the world, will be regarded as part of a warfare system, however infrequently invoked.

In terms of these definitions, the Eskimo (Boas 1888; Thalbitzer 1914, 1923) did not have the institution of warfare; peoples like the Arapesh did have the institution although they avoided invoking it regularly and treated killing, either within or without the group, as ceremonially dangerous (Mead, 1963a).

The Andamanese had warfare (Radcliffe-Brown 1964), New Guinea headhunting societies, like the Iatmul (Bateson 1958), the Mundugumor (Mead 1963a) and the Orokaiva (Williams 1930) were actively warlike societies with rewards for the sanctioned killing of enemies. In such headhunting societies killing of a single member of the other group, by lucky accident, and not on a battlefield, can be counted simply as part of a *permanent* state of warfare. The existence of other relationships between groups, such as intermarriage and trade will not be considered grounds for distinguishing between headhunting, vendetta, ceremonial revenge, and other forms of warfare, but different kinds of hostile relationships between identified groups, which may constitute more or less self-perpetuating warfare. From this point of view, the Manus, who had no built-in institutions that required killing a member of another group, and no adequate sanctions against intra-group conflict between localized clans or intra-village entrepreneurial clusters, were characterized at different periods in their history by periods of purposeful rapine and attempts to drive out or exterminate other groups (Schwartz, n.d.[2]). The Dani (Matthiessen 1962; Gardner 1964; Mead 1964a), on the other hand, would have to be described as a people for whom warfare was so institutionalized that it was self-perpetuating. Many such warfare forms lack such objectives of destruction of property and crops, conquest, extinction, dispersal, or incorporation which have made warfare a device for the spacing out of populations, and for the establishment of larger units within which other forms of domination, paying tribute, slavery, and modified allegiance or actual incorporation as full citizens have been successor conditions.

I also assume that warfare, as defined here, and the distinctions between intra-group and inter-group killing itself are social inventions without a specific biological basis. I assume that we must take into account man's capacity to use symbolic means to define who is and who is not a member of his own group, and that in man—in contradistinction to members of other mammalian species—there are no built-in, culturally independent devices for ritualizing intra-group fighting. Instead, the capacity to symbolize makes it possible for men to socially define other men either as comparable to con-specifics, and so inappropriate objects for killing (although often appropriate objects for physical combat especially between rivalrous males) or as, effectively, non-conspecifics, and either prey, predator, or rival.

The ethological literature on aggression and territoriality seems to me to lack clear discussion of the conditions within which other creatures, non-conspecifics, are neither prey nor predator, but coincidental rivals for the same prey, or the same hunting, nesting, territory or even highway. The occasionally reported "battles" between troops of apes or monkeys, and the controversy between those who claim that there are yearly "battles" between eagles and storks, during the joint migrations over Turkey *(Times,* 1967) would be cases in point. Territoriality which reduces conflict among con-specifics, would, under conditions of temporary or periodic crowding, result in something that looks very like the least organized form of human group conflict and that might be theoretically regarded as the precursor of warfare. There is still a strong case to be made against identifying the social institution of taboos on murder, with any built-in instinctual equipment for the recognition of con-specifics or any built-in aggressive tendency to kill other human beings, or members of other human groups who carry physical indicators or social indicators of belonging to another human group. I would simply argue, as Gorer does (1966a), that man lacks instinctual controls, and not, as Lorenz and Ardrey do, that warfare is an extension of built-in aggression towards rivals for mates, territory or food (Lorenz 1966; Ardrey 1966; Gorer 1967). But I would add to Gorer's argument the factor of symbolization in man, and argue that the identification of an enemy suitable for warfare, is socially analogous to the non-human biologically based identification of prey or predator, in which other human beings are seen as non-human. I would further argue that those forms of warfare that are sometimes identified as play—tournaments, conflicts between individual "champions" of rivalrous groups, American Plains Indians' warfare with death low on the list of counting coup (Benedict 1959), can be seen as analogies to those con-specific rivalries that do not have as their aim, but may have as their by-product, the death of one or the other of the two involved in ritual aggression, and which under conditions of crowding (Mead 1963b), may lead to murder (Calhoun 1948).

The resolution of this argument, which is still being pursued with inadequate knowledge of culture by the ethologists, very preliminary experimentation by the experimental ethologists, and the invocation of selected ethological examples by anthropologists, is essential if alternatives to war are to be scientifically considered. If the claim of built-in biological aggression as made by Lorenz (1966), and adumbrated journalistically by Ardrey (1966), and as assumed in many psychoanalytic discussions (Masserman 1963 passim), were to be substantiated, then the social measures necessary for the prevention of warfare might include ways of modifying the gene pool or radical changes in diet, which might, as Lorenz believes, have serious consequences for the exercise of other valuable human characteristics. In the present state of the evidence there remains the possibility that certain types of aggression may be "built-in" to some individuals—which would leave open the possibility of differential distribution of relevant genes in different populations, especially in very small populations. There is also the accompanying possibility that such behavior can therefore be "read-in" to or programmed culturally into many other human constitutional types, as well as the possibility that there may be constitutional types endowed with built-in controls against lethal aggression where not only con-specifics but also living prey or predators are concerned. It may be that the production of a social environment in which there were no living creatures used as food or pets or work assistants might be sufficient to extinguish the human capacity to kill living things, or, alternatively, might make it socially impossible to modulate and teach the difference between permitted and impermissible killing either of other living things or of other human beings (Mead 1964b).

If we regard warfare as a cultural artifact (a sociofact in Bidney's terminology), which can be used by any human group, but is not specifically biologically underwritten, it may then be described as a social invention, in the same way that the wheel is a social invention, with the probability that it was invented many times by early man in the course of the development of language, tools and social organization (Mead 1940, 1965a). Here one further historical peculiarity must be mentioned: the distinction between the sexes in the use of tools and weapons. Tools are extensions of the manual abilities of both sexes, although they may be restricted in some special forms to one sex or the other. Weapons, designed for hunting, defense, and combat, have been almost completely restricted to males. With a very few brief exceptions, social sanction has never been given to the habitual use of weapons by women, and women have been left to fight, when they fought, with only their natural equipment of fingernails and teeth, or temporarily adapted tools, the rolling pin, distaff, digging stick, etc. This circumstance has not been sufficiently integrated into the ethological discussion. It is notable that all consideration of females disappears when Lorenz (1966) reaches his discussion of human aggression, and that one of the most insightful treatises on the possibilities of innate aggression, *Lord of the Flies* (Golding 1959) creates an artificial society of boys in which females are lacking. It is important to take into consideration the possibility that the biological bases of aggression in the two sexes—in human beings as in other mammals—may differ significantly. The female characteristically fights only for food or in defense of her young, and then fights to kill, and may be without the built-in checks on con-specific murder that are either socially or biologically present in males. Arming women, as has been done in this century in Israel, the USSR, Indonesia and Vietnam, may be a suicidal course.

If war is an invention, we can then examine the functions that it has served in the past. In any discussion of alternatives to war, as in any discussion of sequences of inventions, it is necessary to investigate whether the functions fulfilled by warfare in the past are functions necessary in modern society, and if so what other inventions can fulfill them better. Recognizing the extent of cultural lag in many cases, we may, I think, insist that a functioning invention will be used at least until rendered obsolete by another invention or set of inventions, by the disappearance of the function it performed, or by becoming itself dysfunctional. It may therefore be argued that unless a better invention is found, a previous invention will continue to be used as long as it does fulfill some social function. We must also reckon with the continuation of earlier inventions even under conditions of long obsolescence, as when human labor is invoked in the absence of machines, or during warfare and revolution when people return to earlier technologies. (This was the case in the use of candlenuts for light and a return to bark cloth making in the South Seas during World War II, after both had been abandoned.) It is unlikely at present that the possibility of warfare—as an invention—could disappear from human knowledge.

Therefore, this knowledge has to be reckoned with as one of the conditions in any discussion of the hopes for a warless world. Correspondingly, the knowledge of methods of nuclear warfare has to be regarded as a component of modern culture in the foreseeable future, however much we may succeed in banning nuclear tests or eliminating stockpiles of bombs.

A further question thus becomes: given warfare as a known functional response to a variety of identifiable conditions, what are the necessary conditions under which this invention will *not* be used? Warfare may be used to repel attack, add territory or subjects to one's own territory, establish autonomy or freedom from subordination, provide targets outside the country when the maintenance of power is threatened from within, provide sources of food or minerals, and even, in some cases, provide a market for munition makers or an excuse for the maintenance of a wartime, heated-up economy which serves a group in power. Such a discussion leads to a consideration of what are essentially other forms of warfare: economic and psychological warfare, and the destruction of weapons, buildings or crops rather than persons, without attempting to alter forms of social organization of large groups so that hostile conflict is no longer functional.

One condition which might leave the existing types of hostilities otherwise uncorrected, is the recognition, by all relevant groups, that scientific warfare would result in the complete elimination of the own group as well, and consequently of the values which its members have been educated to defend. We have in some respects approached this condition today, as far as some of the leadership of the industrialized blocs is concerned. Most of the world's citizens, however, are still willing to go to war under nuclear threat, including the citizens of those states whose leaders are best informed about the consequences of nuclear warfare, suggests that the task of convincing people that it is useless to die for something which will no longer be embodied in other human beings, is still very difficult. This can be attributed to the same capacity to symbolize, that has made warfare possible by defining other human beings as non-human, and so preserving side by side the socially cultivated sentiments of cooperation, protection of group members, and the ruthless extermination of members of other groups. The last ten years have demonstrated that the threat of nuclear warfare, and the accompanying relative immobilization of the great powers, vis-à-vis each other, does not, as the world is currently organized, prevent the proliferation of other forms of warfare, or the decrease of violence which may turn to civil war, within national states. It is therefore necessary to distinguish between the recognition that warfare, on a world scale, is not only no longer functional, as it has often been in the past, but actually endangers the entire population of the planet and the recognition of the importance of the development of values that may in time contribute to a climate of opinion that will make it easier to discard war as a political tool. However, these recognitions need not prevent the active propagation of an understanding of the consequences of scientific warfare as part of the preparation of world opinion for the outlawing of war as obsolescent and destructive to *all* participants alike. We may also argue that the failure of the efforts to use the invention of nuclear warfare as a sufficient condition for the establishment of international order after World War II, was due to the absence of other necessary inventions, and alternatives to the political-economic arrangements in this interconnected world.

It is these other arrangements with which the remainder of this paper is concerned. Warfare depends upon the establishment of unequivocal and mutually exclusive identities and loyalties, today represented by national boundaries. As long as there exists a permanent definition of the own group, within which to kill is murder, and others, whom it may be or is virtuous to risk one's life to kill, warfare or the threat of warfare with its accompaniments of uncontrolled violence among smaller nations, or sub-national groups, can be easily invoked.

Various modifications of our present conceptions of the nation state are possible. The present definition predicates the state upon its absolute right and continuing ability to make war on other states. This definition, supported by properly developed sanctions and accepted definitions, could be changed to an emphasis on nationhood, in which the identity and power of each state was a function of the identity and power of all other nations. This is the case where federations succeed in binding internal warfare and strengthening the security, well-being and identity of each group as a function of its membership in the larger group. It is frequently argued that federations have been dependent upon external enemies and therefore are impractical forms to use as models for a single world order. But internal order has been attained by societies without the need of invoking external enemies, once the social forms made it possible to identify all members as equally human and exempt from treatment as non-human. Slaves have been freed, children released from the brutal domination of parents and teachers, women given rights, and minorities given full citizenship, as the social identifications have been altered, in belief and in practice. The definition of nations as owing their status to the existence and prosperity of other nations, their security to the security of other nations, and emphasis upon interdependence rather than independence, could result in concepts of nationhood replacing concepts of nationalism (Deutsch 1963). Such changes in our present world organization would require altering the present appeal of nation-states. We would have to find ways to perform those organizational and identity-bestowing functions now met by nation-states. Substituting multilateral responsibilities for bilateral agreements is one way in which this change can be promoted. A second structural device is the development of multinationality, but it seems unlikely that this would be adequate without further changes in international structures. As long as nation-states are the building blocks of international structures, regional organization, and non-localized power blocks must represent the weakness inherent in their component parts. Any component in an over-arching structure designed to eliminate war must, by definition, not be defined in a way that permits warfare and the definition of members of another group as non-human and suitable for killing. International organizations built of nation-states, in whatever combination, retain this liability of return to warfare. The simple federation model is, for this reason, not a feasible alternative.

Furthermore, if the model of a single hierarchical state is used to represent a possible future world community, we then have to reckon, not with the traditional view of warfare in which the enemy are defined as non-human, but with the cultural acceptance of the less ancient, but equally well-supported social belief in the rights of local, geographically based groups vis-à-vis superordinate groups governing larger territories. This belief, which those who think that territoriality is important trace to animal societies, is, however, also subject to man's capacity to symbolize. The intrinsic right to self-determination and autonomy of a localized group can easily be extended to non-localized groups that consider themselves human—as opposed to the less human or the non-human other. Religious groups have this capacity, and most of them have exercised it; divisions along lines of racial identity, language, custom and political ideologies have also proved as potent rallying points as geographical continuity. It is true that since the invention of the autonomous nation-state such groups have had to capture the state mechanism in order to actually make efficient and socially sanctioned war, so that the cultural appeal of mutually exclusive geographical and ideological identities reinforce each other. But at present, scrutiny of history suggests that the elimination of one without the other will not be sufficient. The current demand for a theology of revolution (World Conference on Church and Society, 1967) is only another form of the old demand for a theology of the divine right of kings and the legitimacy of wars between nation-states in which the priesthoods of the same religion could each pray for victory. Any form of world state within which the components can rearrange their loyalties so that members of other identifiable groups can be defined as legitimate prey cannot be regarded as a social invention that can actually prevent war. Ideas of revolution and holy wars would continue to threaten its stability, just as geographical loyalties would continue to threaten the federation model.

Our organizational task may then be defined as reducing the strength of all mutually exclusive loyalties, whether of nation, race, class, religion or ideology, and constructing some quite different form of organization in which the memory of these loyalties and the organizational residues of these former exclusive loyalties cannot threaten the total structure. The difficulty of arriving at such a conception only attests to the dangerous hold of past models on our imaginations. Even our most imaginative science fiction writers continue to deal either in the fantasies of other planets, against whom the inhabitants of Earth can unite; or superordinate and unbearable forms of world organization against which human beings must finally rebel; or totally superordinate angelic beings—in twentieth-century flying saucers—who because they are super-human, can keep order among us. One of the principal contributions of anthropology should be to distill from our available treasure house of small and unusual social

models—many of them outside the single narrow and steadily con-
verging mainstream of "civilization"—new combinations and new
forms that will release us from our historically limited imaginations
(Mead and Metraux 1965).

The proposals which I am going to make stem from a series of
anthropological contributions to the subject of alternatives to war, in
the specification of necessary conditions and the prefiguration of new
forms (Benedict 1948; Malinowski 1948; Mead 1948). Ruth Benedict
(1948) insisted upon the importance of institutional arrangements
rather than human motives as the essential and modifiable elements in
the consideration of warfare. Gregory Bateson brought warfare within
the formulations of cybernetics, self-perpetuating systems and positive feedback runaways (Bateson 1946), by combining Richardson's
neglected theory of an armaments race (Richardson 1939, 1960), with
the emerging cross-disciplinary language of cybernetics (Von Foerster
1950-1956; Bateson 1947). Geoffrey Gorer (1966b) has concentrated
on the importance of developing smaller, and cross-cutting forms of
group identification, and the relationships between ethology and discussions of warfare. Finally, Alvin Wolfe (1963) drew upon his anthropological training in identifying an emerging form of acephalous
control, against which rebellion or revolt is structurally impossible.

As a prelude to more specific suggestions, which utilize all of
these, I should like to discuss Alvin Wolfe's model in some detail. In
his original paper, called "From Cape to Katanga," he identified a new
form of control over minerals in Africa. This involved overlapping
membership of Boards, each with different geographical centers of
influence, with memberships reaching from Brussels to San Francisco,
and with international agreements (including Moscow) on the subject of the controlled production of industrial diamonds. These
Boards actually had superseded the power of either the former colonial powers or the national governments of emerging African states.
Wolfe showed how this acephalous organization was one which
could neither be joined nor resigned from, based as it was on overlapping membership in which no one membership could be seen as
primarily related to the whole (Wolfe 1962).[3]

A practical version of the acephalous model within which the
components are not sufficiently identified to make warfare or revolution possible, is provided by the U.S. and Canada Eastern electric
power grid. Had this model fulfilled its requirements, it would have
provided an acephalous self-regulatory mechanism of very high
functional ability.[4]

Our new models for world organization can be asked to meet the
following negative requirements: (1) absence of forms of organization

providing any mutually exclusive self-identifications; (2) absence of self-perpetuating, accelerating systems involving positive feedback runaways; (3) absence of the kind of hierarchical, linear, or branching structures, in which the component units can be seen as of the same sort—and so rivalrous—or as presenting organizational lines of fission.

As positive requirements, new models should:

1. Provide order as well as prevent major wars.
2. Provide for the distribution of the essentials and goods of life among *all* the peoples of the planet, in such a way that their common and shared species membership is not violated and so accompanied by denial.
3. Distribute centers of power over organizational functions that will necessarily be worldwide, such as control of food, banking, communication, policing, travel and migration, and protection of the natural environment, so that no two centers coincide geographically. The structures that express these functions should be as structurally dissimilar as possible, in such dimensions as size, internal relationship between organizational levels, number of constituent regions, in order to reduce possibilities of symmetrical conflict among them. None of these structures should command other than professional loyalties.
4. Establish the conditions for self-identification with a small geographically located group, within which all the component individuals can be personally known to each other, to underwrite each growing child's need for identity and security. These needs have been well spelled out (Erikson 1959,1964; Soddy 1961).
5. Establish the conditions for a variety of mutually over-lapping and non-exclusive identifications with larger groups of many kinds, without any single or overriding loyalty.

Finally, there are conditions of order without which it would be impracticable to discuss such new worldwide arrangements, the non-fulfillment of which might seriously prolong the present state of worldwide anarchy, small wars and disorder. It will be necessary:

1. To formalize ways of preventing nuclear war (Kurtz and Kurtz 1967).
2. To establish adequate technological and political means to halt the rapid pollution and deterioration of the biosphere.

3. To establish the technology and the ethics to halt the present rate of population increase and to restore it to a balance with food supplies and human resources of maturity and skill.

4. To increase food production without intensification of the present consequences in the destruction of the biosphere.

5. To establish a world-wide secondary spoken language that will equalize the positions of speakers of all languages large and small (Mead 1965b)—this means the adoption of a politically negligible natural language as a secondary spoken language—and some form of glyphic and written communication which will be independent of lexicographic considerations, like Chinese, but more formal, simpler, and easier to learn and to execute.

6. To find ways in which young males, in an increasingly urbanized environment, can validate their courage and physical competence (Mead 1959) as substitutes for the validations once provided by exacting natural environments and war, in order to prevent the consequences in urban violence that we see allover the urban world today (Mead 1963c).

7. To develop a means of controlling large masses of people which will be effective but non-lethal.

Into all such plans, we should build methods of assaying the unanticipated by-products of taking first steps in any given direction (Bateson 1958). Although general systems theory—as the sophisticated successor of cybernetics—has provided us with both a cross-disciplinary and cross-ideological medium of communication, it has not been self-conscious enough in allowing for changes when it itself is applied. Our knowledge of biological behavior of all sorts, and particularly of human behavior, is so imperfect that long term planning without allowance for multiple feedback often does more harm than good.

NOTES

1. Mead, Margaret, unpublished fieldwork under National Science Founda-
    tion Grant No. GS-642, to the American Museum of Natural History, enti-
    tled "The Cultural Structure of Perceptual Communication, 1965-69."
2. Schwartz, Theodore, unpublished fieldwork in the Admiralty Islands
    under National Institute of Health Grant No. MH-O7675-05, 1963-67.
3. In further discussion of this important paper, it is useful to make two
    points. The control broke down as the Belgian Miners Union Miniere
    attempted to excise the old forms of nationally based exclusive power,
    and the disorders in the Congo have been a continuing sequelae. Wolfe's
    paper, in a revised form was turned down by several social science jour-
    nals, an indication of how ideologically culture-bound the social sciences
    are becoming.
4. Analysis of the 1965 breakdown only serves to underline the importance
    of the model. It broke down because of a mixture of automatic and
    human functions (including mutually contradictory considerations of
    load and cost) and inadequate automatic checks, and the consequences
    of the break down were aggravated by the extra lack of imagination—
    prevalent in many fields in the United States—by which a separate source
    of power to restart the generators had not been provided.

REFERENCES

Ardrey, R. 1966. *The Territorial Imperative*. New York: Atheneum.
Bateson, G. 1946. "The Pattern of an Armaments Race," *Bull. Atomic
    Sci.* 2:10-11; 26-28.
_____. 1947. "Atoms, Nations and Culture," *International House
    Quarterly*, Spring: 47-51.
_____. 1958. *Naven, Second Edition*. Stanford: Stanford University
    Press. (Originally published 1936.)
Benedict, R. 1948. "Appraisals of the Conference," in *The World
    Community*. ed. Quincy Wright. Chicago: University of Chicago
    Press, pp. 303-315.
_____. 1959. "The Natural History of War," in *An Anthropologist at
    Work*, M. Mead. Boston: Houghton Mifflin, pp. 369-382.
Boas, F. 1888. "The Central Eskimo," *Bur. Amer. Ethnol.* Sixth Ann.
    Rept. 1884-1885, pp. 399-669.

Calhoun, J. B. 1948. "Mortality and Movement of Brown Rats (*Rattus norvegicus*) in Artificially Supersaturated Populations," *J. Wildlife Management* 12:167-172.

Deutsch, K. W. 1963. *Nationalism and Social Communication, Second Edition*. Cambridge: Massachusetts Institute of Technology.

Durkheim, E. 1963. *Incest: The Nature and Origin of the Taboo*. Edward Sagarin (trans.), New York: Lyle Stuart. (Originally published in 1897.)

Erikson, E. H. 1959. *Identity and the Lifecycle*. New York: International Universities Press.

_____. 1964. *Childhood and Society, Revised and Enlarged Edition*. New York: Norton.

Foerster, H. von, ed. 1950-1956. *Cybernetics*, (5 volumes). New York: Josiah Macy, Jr., Foundation.

Gardner, R. 1964. "Dead Birds." Cambridge: Peabody Museum, Harvard University. Distributed: New York, Contemporary Films, 16 mm.; 83 min.; sound.; color.

Golding, W. 1959. *Lord of the Flies*. New York: Putnam. (Originally published 1955.)

Gorer, G. 1966a. "Man Has No Killer Instinct," *The New York Times Magazine*, Nov 27:47ff.

_____. 1966b. "Cultural Community and Cultural Diversity," in *The Danger of Equality and other Essays*. Geoffrey Gorer. London: Cressett, pp. 48-62.

_____. 1967. "Ardrey on Human Nature," *Encounter* 28:66-71.

Kurtz, H. and Harriet Kurtz. 1967. "Global Compassionate Power," *Renewal*. June 3-17.

Lorenz, K. 1966. *On Agression*. New York: Harcourt, Brace and World.

Malinowski, B. 1948. "An Anthropological Analysis of War," in *Magic, Science and Religion, and other essays*.

B. Malinowski. Glencoe: The Free Press. (Originally published 1926.)

Masserman, J. H., ed. 1963. *Violence and War: with Clinical Studies*, Vol. VI of *Science and Psychoanalysis*. New York: Grune and Stratton.

Matthiessen, P. 1962. *Under the Mountain Wall*. New York: Viking.

Mead, M. 1940. "Warfare is only an Invention–not a Biological Necessity," *Asia* 40:402-405.

_____. 1948. "World Culture," in *The World Community*. ed. Quincy Wright. Chicago: University of Chicago Press, pp. 47-56, discussion pp. 57-94.

_____. 1959. "Cultural Contexts of Puberty and Adolescense," *Bull. Phila. Assoc. Pysch.* 9:59-79.

_____. 1963a. *Sex and Temperament in Three Primitive Societies.* New York: Morrow. (Originally published 1935.)

_____. 1963b. "Violence in the Perspective of Culture History," in *Violence and War*, ed. J. H. Masserman. New York: Grune and Stratton, pp 92-106.

_____. 1963c. "The Psychology of Warless Man," in *A Warless World.* ed. Arthur Larson. New York: McGraw-Hill, pp. 131-142.

_____. 1964a. "A Savage Paradigm," *Film Comment* 2:14-15. (Review of "Dead Birds," a film made by Robert Gardner.)

_____. 1964b. "Cultural Factors in the Cause and Prevention of Pathological Homicide," *Bull. Menninger Clinic* 28:11-22.

_____. 1965a. *And Keep Your Powder Dry.* New York: Morrow. (Originally published 1942.)

_____. 1965b. "The Future as the Basis for Establishing a Shared Culture," *Daedalus*, Winter:135-155.

_____. 1968. "Incest," in *International Encyclopedia of the Social Sciences.* New York: Macmillan.

Mead, M. and Rhoda Metraux. 1965. "The Anthropology of Human Conflict," in *The Nature of Human Conflict.* ed. Elton B. McNeil. Englewood Cliffs, New Jersey: Prentice-Hall, pp. 116-138.

Radcliffe-Brown, A. R. 1964. *The Andaman Islanders.* New York: Free Press. (Originally published 1922.)

Richardson, L. F. 1939. "Generalized Foreign Politics," *British J. Psych. Mono. Supp.* No. 23.

_____. 1960. *Arms and Insecurity.* ed. Nicolas Rashevsky and Ernesto Trucco. Chicago: Quadrangle Books.

Soddy, K. ed. 1961. "Cross-Cultural Studies in Mental Health," *Identity, Mental Health, and Value Systems.* New York: Humanities Press.

Thalbitzer, W, ed. 1914. "The Ammassalik Eskimo, Part I," *Meddelelser om Grønland* 39:1-755. Copenhagen.

_____, ed. 1923. "The Ammassalik Eskimo, Part II," *Meddelelser om Grønland* 40: 113-564. Copenhagen.

Wolfe, A. W. 1962. "The Team Rules Mining in Southern Africa," *Toward Freedom* 11.

_____. 1963. "The African Mineral Industry: Evolution of a Supranatural Level of Integration," *Social Problems* 11:153-164.

World Conference on Church and Society. 1967. *Christians in the Technical Revolutions of our Time.* Geneva: July 12-26, World Council of Churches. *Times* (London). 1967. "Do Eagles Fight Storks?" August 10:6.

Williams, F. E. 1930. *Orokaiva Society.* London: Oxford University Press.

1968c

THE CRUCIAL ROLE OF THE SMALL CITY IN MEETING THE URBAN CRISIS*

Editor's Commentary

This symposium presentation reflects Mead's intense awareness of the world's population explosion, of the mass migration to the cities, and hence, of the need for intelligent urban planning. Although her work in Anticipatory Anthropology does not generally employ the scenario—a primary method used in Futures Studies today—she does here provide three contrasting urban vignettes that have some aspects of a true scenario.[1] Each such quasi-scenario illustrates the importance of the relatively small city, and explores its advantages over mega-cities for accommodating the housing and social needs of an expanding world population. This accommodation is achievable through united community action aimed at capitalizing on each community's unique or special geographical, historical, and cultural advantages.

In this lecture, Mead anticipates by many years a number of major themes that have since become commonplace among leading urban planners and citizen activists, such as sustainability, restoration, livability, and sense of place.

* * *

The world faces a crisis in building shelter for its burgeoning billions and in designing towns and cities within which they can live safe, healthy, and rewarding lives. We will have to build, within the next twenty-five years, as many more units of shelter as there are now in existence. And most of the housing in the world is obsolete, unsafe, unsanitary, deteriorated, uneconomic, and unlovely. Only the most vigorous international and national efforts will make it possible for us to act with sufficient wisdom, to take advantage of all that we already know, and to set up research that will ensure our learning more in time to meet the needs. We will be building millions of houses, redesigning old cities and building new ones. We will be laying down enormous

*   In: *Man in the City of the Future: A Symposium of Urban Philosophers*, ed. Richard Eells and Clarence Walton (Arkville Press Book, London: Macmillan Company, 1968), 29-57.

stretches of road, laying out new airports, setting up new factories, building schools and colleges to hold the millions who will be streaming into them. That we will build is certain, but how we will build, whether we will take advantage of this crisis to build wisely and well, is not at all certain. The crisis is only newly recognized in all its depth. It gives us an opportunity that will not come again in this century. Only with concerted efforts at every level, involving industry, government, science, and citizenry, can we hope to accomplish what is necessary.

To meet the great needs we will have to use every device to transform ancient cities with camel tracks or carriage roads too narrow for automobiles, to rehabilitate cities that have recently decayed at the center as the result of the flight of the middle class from the cities and the flight of the rural poor into the cities. We will have to promote the growth of well-located small towns, combine cities which have been independent, build authorities which can combine local government units and work within large areas that cross municipal, state, and national boundaries. We will have to redesign our great conurbations, which stretch out through miles of anonymity and disorganization, into focused, well-organized, responsible, large communities with well-designed neighborhoods where children may be reared and old people live in safety among familiar things. We will have to design and build many kinds of new cities.

In this paper I wish to concentrate on just one of our options— the strengthening of the existing small cities of the world so that they can make their contribution to the solution of the problems presented by urbanization. The existing small cities provide us with one of our most valuable bases for new development. They occupy choice sites, at natural crossroads and junctions, on rivers, on good harbors, at places where mountains are passable. They were chosen long ago by natural selection for small settlements, some of which grew and flourished while others withered and died. They have sources of water; they have centers. Those who have lived there have chosen appropriate paths and out of the paths roads have grown. Many of the hazards of the completely new city, where planners lack both a living knowledge of the local peculiarities of wind and sun; rain and tempest, and any certainty as to what kind of people will live there, can be avoided in the old cities. A core population is already there; the weight of the snowfall on the house roofs has been tested and known. When the small city grows, it can grow along lines which have already been tested and tried; new buildings can be placed where the old buildings were or placed elsewhere because the old site has been demonstrated to be unsuitable for the motor age. And as in the physical plant, so in the social; there will already exist old established institutions, clubs and associations, schools and banks and insurance companies, lawyers and doctors. In a completely new city all these have to be imported and built from scratch.

There are, of course, disadvantages in old small cities also. Characteristically, the most ambitious people tend to leave small cities for larger cities. Those who remain are often ultraconservative and cautious. The leaders are likely to have stayed because they have inherited wealth and position too tempting to leave; such leaders are not enthusiastic about change. In their wish to maintain control over local conditions they are likely to oppose efforts to bring in more central or national planning and refuse to recognize the need for larger political units to deal with water, air pollution, river and ocean traffic, air traffic, conservation. Newcomers characteristically come from smaller towns and villages with less experience in small city life. Those few who come to small cities from larger cities are likely to be impatient with the slower pace and more old-fashioned ways, and in turn their impatience will be exploited and resented. If the small city is to be redeveloped to play a role in a rapidly expanding and intercommunicating world, these disadvantages must be faced and means must be found to overcome them. It is because of the advantages, because we cannot afford to neglect a single resource, and because it is in small existing cities that service clubs can play the most decisive role, that I have chosen to emphasize the development of existing small cities here.

There are a variety of ways in which the possible contributions, the drawbacks, and the advantages of small cities could be discussed. I shall be speaking in American terms because these are the only ones that I know well and because this meeting is being held in San Juan, which has been influenced by American experience in city planning. But I am also speaking with full recognition that the problems of other countries will be quite different, and sometimes almost diametrically opposite.

As one way of thinking about what can be done with the small city, I want to discuss a model for a new city with a special purpose—that of attracting high-level research institutions. If small cities are to develop new styles and new attractions for high-level institutions and energetic outside leaders, one of the ways of doing so is to develop new emphases, new kinds of industries to replace dying industries, new and distinctive attractions.

BUILDERS OF TOMORROW

In a recent paper delivered to a symposium on "Research and the Community,"[1] I attempted to elaborate a model of an ideal community, which would be built up specifically to accommodate a series of research institutions. Such a model can be used as a way of evaluating real communities.

The segregation of those with special interests is an old tradition in the United States in the form of communities of the religiously dedicated, communities of artists, communities in which the political Utopians have experimented. But the community of scientists and technicians specifically concerned with such problems as the development of atomic energy, the instrumental bases of automation, the space sciences, is new—only as old as Oak Ridge, Tennessee. These communities have been heavily influenced by the dictates of security and by the demands imposed by location, on the one hand, and by the desirability of such light, clean, high-level type of industry, on the other. "New electronic industries" has become almost a synonym for "desirable industrial expansion," with the undertone of worry over the dangers of atomic power, fall-out from the location of plants or bases upwind from urban centers. Association with defense has also created associations with military installations and the special types of isolation and integration peculiar to the military. The problems of public relations for the formation of these new communities are therefore very complex, and the shape such communities take will affect not only the images of the scientist, the engineer, the machine, and the future of human beings, which are held by the surrounding communities, but also those who live in the new technological communities will reflect these views and come to think of themselves in many of the same ways. The image of the scientist and the engineer drawn by school children whose parents are semiliterate conforms in many respects to the image of the scientist presented in the house organs of great engineering firms, or in the advertising pages of *Science* and *The Scientific American*. The feeling that scientific progress may endanger mankind, involve one in treason, destroy precious human relationships, produce unemployment and regimentation—these are all involved in the way in which groups of scientists and engineers and technicians live and relate to other groups in the community.

The special communities of the past—artistic and intellectual, religious or politically utopian—were related to the local ecology; artists and intellectuals have sought communities that were rural or devoted to special pursuits like fishing and have maintained a relationship with the natives, which was both close and explicitly different. Utopian communities have almost always included "dignified" manual labor, involving the care of plants and animals. The new technical communities have no such immediate relationships with either the people or the natural life of a region where they work. The location is determined by the availability of power, airports, the presence of other industries and other installations of the same sort. The scientists and engineers are themselves a highly selected group who have developed their special interests in high school, often under counter pressures from family and schoolmates, who welcome isolation from other kinds of people and the relaxation of association with those who speak the same language and have the same detachment from other human beings. The demands they themselves will make on a community and the demands, which, in their name and in the name of the state, the nation, and the world, the planners should make for them, are often contrasting.

We may expect that the technical group will want good, modern housing, availability of the services which they consider essential, such as accessible airports, shopping centers, good schools, and some sort of recreation for their families. The presence of others who are technically trained will be regarded as an advantage. Space to move around in, freedom from irksome interruptions due to faulty physical planning or tiresome social pressures, ability to get away when they want to—these they will recognize.

As designers, however, there are other needs which they will not recognize as readily but which are urgent if we are to prevent the further fragmentation of knowledge and the development of a technical elite totally out of touch with the humanities, with politics, with the ongoing life of the world. Because of their high intelligence and technical competence, the other steps, which must be taken on their behalf, must be very high level. Music is the art most likely to appeal to them, and locating a music center or an orchestra in such a community is one way of assuring both a fuller life for the technical group and a diversified human community for themselves and their children. Top technical groups usually contain a few foreigners, and this circumstance can be expanded into specific welcome to intellectual activities related to such institutions as national cultural centers, Casa Italiana, international institutes. The technical community should be keyed into circuits of artistic and intellectual resources. There should be a theater to which theatrical companies can come, a documentary film theater, an art gallery for small circulating art collections, a first-class library able to tap both public and private libraries in the state, circulating collections of original paintings, records, tapes of all sorts. In the center of the community there should be services that can tap the whole artistic and intellectual life of the nation efficiently and quickly and without requiring too much "do-it-yourself" of men who work long hours in laboratories.

The scientists and technicians associated with activities of this sort also need an outdoor life provided for them; if the natural world—whether lake, or stream, or forest—is at their door, they will make something of it, if not for themselves then for their children. Community facilities, if the residential areas are diversified, such as swimming pools, shared by adjacent residents, provide for the kind of implicit democracy in the scientific world. The sports they enjoy most are associated with individual skills, and areas in which their children can develop as swimmers, pole vaulters, runners, and so on, are essential, as is provision for tennis, handball, and the like.

All need for activities that involve bringing in groups of lower-status labor, lower-status employees, maintenance men, and so on, should be avoided in favor of designing high-level services and, if necessary, training programs for immigrants. This will involve the residence in the community of highly intelligent but unskilled and possibly illiterate service people, whose children can benefit from the schools and provide some balance to the possible overintellectualization that will be encouraged in the homes of the technical community.

Among scientists and technicians we find a range from those whose primary scientific work is fed by vigorous and enthusiastic activity in many other fields—artistic, athletic, creative—to those who wish to pursue their special interests with absolute single-minded dedication and who regard all other types of activity—mowing the lawn, serving on a committee, going to a concert, or taking the children swimming—as an interruption. There will also be a certain number of married women who are also scientists and technicians and who will parallel this second group of men in their wish to be relieved from the more mundane chores. For the men who wish to work uninterruptedly, and the women who must carry the double or triple responsibilities of a career, wifehood, and motherhood, there is a great need for adequate community services which will relieve a certain section of the homes from domestic drudgery—nursery schools, an organized source of high-level domestic help, gardening and grounds care, inexpensive food services, a repair service that is always accessible.

It is also a mistake to assume that because such communities consist of well-paid and highly trained individuals, there is no need for community social services, such as a mental health clinic, a small, well-equipped community hospital, and generalized social work services to deal with the emergencies, which will arise. A community is not a real community until people have been born there, married there, and buried there. Provision for birth, marriage, illness, and death—*within the community*—is essential.

These communities must be open to the world to prevent the isolation, fragmentation, and specialization that will otherwise result. This means easy transportation, especially by air, as the ties of such men are wide and the spread of their special interests includes the whole country. But it should not only be easy to get away, it should also be easy for others to come there, and occasions for their coming should be planned. This requires the provision of comfortable and moderately expensive motels and guesthouses, where all sorts of guests—temporary consultants, interns, foreign visitors, and so on—can be put up. A conference center with the accommodations for at least one hundred visitors is also recommended; this will bring groups to the community and favor the involvement of the technical community in nationwide activities.

There are other ways in which the diversification of the community at a high level can be attained: the location of colleges, special departments of universities, special research institutes that complement the principal technical interests represented. Recent developments in areas of California, where new electronic industries, special research institutes, and new branches of the University of California are combined, provide a good model here.

Further diversification can be attained if provision can be made for weekend and vacation facilities for various types of specialists in the arts and sciences who will be attracted by the caliber of the services and the opportunities to associate with a lively intellectual community. The biological laboratory at Woods Hole, Massachusetts, has represented such an attraction. Lawyers, high-level civil servants, journalists, physicians, residents in nearby urban centers, would welcome such a spot. These facilities should be of varying economic levels, suitable for graduate students finishing their theses, and families with many children and a couple of pets who arrive in a battered station wagon, as well as more established and wealthier people.

Communications within the community are vitally important so that everyone will know of the arrival of interesting visitors, the visits of people in the community to other communities, lectures, film showings, special school activities like the National Science Talent Search and Science Fairs, special broadcasts and telecasts. Freedom to move from institution to institution for special lectures or demonstrations is one of the ways in which such a community is welded together. The special technical community can become a lively, self-activated center for radiating intellectual and scientific interest by means of a small daily bulletin, local radio stations, and possibly closed television circuits with provision for diffusion throughout the community and to school auditoriums and places of assembly in other nearby centers.

Every imaginative effort put into planning such communities, and especially assuring the allocation of enough space for all of these activities, will benefit the wider interests of the state by raising the level of education, increasing the supply of future scientists, and assuring the type of community that is valuable for the ongoing economic life of the state.

In recent considerations of the way in which cultural evolution takes place and the possibility of man's taking a more active part in directing the course of his own intellectual evolution, it has been found useful to look for the occurrence of clusters of individuals who stimulate and complement each other's intellectual life. The surest way of developing such groups is to have clusters of institutions that will attract research-minded individuals of many different kinds and give them an environment that provides for their informal and voluntary interaction.

I have discussed here a specific model for one kind of development. Comparable models could be developed for small cities with different emphases—heavy industry centers, trade centers, educational centers, sports centers, and so on. Each type of city would have its special requirements for accessibility, design, and types of necessary diversification. One would be more appropriate than another, as a point of emphasis for small cities in different parts of a country, at different distances from the center of the country, from the capital city or metropolis and from other smaller or larger cities.

TYPES OF SUCCESSFUL AND UNSUCCESSFUL SMALL CITIES[2]

We may next look at contrasting types of cities, "good" cities and "bad" cities, which have developed within the same national economic and political framework. By concentrating on successful and unsuccessful histories within the same national potential, it is possible to highlight some of the factors which have made some small cities good and others bad, and use this analysis to direct the future growth and development of existing small cities.

First, let me consider a hypothetical small city in the middle-western part of the United States, one with a population of over 150,000. What will be said about it is based on conditions generally found in small cities in the United States but is not a description of any particular one. I will call this composite portrait Center City. It has been adding new, light industries for some time. Its local Lions Club has visitors dropping in frequently who bring news of what clubs in other cities are doing and what speakers they have had at their meetings. These guests keep the members of the business and professional community on their toes. It has two newspapers, a morning and an evening paper, expressing different political views. Although they use a great deal of syndicated material that is distributed nationally, each newspaper carries its own editorials, and each has an editor personally known to the townspeople, who can complain directly to him if they do not like his paper's policy. Local issues are aired in the newspapers, and it is very difficult for some activity not in the public interest to go on for very long without an exposure.

Children of all races go to school together; there have been Negro teachers in the schools for twenty-five years; the basketball teams, of which the city has two first-class ones, have players drawn from different races. The salaries of the teachers are high, the standard of the high schools good, and every year high school graduates go away to college. They go not only to the state university and to the many nearby small private colleges supported by different religious organizations, but they also pass national college entrance examinations (and win scholarships for which there is national competition) to famous colleges and universities outside of the state.

The people of the city have seen to it that there is a big gymnasium for basketball games, school dances, science exhibits, educational exhibits, and teachers' institutes. Other meeting places—small halls in primary schools and junior high schools, and parish houses connected with the different churches—are plentiful enough so that there is room for all kinds of organizations to meet. There are three good hotels, which serve the luncheon clubs, Lions, Kiwanis, Rotary, the Chamber of Commerce, the Business and Professional Women's Club, and several smaller luncheon clubs.

Most of the industries are unionized; strikes hit the town only when they are part of a nation-wide strike, and there has never been a labor riot. In fact, there has never been a riot of any kind.

The center of the city is something the people are proud of. There is a wide-open square with a fountain where children play in summer, a memorial to the men who died in the First World War. Around the square are the courthouse, one of the large old churches, a concert hall and theater. The city has its own orchestra and little theater repertory group, and it sponsors a series of concerts given by singers and musicians who are nationally and internationally known. A new shopping center has replaced some of the older stores on one side of the square, but without wrecking the design of the older buildings. Traffic and parking are not too difficult. The city was one of the first to put in traffic lights; the Parent-Teacher Association has organized a corps of women volunteers to stand at the street corners where small children cross to go to school; the city put in parking meters as soon as these were for sale, and so never built up a set of bad parking habits. When the police say that they will pick up and haul away cars parked illegally, this is not just a threat: The cars are picked up and hauled away. Campaigns conducted jointly by the city police and a local chapter of the National Public Safety Association have cured pedestrians of crossing streets between crosswalks, and the City Improvement Society—it used to be called the Village Improvement Society—has put large waste-paper baskets for trash at every street corner, and these are used.

The library is almost a hundred years old, and a society called the Friends of the Public Library keeps up the appropriation for it from local taxes by appearing at City Hall for budget hearings. This group raises a considerable fund, each year, to buy new books, to pay for an extra librarian to work with the children, and to stock the steadily growing supply of tapes and recordings. A new library building, the fourth since the library was founded, is now being planned.

This city always goes over the top in every kind of fund-raising campaign. In the annual Community Chest drive the whole city is divided into sections—residential units and business units—and every citizen is included. An enormous number of local people are on the rolls of a national association for the prevention of tuberculosis and receive, each year, a packet of Christmas seals, for which each person pays a dollar. These seals are both for fund raising and to remind the public of the importance of the work of the association, and all the mail for several weeks before Christmas is decorated with them. There is a small Community Chest, a coordinating committee representing most of the local social agencies. Donations made to the Chest are distributed among the member agencies, so that people do not have to give to each one separately.

The local public agencies, which administer aid to families and dependent children, care for the needy old and blind, and provide health services to the community, have good relations with their state and federal counterparts. The representatives of these state and national agencies—professional, specially trained social workers, educators, public health workers—enjoy coming to this thriving little city and talking with the people in the local offices and giving talks to the service clubs and other organizations interested in the programs for human betterment they are there to foster. These include such concerns as mental health, parent education, air pollution, the education of handicapped and culturally disadvantaged children, more jobs for the unemployed, and the war on poverty. Center City responds warmly to the specialists who come into the community to discuss these concerns.

The schools have been alert to all the new possibilities in special educational programs. There are special classes for mentally retarded children, special teachers for house-bound children—youngsters who are recovering from operations and injuries or are suffering from chronic diseases—and special programs for the blind and hard of hearing. Deaf children are identified early and sent for their education to a nearby residential institution. There is a good foster home program, with more foster parents ready to take children from the public and private children's agencies than there are children to be placed. Unmarried mothers are given sympathetic care and their babies are sent to another city for adoption. There is a good juvenile court, the names of juvenile offenders are never published in the newspapers, and most children brought into juvenile court are placed on probation.

The local branch of the American Association of University Women has established and financed a mental health clinic for emotionally disturbed children. In this association, the high school teachers play a leading role. Most of them have been in Center City for many years and taught generations of Center City children. The city has three private schools, one coeducational, one for boys, and one for girls, all of which began under religious auspices and are now nonsectarian, and a junior community college, which will soon become a four-year college. Its faculty takes an active part in community affairs. There is a small art museum, liberally supported by some of the older families in the community, and an organized society of supporters who work for it, arranging, for instance, for Saturday classes in painting and for public lectures.

People who live in Center City agree that this is a good city to live in. Many young people born and educated there do not want to move away and, in order to stay, will take local jobs at lower salaries than they could earn elsewhere. Young executives who are placed there in branch offices of large corporations often refuse to take the next step up in their organizations if this means leaving Center City. High school teachers qualified for college teaching stay on here as high school teachers rather than go away to university positions.

People are so proud of what their city has done and is doing that it is very hard for them to see that more needs to be done—which is, in fact, a great deal. Interest in international affairs has never been very intense. There is a United Nations Association, but it does very little except plan school programs for United Nations Day. There is a Center City Mental Health Association, which provides a way for interested professional people, like social workers and community-minded doctors, to meet with interested lay people, but no one in this local group seems very much concerned about the State Mental Health Association, and none of them are members of the World Federation for Mental Health.

The recent agitations for civil rights for Negroes have practically by-passed this small city. It is true that it is still hard for middle-class Negroes here to get the same kind of credit conditions that are available for white people or to buy homes in new middle-class housing developments, but relationships between the small Negro professional group, the Negro community as a whole, and the rest of the town have always been so good that it is very difficult to get people to bestir themselves about the problems that are not yet solved. Years ago, there was some excitement over having Negro teachers in the public schools; two were employed and the excitement subsided. There have not been any more Negro teachers added, not because there is the slightest objection to having them, but because they are hard to recruit and those who might be out looking for them are making no effort. The racial imbalance in the teaching corps is evident; school officials have become so *tolerant* that they see no reason for making it an issue.

There is a very small Jewish community, and the rabbi is invited once a year to give the invocation at a meeting of each important community organization. After the inauguration of President Kennedy, when prayers were offered by Roman Catholic, Jewish, Protestant, and Eastern Orthodox clergy, several Center Citizens asked if there was an Eastern Orthodox church in town and found that there was not. A few Spanish-speaking Puerto Ricans have moved in lately, and a community group got together some money to send a teacher to Puerto Rico to learn something about the Puerto Rican children's background.

Only in time of war or some other great national crisis does a "good" community like this wake up and try to become a better community, to compare itself not only with all the neighboring cities, where it already excels, but with national averages for different kinds of achievement. And it will only be thoroughly awakened from its accustomed round of excellent activities if national pressure, exerted through radio, television, and the press is very strong.

In the early 1960's, the national concern about children who drop out of school before graduation pierced the complacency of Center City. The Parent-Teacher Associations, the American Association of University Women, three service clubs—Kiwanis, Lions, and Rotary—the local chapter of the Association for Childhood Education

International, and of the National Education Association, the Mental Health Society, the Society for the Support of the Arts, the City Improvement Society, and representatives of the coordinating council of the Community Chest, all worked on the dropout problem with the city superintendent of schools and his staff of principals.

This meant getting all the national literature: finding out what their own state was doing and, for each organization, what its national office was doing; getting a list of good speakers who could deal with different aspects of the problem; finding out what programs were already going on; deciding whether to try some plan that had been tried or make an innovation.

Someone recalled an innovation made during World War II, when the brighter, older children in the high schools had been organized to help relieve the teacher shortage by tutoring younger children who were falling behind in their studies. It was a plan that had been dropped after the war because teachers, poorly paid and overworked, had developed an overprofessional attitude toward teaching and did not want volunteers to interfere with their attempts to raise standards and salaries. Now that it was clear that an important new national program would require a great deal of volunteer help to get started, the groups working on the dropout problem decided to use students again. When New York City in 1967 inaugurated a plan to pay older pupils to teach younger children who were falling behind, this resulted in national publicity and reinforced the local effort.

Center City, then, has the virtues of the best small American cities. People are proud to live there. They boast that every child gets a chance to go to some sort of summer camp, that their high school graduates have the best records in the state.

But the enthusiasm of its citizens is not the only reason for the prosperity of this city. It is just the right distance from two very large cities in a part of a state where industry has flourished. The plants located here are in expanding industries. The first labor union to enter the town was a particularly enlightened one. None of the local industries were deeply involved in army contracts, so cutbacks and expansions in armaments have not affected them badly. Nor have they yet felt the impact of automation; several of the major industries were partly automated earlier.

The owners of the two newspapers are independently wealthy and, so far, have not had to sell out to syndicates. There have been three competent school superintendents in a row. There is a good, small airport because several of the sons of prominent families like to fly and their demands for an airport were supported by townspeople who thought the city ought to have one. There is an excellent supply

of fresh water; the streets are well laid out, with residential areas
nicely dispersed. Industry is electrified, and the air is not yet polluted,
as it is in so many other places, by the fumes from cars and factories.
And, finally, the city has never had to deal with an influx of people
from terribly disadvantaged areas, people badly schooled, in poor
health, bearing the marks of generations of neglect.

For some of these things, Center City residents can take credit
because, in spite of all these advantages, the town could be in bad
shape if it had not had lively leadership, ready contributions of time
and money, esprit de corps, the loyalty of its hard-working citizens.
But these same citizens tend to take responsibility for everything
good, and to blame everything that goes wrong on "circumstances
beyond our control."

There are unmarried mothers here, juvenile delinquents, frauds
and robberies, corrupt politicians, small but unmistakable slums,
deprived children, broken homes, sex crimes, miserable old people,
high school dropouts, mothers who receive no prenatal care, dis-
criminations against minorities, children whose expectations are
dimmed and futures ruined because they feel that they come from a
background which never has been and never will be accepted.

But when the people of our lively, intelligent, favored little city
have to face these things, they disclaim all responsibility for them.
Failures in school? The parents have probably moved too often. Dis-
crimination? Not among us; it must be those new people. Vandal-
ism? That comes from the glorification of violence and crime on
television and in the movies. *Our* people don't behave like that. Why,
even when we do lock our doors, everybody knows where the keys
are kept.

It is not likely that Center City will produce many ardent reformers, even from among its most disadvantaged and rebellious citizens.
Advantaged or disadvantaged, young people growing up here feel
that it is a good place to live, that if they fail as individuals, this must
be their own fault since theirs is such a good city. It is a city which
may not even produce many young people who want to join the
Peace Corps or Vista; the very complete and adequate social services
of their own town have not awakened in them any sharp awareness
of other people's needs. The Center City post office sends out a flood
of parcels at Christmas time for persons all over the world, but many
of those who mail them gladly criticize the federal government
harshly for "giving away things," meaning by that its programs of
social welfare and foreign aid. A good many people who want every
dollar of state and federal money they can get for local activities they
are interested in, will greet the slightest suggestion from their state

capital or from Washington with suspicion, crying "the federal government is trying to take over the country."

So it is important to recognize that an American community that runs the way an American community is supposed to run can do it almost too successfully—so successfully that its citizens become too complacent. Though it is a city that keeps many of its promising people, it is not a city to which successful people from larger cities would like to move. There is something too provincial about its complacency. This complacency can be challenged if the community is compared unfavorably with some other city of roughly the same size. The accomplishments of great cities have little meaning for Center City, and the achievements of smaller cities stir no interest there. As long as other places of the same size are not doing better, Center City will rest on its laurels, unless something tremendous shakes it out of its self-satisfaction. In such communities, striving has become maintenance, and aspiration has turned into justifiable but self-defeating pride.

But there are other cities of the same size in the United States that present an almost exactly opposite picture. Let us take another composite example and call it Border City. Border City lies not inside a prosperous state but on the border between two states, one much more prosperous than the other. Part of the city is in one state, part in the other. Any attempt to unify services, which need state or national help runs immediately into problems of jurisdiction. Every time someone moves from one part of the city to the other, he goes into another world. He must get a new license for his car, pay a different state income tax, comply with a different set of marriage laws, meet different requirements for various kinds of insurance.

Education on any public issue is difficult in Border City, again because there are two states involved. Whereas in Center City, state, county, and city work so closely together that most citizens do not know where one begins and the other ends, here there is constant dispute over which authority has the right to do what. A sick man may be driven to a hospital, only to find that he cannot be cared for at this institution because he lives on the other side of the state line. If there is a question of public relief or compensation in his case, and the hospital does take him in as an emergency, it may take months of paper work to decide who pays for him. When responsible citizens in the upper, more prosperous part of the city try to clean up conditions they feel are producing a bad environment for their young people, they are continually foiled by the other side, where there is open gambling, much teen-age drinking, open sale of drugs, and a corrupt police force that interferes with their attempts to enforce the law.

Migrant workers, homeless and destitute, pour into the lower city first, then cross over easily and become part of a faceless welfare load on the other side.

Border City started as a mill town, but the owners of the mills soon moved away to a nearby large city. Hired managers, who were often unfriendly to the town, took their places. One industry after another has come in to take advantage of the cheap labor available here, using first immigrants then rural migrants who have followed their friends and relatives into town.

As there were no professional people here, originally, the city has no core of old professional families; no sons or nephews come back to take over the medical practices of fathers or uncles; no young men to go into family law firms. The professional people who do come here do not usually come by choice and do not stay if there is anywhere else for them to go. The schools, long a political football, have a superintendent who seems utterly uninterested in standards of any kind.

A long series of strikes left the union leaders and small business and professional men at loggerheads, with no body of stable, responsible old inhabitants to mediate the differences. Housing is run down, and the few housing developments built during World War II are dilapidated and occupied by families on relief rolls. In most American cities, the local political organization is built with the votes of individual citizens. In Border City, the politicians work for blocks of votes, to be delivered through the leaders of the four principal ethnic groups: a southern European group, an old United Kingdom group, an eastern European group, and a sizable group of Negroes, recent immigrants from the South. There is no attempt to conceal political patronage.

There is an old public library, started years ago by a small, eager college club composed of half a dozen schoolteachers and two ministers' wives. This little group managed to take their plea for a library for Border City all the way to Andrew Carnegie, who built or helped to build so many libraries in American communities. But there is not enough money, now, to give good library service. The librarians are poorly paid; the city council is not interested in appropriating funds. Because of a shortage of staff, the children's room can only be open part of the time.

Instead of the full complement of organizations, which kept Center City humming, there are very few in Border City: some lodges, a dispirited Rotary Club, a few groups connected with churches. The church leadership is weak; assignment to a pastoral charge here is considered a hardship, not a challenge. Most of the schoolteachers come from homes where there were no books; to them, education is a new, almost frightening experience. There is no bookstore in town, no museum, no large hall where lectures could be heard, no lecture series bringing distinguished, nationally known speakers, no little theater group, no concerts. The two newspapers are both owned and operated by a national newspaper syndicate; one is probably going out of business soon because there is not enough advertising to keep it going. There is no institution of higher learning of any kind, no modern industrial plant to bring a corps of lively young engineers, not even a normal school that might become a teachers' college.

The center of the city is grubby and run down, but it does not face the kind of deterioration that larger, fairer cities do because it never had either style or beauty, and there were no old families there to move away and leave houses that became rat-infested slums. The city is not growing and unemployment is rising as industries adopt new labor-saving devices. Large numbers of young people drop out of school to look for work as soon as the law permits them to do so. The fact that the age of compulsory education is two years higher in one part of the city than in the other, because the two parts are in different states, adds to the tension.

The established churches are poorly attended and find it hard to get committees responsible enough to handle their affairs. There are many so-called "store-front churches"—store buildings used by small sects for services because they are too poor to have their own houses of worship or to pay for full-time pastors.

The schools are miserable. The children clique together, perpetuating religious and ethnic hostilities. Those who do finish high school with some ambition for more education will go on to the nearest—the poorer—state teachers' college. Very few will even try for the state university. In the Border City schools there are no teachers to nurture their ambitions, no young people's organizations to stir up their hopes. Returned missionaries, who travel from community to community telling congregations about their educational work with children in other countries, pass Border City by. It is notorious for meager contributions, for never meeting its quota in national drives for causes like the Red Cross.

Here, there is very little hope that sparks will fly or that some young and vivid reformer will raise his head. There is every reason to believe that each of these cities has as many innately intelligent children as the other. But in one of these cities every community agency and institution works for the children, protecting their health as infants, seeing to it that they have good preschool care, giving them stimulating grade school experiences, providing wholesome opportunities for their leisure. In the other city, medical care is poor; there are no nursery schools, kindergartens, or Head Start classes. Aid to dependent children is given without supervision; the primary schools are crowded, poorly equipped, and the children are badly taught; in the high schools, the chief interest is the band.

Both are American cities. Both have access to the same state and federal matching funds for improving, expanding, and introducing all sorts of programs; both have, theoretically, the same access to such other sources of funds and consultation services as national foundations and state and national offices of voluntary organizations. In one place historical conditions combined positively to produce a city in which the sense of community has flourished. In the other, historical conditions have had an opposite outcome. The same national agencies, the same state agencies, the same foundations, the same national organizations, and the same human potentialities were there for each to draw upon. The children have read the same history books in school, and memorized the same sentiments. The same national television shows have been reflected on screens in both cities. But in one, the community was able to take advantage of all this; in the other it was not.

Center City and Border City are not to be found on any American road map, or in any railway guide, because they do not actually exist. They are composite pictures representing the extremes of American community life. Because each community in the United States is free, within reasonable limits, to become the kind of hamlet, village, town, or city that its people want it to be, community life in any one of them can be raised to a very high standard or sink to a very low one.

At present, neither Center City nor Border City seems likely to generate leadership for change: one is too complacent, the other too miserable. The impact of a powerful national program might help to start community action in either place. Cities like Center City do sometimes come out of their comfortable shells, and things sometimes do get going in places like Border City. A small city may receive a bequest, which gives it a college, for example, or a museum, or enables it to employ a magnificent superintendent of schools or a forward-looking city manager. A new kind of industrial plant may come in and its management, used to cities with some life in them, goes to work. But Center City has a long, long start in the kind of institutions that lead to responsible change. It is right here that the state and national program can have an impact. Spurred by knowledge of what is going on in the state, the nation, or the world, they can take the lead in starting a college or a museum, or in bringing in a new kind of city management and a new kind of urban planning.

PLANNED NEW SMALL CITIES

The possibilities inherent in old small cities may be contrasted with the planned new small cities, which are now on the drawing boards or partly completed. Behind the plans for these new readymade communities lies more or less the same assumption: if the physical environment is right, life for the people in it will be good. Such cities, the promoters say, offer a new opportunity to meet the challenge of growth. They stress the economic advantage to the community, the county, and the state through the planned use of space and the careful integration of the new town into the economic structure of the region.

In such designs, there are a number of small towns or villages within the city, with different types of residential neighborhoods in each one. Each will have its own schools, parks, churches, shops, and other appropriate businesses and services. The industries will be, for the most part, very tidy ones—research and development laboratories, offices, and plants for light manufacturing. Each part of the city will be linked to every other part by small buses, traveling on roads especially built for them. The idea is to make the development so completely self-sustaining and so well arranged that everything a family needs will be within walking distance of its home or on a local bus line. It is expected that many people will give up cars altogether, or use them only for trips out of the community. Actually, the local buses will connect with the regular intercity, interstate buses on the superhighways that pass by the town. In fifteen years, one such city, planned for families with an average income of about $9,000 a year, could provide homes for about 29,000 families, approximately 110,000 people. Other new cities are planned to have homes at different prices for families in a wide range of income brackets.

DYNAMIC CITY-INDUSTRY PARTNERSHIP

To Americans who believe that the best communities are created and continually reconstructed by the people who live in them, these new, planned communities are somewhat disconcerting. It is encouraging to turn, at this point, to look at a town that enjoys a remarkably rich and delightful community life because it has a dynamic, working partnership with a thriving industry.

This town is Corning, New York. It sits on the banks of the Chemung River, in one of the prettiest parts of the state. Settled in 1789, it now has a population of about 17,000. Electrical and railroad supplies, tools, saws, and furnaces are manufactured here, but the chief source of pride is the world-famous Corning Glass Works. This is the firm that in 1934 made the 200-inch lens for the telescope of Mount Palomar Observatory in California and produces, among other things, the exquisite and costly Steuben glass.

This company is a small-town family business founded in 1851. It moved to Corning in 1868 and has grown to giant size. It now has, together with its subsidiaries, 45 factories in 15 states. An article about the Glass Works in *Fortune Magazine* for August 1964 describes it as "the company that never left town." Its present chairman and chief executive officer, Amory Houghton, Jr., a young man now only 42 years of age, is the fifth generation of his family to run the factory, having come up through the company with experience in nearly every branch of the organization.

The Glass Works and the town are in real partnership and are equally appreciative of each other. Whatever is done in the community, they do together. From the beginning, it has been company policy to encourage local independence and citizen initiative by giving in such a way that the gifts help the town do its own growing.

Some of the results of this joint venture are widely recognized. There is a good school system, as progressive as any in New York State, which has some of the best teachers in the country. There is a non-profit hospital and a library that serves as a library center for 100,000 people in that part of the state. There are excellent recreation facilities: choral and square dance groups, a glider site, swimming pools, a ski run, and an ice-skating rink, picnic areas and a toboggan slide. All of these are set up for families to use and enjoy.

Contributions from the glass company are more or less concentrated in two areas: community improvement and education. The most spectacular thing it has created cuts across both areas of its interest, and is a service to the whole country, not just the town of Corning. This the Corning Glass Center, a modern Crystal Palace, which commemorated the one hundredth anniversary of the firm and, by coincidence, the centennial of the original Crystal Palace in London, England.

The building includes a large auditorium for community and company use; a lobby where the first casting of the 200-inch lens has been placed upright against the wall facing the entrance, a wall covered with soft draperies of the blue of the midnight sky; one of the most complete glass museums in the world; a Hall of Science and Industry, where the nature and use of glass are shown with the aid of lectures and modern visual aids: exhibits, demonstrations, dioramas, films, recordings, and slides; the Steuben factory, where the visitor can actually see fine hand-blown crystal being formed and engraved; two auditoriums seating, respectively, 100 and 1,100 people. This is not only a center for the display of one of man's great discoveries, the process of glassmaking, it is also a center for the people who work with this material.

The Corning Glass Center is a source of wonder and delight to the three-quarter million people who visit it each year and these visitors have helped the town in many ways. The local stores have greatly increased their businesses since the Center was opened, and the hotels, restaurants, and motels—many of them new—have brought in large amounts of additional revenue. The company has benefited, too, because everything done to make Corning and the neighboring villages attractive to employees and their families makes it easier for the firm to find and keep the kinds of people who meet their very high employment standards.

Contributions made by the company in the field of education are carefully considered for their "seeding" value. High-level national conferences are held in the Glass Center from time to time, meetings which have an influence on national policies in many fields of science and the humanities. These, too, become the concern of the entire community. When the first one was held, to celebrate the opening of the museum, everybody in town worked to get it ready on time, and when the guests came from abroad, a role in the plans for their reception was found for every group in town, including the local fire company, which took over the task of shining all the foreign visitors' shoes.

Opportunities for the in-service training of teachers in the schools are varied and good. A community college was established in 1956 as a unit of the State University of New York. This has had a measurable effect on Corning and the adjacent communities. Since it opened, the library circulation has doubled, book sales in the town have increased, a cooperative nurses' training program has been developed in the Corning hospital, and the college has also set up industrial courses to train for local business and industry.

Seven small colleges in the area are being helped to strengthen their programs through a cooperative venture known as the College Center of the Finger Lakes, the headquarters of which are at Houghton House in Corning. The possibility of establishing a national headquarters here for cooperation in education is being considered. Contributions made by employees of the Glass Works to educational institutions are matched by the company. In 1967, these employee gifts amounted to $66,000.

Grants are made to enable teachers to study in the summer time, not only in Corning but in other company plant towns. About one hundred teachers are chosen from all communities where the company has plants, and the maximum grant is $600. An annual College Day is held in Corning for students, parents, and guidance counselors, to acquaint people with what different American colleges and universities have to offer. Grants are made to the Corning School District for educational television programs in the schools, and small capital awards are frequently made to projects that will become self-supporting, such as a program for gifted students, the Corning Philharmonic Society, and an exhibit arranged by the National Sculpture Society. In 1951, the Corning Glass Works established the Corning Glass Works Foundation to plan and coordinate its wide spectrum of activities in cooperation with the people of Corning and other communities with which it works. In 1964, the Foundation set aside funds for a conference on Africa, in cooperation with the Foundation for Youth and Student Affairs. The meeting was held in Corning and combined discussions with a study of the Corning area, which includes several colleges and universities, and provided an opportunity to become acquainted with the workings of local government in a special situation—an industrial community within an agricultural economy.

In a country with more than 200 million people and more than 18,000 population centers, of all shapes and sizes, there are sure to be communities as complacent as Center City, as depressed as Border City, as efficient as the new planned cities, and as fortunate as Corning, in some degree. As each one is able to take what it has and make what it wants, within the framework of the American value system, the possibilities for growth are very great.

It is in situations like these, as some impetus makes change possible that institutions like the Lions Clubs can have a real impact. They can take the lead in attracting a new and lively industry, in exploiting some natural advantage, in getting a college started, or a new shopping center with a community center. They can, if their attention is focused on their role in urbanization, tip the balance, away from provincial complacency in the good cities and towards growth and development in the bad cities.

THE NEED FOR QUALITY NOT QUANTITY, DEVELOPMENT RATHER THAN GROWTH

But there is one further problem that must be faced if the small city is to play an important role in the future. It must not only hold some of its own best young people, but it must also attract gifted and enterprising people from larger cities, people who will value the advantages that can be found in a developing small city. It must not only maintain the sound institutions that it has, but it must provide for development within them: a small library must become a bigger library; a radio station must be replaced by a TV station; the old opera house or concert hall must become a modern theater; the normal school a four-year college, the college a university, the university add a medical school. As old industries decay, new growing industries must replace them. An old hotel must not be allowed to close its doors until new motels with adequate banquet facilities have been built.

If a city is to have the kind of character that will keep some of its best people and attract others, there must be a sense that it is developing. In the past those cities that have achieved this have done so primarily by a growth in numbers. It is true that some cities have gone steadily downhill without an appreciable loss in numbers, simply by the substitutions of less-able people for the more-able people who moved away. But the cities, which have been able to generate a large amount of enthusiasm, have been cities, which were growing steadily in numbers. But growth in numbers is not what we must aim at today. If the small city is to make its most distinctive contribution, it must remain a *small* city, a city where distances are not too great, a city where all the interested citizenry take part in the same activities, a city big enough for surprises and new encounters but small enough so that all the citizenry feel a connection with the political, economic, artistic and intellectual life of the city.[3] So it is necessary to replace a growth in the number of institutions by an improvement in their quality, higher standards, increased national and international participation, increased ways of attracting outside activities, temporarily or, occasionally, permanently into the community without increasing its size. Those institutions, such as service clubs, who are the promoters of civic well-being will need new forms of reckoning up their progress, in upgrading, in ever higher replacement of the old by the new. Small cities as small cities have a bright future and an important contribution to make. Small cities that become overgrown and unmanageable, air polluted and overstrained, sprawling among uncoordinated suburban developments only add to the problems of today's world. Their essential and challenging problem is how to develop without growing bigger.

EDITOR'S NOTE

1. For background information on scenarios, please refer to page 24.

NOTES

1. Margaret Mead, "Building Communities for the Builders of Tomorrow," in Sterling Forest *Symposium on "Research and the Community." May 1, 1961 under the Auspices " of the New York State Advisory Council for the Advancement of Industrial Research and Development* (Albany: Department of Commerce, State of New York, 1962), pp. 47-54.
2. Margaret Mead and Muriel Brown, *The Wagon and the Star: A Study of American Community Initiative* (St. Paul, Minn.: Curriculum Resources, 1966; reprinted Chicago: Rand McNally, 1967).
3. Margaret Mead, "Values for Urban Living," *Annals of the American Academy of Political and Social Science,* CXIV (November 1957), pp. 10-14; "1. The City as a Point of Confrontation. 2. Megalopolis: Is It Inevitable?" *Transactions of the Bartlett Society,* II (1965), pp. 9-22, 23-41.

1968d

STATEMENT [ON AGING AND RETIREMENT]

Editor's Commentary

During President Lyndon B. Johnson's promotion of his "Great Society," he succeeded in focusing the attention of the American nation on meeting a host of pressing human needs, including those related to the aging of the national population. This selection is a testimony that Mead gave in early March, 1968, before a special U.S. Senate Subcommittee on Aging.[1] It gives us a glimpse into the genuine esteem in which she was held by the participating senators.

Mead's testimony is comprehensive and richly rooted in her anthropological experience and knowledge. It is also fully consistent with the general spirit of the Great Society program. She urges various changes in existing laws or government programs, so that elderly Americans could continue to live satisfying and socially useful lives until the end of their days.

Since old people have personally experienced much change, Mead stresses that they have developed a certain wisdom that they can use to help their children and grandchildren adjust to rapid change, to gain benefit from it, and to minimize its dangers.

In 1968 the American and world situations were in profound strain, pain and flux, which helps explain why the founding of the modern Futures Studies movement dates from about that year.[2]

At this point in time Mead's own positions were also apparently in flux on matters of aging. Thus, the general position she takes in this testimony concerning the value of the elderly in the process of cultural transmission and adjustment, seems somewhat inconsistent with her general position two years later in *Culture and Commitment* (Mead 1970). In this latter work, Mead's emphasis is on grandparents' and parents' lack of background of a type that would be useful in helping the younger generation to adapt to rapid change.

However, this change in position might be more apparent than real. In this testimony Mead does indicate that the grandparental generation, to be fully useful, must have the opportunity for continuing education, so that they may update their knowledge as

* *Proposed White House Conference on Aging.* Hearings before the Special Subcommittee on Aging of the Committee on Labor and Public Welfare, U.S. Senate, 19th Congress (U.S. Government Printing Office, 1968), 70-83.

needed, in order to effectively apply their general wisdom to the new and specific challenges of guiding the young in their current, and rapidly changing, situation.

At the end of the article Mead, then sixty-six herself, describes her interesting affiliation with the Oliver Wendell Holmes Society, a highly creative organization which fostered useful services to the elderly, services designed to allow them to remain relevantly engaged in society.

*   *   *

The Oliver Wendell Holmes Association, through its director, Mr. Sidney Wallach, has made a statement previously before this Subcommittee in June 1967.[1] I need only stress here that the Association has been conducting extensive experiments in education and pre-retirement counseling involving the more educated and more affluent sections of the older members of our population, and that we feel that in the consideration of aging and the relationship between the retired sector of American life and the whole American society, it is important to develop the citizenship and creative potential of this group, who are both articulate—and therefore valuable in pilot projects—and have a high capacity for contribution to their respective communities if they are able to keep abreast of the times.

My special area of competence is that of anthropology. Anthropological contributions to aging include: (1) historical statements of the evolutionary significance of our present period of technological and cultural development in such respects as increasing longevity, infant death rates, physical hardship, disease incidence, etc., all of which are relevant to an accurate evaluation of our present new demographic situation; (2) cross cultural studies of the way in which different cultures have handled work, leisure, free time, and the care and position of the aged; (3) field studies of primitive societies and isolated peasant communities under conditions of exceedingly rapid change, in which these intimately known and intensively studied societies serve as living laboratories; and (4) culture building, the constructions of new institutions which will be more appropriate to the new conditions in which we find ourselves taking into account the present state of American culture.

On the basis of these various tasks of anthropology, I have from time to time taken a diagnostic look at the problem of aging in the United States, using also the position of the older members of a society and the question of rapid change [reflected in] a series of my publications on aging in the context of rapid cultural change, and I append here a list of these publications. I do not think it is necessary to insert them in the record except as titles.

I wish to address myself initially to the question of the relationship between the position of the older members of a society and the question of rapid change. Great emphasis has been placed upon the generation gap and the consequences in mental ill health and social disorganization when there is too wide a gap between the generations. Some specialists have suggested that this is an inevitable concomitant of rapid change. This need not be so. I have followed one small primitive society in the Admiralty Islands. Trust Territory of Papua, New Guinea, since 1928, and made detailed studies of the way in which this sma11 group of Stone Age people—some 2200 in all—were able to transform their culture from a stone age culture to one ready to participate in the modern world—traversing in a little over 50 years a cultural distance which initially took some ten thousand years since the beginning of civilization. I have found that one reason they were able to do this is because they included the grandparent generation within the changes, which they inaugurated.[2] On the basis of this and many other observations on other societies, by myself and other anthropologists, I believe we can say that social change will be smooth just in proportion to the capacity of a social system to re-educate and include the oldest generation within the situation of change. This is so because, unless they are included, they constitute a drag on progress, and that without them, the generations, which are newly involved in the change, have no reliable way of understanding the changes which are occurring. In any rapidly changing society, it is the oldest members who have experienced the most change, know most about it, and are most capable of transmitting the experience of how to deal with change—provided the total society permits them the status from which such experience can be transmitted. Pioneer societies tend to leave the old behind or to neglect them and may then face a generation gap of crisis proportions because they have made the experience of their older members unavailable. This has happened in most parts of the United States—with the exception of small communities where people have lived for many generations, and of special occupations where traditional skills or knowledge are still valued. Because of our overall depreciation of age, even these have shared in the general devaluation of experience. We have come to think of older people as incapable of learning, rigid, resistant to change, and having very little contribution to make to our on-going culture.

I would stress that if we are to survive and develop a more harmonious and better articulated society, it is essential that children should be prepared to expect to learn from older people and later, as they approach maturity and middle age, to prepare themselves for creative contributions to the life of the society. Any effort which concentrates only on the education of the next generation and neglects present generations is building in a self-defeating mechanism through which the growing generation will absorb the failure and pessimism of their grandparental generation, instead of a sense of flexibility and a belief in the possibility of new adjustment, new learning and continuing vitality. Every change in attitude which we wish to initiate, whether it is an attitude towards second careers, constructive use of retirement, responsibility for controlling nuclear war-making powers, protecting the natural environment, controlling the population explosion, or new kinds of elementary education and pre-school teaching, must be communicated simultaneously to every age level, if the desired changes are to be fully effective. I speak therefore not out of considerations of compassion alone, because of the ample evidence that such a large proportion of retired persons in the United States suffer from poverty, isolation and a sense of rejection and futility—which has been well documented in previous hearings—but also out of the urgent need of society itself to maintain a viable relationship among the generations if it is successfully to overcome the difficulties of increasingly rapid change.

I shall be considering the various aspects of the problem of aging and retirement from this over-all position—that it is absolutely essential that we keep the generations in step.

Income

Within the present value system of the United States we are unable to give deference to adult males who are not economically self-maintaining. A loss of the capacity for self-maintenance is therefore inconsistent with the maintenance of status of retired persons, especially retired men, but increasingly of women also. The provision of an adequate income, for health, separate maintenance and self-respect is therefore essential.

Housing

It is a first requirement to provide by every type of effort within the public and private sectors of housing within which older people can live which will permit them closeness but not too great closeness to their relatives and friends, and which will in turn provide children and young adults an opportunity for continued association with older people. We should take steps to do away with age segregation in all its forms; age segregated suburbs, small towns in which the old live on under conditions from which the young have fled, golden ghettos, and institutions within which older People who are ill or disturbed, are separated from the kind of social relationships upon which their recovery and continued adjustment depend. This means diversified housing, housing with facilities of different kinds of care, and housing and town and city planning within which the continuing useful participation of older people—in terms of distance, transportation, organizational style, etc., is specifically allowed for. Here I would particularly like to call attention to the importance for the increased racial integration of our society, of including older people from different racial backgrounds. It is from those over 60 that some of the softening of the new racial antagonisms may be expected to come, from persons who date back to the days when there was more interdependence and less bitterness between members of different races. There are few 50 year old members of racially mixed communities who have not received many kindnesses from members at other racial groups, something that cannot be said about the young people of today, both black and white, who have grown up under completely segregated conditions, and have had no experience of cross racial gentleness or mutual indebtedness.

The successful participation of older people in the great variety of ways that are now being tried out in Foster Grandparents programs, programs of political participation in the affairs of the community, such as that being pioneered in the program of the United Automobile Workers,[3] depend almost completely on adequate housing plans. In turn imaginative housing plans can facilitate and stimulate and promote the kind of participation of older people which can augment their incomes, contribute to the community, and maintain them as alert, healthy and functioning persons during the increasingly long years of their expected lives.

Medical Care

I would reiterate the extent to which today, ill health is a tremendous handicap to the retired, perceived by them as a major reason for retirement although also somewhat mitigated by retirement when they have been engaged in occupations which they found burdensome and fatiguing. We may usefully divide retired persons into those who live more contented lives when freed from heavy and taxing work, those who maintain the same level of health after retirement because other activities replace the former formal job (this includes many creative professional people as well as some workers at every level) and those for whom their work has been so intricately intertwined with every aspect of their lives that retirement is virtually a death sentence. This third is especially true of those whose work has been organizational or administrative in character, which does not, as society is now constituted carry over in any way into retirement.

For the first category—workers who found no satisfaction in their jobs and among whom retirement is rationalized as due to ill health—there is a very great need for better preventive medical care during the years before retirement. Here it may be pointed out—and this is applicable to all levels of income and occupation but most serious for the poorly paid urban and rural workers—that society makes no provision for the regular care of adult men. For infants we have well baby clinics, for school children a certain amount of checking and supervision and for women, as child bearers, continuing expectations of check ups and care. For adult men, however, medical care takes the form of attention to illness, not preservation of health. There is no medical specialty devoted particularly to the care of the male in middle age. Our knowledge of this age group is correspondingly poor.[4] In contrast, adequate physical care is essential if the vigor and reward of the new kind of middle age of which Nancy Simon writes in *The New Years* is to be realized.[5] So in addition to adequate medical care programs for those already retired, preventive measures, regular checkups and increasing attention by medical researchers to middle age is very much needed.

Continuing participation and continuing education

The Committee has already before it statements about the expectation that one third of a lifetime may in the future be spent in education, first in basic education, then in specific vocational education, and recurrently throughout life, periods of further education for career advancement or career change. There is Dr. John Gardner's suggestion of Mid-Career Clinics.[6] And there has been discussion of the importance of giving social security and pension plan credits for periods spent in re-education.

We need several complementary inventions. We need forms within which at any period after fourteen young people who find school unrewarding can find occupations in which they receive adequate supervision and protection and opportunities for some sort of work preparation or contribution to society, from which they can later return to school. Furthermore, we need provision for the return for more education of any individual at any age, and with any number of dependents, who can demonstrate his or her ability to make constructive use of such further education. Constructive use will, of course, vary with age, and for very senior people might be directed only towards fuller citizenship activity, a development of inner resources and the capacity to sustain declining physical strength without becoming a burden on family or community. But in order to realize such a system, we need endorsement and underwriting of the cost of such education for individuals at any age, and adequate provision for care of their dependents. At present there is nowhere for a divorced or widowed woman with small children to turn to finance her further education, and in many parts of the country there is no continuing education even for young adults. Acceptance of the educational needs and rights of retired persons, as is done in California, feeds back into the entire educational system. Scholarship arrangements beginning after fourteen, and relieving parents from the disproportionate burden of educating the country's future citizens just because they happen to be able to afford it, would feed forward into possibilities of continuing education for older people.

Several careers in a lifetime

The expectation of many changes in one's formal work life is one way of preparing individuals for flexible participating in rapid change and for effective handling of the changes brought on by aging itself. This expectation, as well as the expectation that married women will come in and out of the public work world, and required retraining and reorientation, should be built into many institutions, into counseling, training programs in industry, colleges and universities, etc., and also into income tax provisions for example, when cost of fresh education might be an allowable deduction. A serious look should be taken at the need for transferable pension schemes, such as that now provided by TIAA, through which an individual can move, taking his accrued pension rights with him from one institution of learning to another. We need provisions for transfer between the same kind of institutions, as TIAA provides, and also between different kinds of institutions—e.g., between government service, industry and the academic world, between national and international organizations. In addition to transferable pension benefits, provisions to finance transitions, not only in terms of education—as discussed above—but also in terms of security, medical care, and provision for family responsibilities between jobs are needed. If we are to have a society in which the continuingly growing demands for higher and higher levels of skill are to be met, provisions which free men from pension-plan-prisons must be made. Admirable as many of the pension plans of single industries or agencies may be, they all serve to freeze talent, develop rigidities and discourage change.

Together with the cultivation of several careers, other changes can be introduced in the life style of adults; housing which will be appropriate at different stages of marriage, such as planned moves to different sized communities or different climates at different periods. Today, because no such provisions are made, we have a tremendous waste of housing, on the one hand, as older people continue to live on in houses in which they raised a family, unable to either use or take care of them. Older people remain expensively rooted in unsuitable locations for lack of any sense that a move, to another kind of housing, or another part of town, or out of the city, or into the city, is possible. Institutionalization of such arrangements, in retirement industry, in housing, in mortgage arrangements, would all increase older people's receptivity to such moves and changes.

Different types of identity needs

Research during the last two decades, originally expressed in preparations for the White House Conference on children in 1950, has focused our attention on the identity needs of individuals at all stages of their careers but particularly during periods of transition, such as adolescence, marriage, entry into the work world, change of career or retirement.[7] We may distinguish some differing needs of members of the aging population by considering: (1) those who owe their sense of identity primarily to interpersonal relationships with relatives and friends—prevailingly true for women who have never worked and often true for men who have found no satisfaction in their jobs; (2) those whose identity is related to their jobs, and particularly to specific skills or statuses whose contentment in retirement will be dependent on some continuation of this sense of identity, as continued membership in the retired chapter of UAW, continued membership in professional organizations, or continued performance on a freelance or consultant basis; and (3) those whose sense of identity is anchored in their participation in voluntary activities, outside the home, but not primarily job associated, in voluntary organizational life, politics, church affairs, lodges, associations based on common interests, etc. If individuals were assisted in identifying their major source of identity, and to plan their lives in those terms, and if appropriate institutions and public support were available to underwrite them, we might in turn distinguish among (1) those for whom residence somewhere near their kin was most essential; (2) those for whom continued work identification was most essential which would point towards a proliferation of such institutions as the UAW retired chapters and new retirement structure, or emeritus status in professional and trade associations, and (3) the development of new, underwritten forms of voluntary activity, such as Vista, the Peace Corps, the International Executive Service Corps in which the principle of both publicly and privately underwritten national service is extended to give new focus to the lives of retired people and to make possible the contribution of their experience to society.

Revision of present style of responsibility

The present expectation of responsibility is that a couple who have adolescent children will only need to be concerned with their children's education and their own retirement, whereas they may actually today be struggling not only with their parents' problems but increasingly with their grandparents' problems. It is necessary in whatever revisions of formal handling of the new economic provisions we make—in income tax exemptions, in social security payments, in negative income tax or guaranteed annual income—to recognize the shifting center of responsibility and alleviate the terrific burden on the middle aged group—that group which will be relatively the least numerous in the next decade. Relief can be given to this overburdened age group, for example, by removing their responsibility for their late adolescent children's education, by more adequate multi-serviced housing—and most of all by income maintenance throughout adult life.

Shaping children's expectations

If old age is to be regarded differently, children from the earliest years must have opportunities to value older people. The presence of grandparents or surrogate grandparents is essential. Furthermore recent studies have found that it is those older people, who remain in close touch with children and young people, who are most flexible, most alert and most open to change themselves.[8] In institutions of all sorts, schools, hospitals, recreation centers, playgrounds and parks, provisions should be made to combine the very young and the responsible and alert old, so the children can stimulate the older people and the children receive a hopeful picture of old age. An outstanding difference between my generation and the next generation is our experience of old age; those old people whom we knew were on the whole in full possession of their senses. This next generation has had the spectacle of old people, helpless, paralyzed, bedridden, unknowing. Although these may only constitute a tiny percentage of the aging population, they are a frightening spectacle to younger people. Exposure to the alert old, and new provisions which will make it possible for younger people to anticipate and guard against this type of helpless dependency for themselves—would do much to alleviate the present dread of the possible terrible dependency of helpless old age.

Distinguishing among the aged in terms of biological experience

Today most discussions of the condition of the aged are couched in terms of chronological age, with subordinate allowance for marital status, and existence of living relatives. It is important to introduce a further set of distinctions as to whether an old person has no children, children but no grandchildren, grandchildren, or great grandchildren. Much of the controversy about what proportion of older people prefer to live quietly by themselves and what proportion desire the near proximity of children would be solved if we asked, has this couple already taken responsibility for two generations, children and grandchildren, and so now feel entitled to withdraw? Furthermore the type of engagement in life of the childless and single persons shows very definite differences from those with living descendants.

The question of leisure and free time

Many of the discussions of free time treat our increasing amount of time that is not spent in remunerative work, as something entirely new in human history. Actually the requirement that man had to work long laborious hours every day for most of his life has not been universal. Farmers in cold climates have always had long, somewhat empty hours in winter. Even nomadic hunters have periods of plenty in which feasting and ceremonial fill their days. There have been peoples for whom a few days fishing or hunting provided months of food. We have ample evidence that without free time the arts cannot flourish, but no reassuring evidence that the existence of free time necessarily leads to creative activity. This depends upon the culture. If we wish the increasing amount of free time that we expect to be available to be expended in the enrichment of individual lives and of the life of the community, this must be seriously planned for beginning with children's early education, and the *immediate* provision of community facilities and support of the arts.

It is furthermore important to realize that as the time spent in remunerative activity is shortened, by work day, work week, or working life, many other forms of activity are presently imposed on the population: driving three and four hours to work, putting together prefabricated objects, keeping the government's books in carrying out endless tasks demanded by bureaucratic arrangements in connection with taxes, licenses, insurance, repairs, property transfers, etc. Calculating the free time available by simply subtracting the hours at work from the hours in a day gives a completely fallacious result, as does the practice of speaking of women as *working* only when they are engaged in remunerative employment outside the home. Men are becoming increasingly involved in the performance of the same kind of non-remunerative, necessary maintenance tasks, which now take up the time of women who live at home. The attitudes of retired persons towards tasks of this sort will greatly depend on the way in which they are conceived, as frustrating work or as a comfortable accompaniment of more free time, both for work essential to mere subsistence and work performed with genuine sense of enjoyment and fulfillment; empty time, leisure time—time that an individual has the capacity and resources to spend as he chooses—and do-it-yourself time, in which the society imposes more and more unremunerated but socially required tasks on the individual, would improve planning for the future of the entire population and for the aging in particular.

Transitions

Traditionally we have made the most important transitions in the life cycle, abrupt and conspicuous, entering school, graduation from school, entry into work, marriage, moving to a new job, and retirement have had this abrupt character. The contemporary trend is towards the reduction of such sharp contrasts; pre-school precedes regular school; work is being interpolated into periods of later schooling; young people slide slowly into those commitments which end in marriage, in contrast to the earlier style of a long definite engagement and a marriage which marked an extraordinary difference in their lives. Less has been done to reduce the suddenness of retirement in addition to pre-retirement counseling, which should begin many years before retirement, different sorts of transitions, from full time to part time work, from executive positions to continued participation on a skill or knowledge basis, should be introduced.

Many parallel changes could also be introduced into voluntary and political activities. Politically we should have a high and functioning place for former presidents, former state governors, former senators. In voluntary organizations the end of high office should no longer mean the end of participation. *Retirement should cease to be a status and should instead become a process.*

Strategy of changing the conditions of aging

Changing the conditions of aging gives us an opportunity to make major changes in the whole of our society. When archeologists find the skeletons of early man, and find the bones of an individual who had obviously been injured and yet survived, we know that human compassion had developed to the point when the wounded were fed and cared for. When we find primitive people carrying their infirm and ill and wounded people many miles in their arms, as the Bushmen of the Kalihari desert do, we recognize a higher state of social organization and social conscience than that of people who, like some other contemporary primitive tribes, abandon their sick and infirm. As civilization advanced, respect and care for older people could be implemented in more and more ways. However, with the industrial revolution and the substitution of wage contracts for other forms of economic relationships, society again became callous towards its aging poor. Today, in our affluent society, the treatment that we provide for our older people becomes a measure of our successful embodiment of our ideals in our practice.

But changed treatment of older people can also induce changes throughout our society. As we expect less remunerative work and less productive labor from older people, we can also emphasize the importance of other aspects of life, community service, contemplation, the arts, as appropriate forms of human behavior. Just as the recognition of the value of the lives of children has transformed the social practices of many parts of the world, so a renewed recognition of the importance to a changing society of those who have experienced the most change should transform our attitudes towards the whole life cycle. By changing the expectations of the young towards old age, we change the young themselves, giving them new time perspective and their characters new depth. The position of the aging is a point of leverage in the necessary transformation of the United States from an industrial to a post-industrial society, from a society demanding many hours of human labor, to a society based on machine production which can set men free for other things, from a society short of all the services, which individuals perform for other individuals, education, nursing, rehabilitation, companionship, and inspiration, to a society where we can afford an increasing number of human beings for just these human person-to-person services, from a society where the majority live in insecurity and anxiety, into a society with a floor below which no human being is allowed to fall and an ever more elevated ceiling towards which men who live longer, have healthier bodies and better educated minds, living within a society which is better related to its natural environment, and balanced among its generations, will have an ever growing chance to make its aspirations manifest.

In conclusion, we may say that in stable, slowly changing societies, the more the most senior generation are included with the ongoing structure of society and the more power that they have, the more stable, the more rigid and the less innovative these societies will be. But, in a rapidly changing society, especially when there are immense changes within one generation as is the case today, both in the emerging nations and in the United States, then the more completely the senior generation, with the most experience of change, can be included, the greater that society's flexibility and ability to accomplish transitions from one state to another will be. This priceless experience of older people can only be incorporated if they are accorded adequate economic status, appropriate living conditions, adequate medical care, and institutional provision for participation. We have as yet accomplished none of these things. Both at the most primitive and at the most modern level, the care a society gives to its aging population is the hallmark of its achievement of the fullest humanity possible within its stage of technological development.

SUPPLEMENTAL STATEMENT OF
DR. MARGARET MEAD

The Oliver Wendell Holmes Association is a voluntary organization devoted to providing certain kinds of special experiences for a group of educated and responsible citizens who have retired or will retire in a few years. For those who have retired, we provide seminars and institutes, which encourage a continuing creative life with intellectual and cultural content. We also are experimenting with employee programs on pre-retirement. We hope to develop a reservoir of highly qualified manpower and woman-power (chiefly as volunteers) to help deal with the many proliferating national problems. By keeping alive the informed interest of those citizens who formerly often retired in emptiness, they become a valuable resource to society, the community and the nation. We feel that it is most important to develop the citizenship of this group who have adequate income, extensive experience and a high level of previous education. They are especially important in pilot projects because they are articulate and have had disciplined experience of responsibility and leadership. We believe that the proposed White House Conference should devote attention to the need for institutions, which will provide our society with this kind of leadership.

The measure of the success with which a society meets its goals is found in the provision that is made for those who most need its care—infants and children, on the one hand, and the aging on the other. We have now come a long way, since the White House Conference on Aging in 1961, in providing medical care for the aging. Our paramount tasks today are to provide them with an adequate income, and housing, which will make it possible for them to use an adequate income constructively.

I wish to emphasize particularly how deeply a rapidly changing society like ours is dependent upon the ongoing participation of its alert and experienced older people. In the stable, slowly changing societies of the primitive and peasant world, the greater the dependence on the wisdom of the old men, the more stable, the more flex-

ible and [adaptive] the social order. The opposite is true in a society in
which changes are occurring within the lifetime of one generation.
Here, *only* the older people have the full experience of the way of life
from which we have recently come, on the basis of which the future,
which is emerging with such dismaying speed, can be met and
enjoyed. It is they who have the most experience of change, and if
they continue to participate in the affairs of the nation, they who can
provide the models for change. *Man today is born in one kind of society,
lives in another, dies in still another.* If those who have lived with and
absorbed the changes, can continue to grow, to understand, to coun-
sel, in terms of the new technological and social changes, the society
is able to make a more constructive and painless transition. My experience in following the course of transformation of small primitive
communities who must cross thousands of years in a matter of
decades, suggests that the more the senior generation is included, the
more rapid and successful the transformation can be.

To accomplish this essential inclusion of our older people, we need
income maintenance, which will give them dignity, independence and
the means for social participation. In the United States, economically
dependent men do not receive respect, and research shows that independence and health are the deepest needs of older people. Housing
which provides for living, close to children and young people and near
centers of education and activity, is equally essential. We need new
social provisions for the continued inclusion of older people within
significant activities, as members of unions and of professional associations, and as active participants in voluntary activities specially
designed to tap their skills. The Foster Grandparent Program is one
example, programs in which retired executives contribute their skills to
new industries or new political institutions in the emerging countries
is another. Continuing education all through life, publicly underwritten and available, will make career changes in midlife more possible,
and prepare men and women for continuing learning. A group of
aging people, with no status as effective family members, responsible
workers, or full participants in community activity, are a social liability, making tremendous drains on the strength, the work, and the ability to participate of the middle aged, and limiting what they can do for
their children. The same group, financed, housed, and continuingly
educated, become an asset. For their own future, and for the future of
our sorely strained, rapidly changing country, we cannot afford to
neglect them. The elderly poor today live in dire need, the elderly affluent in unwilling disengagement, the elderly skilled and wise sit with
empty hands and no listeners for their wisdom. If we can correct our
pioneer tradition in which the aging were set aside while youth went

on, and include them in our country where there is productive wealth enough, and should be will enough, for all, we can enormously speed up our successful adjustment to change.

In simple societies, people needed children and grandchildren, or they perished for lack of food and care. Today, older people still need society's care, but also children and young people need grandparents, real and surrogate, more than they ever needed them before. The need of our aged and retired population is great. The need of society is even greater. *We must ensure that retirement* is *changed from a state to a process* and that we have all that they can give us, as they live longer, in better health, alert as well as alive. The young stand, bewildered in a world they did not help to make. Those of us who have seen it change, from the oil lamp to the fluorescent lamp, from the horse and the steam engine to the jet airplane, from the telegraph and telephone to transmission by satellite, know how it happened, what we left undone, how we could have done it better. In today's world we cannot afford to make the same mistakes over and over as we are doing today. In today's highly mechanized, interdependent world, where man, and Americans especially, must keep safely locked up weaponry that could destroy mankind, we can live very well, but we also live dangerously. Life has become a parachute jump; we need all the experience and expertise we can find, to assure that new learners are taught well enough to get it right the first time.

EDITOR'S NOTES

1. Ironically, on the final day of that very month, President Johnson abruptly announced to a surprised nation that he would not seek re-election, thus tacitly conceding the stubborn fact that overall American resources were not sufficient to fund both the promotion of the Great Society and the continued prosecution of the war in Vietnam.

2. For background information on the Futures Studies movement, please refer to page 7.

NOTES

1. Older Americans Act Amendments of 1967, hearing before the Special Subcommittee on Aging, U.S. Senate Committee on Labor and Public Welfare, June 12, 1967, p. 133.
2. Mead, Margaret. *New Lives for Old: Cultural Transformation, Manus 1928-1953*. New York: Morrow, 1956; reprinted with a new preface 1966, Apollo A-124. New York: Morrow.
3. *Retirement and the Individual,* hearing before the Subcommittee on Retirement and the Individual, of the U.S. Senate Special Committee on Aging, Ann Arbor, Michigan, Pt. II, July 26,1961, p. 435.
4. Soddy, Kenneth. *Men in Middle Life: Cross-Cultural Studies in Mental Health.* London: Tavistock; Philadelphia: Lippincott, 1967.
5. Simon, Anne W., *The New Years: A New Middle Age.* New York: Knopf, 1968.
6. *Retirement and the Individual,* hearings before the Subcommittee on Retirement and the Individual, of the U.S. Senate Special Committee on Aging, Washington, D.C., Pt. 1, June 7, 1967, p. 7.
7. Erikson, Erik. *Identity, Youth and Crisis.* New York. Norton 1968.
8. Studies in Allopsychic Orientation. NIMH grant No. M-3303 to The American Museum of Natural History, in preparation.

REFERENCES

Mead, Margaret. "Cultural Contexts of Aging." In *No Time to Grow Old.* New York State Legislative Committee on Problems of the Aging, Legislative Document No. 12, 1951, 49-51.

Mead, Margaret (ed.) .*Cultural Patterns and Technical Change: A Manual prepared by the World Federation for Mental Health.* Tensions and Technology Series. Paris. Unesco, 1953.

Mead, Margaret. *New Lives for Old: Cultural Transformation, Manus 1928-1953.* New York: Morrow, 1956; reprinted with a new preface 1966, Apollo A-124. New York: Morrow.

Mead, Margaret. "The Pattern of Leisure in Contemporary American Culture," *Annals of the American Academy of Political and Social Science,* 313 (September, 1957), 11-15.

Mead, Margaret. "New Thoughts on Old People," *Council Woman,* 22, No.4 (October, 1960a), 4-5.

Mead, Margaret. "Work, Leisure and Creativity," *Daedalus* (Winter, 1960b), 13-23.

Mead, Margaret. "Outdoor Recreation in the Context of Emerging American Cultural Values." In *Trends in American Living and Outdoor Recreation.* ("Reports to the Outdoor Recreation Resources Review Commission," No.22.) Washington: U.S. Government Printing Office, 1962, 2-25.

Mead, Margaret. "Aging Differently in the Space Age," *Proceedings of the Second Annual Governor's Conference on Aging, May 2, 1963, New York City, New York State Office for the Aging.* Albany, New York: 1963, 3-13.

Mead, Margaret. "Leisure Is for Recollecting in Tranquility," *Nova,* 1, No.3 (May, 1965), 62.

Mead, Margaret. "Changing Cultural Patterns of Work and Leisure." In *Seminar on Manpower Policy and Program, February 16, 1966.* Washington: U.S. Department of Labor, 1967a, 3-16; discussion, 17-38.

Mead, Margaret. "The Changing World of Living," in "The Emotional Basis of Illness," *Diseases of the Nervous System,* Suppl., 28, No. 7 (July, 1967b), 5-11.

Mead, Margaret. "Ethnological Aspects of Aging," *Psychosomatics,* 8, Sect. 2. (July-August, 1967c), 33-37.

1968e

SOME SOCIAL CONSEQUENCES OF A GUARANTEED INCOME*

Editor's Commentary

This item is a chapter in a book edited by the late Robert Theobald, economist and pioneering futurist. It dates from the turbulent Sixties, when America's cities were exploding with ethnically rooted riots, and President Johnson, in seeking to build his "Great Society," had redefined poverty as a problem to be solved, rather than a condition to be ignored or endured. At this time the idea of a guaranteed annual income enjoyed active support from a wide array of organizations, left and right, within the American policy establishment. There was broad agreement, which Mead ardently shared, that something had to be done about income disparity, and about getting people out of the trap of poverty and hopelessness.

Mead is careful to label her contribution as an examination of some of the social needs for, and projected social consequences of, a guaranteed annual income. She stays away from any attempt at the kind of complex quantitative economic analysis that was also needed (and at that time was unfortunately inadequate) in order to pencil out and project economic costs and benefits to the individual, and to society.[1] Indeed here, as generally in her writings, she makes her argument in almost purely qualitative terms, even though a certain amount of quantitative social analysis could have strengthened that argument.

Mead proceeds to supply several pages of interesting, and often subtle, social projections about how a guaranteed annual income could, would or should impact American life. Her presentation does, though, have a weakness, namely that her projections are almost all of the "optimistic," or "most probable" type. She gives only minimal attention to plausible "pessimistic" or negative projections. If she had done so, her paper would have been even more powerful in stimulating her readers' proactive thinking. Even so, her sociocultural approach is a highly useful balance-weight to the strong tendency among many politicians and

*   In: *Committed Spending: A Route to Economic Security*, ed. Robert Theobald (Garden City, NY: Doubleday, 1968), 93-116.

social scientists—then and now—to think about issues such as these primarily in political or economic terms.

Although the guaranteed annual income never passed Congress, in the years that followed, various legislative proposals were made, aimed at producing broadly similar results. In 1975, during the Ford Administration, the Earned Income Tax Credit was enacted into law. This law was expanded in 1986 under President Reagan, and further modified in 1996 under President Clinton.

* * *

It is characteristic of modern industrial societies to establish a close relationship between the amount of work a man does and his subsistence—as well as that of his wife, his children, and perhaps also his parents. In contrast, most of the societies that the world has known have, throughout history, linked the amount and kind of work done to the subsistence of a group, rather than that of an individual. At every level of civilization it was necessary, of course, to get enough work done so that the group was provided with food. When enough work could not be done, the consequences were serious indeed. This might happen because there were too few hunters in proportion to the number of women and children who had to be fed. It happened among the Eskimo during the period after a death, when an entire group would become hopelessly entangled in some physical and religious situation that made hunting impossible. It could also happen to them between seasons, when the snow house melted and it was not yet the season to go elsewhere for another kind of hunting. But when the hunters could hunt, there was food for everyone. The lazy, the improvident, the mentally defective, and the insane were fed from the work of the vigorous, the provident, and the ambitious. The idea that anyone should not receive basic subsistence, food, water, and shelter—so long as there was anything left to divide—is a modern savagery.

It is true that among the Eskimo, the old were sometimes abandoned at their own request when, no longer productive, they felt they were overstraining the slender resources of the group. Among food gathering and hunting peoples, drought may sometimes force the entire group to walk many miles to a place that has in the past produced food even in time of famine. If no food is then found, and the group must travel many more miles, some of the old and weak would have to be left behind. But even when the hunters have searched hungrily for days, while the rest of the group waited just as hungrily at the camp, there was still compassion for the unfortunate. When the Bushmen of the Kalahari Desert went on such a search for food, and one of them broke a leg, the others would attempt to carry him until food was found.

So since the beginning of man's history, men have cared for other men and assured each other of the basic necessities of life. Certainly there were times when the old had to be left to die, and sometimes even the dying had to be abandoned—although this has been reported only for people whose social relationships were deteriorating. Very often, too, not all the babies born were saved. Sometimes they were not saved because they were born while a nomadic people was making a forced march to reach new grazing grounds in time to save their herds. Sometimes they were not saved because the mother already had another baby, a weakling who commanded all her care. And sometimes they were not saved because the baby born was the wrong sex to balance marriages in the next generation. But those who were allowed to live were fed.

The idea that any human being would be so cut off from all other human links that even food and shelter were denied him is a by-product of civilization. (Civilization itself was a direct consequence of man's ability to store food, build great cities, organize large areas, put armies of conquest in the field, and bring in other groups as tributary relatives and slaves.) Stated simply, with civilization and affluence for some came poverty and vagrancy for others, and such institutions as charity—through whose practice the wealthy acquired credit in heaven. With civilization there also came the beginning of poverty that was all the more bitter because it was experienced alone and not shared with other human beings. A group of Eskimo, sitting in their melting hut with no food and the lamp going out for lack of oil, was desperately unfortunate—but not poor. Poverty is the other face of affluence. The Eskimo became poor only when he encountered the European's superior technical equipment and guns, or more lately, his airplanes, radios, and tape recorders. And this poverty is experienced by the Eskimo only when he moves into the European orbit and lives on welfare. Historically, it has been common for civilizations to create poverty by bringing into their orbit people of a different subsistence style and assigning such people an inferior place within the civilization. In time, the subordinate people are no longer close enough to their former means of livelihood to revert, should the need arise, to primitive hunting and food gathering. They become so dependent upon more complex social organizations that when these break down almost completely in times of war and famine and pestilence, descendents of once self-sufficient peoples die by the hundreds of thousands—and sometimes by the millions.

It is thus possible to regard poverty, and mass death from starvation, as by-products of civilization. But the peculiar set of ideas that accompanies the growth of industrialization belongs more to our own

Western history—and here I refer to the way we have coupled the amount of work a man does to his right to remain a viable member of the human race.

It is not difficult to trace the evolution of such concepts. As industrialization developed, the poor (multiplying in rural regions that could no longer support them) crowded into the cities. Here, so long as their survival depended on their accepting any work at any price, they were welcomed as cheap labor who could keep the wheels of industry turning. The old ties these rural poor had once enjoyed with extended kin, the neighborliness of villages, the protective largesse they had been able to count on from the manor, the castle, and the monastery—all these were swept away. The right to exist became associated with the willingness to do any kind of work that was available. This brings one to a point historians are still debating, and perhaps will argue for years to come. What is the relationship between the Protestant ethic—the insistence on work and a post-ponement of pleasure, as a condition of acceptability to God—and the industrial and technological development in Northern and West-ern Europe? There is no doubt that the two went hand in hand. In a sense, the relative poverty of the Mediterranean countries (which did not share fully all the benefits of the Industrial Revolution) may be regarded as more endurable. For it was still a shared poverty, and from their pitifully inadequate supplies, the poor gave food to those who were hungrier than they.

In the United States, the unremitting demand for cheap labor meant that almost everywhere and almost all the time, the poor could survive without benefit of either the old type of kin ties and institutionalized religious charity, or the local work house provision for the needy. European countries began to experiment with various sorts of social insurance, designed to replace on a governmental basis the older forms of responsibility for the needy. But the United States ignored such social reforms and was able to survive until the Great Depression with only such simple laws as England had invented by the end of the Middle Ages for the care of the occasional needy old man or old woman, or unadoptable orphan. The United States was able to do this because this country still offered virtually untapped resources and vast amounts of free land to a population growing in numbers through immigration as well as natural increase.

Essentially, our ethic was as harsh as that which prevailed in Eng-land during the early days of the Industrial Revolution, or in Ireland, during the potato famine. Yet it seemed less harsh because of the sense of space and opportunity, which was so integral a part of early American life. The sense of wider spaces into which everyone was free to move, and a faith that opportunity waited just around the corner, was instilled into Americans. It did not matter whether he was a three-generation native living in a log cabin where the wind whistled through the chinks while pine logs provided a bright blaze, or a recent immigrant packed into the noisome slums of New York City's Lower East Side. American school children learned to recite verses celebrating Opportunity, which claimed:

> They do me wrong who say I come no more
> When once I knock and fail to find you in;
> For everyday I stand outside your door
> And bid you wake, and rise to fight and win.[1]

Or this:

> Master of human destinies am I!
> Fame, love, and fortune on my footsteps wait.
> Cities and fields I walk; I penetrate
> Deserts and seas remote, and passing by
> Hovel and mart and palace—soon or late
> I knock unbidden once at every gate!
> If sleeping, wake—if feasting, rise before
> I turn away. It is the hour of fate,
> And they who follow me reach every state
> Mortals desire, and conquer every foe
> Save death; but those who doubt or hesitate,
> Condemned to failure, penury, and woe,
> Seek me in vain and uselessly implore.
> I answer not, and I return no more![2]

The Great Depression challenged, for the first time, the belief that if any man were willing to work, he could find work to do. It challenged the belief that if any man could not feed himself and his family, it was because he simply was not willing to work at *anything*. Although the Great Depression did bring in legislation that provided minimum insurance against starvation for most Americans, it did not truly change the attitudes that prevailed before the Depression. Not only do these attitudes still prevail, they are today complicated by three generations of families who have endured the humiliations and deteriorations of our present system of welfare.

We still employ the workhouse psychology of Tudor England. We will take care of those within our gates when we must, at least to the point of preventing death from starvation, or seeing that lack of shoes does not keep a child from attending school. But we resent any increase, by migration or birth, of those who must be cared for by the people of our city or our town. And we resent a corollary fact—that there are today many essential services that go unperformed because no one can be found to do the work, and this at the very time when so many are on welfare.

Historically, we are a country where the eager immigrant turned his hand to any task at any wage. We have never really adjusted to the combination of a legal minimum wage and an unemployment insurance policy that insists only that a man should find the kind of work he is trained to do. This combination is even more difficult to accept since it co-exists with a welfare system that will continue to support the unemployed engineer, insurance salesman, or truck driver when their unemployment insurance runs out—even though there are plenty of dishwashing jobs that need to be done.

The American ethic, shaped in the styles of the open frontier and the land of golden opportunity for the determined immigrant, had its peculiar imperatives. It insisted that a man, no matter what his status, should be willing to turn his hand to any task. It insisted that the newcomer to our country, or a region of our country, should be willing to begin afresh, at any level. The traditional respect for the man of humble beginnings perpetuates this feeling. So does the fact that in the United States, maturity for a man is essentially economic. When a man can support himself in a manner that includes the support of his wife and children, he is counted a man. If he loses his job after marriage and must again be supported by his parents in their home, as happened to so many men during the Depression, he temporarily returns to the status of a minor—a status he may leave by again becoming economically independent. The American belief that maturity is reversible played a role in a mayoralty campaign not many decades ago, which was based on the threat that King George was again about to take over the United States, presumably because we were not doing too well economically.[3]

Of course, we have not really abandoned any of our essential beliefs. We still believe that it is wrong for a man, or an unmarried woman, not to be gainfully employed. The rich man who makes token trips to a brokerage house, or engages in politics, may be making only symbolic gestures, from the standpoint of the relationship between his income and his earnings—but he has to make them. We still believe that there is something wrong if a man is supported by his parents after he completes graduate or postgraduate training, however well they are able to support him. And students, anxious to escape the dependent position of being supported (and controlled) by their families, accept support from their wives—only to find that this transforms their wives into parent figures to be abandoned when degrees are obtained. Uncounted hundreds of thousands of families live on less than they are entitled to in terms of present welfare concepts, because they still insist upon being self-respecting, self-supporting persons. Meanwhile, those who advocate that we control the right of the poor to have children point with horror to the fact that families in which fathers do have jobs still need welfare help. In their view, the right to marry and have children is inextricably involved with the right to act and live as a mature man, and is based on total economic and social self-sufficiency.

This genuinely pioneer view was made obsolete long ago by the urbanization of the country. But by extension, we also deny mature status to students, who are not considered to be earning a living, no matter how hard they may be working to prepare themselves for a career essential to our economy. We still treat them as sub-citizens, whatever their age. The scholarships and fellowships we extend to them are based on a means test and treated like a dole. University students often find difficulties in renting a home, getting a telephone, or voting-rights that are accorded to an economically self-sufficient high school dropout working at the lowest-level job.

A further expression of the American ethic that a man should work his way up, should begin at the bottom of the ladder, and should be willing to begin over and over again is found in our treatment of young Americans who grow up "too fast" (this was the perspicacious comment of a woman juror in the first trial of Alger Hiss) .We have small sympathy for those who fail to pass through the appropriate apprenticeship stages in any occupation—stages that by common agreement we make difficult. Each stage in education demands that students begin all over again, as "freshmen" targets for upper classmen hazing. The young man who completes a professional degree must begin again at the lowest rung of the ladder, and nothing is more dangerous to academic success than to omit such stages. Deans and heads of departments carefully balance the amount of suffering at each stage; those who have not endured the proper amount of suffering cannot compensate by pointing to their research work or different experience.

The convention that the good immigrant takes whatever he can get and makes his own way—once applied to peasants coming in droves to the United States—continued to be applied to the highly educated refugees from Europe, throughout the Hitler period of the 1930s and early 1940s, and even to some of the refugees after the Hungarian uprising in 1956. Educated men, while being given hospitality by their economic peers, were still expected to accept menial jobs at once, while they laid plans to resume their professions.

The demands that we make on those who have inadequate education, health, motivation, or opportunity help to perpetuate an ethic in which subsistence is inextricably tied to a paid job, except for retired persons, married women, or widows and spinsters living on the accumulated savings of some man's previous earnings. And this ethic insidiously encourages the belief that if people didn't *have* to work, they wouldn't. All proposals for a guaranteed annual income, however phrased, conjure up, on the one hand, the loss of independence and autonomy, and on the other hand, an army of people living on welfare, without the slightest interest in taking jobs that are waiting to be filled. Work, to be work, must be a duty, and not a pleasure. Rich and poor alike are seen as being goaded by a variety of pressures into doing some work, and all are believed anxious to do as little as possible.

We have been unable to revise our ethic fast enough to fit our changing condition. The unadorned truth is that we do not need now, and will not need later, much of the marginal labor—the very young, the very old, the very uneducated, and the very stupid. This fact continues to go unrecognized as we talk about "full employment." The temporary stringencies of a wartime situation obscure the fact that our economy will need fewer workers per unit of output with every year that passes. The old need for cheap labor is fast disappearing, and with it the ability to coerce people into taking ill-paid, unsafe, and low-level jobs by the physical threat of starvation, and the psychological threat of a loss of self-respect and autonomy. As minimum wage laws go into effect, machinery simply replaces human cotton pickers in the Southeast—and New York and Chicago have more mouths to feed. The motive power of the need for self-respect does not act on the new migrants to the cities as it acted upon our pioneer ancestors, and upon the recent wave of highly motivated immigrants from other lands. People who have lived a marginal life of' peonage and dependency in unicrop economies, where the gains from production and consumption were both drained away from their lives, have not been schooled in a major commitment to autonomy. They want to eat. If these migrations had occurred at a time when society was still willing to starve them into working, and then pay them starvation wages, the results would undoubtedly be different. But today we are caught in the midst of a half -realized ethical revolution; we are too rich and conspicuously affluent to bear to use starvation as a weapon. Yet we are too traditionalminded to realize the drastic revisions we will have to make to bring our social expectation in line with the facts of our changing technology.

Like all colonial peoples, we have attempted to preserve certain elements from our ancestral culture. These ways of thinking and being tend to continue despite new situations to which they are inappropriate. Such discrepancies between the ethic and the reality have been maintained for hundreds of years. We can be forced to examine our ancient premises by crisis or threat of crisis—such as is now presented by pollution of the human environment, by the chaotic state of the inner cores of our large cities, by the population explosion, and by the need to readjust our methods of distribution to fit changes in production that are the concomitants of automation.

Since the changes in our distribution patterns will have to be made by the federal government, the revision in our ethic must necessarily be nationwide. Glaring contradictions result when a government policy is inadequately supported by discussion on a nationwide level. All through the late 1930s and 1940s, for example, children studying history were not taught anything of the events that took place in this country after 1932. This period was neglected on the assumption that as soon as a Republican administration came in, it would, of course, sweep away all the New Deal legislation—so why bother to teach it?

We may feel a kind of dependence upon, and expect to give loyalty to, our own locality, our state, or our country. But the view of a nation cross-cut with regional administrative lines (so real to the special Washington office of the agency involved) has no reality for the country. Each attempt to assume greater federal responsibility is fought as an increase in bureaucratization. Those who advocate federal responsibility for slum clearance, schools, or welfare in one area of the country will fight against it in another area where the same conditions prevail. They will do so in the face of the obvious inability of localities with very different resources to cope equally with a national burden.

For these reasons, when we discuss the possible effects of some form of guaranteed annual income, we must do so in terms that have meaning for the nation, and that can be disseminated by the nationwide news-dispensing networks. As we have accepted the right of every resident in the United States to a minimum of subsistence help—however inadequate and niggardly it often is, and however grudgingly it is given—it will be necessary to accept some extension of this principle. As the people of the nation take the burden from the people in small towns, poor cities, and needy states, new definitions of responsibility will be required. Unless these responsibilities are defined in terms meaningful to the entire nation, they will be successfully fought and evaded. It may be argued that the cost of the undeclared Vietnam War and the increased draft quotas are so deeply resented because the nation as a whole is not involved in the war. In an all-out war we have the greatest awareness of ourselves as a nation, and the least resentment of Washington. Yet, in a situation of total war, people not only have to contribute resources, labor, and military service, but also want to contribute to the outcome of the struggle. A guaranteed annual income would provide the same kind of total involvement—not only would everyone be taxed, but everyone would be involved personally as a participant. Both contributing to, and receiving, a guaranteed annual income could and should be viewed as greater participation in the life of the nation.

It is therefore necessary to see first how a guaranteed annual income would affect the definition of citizenship in the United States. At the present time, citizenship is an internationally oriented concept; it is something that birth in the United States confers, as compared with the citizenship conferred or imposed by birth in other countries. American citizenship is seen as something that natives of other countries may acquire, but also as something that Americans, both new and old, for example, can lose by serving in the armed forces of another country. It gives one the right to a passport and to protection abroad. Also, there are a lot of things that someone who is not a citizen cannot do—notably, work in governmental contexts of any sort, or receive scholarships and grants designed for Americans. But whenever he is home in the United States, the American feels only a weak relationship between his citizenship and his sense of participation in the nation. This has been accentuated by attempts of the extreme right, and sometimes the extreme left, to promote their partisan causes by the use of nationwide identifications and American historical symbols. Thinking in nationwide terms has almost become confined to extreme ideological positions.

If one interviews Americans about the domestic implications of being an American, one sometimes gets vague and general answers about how good it is to live in a free country or in a country with such a high standard of living. Sometimes the respondent is quite specific, giving particulars about being glad that he is not a citizen of some other country "living under a dictator," or how he can "get a job with the city," in contrast with the non-citizen, who cannot. Significantly, it is not the individual citizen who makes widest use of American symbols, but those groups, whether left or right, who are either concerned with importing a "foreign ideology" or preventing its importation.

If we are to have a guaranteed annual income, it is clear that it must be inclusive, and it must apply either to every citizen, or to every resident. If it is seen as the opposite face of taxation, then as foreign residents are taxed like American citizens, the all-inclusive category should be *resident*. Those who live here, and are taxed here, share together in the benefits a rich and productive country is able to assure every adult member of the society and, directly or indirectly, all children. Whether citizenship or residence is the criterion, we may have to deal with the problems of immigration. We must answer the question of whether such recognition of full participation in a society, still nationally bounded, is compatible with the same kind of hospitality that prevailed when the country needed cheap labor. This earlier condition, combined with our tradition of giving religious and political refuge, has left us as residue a certain amount of hospitality, even in today's world.

If we are to avoid the psychology of the English Tudor town, where the sick stranger was carried out into the fields to die, so that the town would not have the expense of burying him, we will need some way of reconciling the freedom to come here with the freedom to live here and share in a guaranteed annual income. And we shall need to develop an ethic based on generosity and a sense of affluence and abundant resources. In time, there will be fewer tendencies toward limiting what we can give to others, because we have given so much to ourselves. At present, however, it might be well to stress how the well being of the country would be served by a guaranteed annual income that would stabilize the economy by ensuring it a steady group of consumers. It would help the picture if immigrants are seen as valuable consumers, as once they were seen as valuable in the production process. The total economy can be stimulated, through the development and use of machines, to meet the needs of the new consumers. If these measures were taken, then we could work on other major stabilizing mechanisms such as establishing the best ratio of men to land, and controlling the growth of metropolitan clusters.

What would be the consequences of a guaranteed annual income? It is apparent that its impact on different groups in the population would vary enormously. The first impact would be upon men of wage-earning age. (The position of the retired has already been drastically altered by social security and Medicare; the position of children will be a function of the changed position of adults.)

There is an increasing tendency for young men to assert their maturity by marriage and fatherhood. But when such actions are combined with economic dependency, they are excused only if the young husband and father is a student or is obtaining further training. To be a respected member of American society, a man must earn a living and provide the major part of the support of his wife and children. In the same context, the money he earns should be enough to keep them all; any money his wife may earn should be complementary, but not primary. (So strong is this feeling that many men are unwilling to have their wives work, for fear someone will think they have to work—and this would impugn their own capabilities as mature men.) This belief that a real man can support his family all alone is of course shared by women. To the degree that a wife has to support her husband and children, she loses respect for her husband's manhood. Among the urban proletariat of all racial attributions, the inability of the men to get jobs reduces their effectiveness as husbands and fathers. This has a variety of implications that have recently been spelled out in many analyses of lower class family structure. But some of the older consequences have not been as fully spelled out, as, for example, in the mechanics of gang formation among boys in the slum areas of American cities. In such areas, the normal American socialization pattern—in which the parents are audience to the exploits and successes of the child—is lacking, because the father lacks the respect of his children. The boy with leadership qualities, robbed of the adult audience he would normally enjoy, turns to younger boys for his audience, becomes a gang leader, and by so doing seals himself off from the normal paths of advancement in American life.

Our discussions about the weakness of family ties in urban slums (often directly counterpointed to the strength of such ties in the same population before migration from the rural South, rural Puerto Rico, or Ireland) has not been correctly focused. It has dwelt almost entirely on the weaknesses in the family structure, rather than upon the essentially economic nature of those weaknesses. If men—in a society that has defined its men as providers—are unable to provide either money or services to support their families, the family structure breaks down. Then we get the fatherless families, the ADC [Aid to dependent Children] mothers, and the adolescents who face a difficult and often devastating choice. They must decide whether to play the role their fathers should have played, and help support their mothers, or by rebelling against this position, to assume instead the role their fathers are actually playing a role of dependency and irresponsibility.

A guaranteed annual income would provide such fathers with an ability they once had in rural areas but have forfeited by failure to find jobs in the city—the simple ability to provide for their families. Their relationship to their wives and children would be stabilized at the center. Their manhood, instead of being called to question, would be reaffirmed. From this stability, they could go on to look for forms of employment from which they could hope to improve their position—now that they had a position capable of being improved. This kind of stabilization is urgent and imperative, unless we wish by some means to attempt to dissociate the father from any provision of a livelihood for the family, and reduce his role to that of the mother's partner in sex and procreation. Welfare, doled out so that his wife and children will not starve, is an incentive to absenteeism and parasitism. (One cannot anticipate very much success for the efforts of those who would have welfare agencies treat the matter more sympathetically, and who insist that any sex partner of the wife be allowed to share her home—so as to contribute social, if not economic, stability.)

At present, it is difficult to predict whether a guaranteed annual income for presently resourceless families might increase their fecundity. To the extent that the men were stimulated to add to their small reliable subsistence incomes, this should not be the case. To the extent that absolute hopelessness encourages a resort to the one fully human power left to the poor, reproductivity, a decrease in despair should provide a check on reproduction. To the extent that middle class models continue to emphasize large families as the perquisite of affluence, there might be a positive relationship with the family size of those men who were stimulated to greater effort by the provision of basic security, and a negative relationship where a guaranteed annual income was taken as adequate and no need was seen to make any further effort. A relationship between ambition and larger families would not in itself be evil, and could be corrected by changing trends in middle class ideals about family size.

The greatest effects of a guaranteed annual income on individual and family stability might be expected to appear among the most recent migrants to the large cities. These new migrants have not yet lost a style of life in which men who provide for the family in other ways than earning money are nevertheless respected. The smallest effects might be expected among those who had lived in either urban or rural slums for two or more generations, and among whom responsible behavior patterns for men are lacking. There is probably no justification in any claim that a guaranteed annual income will do anything more for such people than to substitute a more bearable, less expensive, and more dignified form of welfare. But their children would be on a better basis with other children—not separated by a gap because of the source of their income.

In the lower middle class, the guaranteed annual income would make itself felt most by relating the members of the middle class to the rest of society. It would reaffirm the fact that their comfortable way of life is related to the prosperity and productivity of the country, and not simply to their own virtuous industriousness and saving habits. Also, as many new middle class families actually have no savings, and live on an essentially lower class pattern of installment buying, a guaranteed annual income would provide this group with a greater sense of security. In so doing, it would convert them into more stable citizens, less suspicious of their own community and their nation. The anxiety that goes with fear of losing a job is greater in the middle class, where the idea of not having work is inconceivably awful, than among the very poor. The special provision for Committed Spending that would cushion the effects of loss of expected salary level, as well as dealing merely with immediate job loss, becomes particularly important for those who have saved and planned and are then confronted with the types of unemployment that accompany technological changes and large-scale reorganizations.

This is so even in the upper middle class. Here I include the professional and upper managerial groups, highly motivated and able individuals who have reached their present status by consistent effort, often combined with large amounts of familial support. This is not a group with whom we ordinarily associate the kind of insecurity with which the Guaranteed Annual Income is designed to cope. Nevertheless, in today's fluid, rapidly changing world, it is particularly members of middle management and liaison who are most seriously endangered. In the United States, it is possible to identify a new class of the previously successful who, sometimes in early middle age, are bypassed in the course of social change, with long compulsory periods before new und even partially satisfactory employment is found. Committed Spending will make it easier for them to make such transitions and reduce the sense of bitterness and injustice that now characterizes many of those who find themselves suddenly in transition, where they had expected continuous promotion and success.

Although the upper middle class is characteristically motivated far beyond considerations of immediate economic gain, sharing a core of security with workers whose industriousness they have so often questioned should have ethical significance. Many of the upper middle class already work many more hours than their contracts call for. But even for these, it will make it easier to know that their less fortunate classmates and associates are not being forced summarily into sudden violent reorganizations of every aspect of their lives, and to know that they live in a country where not only no one is hungry, but where no one is demeaned. The extra economic efforts, which are almost an automatic accompaniment of middle class status today, will be played in a wider context.

The small but important upper class in the United States has always been faced with a society lacking a responsible role for its fortunate elite—a society that presented its upper class with nowhere to go but down. There has been no consistent, continuous role for members of our upper class families. There has been the additional handicap that they belonged to families and not to a nationwide class. It is not yet clear whether a guaranteed annual income can be made to give them a new sense of freedom of choice. But a society, in which all occupations are followed by choice, and none by threat of starvation, is intrinsically closer to an aristocratic ideal of responsibility.

Now we may turn to women, and consider the effects upon them. Are women, upon becoming adults, to be given a guaranteed annual income just as would be given to a man, and then suddenly disenfranchised and reduced to dependency level if they marry? This seems to be our present trend. Single women are increasingly treated as individuals in terms of jobs, protective legislation, and social benefits, but those who marry are no longer treated in the same way. We are fast approaching a stage in which married women can, in a sense, be compared only to nuns in the Middle Ages—set apart, subject to separate rules, and condemned to physical labor as a condition of following a chosen way of life. Women who are not married are treated as responsible individuals and presumably might be given a guaranteed annual income just as any mature man would be. If they had any dependents, as so many women do, these could be treated as the dependents of a man are treated. (This is not so at present, where, for example, a man is permitted to take his wife overseas, but a spinster does not have the same permission to take a mother or a dependent sister or niece.)

The decision as to whether women should be treated as full individuals, married or not, would be a crucial one. Giving them such status would conflict with many of the articulated motivations in favor of a guaranteed annual income, such as reinforcing the manliness of men and preserving the family. The dependency of the wife has been such a significant element in our idea of the family that it will be difficult to substitute a status for women based on choice rather than on economic advantage. If, on reaching majority, each woman were to be assured a guaranteed annual income for life, and given the same security as her brother, both instituting and continuing in marriage would be matters of free choice. The status of a family would be that of two adults, freely joined to rear their children together. The standard of living would be calculated on the contribution of two adults to each family, and the family would not be dependent upon some archaic survival of a theory that two can live almost as cheaply as one. As we have adapted to the idea of women working, partly due to the rising standard of living and partly to an insistent demand for cheaper educated labor, we have merely substituted work outside the home plus domestic drudgery for total economic dependency. So, today, the demands made on a married woman who works outside the home are almost impossible to meet. If all women, married or not married, had a guaranteed annual income, we might expect to see fewer mothers of young children working outside the home and consequently far fewer unsupervised and uncared-for children, overworked mothers, irresponsible husbands and fathers, and women aging before their time from carrying a double load. We might expect, if women, married or unmarried, were given a guaranteed annual income, that fewer married women would work full time, and that perhaps more of them would work part time as choice replaced coercion.

The effect on the young adult, male or female, would perhaps be the most striking. At present, the social worker is plagued with a series of discrepancies. Neither boys nor girls are really welcome at home after they have reached physical maturity. In the social classes where they can afford to go away to college, they survive in an uneasy dependency—sometimes even after their own marriages. But where they must live at home, whether they work or continue in college, an overwhelming proportion of young adults are pushed toward marriage as an escape. This results in premature parenthood, too heavy a load on young men who attempt both to support a family and to obtain further training, and often also in too-large families. At present, service in the armed forces is the only other escape for young men, and there is no other escape for the girl who cannot go away to school. There are also further contradictions in our demand that young people continue in school, as a service to their country, and in our refusal to pay them for doing so. While boys who are out of school perform unskilled and trivial tasks and are paid as men, students are submitted to a means test, and the best fellowship available for the most gifted student is not supposed to equal what he would earn "if he worked." Parents who can possibly afford it are still supposed to finance their children through college.

There is a tremendous discrepancy between the possibilities of support in higher education for those who early make a career choice, and for those students who are slow in settling on one particular career line rather than another—yet some of those who are slow to decide will later be our most valuable thinkers. Only with affluent parents behind them, do they have much chance for the kind of exploratory educational period they require. If each young man and woman reaching eighteen years of age had his or her own guaranteed annual income, then the questions of education, work, and marriage would fall into place entirely as matters of choice. To facilitate that choice further, we might also initiate some system of nationwide service that would acquaint young people with the possibilities for different kinds of careers in different parts of our country and the world.

Today we are not able to support our artists, our composers, our poets. The richest nation the world has ever known has a handful of scholarships, a miserable little collection of prizes and grants. It offers its gifted individuals nothing except a chance to work at some other occupation and give the time left over to the arts. With a guaranteed annual income, young people would be able to spend the time necessary to perfect their skills. It would put an end to composers becoming night watchmen, and poets trying to support themselves as silk-screen craftsmen. This support would be their right, as it would for any other citizen, and would not have to be debated as a matter of patronage. A poet, like anyone else, would have a right to subsistence and the right to choose to do something unremunerative the rest of the time.

For this is the crux of the matter—the right to choose to spend one's life in a way that society does not remunerate. In certain stages of industrialization, especially before the introduction of automation, every hand was needed to produce and to build up capital goods. It was not possible to encourage "unproductive activities" in societies still struggling to industrialize. Where this is so the arts must be subsidized if they are to survive, as in the countries of Eastern Europe, and to some extent fettered by the state. But where there is no longer a shortage of labor, this need not be the case.

To free the arts, we should have to exorcise the belief that it is morally dangerous for anyone to choose to do nothing—that is, to choose not to make money. This belief has been terribly strong, and it has been reinforced by the low level of opportunities available to fill the growing leisure of the formerly overworked classes—people who never had a chance to develop taste or skill. To learn to believe that leisure can be a good part of life, and that it can be filled with activities of a high artistic, social, or spiritual nature, will require both a change in belief and a change in the opportunities that are available. There must be a substitution of a great deal of locally based activity for the present mass-produced recreation. But to have good little theaters, for example, there must be many people who are free to devote their time to building and developing them. Guaranteed annual income would provide for this.

The twin of our belief that time not spent in gainful employment will corrupt the soul is our fear that if men are not coerced by threats of ignominy and dire poverty, they will not work. In such a case, it is believed that all the dull, unpleasant, routine, and degrading tasks that must be done will not be done. It is undoubtedly true that if a man does not live under dire threat, he will ask more of his job. He will not tolerate unsafe working conditions, a degrading work situation, a job that defines him as less than human. Members of minority groups will refuse to accept jobs that are defined as appropriate only for those of low status. Factory work once liberated men, and particularly women, from the domestic drudgery in which they had neither dignity nor rights. This trend, which has already gone very far in the United States, would be accelerated with a guaranteed annual income. No one would accept work in which human rights are disregarded. Every task would have to be made worth doing, if it were to be done at all. Every task would have to provide some desired reward, a fair return in money, good working conditions, a sense of purpose, dignity, and participation.

We will have to give up the belief that men work only for money, and realize that men also work to do something together, to have a purpose in life—a purpose that is provided for the mother of young children by her home and that an increasing number of older married women now demand also. Idleness as a full-time occupation produces dullness and ennui, and people can be trained to put up with it only by the most extreme measures—such as certain kinds of compulsory military service, imprisonment, or hospitalization. But also we have to see that necessary tasks are fit to do. If everything that can be done by a machine is done by a machine, and work itself is necessary and remunerative, dignified and safe, there is no reason to believe that the majority of Americans, deeply committed to the possibilities of bettering themselves, will not elect to work. Of course, all such work must be remunerated above the guaranteed annual income. A man would not give up his guaranteed annual income when he worked, but would simply supplement it; in the case of those who made large salaries, the guaranteed annual income would be counted against taxes.

In Britain after World War II, it was difficult to raise production because the workers had everything they had learned to want that it was possible for the country to provide. As a result, they simply refused to work overtime. They would have worked for better housing, but this was not a practical possibility. This is not the case in the United States. A people to whom moonlighting is almost second nature would not abstain from work and live on a subsistence level. A United States with a guaranteed annual income would be a United States of tremendous productivity—a total population with a guaranteed annual income would assure an enormous and steady mass market, and a continual output of more and more desirable goods and associated services. People would, as some of those on welfare do now, refuse jobs that had neither good pay nor interest nor social importance to recommend them. We have had to pay school janitors more than teachers to get the jobs done. We have had to glamorize the role of the airline hostess to get well-educated and responsible girls to combine high responsibility with the daily performance of onerous, menial tasks. The fact that good restaurants fail to get waitresses while girls compete for the airplane hostess jobs is simply a comment on the way waitresses are exploited in restaurants. It does not point to any inherent unwillingness to work on the part of those who quit. A poor job cannot encourage those who have experienced a long and demoralizing life among others who were also on welfare to strive for self-realization. But we need not argue from this—from the boy on the corner who refuses five dollars to shovel some snow— to any fear that in a society where subsistence is a right of every citizen, rich or poor, the provision of such subsistence would make people unwilling to work.

There would be those who found the guaranteed annual income sufficient and went fishing, or painted pictures, or devoted themselves to some form of religious work. There would, undoubtedly, be those who drank it up, or gambled it away, or who spent their days at the races or their nights in the numbers racket. Large mass societies, like much smaller and simpler societies, have not learned how to bring up every child so that he or she will fit into the adult world, instead of into some illegal and disapproved nook that is also provided. But the danger that we shall be underwriting the failures of skid row is trivial compared with the benefits the guaranteed annual income would give us. It would provide dignity for every citizen and choice for every citizen. It would free us from the stigma of poverty and the demoralization of welfare, and turn our affluence from a reproach into a point of pride among nations.

EDITOR'S NOTE

1. For an expert political and economic commentary on the complex specifics of this matter, see Dennis J. Ventry, *The Collision of Tax and Welfare Politics: The Political History of the Earned Income Tax Credit, 1969-99*. Washington: The Brookings Institution, 1999.

NOTES

1. Walter Malone, "Opportunity," in *The Best Loved Poems of the American People,* ed. Hazel Felleman, (Garden City, N.Y.: Doubleday, 1936), pp. 100-1.
2. John James Ingalls, "Opportunity," in *Poems That Live Forever,* ed. Hazel Felleman (Garden City, N.Y.: Doubleday, 1965), pp. 411-12.
3. For girls, maturity is attained by either marriage or by economic independence, and so presents a different problem.

1969

MAN ON THE MOON*

Editor's Commentary

Mead and Métraux wrote this article for the lay public in the days shortly before Neil Armstrong set foot on the moon. The article is an interesting expression of anthropological insight. It is also an expression of Mead's typical enthusiasm for the American national future that, to some scholars, must have seemed tinctured in a romantic cultural boosterism.

Her enthusiasm is, however, not just about what a moon landing would do for America, but also for what it would do for all of humanity. Here she cites the need to overcome "future shock," and compares it with the need to overcome "culture shock." These two terms have a broad similarity to two key terms used in this book, namely tempocentrism and ethnocentrism.[1] Mead believes that these two shocks must be transcended, for the good of the entire human species. As she sees it, "this new exploration—this work at the edge of human knowledge—is what will keep us human. It will keep us from turning backward toward ways of thinking and acting that have separated men from their full humanity."[2]

This piece sets Mead starkly apart from many more traditionally oriented anthropologists trained during the 1920s or 1930s—or even much later—in the way she welcomed change and adventure, and dared to imagine future national and global possibilities in sufficiently explicit terms to provide the basis for intelligent discussion.

* * *

The day a man steps onto the surface of the moon, human beings will be taking a decisive step out of the past into a new reality.

Long ago our ancestors lived on very small islands of the known, scattered on an unknown planet. The whole of a universe could be encompassed in a hilltop and a valley, the steady stars, the wandering Pleiades and the waxing and waning moon. Mountain walls, vast

* First published in July 1969. Available in: by Margaret Mead and Rhoda Métraux, *A Way of Seeing* (New York: McCall Publishing Company, 1970).

plains, dark forests and the fringing seas cut off little groups of men from knowledge of what lay beyond their own familiar patch of earth, and the arching sky was accessible to them only in fantasy.

Today the deeply important thing is that the same set of inventions that is opening the universe to exploration also has made our world one, a bounded unit within which all human beings share the same hazards and have access to the same hopes. This is why I think the moon landing is a momentous event.

But as we wait for the astronaut to take that first step onto a part of the solar system that is not our earth, it seems to me that our vision is faltering. We have followed each stage of this venture into space. Through the camera's eye we have already looked down at barren stretches of moonscape and we have seen our own world, a small, shining globe in space. But as the first climax approaches, wonder at the unknown and a sense of the magnificence of the achievement are dimmed and tarnished by doubt and the feeling on the part of many people that "all this is meaningless to me."

The same questions have been asked for a decade. Why go to the moon? Why spend all that money on a space program that will change no one's daily life and solve none of the problems of human misery on earth? Can't we put the same money to much better use here? Why not put the earth in order before we take off into space? Who cares whether we or the Russians win this "race"? With the danger of nuclear warfare and the menace of uncontrolled population growth—both the outcome of modern science—confronting us, why should anyone get excited about one more technological success, the landing of a man on the moon?

These are the wrong questions to be asking, I think. They are evidence, it seems to me, that we are suffering from a failure of the imagination a failure of nerve that psychiatrists are beginning to recognize as *future shock*. It is well known that people who go to live in a strange place among strangers whose language and manners are incomprehensible often suffer from culture shock, a state of mind in which, alienated and homesick, they temporarily lose their ability to take in new experience. In somewhat the same way many people are shrinking from the future and from participation in the movement toward a new, expanded reality. And like homesick travelers abroad, they are focusing their anxieties on home.

The reasons are not far to seek. We are at a turning point in human history. What is required of us is not merely a change in our conceptions, but also in our sense of scale. The only parallel to the situation with which we are confronted lies five hundred years in our past, just before the great era of world exploration.

Then, in the 1440s, Prince Henry—an extraordinary technologist whom we only vaguely remember as "Henry the Navigator," brother of the king of Portugal—gathered around him a great company of scholars, astronomers, map makers, pilots, instrument makers and craftsmen in Sagres, on a lonely promontory reaching out into the unexplored Atlantic. They created a new science of navigation and invented a new kind of ship, the lateen-rigged caravel, which could make headway against the winds and was designed for long sea voyages. Up to that time ships navigated from island to island or from point to point, close to shore; where this was impossible, few men sailed intentionally.

For forty years Prince Henry sent ship after ship into the Atlantic and down the coast of Africa, hoping to solve the "impossible" problem of circling the continent. His were not the first craft to reach the nearer islands or to attempt the African voyage or even to rove the open Atlantic. But the men who sailed the caravels were the first to study and plot systematically the winds and currents off the African coast and, eventually, on the open seas from the North to the South Atlantic. And it was from seamen trained in Sagres, only a few years after Prince Henry's death, that Columbus learned his seamanship.

Prince Henry and his company of scientists and technicians formed one of the small clusters of men whose work began the transformation of the world. They solved no immediate problems. The Moors, against whom Henry fought as a young man, still were a threat to Mediterranean Europe when he died. The Portuguese inventions made feasible long voyages of discovery, but no one knew what lay ahead. And certainly no one could foresee that the greatest innovation was the new approach to problem solution, which combined theory and the deliberate creation of a technology to carry out practical experiments. Only today do we fully realize that this linkage of science and technology in the thinking of Prince Henry and others of his time made possible a world in which people could believe in and work toward progress.

The parallel, of course, is an imperfect one. Where it breaks down most seriously is in the number of people involved. In the fifteenth century only a handful of men were aware of the tremendous breakthrough in knowledge. Today in an intercommunicating world, millions of people enter into the debate and are part of the decision-making process that will determine how we shall deal with the knowledge, the anxieties and the hopes that are part of this contemporary expansion of reality. And it is extraordinarily difficult for vast numbers of people to move simultaneously toward change.

We could slow down and wait. We could turn our attention to the problems that going to the moon certainly will not solve. We could hope that, given time, more men would become aware of new possibilities. But I think this would be fatal to our future.

As I see it, this new exploration—this work at the edge of human knowledge—is what will keep us human. It will keep us from turning backward toward ways of thinking and acting that have separated men from their full humanity. For humanity is not to be found by going back to some Golden Age when communities were small and the people living in them knew and trusted (but also, in reality, often bitterly hated and despised) one another. Humanity is not to be found in any kind of romantic retreat, in any denial of present reality, in any decision to rest within the known.

Humanity lies in man's urge to explore the world. It lies in man's unique drive to understand the nature of the universe within which he lives. It lies in man's capacity to question the known and imagine the unknown.

Step by difficult step men expanded the world they knew to include the whole of the planet and all men living on it. In the seventeenth century, men's conception of the universe was transformed by the telescope, which brought the moon and the stars nearer, and by the microscope, through which the once-indecipherable nature of matter was made intelligible. Once men could count only the smallest collections of objects, and until our own generation the organization of vast assemblages of facts was an infinitely laborious task. Today the use of computers allows men to think about organized complexity on a scale entirely new. And now, finally, we are moving out from the earth as living beings, in the persons of the astronauts, to experience space with all our capacities, our wonder and thirst for understanding. For the first time we are exercising in full reality what has been truly called man's cosmic sense.

Each stage of discovery has enlarged not only men's understanding of the world, but also their awareness of human potentialities. So I believe we cannot stop now on the threshold of new experience. We must put our knowledge to the test. Human potentialities, unexercised, can whither and fester, can become malignant and dangerous. A society that no longer moves forward does not merely stagnate; it begins to die.

The exploration of space does not mean neglect of the tremendously difficult problems of our immediate environment. It will mean, I think, the development of a new context within which we can look for viable solutions. Up to now, our ideas about what can be done have been either utopian or essentially parochial, while the problems themselves affect the well being of human beings everywhere.

It is no accident that the Soviet Union and the United States, the two largest organized modern states, have built and launched the first

successful spacecraft, while the governments of the 180 million people in the Common Market countries of Western Europe have continued to bicker divisively and ineffectually over which stage of a
shared rocket should be built by whom and have been unable to find
ways of coordinating their efforts. Nor is it an accident that these two
countries are moving ahead so fast in changing and raising the level
of education—though in this we still, by far, lead the world.

In part the success of the Soviet Union and the United States has
resulted from the fact that these two countries have—and have been
willing to commit—the resources in money and men and organization necessary for so large-scale an enterprise. In part it is owing to
their orientation to the future. Soviet and American men and women
have no monopoly on talent. But each of us, as a country, has been
able to attain the precise and magnificent large-scale co-ordination of
effort necessary for building spacecraft and for becoming pioneers in
the space age.

The very thing that has made the space program successful, but
also in the eyes of many people boring, is awareness of the crucial
importance of detail. The rehearsals, the repetitiveness, the careful
steps, the determination on absolute precautions and the participation of the citizenry in something that might, but must not, go
wrong—all these things also are essential to the success of an enterprise on a new unprecedented scale.

No country, as yet, has fully recognized the fact that the scale of
our major human problems is not local or national but regional or
worldwide. No country has realized that we must simultaneously
include both extremes—the individual and all men—in working
toward social solutions. Individual human dignity can be assured
only when all men everywhere are accorded and accord to others
their full humanity. National solutions are inadequate as they are
based on past conceptions of human differences, uneconomic uses of
resources and barriers to communication that no longer exist.

We have yet to discover how to co-ordinate effort to solve social
problems on the scale that will be necessary. This will mean, as it has
in the space program, work with small models, new kinds of simula-
tions and trials and intensive learning before we move into large new
systems of organization with planetary repercussions. No more than
the fifteenth-century men who opened the seas to exploration can we
see what lies ahead. But unlike the early explorers, we have learned
how to direct our efforts.

The lunar landing will be a triumph in its own right. But at the
same time nothing can demonstrate more cogently, I feel, that there
is an intimate and inescapable connection between man's pursuit of

his destiny and his attainment of his own humanity than the intricate technological co-ordination combined with individual human courage that characterizes both the American and the Soviet space programs. There is no reason for alienation from experience that will enhance our common humanity. Voyages to the moon—and beyond the moon—are one assurance of our ability to live on the earth.

EDITOR'S NOTES

1. For an explanation of the term "tempocentrism" please refer to page 16.
2. This somewhat poetic term "full humanity" will probably strike some readers today—as it must have in 1969—as too loose and subjective. Yet, to Mead's credit, she does go to some lengths to explain what she means by the term, so that we have a basis upon which to agree or disagree. Today, thirty-five years later, I find myself wishing that she had included explicit examples of possible negative effects that she believed space exploration could, would, or might produce—such as the militarization, pollution, or inappropriate commercialization of space.

1970a

EDUCATION FOR HUMANITY*

Editor's Commentary

In this item Mead advocates an approach to education that takes into account various changes she anticipates in world conditions. True to anthropological tradition, she reminds her readers that there is but one humanity on this earth. She advocates an approach to education designed to reach and benefit all of that humanity—free of the arrogance and rigidity of the past, and free of ethnocentrism. She envisions a world where education is life-long—where both students and teachers are expected and enabled to continue learning and growing throughout their lives.

*   *   *

My mandate is to discuss "Education for Humanity," which might be taken to mean either Education for all of Humanity, seen as all of the human race, or Education for Humanity, that is, an education that increases the humanity of those who receive it. The second sense of the word, as it has been applied, in English, to the *humanities* has too often been exclusive and elitist and arrogant. But I believe a fair case can be made today for the coincidence of any education designed to increase the humanity, literally the humane outlook, of its recipients with the need for universality. Any education that takes for granted the superiority of any group, national, continental, racial, religious, or ideological, over others, contains within it the seeds of "man's inhumanity to man". As the world has been explored and all peoples have been put into communication with one another, *man* now includes the inhabitants of the most remote islands of the sea. No country, therefore, however ancient and honorable its tradition, or however advanced its contemporary technical or political develop-ment, is justified in considering either reinforced perpetuation of its former systems of education, or innovation in the field of education, without including the effects of such activities in other countries.

* In: *The Place of Value in a World of Facts*, Nobel Symposium 14, ed. Arne Tiselius and Sam Nilsson (New York: Wiley Interscience Division, 1970), 419-427.

However far apart in technical development, however opposed in ideology, however contrasting in ethos different countries may be, what happens anywhere in the world today is significant for the whole world. Those who innovate, whether in a technical or social field, in taking responsibility for the foreseeable effects of their innovations, now can do no less than to take into account the whole world—and all the inhabitants of the six continents and the islands of the sea.

Planning for the planet can be modeled on responsible national planning only to the extent that there is no distinction made between internal and external influences. Today most national planning considers only such matters as trade, possible military attack, and rivalries, which assume that, in a sense, nations are not part of the same system. Therefore even the most complete national planning, whether in small homogeneous advanced societies or in great conglomerate societies like the USSR, the US, India and China, cannot provide the kind of model we need. To date, the activities of United Nations commissions have implicitly assumed standards developed in some particular part of the world, usually Euro-American, as the standards to which other peoples should conform. The inclusion of particular religious philosophies has been limited to veto positions, as in the case of Roman Catholic views on birth control, but it is rather as exponents of particular styles of modernity that countries from the world outside Europe have spoken. We have at present no mechanism by which the traditions of the entire world can be included on anything like an equal basis. This means, in effect, that responsible bodies like this symposium are continually planning for other people, but not with them.

The recognition that we represent only a small and differentially articulate part of the human race alive today on this planet, and that everyone here has been educated within a single tradition, however much that tradition may be predominant in the world's current scientific and technological advances, imposes certain limitations on our deliberations here. They must necessarily be tentative and cast in such a form that other peoples can systematically be included within the development of any particular feature of the plan or of the very direction of the plans themselves.

So while it is true that we may be, in information terms, somewhat ready to think about the rest of the world, this may only make our plans the more destructive, just as the ethnologically trained missionary is more efficient in the destruction of the local religions, the practices of which he not only abhors, but is equipped to ferret out for abolition.

Including the entire planet has other implications. Each step we may inaugurate, assuming that some recommendation of this symposium were to be accepted effectively, somewhere, within the part of the world that we represent, will have effects elsewhere, as it is observed, disseminated, copied, reacted against or rejected by the rest of the world. No experiment of consequence can be conducted in secrecy today. Those who would attempt such secrecy are themselves injured by what becomes, inevitably, a lack of generosity. No ideological division prevents groups theoretically opposed to each other from watching each other's procedures very closely. So, in any serious attempt to think and to plan, the inclusion of all foreseeable results includes not only such matters as differences in scale, the state of the existing culture, the sources of previous changes, as South American countries looked to Spanish and French models of higher education, or Japan, at an earlier period, looked to China, but also the nature of the response that is likely to occur, slavish imitation, irresponsibly poor copying, violent rejection couched in religious, nationalistic or ideological terms, or symmetrical types of nominal rivalry, as when the United States tailors its scientific education to a supposed model of scientific education in the USSR.

In this paper I shall use the word education as inclusively as I know how to include *purposeful* teaching and learning on any subject and at any age, and conducted within any institutional setting. Such an inclusive definition overrides the traditional type of discussion in which education is something that is done to children, or young people, or adults who have been poorly educated and must be brought up to the standard attained elsewhere by children. It also overrides the frequent distinction between education and training. Most uses of the idea of training treat human beings as objects, training them, as one would a race horse or a sheep dog, to perform some specialized task, in contrast to educating them as whole beings. On the other hand, it is possible to speak of educating an animal, as the puppies who are to become guardians of the blind are educated in the United States by being reared in a family of children—a purposeful attempt to produce the kind of upbringing, which an Eskimo husky puppy receives among Eskimo children in an igloo. It is also useful to distinguish education from two other social processes: socialization, the adaptation of a human child to a social environment; and enculturation, the adaptation of a human child to its particular cultural environment. Socialization and enculturation are descriptive terms for processes that occur in all known societies. Neither term implies consciousness on the part of teacher or learner, nor specific and articulate goals. Education as I am using it here, is a goal-directed conscious process on the part of the teacher, or learner, or both, in which a change is envisaged in the learner. We have not, historically, envisaged a change in the teacher, except as greater proficiency came from something loosely defined as "experience" or "practice." We have usually been willing to call any system educational in which there was a stated goal for the learners, whether or not those goals were achieved or shared by the learners themselves.

It is also useful to realize to what extent teaching is peculiarly characteristic of man. With the use of words and the conception of distant goals, man can consciously impart information or behaviour patterns to those he wishes to teach, while among animals, the invocation of future or non-visible actions has to be built into face-to-face procedures, or into genetically transmitted mechanisms.

Every known human society however simple conducts some education, that is, there is a conscious attempt to teach certain things to the young, and this is sometimes extended to the stranger, the immigrant, or the married-in adult. What is taught varies widely. It may be formal gender, in a language, which has multiple noun classes; it may be large amounts of rote material, which include ancestral myths, or genealogies; it may be the names of plants; or a repertoire of hundreds of different color distinctions. Whenever there is differentiation of the behavior of any class of persons in a society—between the sexes, between age groups, between occupational groups—these differences bring into consciousness the associated behaviors so that behavior tends more to be taught and learned consciously, than to be simply absorbed without conscious attention. Such educational procedures can be treated as the precursors of schools, with occasional occurrence of institutions with the attributes which we at present associate with schools, where a group of identified learners are gathered together in an identified place and taught some identified body of materials, or skills, by individuals designated to do so. So periods of initiation of an age grade, by an older age grade, have been called "bush schools" in describing traditional African societies, and the ancient Polynesians, intent on preserving their traditions, had recognizable schools among the Maori of New Zealand and in old Hawaii.

All schools that we know of, whether in our own tradition, reaching back through the Mediterranean to the Middle East, or the schools of the ancient civilizations of Asia, Africa and pre-Columbian America, have been based on the assumption that the learners were being taught something that was already known to the teachers. The addition of script gives further emphasis to this position; what is known is written, and the teacher having learned to read it, and possibly to interpret it, teaches the pupil to read it, and possibly to interpret it. Such exercises in the mastery of the known may also include exercises in mental agility, in working out new philosophical or ethical problems, or those postulated but not solved by the traditional material. It has also been characteristic of the existence of schools, now taken in the widest sense of the word to include universities or lifelong centers of religious learning, that there was the possibility of a pupil becoming a greater teacher than his master, but the classic assumption was that the pupil who excelled, understood better or engaged in more brilliant exegesis, or had access to more reliable sources of inspiration from some authoritative supernatural source.

What we are facing today is a later stage of the changes in education which have been introduced wherever science has been included, and the idea of the production of something new incorporated within the traditional educational structure. But because scientific education has had to operate within a structure designed to communicate only what was known and accepted, and that primarily with the use of script, even scientific education has been heavily imbued with the idea that those who know, teach what is known to those who do not know. The process of discovery has been masked by a system of learning within which experiments, the answers to which were known, were repeated over and over again by generations of students, and often the search for the new has masqueraded either as comparable to the traditional contribution of a historian who discovers a new fact, or as research stimulated by practical demands for technological application. The unwillingness to view science and technology as a single process, and the attempt to dignify science as one of the pure scholarly traditions in which men sought truth for its own sake, has further obscured a reality of modern education—the fact that in a world in which we can consciously state unsolved but soluble problems, education has changed. The old system designed to teach what is known to those who do not know, is no longer viable. What we now need, in recognition of this changed milieu, is a changed form of education itself but that form has not been invented. There have been sporadic recognitions of the need, the search for ways of identifying the particular idiosyncratic and age-connected capacities of individuals, especially of young children, begun by Binet and pursued by Piaget, Lowenfeld, Inhelder, and Bruner; the attempts to build curricula in which exploration and discovery will supplement the present emphasis on rote learning; and the emphasis on the university as the scientific center of modern society responsible for innovation, experiments in teaching skills and materials taught to children and, in some societies, to adults in an adult form. All of these small exploratory attempts have, in one sense, been attempts to widen education but at the same time to contain it within a proliferating institution, with its heavy weight of traditional practice and vested interests. Very seldom is there any question raised as to whether indeed there should be a class of people called teachers, whose life-long occupation is to impart selected materials to identified learners, nor has there been any very thorough questioning of the position that education consists of an interchange between those who know and those who do not.

Yet these are two assumptions, which the contemporary condition of society on this planet calls severely in question. In highly traditional countries, and in countries where literacy is rare or non-existent, teachers are trained to impart very special bits of knowledge or proficiency; the whole thrust of what they do is a function of their not deviating in any marked extent from the way they were taught themselves. New subject matter may, of course, be introduced, provided that it is completely absorbed within the old system of teaching. But any attempt to introduce new subject matter, which brings into question the old method of teaching, produces trouble. I believe the position can be supported that when the teacher is able to teach as he or she was taught, children, and adults, learn successfully whatever it is the school sets out to teach, regardless of the method of teaching. Children learn to read by chanting in unison, by learning to sound the alphabet, by drawing letters in the air, by associating words and pictures, generation after generation, as long as there is no marked discontinuity between the world in which the teacher learned and that in which the pupils or students live.

Even the teaching of science survived its assimilation to the traditional dependence upon print and verbal demonstration, and its failure to incorporate first hand observation, exploration and discovery. The educational system firmly embedded in a cultural tradition in which the major premises were unquestioned, worked. It did not, it is true, produce a literate public who understood the science that was transforming the world about them. It did not produce legislators or civil servants or military men who understood the new scientific ideas and the new technology. It educated groups of young scientists who were able to tolerate the rituals to which they were exposed, and who became on the whole alienated from many of the "humane" values to which they were exposed in the rest of their education. The split between appropriate scientific education and the rest of the educational process has now produced, in the most scientifically advanced countries, a reaction against science and technology. We have the situation of a decided reduction in the proportion of young men who wish to go into physics, with outbreaks of anti-rational cults, in which individuals who were never taught what science is really about confuse it with the mistakes of irresponsible and uncontrolled technical development leading to worldwide dangers of scientific warfare, pollution, population explosion and famine.

This rejection can be, at least in part, attributed to a split in our educational procedures in which methods appropriate to replicating the past were applied in fields where the main purpose is to expand and thus change our view of mankind and the future. If a student wishes to be a scientist, he is still required to exclude a good deal of relevant human life from his consideration, and the average person feels he can reject the findings of science the way he could reject the words of some religious leader recorded hundreds of years ago.

These confusions so conspicuous currently in those areas most touched by science and technology, and among those who go on to so-called higher education, are multiplied in attempts to extend specific styles of education designed for the members of particular classes, within particular historical traditions, to the members of other classes, or other cultures. These extensions have not, of course, always been from an elite to a group of less standing and power—the attempt to educate illiterate governing groups by specialized scholars has also occurred—but the typical extensions in this century have been from imperial peoples to colonial subject peoples, from the town to the country, from superordinate racial groups to subordinate racial groups, from the skilled and the more well off to the less skilled and the poor, from men to women, and paradoxically, from the up-to-date young to their behind-the-times elders. In all of these cases, the dependence upon the past as a model has been combined with an assumption of superiority of those who taught, or whose culture was taught, to those who were taught.

So to the hierarchical superior status that past knowledge held over present living was added the assumption that knowledge, inaccessible to one's forebears of the same race, sex, age or status, made those who received the new education, in some sense, both superior to their forebears and inferior as parvenus. With all of these extensions has gone a whole set of attendant circumstances, the attempt to train, rather than educate, a sufficient number of teachers; the recruitment of teachers who had not received the same type of enculturation as teachers in the past; the downgrading of teachers; and the perpetuation of a variety of exclusionist stereotypes, ranging from beliefs about the innate capacity of people of different "races" to handle abstractions to an insistence that women learn typing rather than mathematics. The more the egalitarian demand grew for previously dispossessed groups to share in the education that had been associated with elite status, the more distorted, unreliable and muddled the educational system became. Today, in many parts of the world, including the United States and parts of Europe, the very educational practices that were designed to bring a large proportion of the citizenry of a country into fuller participation in the society serve instead to isolate them; schooling designed for those who are believed to be less capable or less appropriately aspiring, conveys, sometimes almost with conscious intention, lower aspirations and lower self-esteem. In reaction against such educational systems we find the types of symbolic egalitarianism in which students in countries that have recently acquired Euro-American types of education, write theses, which are meaningless caricatures of what a thesis should be. Conversely, there is the demand in the United States that black students be admitted to higher education regardless of their preparation or intellectual level, finally completing the transformation of the degree from a certificate of special educational attainment into a badge of social and economic acceptance.

A third feature of the present day worldwide scene is found in the changes accompanying the definition of education as age-related. Schools have traditionally discharged the role of mass childcare as well as education. They were places where the young of elite groups could be protected, and the young of people of all ranks could be cared for, during a large part of the year. They have become, in some technically advanced countries, ways of protecting trade unionism by keeping the young out of the competitive labor market, and, as such, a late school-leaving age and compulsory retirement complement each other. They have provided a means for the entire child population to be given minimal health, and sometimes, dietary supervision. All of these primarily care-taking functions replace the family and kin group and are not primarily educational at all. The greater the emphasis on these caretaking functions, the more complete the emphasis on education as something that is done to and for children and early youth. Attempts to extend the school-leaving age are joined not with the educational needs of the young but with worthy attempts to reduce child labor, protect young people from corrupting circumstances, and supervise their health. Only in those countries where there is an ideological emphasis upon giving greater power and prestige to some new elite drawn from the peasantry, the proletariat, or some primitive political hierarchy, is this association between education and childhood and youth temporarily set aside, and then the educators discover that adults can sometimes learn in a few weeks what it takes a child a year or more to learn, or that appropriate motivation enormously short cuts the kind of learning traditionally insisted upon for the captive young.

Yet the conditions of the contemporary world, with the tremendously accelerated rate of change and worldwide interaction by mass communications and transportation, actually mean that where once children, and later, in more complex societies, adolescents, and still later, young people in their 20's, could be taught, once and for all, what they needed to know, there is now a demand for continuous education and re-education for people of all ages. Unlearning is becoming almost as important as learning. If this condition is once realized, schools will have the potential of being transformed from centers where a few adults, officially committed to teaching, teach a mass of children and youth, committed to learning simply by age status, to centers where many people will be learning from those younger than themselves, and where possibly the most effective form of learning will be teaching across age lines in both directions. Under such circumstances, possibly some of the other contemporary functions of schools, as caretaking institutions for children and early adolescents, as weaning institutions for late adolescents, may be minimized or shifted to other institutions. Or, alternatively, education may be diffused throughout the society, and apprentice-type learning, but with the added possibility of the younger teaching the older, may replace its current forms.

With these other shifts, we may expect that the preoccupation of educational institutions with the written word, which has characterized them since script was invented, may give way to other forms of education, in which visual and auditory experience may replace the peculiarly linear nature of learning from script. Both ease of communication and ease of travel are producing a demand for more simultaneous and wholistic experience and for the kind of thinking in which the entire individual is involved. If this occurs, the present hierarchical position given to script will vanish, and other forms of learning, whether it be of a painter or a dancer or a programmer, will be given recognition. The tremendous dependence upon script that has characterized all the high civilizations and molded our forms of thought and determined the limits within which we could develop, can now be broken. This will admit individuals with many different kinds of minds into full participation in building a new kind of culture. It will overcome, probably in a variety of ways, including a second worldwide spoken language, and possibly a new idiographic system with multiple linguistic reference, comparable to the present notation system of the sciences, the present divisions among peoples due to differences in mother tongues, but without destroying those mother tongues.

The new humanity, toward which we are struggling, is essentially based upon valued diversity and absence of hierarchies among peoples, races, ages, sex, the senses, and the traditions within which mankind has flourished. It is based upon placing the unknown future in the forefront, and seeing the pasts of different peoples, as routes, none of which is to be discredited, to a present in which we can work for a shared future.

1970b

KALINGA PRIZE ACCEPTANCE SPEECH

Editor's Commentary

In 1970 Margaret Mead became the first woman to win the coveted Kalinga Prize. This prize, endowed by a wealthy benefactor from India, was described as follows: "The Kalinga Prize for the Popularization of Science is an international distinction created by UNESCO in 1952. The recipient of this annual award must have distinguished him- or herself during a brilliant career as writer, editor, lecturer, film producer, radio/television programme director or presenter, through his/her talent in interpreting science and technology for the general public."

This item is her acceptance speech, and finds her at her oratorical best in visualizing a future world loaded with new challenges and new opportunities. Among the challenges she addresses are population growth, endangerment of air and water quality, depletion of nonrenewable resources, and social inequity. Among the opportunities she envisions are the new information and communication technology, and the general inventiveness of science and technology.

In keeping with the goals and spirit of UNESCO, Mead urges that the wisdom of science, and of humanism, be brought together. She calls for the new information technology to be utilized for the benefit of all, in such a fashion that communication can be truly global. This would enable all humans regardless of culture to participate in the quest for common human goals, without the despoliation of local cultures, even those with very few members. She also renews her call for linguistic science to designate and develop a common international language.

* * *

I am deeply appreciative of the recognition that has been given me and the occasion provided for emphasizing some of the new tasks that confront the world community in the responsible use of the findings of science for the continuing survival and the increasing well being of mankind. As I join the ranks of my illustrious predecessors, the previous recipients of this award, Sir Julian Huxley, Bertrand Russell, Konrad Lorenz, Arthur C. Clarke, Gerald Piel and many others, I believe that there are a number of urgent tasks before us, tasks which

Unesco is in a position to emphasize. I will also stress activities, which are congenial with the long historical contribution, which India has made to our store of cultural solutions to the harmonious co-existence of diverse groups of peoples within her borders. In all of my remarks I will be speaking within the framework of a desirable world where certain agreed upon universals make possible the continued co-existence of unique historical cultural systems, each of which has something valuable to contribute to the world.

First, I believe that we should substitute for the present tendency to characterize technologies and social arrangements, which draw upon science as *rational,* and those assumptions and practices which draw upon the arts, the great religions, and the active commitment of groups of men to the perpetuation of their historical cultures, as *irrational.* This introduces a dichotomy, which disallows depths of emotion, the potentialities of artistic expression and the vigor of action which has been associated through time with love of country and commitment to succeeding generations. I believe that instead of dichotomizing human social behavior, in such matters as the protection of our endangered planetary environment, or the attainment of a balanced degree of population increase, or the reduction of armaments which by their very existence threaten the survival of mankind, we should speak not of *rational* as over against *irrational* measures, but instead of *responsible* as over against *irresponsible* measures. Under the words, *responsible,* I would group the use of the best scientific knowledge and the best available techniques, the invocation of deep feeling and the fire that can be provided by devotion to kin and country, forebears and descendants, the close and dear association with contemporaries and colleagues, the inspiring realization of the oneness or mankind, and action powered by this combination of knowledge and sentiment. Only so, can we see that there is no necessary opposition between our historical sentiments of deep unanalyzable devotion to our own ways of life, and the need for worldwide cooperation in common and terribly urgent tasks. Science and technology based upon scientific discoveries have now provided us with a new means for realizing man's most ancient needs for survival, as groups of identifiable human beings, and those who embody traditions developed through centuries of human effort, the inspired imagination of genius, and the suffering and endurance of countless generations. Today we can feed the hungry, shelter the homeless, protect our children while they sleep, and create conditions in which every child born will be a wanted child, given a full chance as an individual and as a potential contributor to our common human cultural and biological heritage. We now have the means to do these things.

The knowledge that we have these means, even more than the exposure of the suffering and disadvantaged peoples to the sight of abundance and affluence, has given rise to the great surge of hope throughout the world. But it has also provided a rationale for despair, as people see their own countries, or their own fellows, sunk in sloughs of deprivation, which can no longer be defined as the inevitable consequence of our humanity. In the fever heat of alternating hope and despair, a mere call to the rational disposition of irreplaceable natural resources, the protection of the environment against irreversible deterioration, the establishment of population balance in the face of runaway population increase, is not enough. Recognition of the necessities for such rational action that is of the utilization of the findings of science and the capacities of modern technology is not enough. Genuine passion, the passion that comes from man's deepest and earliest commitments must be invoked and embodied in action, visible, palpable, dramatic and standing as living witness to a wider, and deeper concern for the whole and for each precious part, each language, each cherished belief, each cluster of living human beings, united to each other in communities so organically related that tearing them apart is like tearing apart the organs of a living body. Our action, at once informed and passionate, must include not only concern for each living human being, and for each living tradition, but also for each living community. Each year of experience in the great adventure of making an inter-communicating and mutually endangered set of once separate societies into a world wide community brings us new insight into the requirements of the tasks ahead. We have reached the point where each country is endangered by disaster to any one of the other countries on this planet, but we have yet to translate this frightening interdependence into the kind of relationships which provide security and joy in living and acceptance of sacrifice even unto death which have been previously provided in separate cultures.

I wish now to outline a few of the ways in which I believe we can improve our efforts to establish such a world culture. But first I wish to emphasize that I am not urging a world state, as the model of the state inevitably included a position vis-à-vis one or more other nation states, in uneasy co-existence, or muted hostility and rivalry. On our small and endangered planet the continued existence of opposed segments is a poor solution to the problems of survival. Nor can a planet, isolated in our solar system, however much it may be one of many inhabited stars throughout the galaxies, depend upon an organization primarily designed to protect against enemies, and almost inevitably leading to competition for hegemony, and invitations to revolt. I believe that we need better models than the nation state, and better models than federation of previously sovereign national units. We have yet to develop such a model in which activities, rather than spatial entities, which are bounded and mutually exclusive, can be interwoven over the surface of the globe, transcending other lines of allegiance and participation. But we have faint beginnings of such networks in the way in which the different members of the United Nations system are located in different countries, and represent both the attempt to satisfy universal needs, and the unique capacity of single great cultures: France for Unesco, Switzerland for the World Health Organization, Austria for the International Atomic Energy Agency, Italy for the Food and Agriculture Organization, are united in efforts to meet some of the recognized needs of mankind. Internationally organized economic enterprises, and internationally organized groups of workers, provide other partial models of the way in which a mesh of institutional solutions to world wide human needs might be established, within which the conflicts between the center and the periphery common to all present forms of organization, could be mitigated by the distribution of many centers in different parts of the world, each a center for one of the universal needs of mankind, essential to the whole, but unable to satisfy that need alone without the other institutions organized to meet other needs. To date, our political imaginations have been shackled by historical models of empires, nation states, centralized and stratified bureaucracies, all of which have arisen during a period when the planet was divided up among many peoples who only intermittently communicated with each other. None of them are appropriate for an explored, owned and shared planet, on whose continued fertility and beneficent waters and sheltering atmosphere we are all dependent.

I shall now turn to more specific and narrower tasks; I believe we need to inventory all of these dimensions of the physical universe, on the accurate measurement of which the achievements of science and science-based technology depend: weight, length, volume, units of time and space, and units of artificial constructs like currency, architecture and engineering. It is absolutely essential that a single system of measurement and symbolization be used around the world. Significantly, there is no need for continuous simultaneous translation in the international congresses in those physical sciences where the agreed upon sets of symbols are used worldwide. It is necessary to extend these systems, steadily, to every field of science and science-based technology. In my own field I would mention particularly the need of an agreed upon geophysical calendar, to use as a base and a point of reference for the various calendars now used in different cultures, and the need for a culture-free terminology to describe human beings' biological relationships, presently described in ethnocentric abbreviations of English kinship terms. A failure to make such world-wide sets of symbols, freed from cultural particulars immensely hampers the spread of scientific knowledge and science-based technologies, emphasizes and exacerbates the worst aspects of nationalistic chauvinism, and imposes huge economic burdens on many parts of the world. The failure of the United States and the United Kingdom to adopt the metric system when it was invented is a case in point, as is the insistence of different nations upon calendars based on the birth of a prophet of the dominant religion, or upon events in their own political history. All of these can be preserved for ceremonial internal use, as archaic technology is preserved within meaningful religious and political rituals, while a world wide and rationalized terminological system continually expands, as our ability to measure different aspects of reality increases with the advance of science from measurement of physical events to the measurement of human behavior. Every year that such rationalization is delayed puts a greater burden upon mankind's ability to use scientific findings for human ends.

Second, we need to invent a written language which is independent both of existing scripts and existing spoken languages, which gives no special advantage to the linguistic style of any part of the world, which permits the visual presentation of ideas, in the same way as Chinese script transcends the different spoken languages of China. The availability of closed circuit television means that with such a new written language, complex ideas could be communicated without the need for laborious and inexact and approximate translations, to groups who differ profoundly in language and culture.

Third, such a written language, which would have no single equivalence in words, needs to be complemented by a shared spoken language, which can be learned as a second language by an increasing number of the world's people. Such a language should not draw on any linguistic area of the world in a way, which would give any group an advantage, and it should be based on a natural language, which has itself been adapted through centuries of use to the needs and capacities of men, clever and stupid, profound and shallow minded, as spoken by the childish, the senile, and even the mad, as well as poets and song makers and philosophers.

Only by developing universal symbolic communication independent of any present spoken language, and a second spoken language with an appropriate form of script, can we hope to preserve the little as well as the widespread languages of the world. Without it, the widespread languages will contend together for victory, and those who speak less widespread languages will be condemned to second-class linguistic citizenry struggling always a step behind the native speakers of the "official languages" of international communication. Only by insisting upon the development of two such forms of communication can we prevent grievous injustice and inequalities, and preserve the precious capacity for intimacy and poetry and religion, which are so intricately related to the mother tongue, the language learned in infancy.

Fourth, we need to find ways to express comparisons between achievements of nation states, or subdivisions of nation states, in ways, which are less gross and invidious than statements about literacy or gross national product or rate of population increase. The significance of such measures is obscured when nations or cities are placed on single scales, so that they appear to be arrayed in hierarchical sets of superiority and inferiority. We need instead measures which reflect the complexity of each culture, the way in which the level of education is related to the demands for that education, the rate of population increase to maintaining a balance between the number of young and the number of skilled elders necessary to care for them and teach them, and the way in which such a ratio of youth to age is itself related to the natural resources of a country. Ratios which reflect types of internal balance or internal change themselves very different in detail, would provide less invidious bases for comparisons, and would emphasize variety rather than uniformity of technical and social solutions.

Fifth, as the process of urbanization spreads over the world as men forsake the isolation of rural living which has been the accepted life style of the majority of men since the agricultural revolution made it possible to live a settled life, we need new ways of balancing the importance of the small, interdependent community, larger than the family and smaller than a city, in which children can be reared to be full citizens and old people find again the small scale in which they knew in childhood where the adolescents and the mature, wearied by the impersonality of the modern rationalized forms of education and work, may return at nightfall to the many-dimensional satisfactions of a known and cherished human scale. In our search for mobility we have reduced life to too small units, to the single family of parents and children, a unit marvelously adapted to the exploitation of man by man, in soulless systems of production and consumption, in which each fragile household becomes dependent upon large scale industrial and political bureaucracies. We need in the greatly accelerated planning and construction of new cities, and the replanning of old cities, to construct new urban systems in which small face-to-face communities can be maintained and where the countryside and the wilderness may be again accessible to man. Such communities need not become the static, self-perpetuating villages of the past in which people died in the beds where their grandfathers were born, and old rivalries and old expectations limited and defined the scope of each individual's ambitions. They can be open, based upon choice rather than biological kinship and occupational imperatives as in the past, and still provide the security and diversity of personal relationships once provided by the wider kinship group and the small village.

But as we redesign space to match the opportunity provided by modern methods of transportation and communication, we must also come to transcend space as the regulator of our political relationships and our capacity for shared activity. The new realization which has come with frightening suddenness, that air and water are also limited, and may be irreversibly damaged so that the planet becomes uninhabitable, has given us, with its new sense of limitation, new possibilities for the elimination of warfare and for worldwide cooperation. As long as our major concern was for space, for the establishment and the maintenance of boundaries, there seemed no reliable basis for worldwide cooperation among peoples. Each group's gain was another group's loss, as the struggle for absolute sovereignty over territory ranged back and forth through the ages. The size of the units changed but the nature of the struggle did not. Two men cannot stand on the same space; two nations cannot exercise exclusive sovereignty over the same territory. But now that exploration and the scientific analysis of outer and inner space have brought us to a fuller understanding of the nature of the atmospheric shield which protects this planet, and the function of the great oceans in keeping it at a temperature that makes life possible, suddenly the very limitation, which on the ground seemed to make conflict inevitable, has released man to recognize a genuinely shared and common life-giving heritage of air and water. Just because of the fragility of the whole life support system of this small planet, we now know that we are bound together in a common fate, long proclaimed by prophets and poets, now for the first time spelled out for us by the painstaking and breath taking advances of science.

Far from setting up an opposition between science, and the older, deeper commitments of man to love, to passion, to joy and to sacrifices, these new realizations make their attainment more possible. In the past, the only way in which we could extend the taboo against killing a member of one's own group was by increasing the size of the group itself, at the expense of other groups, until huge states of many millions confronted each other, each protecting its own millions against the millions of another state defined as predators or prey, beyond the limits of human brotherhood. Today, with air and water, which we now know, not only can be but must be regarded as the common possession of the whole of mankind if any group is to survive, the old imperatives of territoriality become the ground upon which we stand as we share and protect an atmosphere and oceans held in common.

Even as we cherish the differences in the historic traditions of each people, we can recognize, that while the past of peoples who were bound to small parts of an unexplored and unrealized planet, separated them one from another, the future, as yet uncharted, unsung, the property of no single nation, dependent upon our planetary ability to protect our earth, can unite us just at the moment when the tremendous advances in knowledge and the extraordinary extensions of planetary communication and space exploration seem to have introduced a terrible division between the elders, born into a divided, earthbound, tradition-limited world, and the young, who have lived intimately with the earth seen from the moon, seemed to threaten the necessary continuities of the whole of our society, this vision of our small and fragile planet has instead provided a sense of the future which old and young can share. I believe it is possible to cherish the past, to save our own special and diverse traditions, our mother tongues and our culturally specialized aesthetic styles and religious visions, and the different symbols which have united men born in the same period and still bind the generations together, if we lay enough emphasis on that which all these divided groups share, a future to which we must all commit ourselves, in interdependence on our small and precious earth.

1971

A NOTE ON CONTRIBUTIONS OF ANTHROPOLOGY TO THE SCIENCE OF THE FUTURE

Editor's Commentary

The genesis of the interdisciplinary field of Futures Studies, as understood today, is frequently dated to about 1968, when much of the Western world was aflame with anxiety and protest.[1] In Europe, university students were in open revolt against various aspects of their academic tradition that they alleged to be outdated, pretentious, irrelevant or undemocratic. In America, there were massive protests against the war in Vietnam, and dramatic eruptions of rioting over the assassination of the Reverend Martin Luther King, Jr. The year 1970 saw the first Earth Day, which added a powerful impetus to the emergence of a worldwide "green" movement.

There was general awareness that the world was in serious trouble, and that the future looked perilous. This awareness, and the conviction that anticipation and visualization were needed, became important factors in the emergence of an identifiable Futures Studies movement.

Characteristically, Mead was at the forefront. Here she contributes an article to a book of writings on human "futuristics." The book was conceived at the University of Hawaii, one of the earliest academic centers for Futures Studies, and edited by two prominent pioneers of the movement, Magoroh Maruyama and James A. Dator.

In the thirty-two years since Mead wrote this article, anthropologists have become considerably more receptive to the futures approach. More of them have been producing research products at least partially in the anticipatory mode. Mead's recommendations for how such anthropological input could be used to improve the hybrid field of Futures Studies are as relevant today as when she wrote them.

* * *

* In: *Human Futuristics*, ed. Magoroh Maruyama and James A. Dator. (Honolulu: Social Science Research Institute, University of Hawaii, 1971), 147-149.

Anthropology has to this date made very meager contributions to man's developing concern with the future. It may therefore be useful to suggest some of the distinctive contributions which anthropologists could be prepared to make. This is an area of scarce manpower, and I suggest that it will be uneconomical for anthropologists to attempt to supply techniques, insights or energy for action, which can be provided by other disciplines.

We may consider the contributions of anthropology to the field of human sciences as:

- history, which gives us a better grasp of the processes of change in the past, including the nature of man himself (in such controversies as those spearheaded by Lorenz or Ashley Montague), the nature of change, and the historical background for today's world;
- a comparative critique on the nature of man, his innate characteristics, his capacity to learn and to change, which will correct culture-bound theories of those behavioral science disciplines developed within Western cultures;
- new theories generated by intensive research in small, relatively closed societies where inter-generational relationships can be closely examined;
- a source of new designs for living for the extensive worldwide culture building which is needed in today's interconnected planetary system. This list of possibilities is not exhaustive, rather it is presented as a means for further discussion.

Methodologically, anthropology (including archaeology, linguistics, cantometrics, etc.) has three special contributions to make:

- data on very, very long runs, which can lay the basis for necessary allowances for changes of scale in innovation;
- a disciplinary habit of dealing with wholes—whole tribes, whole villages, whole cultures, the whole of the culture— which is an excellent preparation for dealing with the whole planet;
- a disciplinary practice of working with living people, without a break between the collection of the raw data—by interviewing, observing and participating—and the final analysis. This practice is useful in counteracting the treatment of men of the future as either statistics or science fiction monsters. With the familiarity that anthropologists have with the ways individuals express the entirety of their culture, they

should be able to specify the gaps in prediction whenever the information on the projected future is inadequate.

The requirements for a science of the future in turn may be described as follows:

– responsibility, the creation of the same kind of responsible relationship as that now held by a specialist in the cultural sequences of the American Southwest, present knowledge of Neanderthal man, the specialist in the renaissance in Italy or Ming pottery. It would seem possible to demand the same meticulous attention to the known and responsible avowal of the unknown as we ask of a first-rate archaeologist, ethnographer or historian. No speculation about the future should be advanced without a competent knowledge of what may in fact be competently predicted. (Examples: the appalling presentation of the probable use of fossil fuel in the rest of the twentieth century, presented at the American Association for The Advanced Science's centennial meeting in 1948; predictions about the use of gasoline and natural gas which do not take into account the consequences of the exploitation of the present technology, in pollution, risk, etc.) Speculation should be separated from hard data;
– a disciplined allowance for the extent to which the whole system of human cultures is subject to feedbacks and unpredictable incursions of innovation, concatenations of events, and the dependence of this planet on wider cosmic systems;
– a careful recognition of the importance of self-fulfilling prophecy and the way in which all predictions about the future, if circulated and given credence, become actual factors in the shape the future will take, contributions to despair, hope, carelessness, inertia or effort, as the case may be;
– a scrutiny of all planning as a component in the future of the particular system to which the planning is directed. (Here the ethics adopted by the Society for Applied Anthropology in 1952 can be invoked—responsibility for the longest time perspective and the greatest spread of any innovation or consciously induced change which can be foreseen by the innovator.)

To these I would add one further, more controversial but important requirement—a search for a balance between conscious and unconscious purpose, with the hope that neither too much planning, in itself inevitably somewhat linear, nor too much institutionalization of effectively linked behaviors will occur (Bateson 1972).

It will be important to recognize the different levels of possible participation of anthropologists in the science of the future, as for example, in the problem of world population control:

- provision of carefully collected materials on fertility control in well-studied small societies or sectors of larger societies;
- provision of comparative material on the interaction of such cultural factors as sex preference, age of marriage, fear of loss of virility, status of the elders, within closely comparable cultures;
- the study of attempts at population control as part of the cultural systems within historical cultures;
- the attempt to build a worldwide ethic suitable for rich and poor and all races, religions and ideologies;
- the integration of the effects of modern medicine and social responses to the demand for population control, and the changing roles of men and women in the future.

If each of these levels (1- 5) of scale of enquiry were to be consciously related to the problem of world population in the future, it would not be necessary for those anthropologists and archaeologists who prefer to work at the micro scale, to be personally involved in world problems, but they would work with a sense of responsibility for the way in which their results could contribute to the whole.

It is an old practice of the field ethnographer and the archaeologist to carry in mind the needs and interests of many specialists far beyond their own fields of enquiry, and also to recognize their responsibility to a future when the material, which they are collecting or studying will be forever gone beyond recall. It should not, therefore, be difficult to include in the working inventory for field research, ways of tagging information which is specifically important for certain problems which are at present part of the scope of predicting and planning for the future.

Anthropologists have traditionally dealt with materials of such complexity that any attempt to reduce them to a few variables has been frustrating, if not downright misleading. The possibility of shifting to far more delicate methods of measurement, and to the sophisticated use of a great number of variables should be rapidly included in our methods of field collection, and our analysis of our materials. There can be no science of the future without the use of the computer—with the term computer taken in the widest sense—especially for simulation.

Urban planners at present, who necessarily build for the future and bind the future, are making, explicitly or implicitly, assumptions about human capacities to stand crowding, to live among strangers, to move out and away as far as technology renders possible. One device for the integration of anthropological research into the science of the future is through an active concern with the design of the new emerging urban systems, for which we have as yet no name, which will involve not only entirely unprecedented combinations of open space and building, but unprecedented opportunities for human development.

It is possible that the greatest contribution that anthropology can make will be to keep men's imaginations open, as they tend to let the predictable hardware coerce the form of the software.

EDITOR'S NOTE

1. For background information on the Futures Studies movement, please refer to page 7.

REFERENCE

Bateson, Mary Catherine. *Our Own Metaphor: Effects of Conscious Purpose on Human Adaptation.* New York: Alfred A. Knopf, 1972.

1973a

THE KIND OF CITY WE WANT*

Editor's Commentary

This selection belongs to the field of "ekistics," a term derived from the Greek word "oikos," meaning settlement or home. Ekistics is the scientific, comprehensive, and interdisciplinary study of human settlements in all their variations, with the goal of improving such settlements in the future.

A leading figure in ekistics was Mead's Greek friend Constantinos A. Doxiadis (1913-1975), an architect and urban designer of great energy and creativity. Mead, deeply aware of the rapid urbanization of the world's population, was enthusiastic about ekistics and did considerable work with Doxiadis. This item consists of remarks she made at a conference organized by her friend, in which she points out that some of his designs for urban settlements were based on assumptions that were in fact culture-bound—rather than, as Doxiadis evidently assumed, universal or natural.

Mead's remarks, though not tightly organized, convey considerable insight into how people really live their lives—insight of the very type that many urban planners need, if the human settlements they design are to serve real, rather than imagined, human needs.

* * *

I want to address myself particularly to points not of my disagreement with the design that Dr. Doxiadis has presented, but to supplement a few things, many of which I think have been taken for granted. For instance, Dr. Doxiadis has shown us a picture of every family living in a courtyard, each protected from noise and danger but every family cut off from every other family. This is exceedingly frightening to an American because our typical American design is to have an enormous lawn with no fence and then a big veranda to let people in by degrees. We don't put up walls, as walls are frightening to us, although walls are considered protective in Greece and all through the Middle East.

* *Ekistics*, Vol. 35, No. 209 (April 1973): 204-207.

The assumption of the courtyard diagram, basically, is that the people already know each other. This is not the way you build a city of strangers. This is the way of life in a delightful Greek village, where generations have lived for centuries, and then the walls don't matter. You already know everything about the person next door and their grandparents and their great-grandparents. You know just how they are going to behave and also that probably one of their children will have a harelip or something. These are the non-delights of living with the same people for a thousand years.

We have heard some discussion about the joys of living in multi-family households, but one of the reasons that people go to the city is because they are tired of all these people they have always known. They want to get away. They want to start a new life. We see this when we study the reasons people move to the cities in different parts of the world: one of the reasons is always to get away from the neighbors. Now, neighbors and relatives are taken for granted in Dr. Doxiadis's design. There is no discussion of where they come from or how you get them. You know that God gave them to you, and there they are.

To take another example of much the same thing, all the modern planning that is being done virtually all over the world is assuming the existence of the individual family as a unit, with no relation to anything else at all; and everyone had better be married, because there isn't any place for anyone else. We have had a discussion about what we do with adolescents. Do we send them all to Woodstock, or some related spot? (Certainly, I mean send them. They wouldn't go of their own accord if the society wasn't alienating them.) And what do we do with widows, what do we do with single people, and divorced people, and childless people? There is no place for them in the kind of planning where every single house is supposed to be a family of perennially young children. I notice they never grow up. Every little family has its lovely little children in a nice, close little spot; and then the baby moves out from there, slowly, until he finds another little family with some other little children; and then we don't know what happens to the family until they get aged. When they get old they use the nice courtyard again. But there's about 40 years in between that's left out; and in most projects there is no planning for the variety of people who make up what I would call a real community.

Real community is based on memory. It is based on people who have known each other over time. In a small community you get too much memory, and you want to run away from it, but nevertheless I am now talking about the ways in which societies are organized. What happens when young men bring their wives into their own small group, or what happens when the young men have to go into their wives' groups and make new friends? The community is based on shared experience over time, that is continually revivified by comment, by reference, by telling the story over again. People in small communities are not bored; the thing that is infinitely and absolutely boring is living among strangers shut in with a television set. In this condition you need something new every minute, because life has no meaning, no past and no future, and there is no interest in repetition. The reason that nomadic people find it so hard to settle down into a nice well-organized proper settlement is because it is so boring. In nomadic life there is continual interest in looking at every blade of grass and finding that every blade of grass is different. When I take my granddaughter on a walk she is searching for variety on every sidewalk. But then she finds a piece of paper that has been around some chewing gum, and you have to say: "Don't pick it up; it's dirty;" in effect, stop looking.

I have been to two conferences in the last month dealing with the question of integration in the modern city, for it is of course one of our prevailing desires today to try to build a city in which the poor and people of different racial groups are not discriminated against; are not boxed up in the ghettos and denied access to all that the city offers, but have good housing and freedom to move around. But the discussion centers all the time on individual families, and we hear the parallel demand for the right of people to live near other people who are like themselves.

In many parts of the world we are so preoccupied with the horror of the ghetto conditions under which people have been forced to live (simply because they were black or red or brown or low caste or poor) that we have lost the other part of the picture; that they need to live with people something like themselves, and people with a past that they share, and that in the center of every community there need to be groupings of people who have come to know each other and have selected each other.

The two bases of close association, that we find everywhere in the world, are kinship and friendship. In very small communities, it is very hard to invent a friend that is not a relative. But it can be done, and people do it. A man or a woman can pick out one of their numerous relatives and say he or she is my friend. They may even swear blood brotherhood for somebody who is also a third cousin. But they have picked them out and made them different.

There was a motto that used to hang on the wall when I was a child that said: "It is God who makes brothers and man who makes friends." The right to select usually begins in adolescence (sometimes in play groups): the right to select people that you care about and wish to spend time with, and the acceptance of the relatives that the good Lord gave you—which is a way you learn to tolerate human life. And people, who don't have to learn to accept those relatives that they wish they didn't have, lose one of the great capacities of humanity, which is to learn to accept human beings (male and female in all ages) just because they are there.

What I would like to include in designs for the cities of the future is a way to make it possible for people to come together and form the nucleus of new communities, as well as to move around in the cities. This is taken for granted in Greece, in Italy, even in Calcutta. People move from one village to one spot in the city, where they find their relatives and friends; or where they hide from them, whichever they prefer. But if you are hiding from your relatives, you know they are still there, and you have not lost them; you are just staying on the other side of town. We have no allowance for this at present, for it means a good many other things. It means that people would not live in houses designed for nuclear families. But there would be "congeries" of different kinds of houses. Some would be houses for a small nuclear family; some would be the right size for a couple who have no children, or for a couple whose children have left, or for a single woman or a single man; or for a bunch of kids who would like to put their sleeping bags down and do not want any more space at that moment. A group of older people might stay there more permanently.

We need to know at what age you need familiar surroundings. This is certainly true of small children, and it is also true of much older people, and these can provide continuity for the young people going out and coming back and going out again.

I think one of the reasons that 10,000 communes in the United States have failed in the last 10 years (the figure varies depending on what you call a commune) is because they were all young people on the edge of exploration and change and seeking life styles of different sorts. There were no older people to give continuity, and you need older people both to provide continuity and to give the little children a sense of community. I will give a short story, which I think illustrates this point rather acutely. I was walking along a street with my two-year-old granddaughter and we stopped in front of a flower shop, and she looked in the window and said: "Never be a cat." Now the usual approach of a visiting grandmother might be: "Yes, deary, and see the pretty doggie." Because she would not have a clue what the child meant. But I knew what she was referring to, because she had been sung the same song I sang her mother. This was a little children's song that has been sung in America for 4 or 5 generations: "Always be a pussy, never be a cat. They call me pussy willow, and what do you think of that." And there were pussy willows in the window (they are plants that have flower buds that look exactly like little gray kittens). Now, that is what a child needs. I mean, when she said: "Never be a cat" she expected me to know what she was talking about. And we are exposing children today all the time, everywhere, to adults who don't know what they are talking about, because they don't know what was said or sung yesterday; they don't know what happened yesterday.

The need to be bound to the past is, I think, a basic human need. To remember, and have somebody remember, that you had red shoes when you were two and you walked out in the snow with them. And this time when you are four and you have red shoes, you had better be bright enough not to walk out in the snow. This is what has made people human: this is what has made it possible for them to build rituals, because rituals are relationships to repetitive experience in your own life and in other people's lives.

When I went back to New Guinea after 25 years, to a village where I had lived for seven months 25 years before, my various friends asked two questions: "Did you remember anybody?" and "Did anybody remember you?" Now, those are the most idiotic questions that you can imagine, in talking about people who, for the seven months I was there, knew what I ate for breakfast every day; people to whom I could say 25 years later, when I heard the name of a place: "I don't think I ever went there." "No, you didn't." Or people would say to me: "But you remember him! Why, he was in the second row behind us at that wedding we went to in Patusi" (25 years ago in another village). And I do remember, because I learned those people, and all about them and how to live with them, with a terrific intensity, because they were the material that I was working with, and was going to work with for years. So our memories interact when I go back. Someone will mention a name and I say, "I don't remember that name." "No, you called him so and so." (This is when somebody had nine names, and I used to memorize the nine, but usually only used one). Or I come ashore and an old woman appears with a duck. This was in 1967, and I had been there in 1938, and the duck was in return for a pearl shell that my husband had given her dead husband in 1938. That debt had stayed in her mind all those years: one pearl shell deserves a return of one duck when they come back again. This is community. This is what the human race has lived with always. This is what people lose as small children if we take it away from them in the way that we compose towns.

Now, I don't think this means you have to live in the same place all your life, any more than I believe you have to own your house and stay there. But it does mean that you have to grow up as a child in a community that has some center and focus and set of relationships and that has to be held together by the members of the third and fourth generations: not necessarily your own grandparents but somebody's grandfather. I don't believe that we are ever going to go back to the extended biological family, but we need three generations to give a sense of the past so that we can have a sense of the future. The unit of memory is about five generations: from my grandparents to my grandchild. Because I saw my grandparents, I can tell my grandchild about them. This is the human link in society; and if we rob people of this link, we rob them of a part of their humanity. I want to emphasize again that this means you have got to let people have their own kind of choice of where they will live. We have to have an openness which makes it possible for three young men who went to medical school together to say: "We'd like to live in the same town," or for people to live near their godparents, or their cousins, or whoever it is that they care about and want to live near. This makes the difference between what Harlem was forty years ago in New York, when it was still a neighborhood, and today. Then it was uncomfortable and miserable and there was bad housing, but people were human beings, and it was a gay place. Today nobody knows anyone else and they're afraid of each other, and they're pushed around from one spot to another, and community is lost; and we find this happens everywhere.

What do we have to do now, to try to prepare children to be able to build the kind of cities that we want in the future? Because the kind of cities we are dreaming of will not get built in most places tomorrow. How are we going to bring children up with some sense of the cities we want? And here I want to emphasize very strongly that, although babies may live in one room, everything around them comes into it. If there is somebody coming from the sea they smell the brine on their shoes when they come in, and if they are not taken up to the roof to see the stars, they see people who have been up to the roof. From the moment it is born, and probably before, the child receives an imprint of the total society that it lives in. This imprint may come in very specialized ways. But it is all there from the start. So that if you live in a town where there is no center, that child will grow up with a feeling that there are no centers anywhere; just as in the United States people who have grown up in the city find it very difficult to live in a small university town where there is not any "downtown." They are lonely. If you have lived near a river or lake you are imprinted to want water somewhere, and to feel the water when it is there.

The man-made city and the natural landscape become part of the child's world very early. We can demonstrate this by giving the child materials to build a world and see what it makes. So what are we going to do with children who grow up now in our anonymous and terrible cities? In the Natural History Museum of New York there is a flight of stairs that goes down to the big room where we have a great model whale and children just hurl themselves down those steps towards the whale. You see, they respond to this new kind of situation.

Fifteen years ago I thought that one of the most important things to do with children was to give them aquariums in school or in the home, because there they could see a bounded life and they could learn about the boundaries of natural systems. Now I think the thing to do is to build some kind of biosphere filled with living things, where they can see the effect of their own breath when they enter the place, and see what happens with the change in temperature, and begin to realize that they live in a fragile world that is totally interdependent. We have to think very carefully about preparing the kind of children that we want to have live in the future.

One of the other points that I would like to introduce is the fact that man, who has always been earthbound and will always be earthbound (due to the fact that he has got to lie down or stand or sit on a solid piece of space), now shares an atmosphere, which cannot be bounded, which cannot be staked out, which cannot be defended in war and which is completely shared around the earth; and that what we want to do is to build cities and towns in which that shared sky (the important thing is not the sky that you see through your window; but somehow we have got to get the notion of shared sky) must be protected for everyone or it cannot be protected for anyone. In the past, men have had to fight each other for space, (I say have had to fight because, in one shape or another, that is what it has been, even though they managed to be peaceful for long periods) because if that is your town it cannot be my town and if this is my field of potatoes it cannot be your field of potatoes. So we have had a conflict between local loyalty and love of country; and love of kin and world citizenship and world loyalties. This is disappearing as we realize that we share the atmosphere and the oceans, and that these cannot be defended in the same way. We need to build cities with the kind of open space and the kind of shared space that will give the future citizens of this planet a sense of this shared atmosphere, which cannot be divided by boundaries.

1973b

PROSPECTS FOR WORLD HARMONY*

Editor's Commentary

> This example of anthropological wisdom and visioning is excerpted from Mead's Jawaharlal Nehru Memorial Lecture, which she delivered in New Delhi on November 13, 1973.

*   *   *

Anthropology is the science of mankind. Our students learn to think about human beings living in whole communities by doing their field work in small, isolated communities, far from the influences of the modern world. But having learned to think holistically, we then are turning to think about the greater community of mankind, including womenkind.

As we have come to know the whole of the planetary community, to know that all human beings are members of one species, and that all human groups can learn what any human group has developed, or consciously invented, so anthropology can provide an integrating element in the coming synthesis of science and philosophy, of the arts and humanities.

Although the great thinkers of mankind have realised that we should think of mankind as one, we have only explored this planet, and found and known those who lived in the most remote jungles and mountain fastnesses since world war II as scientists rather than as philosophers.

And it is only since we have been able to see the earth from the moon, that we have fully appreciated how small, how lonely, how vulnerable our earth is.

Planetary Community

But, at the same time, the exploration of outer space has given us a new understanding of the atmosphere which surrounds and protects

* *Indian and Foreign Review* (December 1973): 20-21.

life on earth, and has given us a new region to share, in which there are no frontiers, no boundaries, no ways of barricaded one part off from another. Where oceans and mountain ranges and rivers have separated the peoples of the earth and taught them to range themselves against each other, each defending their own territory, the graves of their ancestors and the future of their children—the atmosphere is the air we all breathe together.

If it should become poisoned by the acts of any nation, all will suffer in the end alike as toxic substances destroy our protective cloud cover and life perishes on earth. So a knowledge of our planetary community gives us more than a knowledge of who we are; it gives us a new medium within which to work out new forms of interdependence. Warfare is a human invention, based on human beings ability to conceptualize those whom we have never seen, as more or less human than ourselves, as prey or predator, or as fully our fellow citizens, our brothers and sisters, our valued neighbours.

We can now go a step further than the imagination which makes it possible to think of everyone in India, in the United States, in the commonwealth, in the USSR or in the people's republic of China—as fellow citizens—and all of these are great feats of the imagination!— and begin to think of all human beings on this planet as those whose fate and future are inextricably bound up with our own.

This is an aspiration—an aspiration which can become a genuine practical possibility because of the means of modern communication which make it possible to send news around the world faster than a messenger could once cross a city. India's decision to give all her people access to television is an example of the way in which the new methods of communication can give isolated and rural people a share in the developing world community.

New Political Forms

But while our shared communications, our airlines, our television satellites, our earth watches and weather watches, bind us together with new technological cords, it is ever more important that we should devise new political forms that will make it possible to live in harmony, conserving the scarce and irreplaceable resources of the planet and lowering the stress which the production of energy puts upon our waters, our earth, our atmosphere. To build a harmonious world, we will need to draw on the distinctive genius of every people and particularly upon the genius of the great societies which have already found philosophical views and social conventions that have permitted previously hostile peoples to combine into one.

Each great society has done this differently by federation, by centralization, by decentralization, by religions that incorporated differences into one common siblinghood, by process of emigration and immigration, occupational differentiation or egalitarian similarity of training, aristocratic, oligarchic, democratic, socialistic, communistic political devices.

Each system, and each period in ancient societies like those of Asia has make its contribution to the wisdom of mankind on which we can draw for the new inventions that are needed. For each of the ancient and modern systems of society, within which we live an unquiet but hopeful life today, is a partible system. Each of these systems was born in a special environment, at special time in history, and each assumed that the members of other societies who followed other systems were enemies, to be converted, overcome or in some case annihilated.

We do not yet have an political system, nor any religion that has proved fully capable of providing a base for all the people of this planet to live together without destroying each other or the earth on which they live.

Respect For Others

I am going to suggest some of the steps that we may take, steps which come from having studied many very small societies in great detail, and from having tried to relate what I learned to the needs of the USA, my own country, and to an understanding of other countries.

I believe that we need to view every culture, the complete way of life of every society, as representing some but not all human capacities. Even if we aggregate all the great cultural achievements of every society, we can expect that there are many human capacities which have been left untapped, for all the ages that human beings have lived on earth.

But just as every great civilization has grown from contacts between many smaller and older societies, so if we consciously seek to learn from every existing society, we may expect new cultural forms to emerge, suitable to the newly understood world in which we live, suitable to the new inventions which science-based technology has given us, suitable to our new vision of planetary humanity.

But this can only happen if no existing society tries to overwhelm others with its own distinctive style, and if each is willing to respect the other. This respect must include different kinds of perception, so that societies are no longer seen as just bigger or smaller, richer or poorer, younger or older, but instead as complementary to each other in their potentialities and their achievements in the promises inherent in their past and their future.

Here, we may look to India for many insights in the way in which complementarity and difference in skill and occupation have been woven together. The more complex a society, the more each member incorporates not only the part that he or she represents, but also the roles and life styles which he or she does not follow. We must, in the future, learn to so incorporate in each human being's mind, valuable qualities of those whom one is not, as men and women incorporate a knowledge of their complementary roles.

But if this incorporation contains ideas of hierarchy, of mutual contempt or devaluation, then it cannot serve as a world model. Nor can the single ladder type of egalitarian education which has been spreading over the world as a Euro-American pattern—valuable as it has been in becoming the basis for universal literacy—be a complete model. And among the great religions, there have been emphases, on past life, on present life, on future life and each has carried great meaning.

Not Much Time

No one social system has been able to encompass all the needs of the world, a world in which we did not in fact yet share a common fate. In the past if a whole continent had been destroyed, the people of the other continents would have survived to carry on the development of human civilization. Today this is not so. Our shared atmosphere, so fragile, so subject to pollution and contamination, this air we breathe together, gives us a new realm in which to develop far beyond our development so ar. And I who have seen those who lived two generations ago, as preliterate, technologically very primitive and isolated people, now come into the modern world, bringing their distinctive qualities with them, have great faith that we can do this.

There is not much time. The atmosphere we breathe is in danger, our planet reels beneath the blows our unthinking use of technology has given it, there are not enough strong adults to care for the millions of infants who now survive where they would once have died; the danger of annihilating war is not yet met.

But just because the situation is so urgent, just because so many millions are so hungry, just because a pall of warning smog hangs over the great industrial cities, just because it is so urgent to find solutions we may hope that we may be impelled to find them.

If there were more time, we might do nothing. Because time is running out, because we fear for our children and yet hope for all they could become, we have the impetus to find new solutions. In these new solutions each culture can play, must play, if we are to have one world, a special and unique part.

1974a

OPENING ADDRESS [TO THE SOCIETY FOR GENERAL SYSTEMS RESEARCH]*

Editor's Commentary

In this selection, Margaret Mead is addressing a European conference of the Society for General Systems Research, later known as the International Society for the Systems Sciences.[1] She had been among the founders of this organization some twenty years earlier, in partnership with such scholars as Gregory Bateson, Ludwig von Bertalanffy, Kenneth Boulding, Ralph Gerard, Warren McCulloch, John von Neumann, Anatol Rapaport, and Norbert Wiener. Other scholars who have subsequently played prominent roles in the society include Bela Banathy, Stafford Beer, Peter Corning, Heinz von Foerster, Ervin Laszlo, Harold A. Linstone, James Grier Miller, Harold Odum and Ilya Prigogine.

The date of this speech is 1972, two years before Mead became the Society's president. Today, after roughly five decades, she remains the only woman, and the only anthropologist, to have been so honored.

In this address Mead speaks informally, in slightly hyperbolic fashion, about where she wants this interdisciplinary field to go, and how it might contribute to the resolution of anticipated global crises. In the process, she also makes clear how natural it was for her to transit from the holistic study of small isolated non-literate sociocultural groups, to the holistic—and systemic—study of complex and global organizations.

* * *

My reasons for being here and speaking on this platform are twofold. [The first is that] I have spent most of my life studying very small isolated communities, which provide very good models for thinking about whole systems; they are small enough so that one can encompass them and it is impossible to discuss them without discussing every aspect.

---

* In: Advances in Cybernetics and Systems Research: Proceedings of the European Meeting, ed. F. de P. Hanika et al. (London: Transcripta Books, 1974), 1-4.

If you try to study a small primitive community but forget where the fish come from, or forget the state of the soil, or forget the number of people, or forget the age constitution of the group, or forget their nutritional status, or forget their beliefs and practices, you don't end up with anything; you end up with a very unsatisfactory partial statement again.

Furthermore, people who have been working with small groups have gradually been expanding their recognition of the size of the system that has to be taken into account. Thus, if one looks at the anthropological work of fifty years ago, the unit was the tribe, and then for quite a while, because anthropologists went into what they called micro-study, it was the village; then they began to move outward again, especially as these very isolated peoples became part of the world system of trade, political interaction and communication. Today, there are virtually no isolated groups.

Recently, Americans have gotten very excited, because a tribe was found in the Philippines that had been out of contact for a very long time. I think the tremendous excitement at finding a tribe with whom nobody had spoken recently (maybe for the last 300 or 400 years or something like that) was part of the recognition that the world had become one system. As anthropologists, we have gone through the full process, of first studying small, isolated groups and then considering in what ways we cannot consider them as isolated and now, watching them being drawn into a planetary system.

That is one of the reasons for my being here. The other is that I was part of the original group (with Norbert Wiener, Warren McCulloch, John von Neunann and Gregory Bateson), who did the first thinking about cybernetics as a cross-disciplinary *language,* which is what we meant it to be in those days. We meant it to be a model, which would unite people from every discipline, from physics to sociology, within a set of dimensions that could provide for common communications. We picked it, also, because it was a model, which we were beginning to realize to be important as we moved from linear thinking to circular thinking, and also because the mathematics with which we could begin to think were already developed.

I was later present at the time of birth (and I think that is what it should be called) of the Society for Research for General Systems in the United States. I proposed at the time that we do a little general systems thinking about ourselves, and before we formed the society, we take everything we knew—which was not much—that had come out of cybernetics, and all we knew about the properties of systems and boundaries and things of that sort, and apply them to the society.

And they only laughed and said: "You mean, that we should think about ourselves?" And nobody has, as far as I know, since.

The only organizational point I would like to make today, when people are here from various societies and different countries and different groups and institutes and associations, is that we had better do some thinking about ourselves. Organized science has a very definite relationship to the forms in which it expresses itself.

The existing organizational forms for the development of a general systems theory or cybernetic theory reflect inchoateness by the way in which ideas of systems have spread into all sorts of places, having done so simply because some individual got interested. But extreme national and ideological boundaries impede, at present, the inclusion of research from different parts of the world.

I am not going to discuss this further, but, having this opportunity of speaking to a European audience, I want to say that this is something that we should think about. Nor should we have journals that just imitate something that the Royal Society of Great Britain invented many years ago. I am not sure we should have journals. I am not sure in what form we should communicate with each other. I am pretty sure it should not be tapes, because they take too long, but some form of coded tape might be more suitable than linear print when we are trying to think about something that is non-linear. I believe that unless all the people that enliven and stimulate this kind of thinking in different countries begin to think about the relationship of the form of organization of human beings to this form of thinking, the thinking itself won't get very far. It seems to me to be one of the first lessons of general systems theory that you have to deal with isomorphisms at different levels.

I had hoped, about ten years ago (and then advanced very briefly the idea) that we might be able to cross ideological boundaries which are on the whole, at present, the most important communications boundaries in the world. We might be able to cross them by using cybernetics as a language, as value-free as physics, for physicists can meet and discuss a problem in physics, irrespective of the nations they belong to, or the military positions relating to their ideological disagreement, as they exist at the time.

We did discover, I think it was at the Atoms For Peace meeting in Geneva, that physicists did a better job communicating across ideological boundaries, simply because of their command of a superior language in which they could work without having to use words. All this was useful, of course, when the participants did not know each other's languages, but it was also useful inasmuch as, by avoiding the use of everyday language, one does not introduce ideological loadings into the situation.

I remember years ago we had an international conference in the field of mental health, and the cost of interpreters was the highest cost. An international group of biochemists were meeting right after us and we wrote to them and asked them to share the cost of interpreters. And they said: "What interpreters?" They were just going to write formulae on the board; they did not need any interpreters at all.

I advanced the idea of using cybernetics in this way after an informal US-USSR conference in 1961, but soon after, some militarily sponsored organizations in the United States started to study cybernetics as used in Eastern Europe, and very rapidly the position of cybernetics was transformed into an ideologically compromised method. And I think this is the most important thing I want to say: There is not, as far as I know, any difference between cybernetic thinking in the Soviet Union and cybernetic thinking in the United States, when it is done rigorously. Certainly Norbert Wiener had no difficulty communicating with people in the Soviet Union, and he was an enormous stimulant to the growth of cybernetic interest there.

But, you can transform something from the outside. You can give it a label, or coding, and change its position. And so, instead of being a possible form of cross-ideological communication, in the early 1960's cybernetics again became a kind of ideological barrier. It was then that I became convinced, when considering the possibility of *cross-ideological communication*, that it would not work unless there was also a shared goal—that it was no use merely to have a *language* that could be used.

I still think that general systems could be THE language with which we could talk between different, advanced ideological systems, and between more and less technologically advanced political systems in the world. If we could teach now a sound general systems approach in the universities of the emerging countries in Africa and in the universities in Asia now undergoing a process of transformation, this would provide a basis for communication among people moving from one place to another. So people from Nigeria or Thailand could come and participate, as you ask their physicists to come and participate in an ordinary scientific discussion with other physicists. But the range would be much wider, and it would be possible to include social and political problems for which we have no vocabulary at present, nor a set of symbols everybody agrees on, and, therefore, no way of communicating at all.

But you still have to have some reason, some goal, some common framework to set this up. But suppose everybody did agree to teach something about general systems, say, that one must look and see what size the system is that one is thinking about, or something on one's choice of units, or the choice of boundaries for every single thing you study whatever the circumstances, whether it is political change or the introduction of Miracle Rice or Miracle Wheat. If only we could introduce this idea and have it as much a form of common education as arithmetic is now around the world! They all learn something about arithmetic. I have seen people from a society where they can only count to twenty, once exposed to ordinary Western schooling, grow into individuals able to graduate from university.

I think there are reasons why it is possible to go from a society in which you can count only to twenty to be able to learn mathematics in one generation; because we are working in a type of system in which the human brain is capable of adapting, if there are not too many prejudices in between. But everything we say about economics or political science or sociology or anthropology is nationally or culturally loaded, so that communications are almost impossible; what we get are beautiful representations of national style. And you can study France just as well by studying Levi-Strauss as by studying French villages; you find the same properties. So, provided we could introduce general systems, I think we would have a new way of looking at any phenomenon of any size whatsoever.

Now the need for a systems approval applies, of course, in medicine just as much as it applies in wider fields like urban planning. In the United States we went through a long period when we had isolated organs in the body so completely that in the hospital, doctors referred to "That Liver in bed fifteen." Then we spent fifteen years getting the livers back into the bodies, and we spent another ten years getting the body back into the family. And, we have just about got the family back into the community. Now, we are struggling to get them into the world, because the repercussions of a style of health care developed in one place can be disastrous when applied uncritically to another country.

I think everybody here would agree that you are going to think in general systems terms. This is a form of thought and has methods of representation. They are woolly, and everyone draws their own diagrams, with a few arrows and a few black spots and a few bits and pieces that make them look like something, but we *are* arguing with something that we have in common, something that could be developed into a cross-cultural, cross-national, cross-ideological, cross-special-interest language, in which you could explain to any one part of the community what you are talking about. But if we are to do this—I am now speaking as a social scientist looking at the world—I think that we have to have some shared goal, within which this type of communication can take place.

It looked as if the survival of man in the late 1950's and early 1960's in the face of nuclear threat might have been a sort of goal. It turned out not to be, and today this issue is, I think, virtually inoperative in many parts of the world, because people decided that the major powers may not throw bombs at each other, and if they try they will activate the hot line and stop it before it involves the whole world. A very large proportion of the world no longer feels concern or worries about nuclear catastrophe; the issue has settled down to a duel between major states, and interest in targets, which has taken away from us any fear of the world not surviving a contest between the superstates.

So, that opportunity was missed. Then came the environmental crisis and the recognition that we are seriously stressing and endangering the environment of this planet, and may be stressing it to a point it will not stand—with varying doomsday predictions ranging from 15 to 75 years from now. But I do not think that anybody who is studying this problem—and I do not mean people who are reading Jay Forrester; they are just reading Jay Forrester and having a panic—but those who are really studying the problem, can fail to see the danger of the greenhouse effect, or of the DDT and PCB that recent studies have found in the deepest point in the mid-Atlantic, beyond doubt having been carried there by air. These things point to a major danger and are intimately related both to what we understand a general systems theory to be, and to a goal that can actually be shared by any people anywhere on this planet.

At present the Stockholm United Nations conference on the Human Environment is being pulled in every kind of direction, due to the fear of the emerging nations that the industrialized nations will use ecological considerations as a reason for slowing down help, or because of a belief that ecology is only something for the industrialized nations to care about. So they say: "Give us 1% of your gross national pollution and we shall be very happy." In fact, however, we should be able to communicate to them that within fifty years from now, the point as to who started the pollution, or who felt it first, or who had a nice standard of living while they were doing it, will be relatively unimportant, as there will be nobody to listen to incriminations of this kind. This deprives them of importance.

So we now have actually a shared problem which is planetary and does involve a system, since one can certainly speak of this planet and then of its relation to the solar system, with certain elements of a closed system, and of the relations within the two.

EDITOR'S NOTE

1. The objectives stated in the original by-laws of the Society were:

    – "to investigate the analogy of concepts, laws and models from various fields, and to help in useful transfers from one field to another;
    – to encourage the development of adequate theoretical models in fields which lack them;
    – to minimize the duplication of theoretical efforts in different fields;
    – to promote the unity of science through improving communication among specialists."

    The current website of the ISSS defines the organization as:

    a broadly based professional society of scientists, philosophers, educators, futurists, humanists, business and policy practitioners, artists, writers, and many other professionals from diverse endeavors, who are drawn together by a common interest: understanding and interacting systemically with reality. Our basic approach is both scientific and philosophical in the broadest and most evolutionary sense of the scientific enterprise. Science and humanities are evolving new paradigms, most notably a systemic view, and ISSS is at the forefront of that evolution.

1974b

CHANGING PERSPECTIVES ON MODERNIZATION*

Editor's Commentary

This item is an edited transcription of an "opening paper" that Mead delivered to a symposium on modernization conducted at the University of Rhode Island. In it she summarizes much that had been learned by anthropologists and others about the phenomenon of planned modernization. She focuses on the three decades following World War II—a period of unprecedented attention to the systematic promotion of modernization and development in what had become known as the "Third World." She examines both positive and negative impacts of organized programs sponsored by governments and non-governmental organizations in the heavily industrialized nations, to bring to economically less developed nations what the former defined as progress. During these three decades numerous approaches were tried, only to be found wanting. Mead does not hesitate to criticize, and spares no academic discipline, including her own.

Although lacking in quantitative analysis, the paper presents an otherwise useful summary of accumulated anthropological wisdom of a type often absent in the works presented by economics, technologists, diplomats, lawyers, and others who plan and administer development programs.

The editors of the volume in which this article first appeared, Poggie and Lynch, introduce Mead as follows:

> … Dr. Mead's career as an anthropologist spans nearly a half-century and gives her a unique vantage point from which she describes changing thinking concerning social and cultural change. Probably no other living anthropologist has had comparable firsthand experience with modernization …

* * *

In considering modernization I think it would be useful to emphasize what it is that we can learn at this unique period in history. If we do not take advantage of this opportunity we will never again be able to

* In: *Rethinking Modernization*: *Anthropological Perspectives*, ed. John J. Poggie, Jr., and Robert N. Lynch (Westport Conn.: Greenwood Press, 1974), 21-36.

learn about ourselves in the same way. Spread out in front of us and accessible to use at this moment is every stage of technological development. We also have today almost all the varieties of culture contact that have ever existed and all their different forms. These range from individualized culture contact situations such as the single ambassador from a developed country to a less developed country, to a missionary, modernizing government official, or emissary of a particular industry, and to the massive sorts of contact that have gone on since World War II.

The one case of massive culture contact that I studied involved the Manus of the Admiralty Islands in Papua New Guinea. Some 20,000 people with twenty different languages had box seats watching two million Americans go through their small archipelago and were exposed to the whole paraphernalia of a modern technology. They hung from the top of the operating room watching operations; on ships they were up on the bridge with the captain; they were down in the engine room; and they had a type of instantaneous access to complex technology, which nobody with a simple level of life has ever had before. In New Guinea the contacts since the war have been even more striking. We have had instances of people coming through three different groups of interpreters—three language mediations—before they could talk to an outpost of the Trust Territory government. Some of these people arrived stark naked, because as yet they had had no means of getting clothes; they had washed the pig fat out of their hair and were perfectly prepared to put on full European dress at once. They knew that the Europeans (Europeans are what we call Australians in New Guinea) do not like pig fat. They also said that they had decided they would like a school and a hospital. They had already built the buildings and asked if the government would please send them the necessary officials tomorrow morning. Crossing boundaries of thousands and thousands of years within two or three days' walk has never happened before because there has never been the complexity of technology that we have reached today, accessible to people at very simple technological levels. We also have an opportunity to compare these transformations with the effects of sixteenth and seventeenth century European exploration and colonization.

I recall, just a few years after World War II, a time when Arthur Raper was talking about some small spot in the Middle East, and he said that nothing had happened there since "the Romans had a Point Four program." As I reviewed the set of papers that have been assembled here, I became acutely aware of the difference in the processes of modernization that have accompanied different levels of technology in different periods in history. We will be organizing our discussions around the concept of modernization. What we actually mean by modernization today is a post World War II phenomenon. We are dealing with an order of diffusion that has never occurred before. One of our tasks here is to sketch in the dimensions of how the phenomenon we know as contemporary modernization, differs from social and cultural change in the past. We now have worldwide information systems, and we must recognize that today's very rapid purposeful diffusion has different results as compared with the effects of earlier diffusion.

When some people talk about modernization they place particular emphasis on how large societies transform small ones, an approach which still expresses a good deal of the climate of pre-World War II opinion. At that time anthropologists and sociologists, on the whole, felt that most of this transformation was alien and imperialistic and negative, that the small societies were being transformed against their will by the great societies. It also represents the present wave of feeling that we find among contemporary students who are again asking the kind of questions that were asked in the 1920s. "What right do we have to go and transform these people who are living this beautiful life?" All these questions are coming up again.

For example, we have the question of the right of the Eskimo to live in a technologically archaic fashion requiring an incredibly large land area to nourish each individual, being counterposed against the desire of people who want to put a pipeline through parts of Alaska. The present climate of opinion coincides with a worldwide technological and communication expansion that brings what happens in these small societies into quite a different juxtaposition with national and international affairs. I think if—even in the early 1940s—anybody had suggested the possibility of national decision makers having to seriously consider the rights of small societies they would have been considered naive. Yet today, we are considering the right of the Eskimos in Alaska to hunt as they have hunted for thousands of years, a right to be protected from any of the advances of civilization except the ones they happen to want. These rights are being weighed against the claims by the power companies who must fulfill the energy needs of millions of people.

A second example is the discussion in the Southwest about strip mining on Navajo land to feed a power plant producing power by archaic methods that happen to be cheap at the moment. It has been possible to persuade some of the Navajos that the employment the power plant and strip mining have brought into the area is worthwhile because the amount of local pollution is reasonably slight. The power that is being produced is being sent to southern California where the pollution laws would not permit anybody to build a power plant of the same sort. I think these two cases dramatize the new relationships between the environment, our concern for the environment, the growing demand for power, particularly in the modern world, and the ethical questions that are being discussed at the present moment.

ANTHROPOLOGICAL ATTITUDES TOWARD PURPOSEFUL CHANGE IN HISTORICAL PERSPECTIVE

It is useful to go back and look at the history of anthropologists' attitudes towards purposeful cultural change from just before World War II to the present. It was, so we thought, reasonably clear in the 1930s and early 1940s that the thing that anthropologists should do was to protect backward societies or isolated peoples from too rapid change. We thought slow change was better than fast change, that less change was better than more change, that it was a pity to disturb the life of isolated peoples who were reasonably balanced in relationship to the territory they had and the technology they were using. We thought it was a pity that this balance should be altered by the inroads of larger systems, parts of which were incompatible with these small systems.

The American Ethnological Society had its 75th anniversary in the early 1940s; this was before the [atomic] bomb, before we had explored the world completely, before we had really begun to relate ourselves to outer space. However, we were thinking about the possibility of an international organization to succeed the League of Nations and people were already talking about the possibilities that later led to the formation of the United Nations. It was clear then that this would lead inevitably to some discussion of the fate of the small societies in the world. I read a paper (Mead, 1943) at that meeting in which I proposed that we treat the small island societies in the Pacific as laboratories for the training of international civil servants; that we face straightforwardly the fact that somebody was going to insist on some kind of relationship to all the small islands, including the islanders themselves, who are usually left out of most of these discussions.

There were no inhabitants of small Pacific islands who did not want some of the things from civilization once they had seen them. Any belief that they liked lighting the house by candle nuts and dressing in bark cloth was rubbish. I have never seen a group of people who want to dress in bark cloth once they have had cloth. Bark cloth is a very inferior form of material, except for its value to tourists. I suggested there would be certain things that they would want—for exam-

ple, some medicine, some means of lighting, and a few other things—
and, given the power situation in the world, every square mile of territory in the Pacific would eventually be of interest to some political
power. There was no way in which you could put the islands of the
Pacific outside the spheres of competitive political influence. This was
before we knew about space travel and before we realized that our present Trust Territory in Micronesia is some of the most valuable real
estate in the world. There is just a little land above the surface; you
look at the ocean and you see just little spots of islands. Yet this is one
of the best takeoff places in the world for anyone serious about traveling in outer space. This possibility has enormously transformed the
meaning of these little islands from pre-war times, when they were primarily refueling and air bases for possible military operations. Therefore, given the fact that small islands were going to be politically
important to somebody, some disposition was going to have to be
made of them. This is something that I believe we are still not facing.

It is impossible for any group of people to be living at any level
in any way without affecting the rest of the world today. If we decide
to let every Eskimo have a large number of square miles in which to
hunt with a harpoon, this immediately affects decisions made all over
the world; it might even affect international oil concordats and the
kind of power plant Consolidated Edison builds in New York. Clearly,
the fate of each small primitive people has become inextricably intertwined with what is going on in other places.

What I said in 1942 and 1943, therefore, was that some great
power or group of great powers is going to have to nominally preside
over these islands. If we turn them into trust territories, for instance,
let us turn them into laboratories for training international civil servants. We could require anyone who was going to work in the international field under the proposed new international organization to
function as the chief emissary of the outside world on these islands,
and do what the people want. If the people wanted to move fast, he
could help them move fast; and if they wanted to resist outside influences, he could help them do so. However, he would have to work
with them over a period of time and find out what it was like to live
in a totally different culture.

From the back of the room an anthropologist, who at that
moment was clearly associated with communism, stood up and said
that this was an outrage; this was a denial of the full right of the peoples of the Pacific to share in modern technology and in all its results,
and he felt that they had a perfect right to modern plumbing! If my
critic hadn't mentioned plumbing, I am not sure I would have
grasped the whole position, for anybody who has ever been on a

Pacific island knows that what they do not need is a bathtub; they have the whole Pacific Ocean to bathe in every day. It was a dramatization (remember this comment came from an anthropologist and a very well educated one) that very graphically illustrated the climate of opinion that was developing in the world regarding the rights and privileges of small societies in relation to technology. People who lived on an island two miles by three lapped by the Pacific Ocean were nevertheless going to have bathtubs!

TECHNOLOGICAL MODERNIZATION IN ONE GENERATION

I saw the writing on the wall clearly enough at that meeting. I went away feeling that we were going to hear technological modernization advocated for every country in the world in one generation. This, I said, was what was going to be the climate of opinion in the postwar period, and indeed it was (Mead 1956). Consequently I realized we might as well settle down and face it; this was what we were going to be up against. What it amounted to was glorification of modern technology. This is one issue on which the United States and the Soviet Union agreed completely. At that time they both assumed that economic and technological advances were invariably good, unmitigatedly good and that it was romantic to believe anything else. The industrialized nations of the world must make available to everybody else running water, followed by airlines, steel mills and all the rest of it—immediately. The fact that the Soviet Union and the United States were rivals did not change this; it simply meant that people could play one off against the other. We went to underdeveloped countries and told them what to ask for from the Soviet Union, and the Soviet Union sent emissaries telling them what to ask from us. So they asked for a dam from one country and a steel mill from the other.

At this point a lot of people predicted that if it had taken the Soviet Union thirty years to industrialize and it took us one hundred, India could probably manage it in fifteen and China in ten. It is very hard to credit these predictions today, but they were all over the place immediately after World War II. Furthermore, it was claimed that new nations, whether composed of peasant or tribal peoples, would not have to be put through the same agonies that industrialization had meant for the workers in Britain, Western Europe, the United States and the Soviet Union. This would not have to happen because what the developed countries had taken out of the hides of their workers was now in the form of capital, which could be nicely transferred to all the other countries, and they could have the benefits without any of the agonies. We were going to export the technological advantages of modernization to all parts of the world.

EVOLUTIONARY STAGES OF MODERNIZATION

There were also a variety of discussions as to whether every country had to go through the same evolutionary stages. We heard a lot about cultural evolution, whereby a developing country might undergo relatively rapid changes that have taken thousands of years in other places and not follow the same sequence of stages. For example, if you go into a country where it is very hard to build roads and even harder to build railroads, you do not build roads and you do not build railroads, you just build airports. And you turn your transport immediately into airplane transport and skip the intermediate stages of railroads, roads for trucks, and all the rest of it.

This type of development depends again on ideology. The Soviet Union firmly believes in its own scheme of evolution, and its own scheme of evolution contains a large amount of mythology just as ours does. They believe that there was once a lovely primitive form of communism, when things were collective and the sexes were equal (This is being invoked by Women's Liberation today as another piece of mythology). Then the dreadful institution of private property and patriarchal kinship were invented, and we had the whole growth of this evil capitalist society. In reaction to capitalist society, socialism goes back to more collective goals. In dealing with really primitive people, like some of the Siberian tribes, the Soviets have systematically yanked them out of any collective generosity they had had, and put them into the nastiest form of private property that they could think up so they could get over it and move to a collective system. (Films of these policies in Siberia were available in the 1920s but these aspects of Soviet policy are still imperfectly documented.) Now this is the grossest form of ideological evolutionism, the belief that there is an inevitable course of social evolution, and you can only get the right kind of societal collectivity if you first have the wrong kind of capitalism; you could not possibly get there by any other route.

We ourselves do not recognize that we also have an ideology, because it is so technological rather than articulately political. I remember once years ago Kurt Levine saying very worriedly as a German who had come to this country, "Why do Americans have no *Weltschmerz?*" I answered, "Because we have no *Weltanschauung*. " Now today we are overdosed with *Weltanschauung,* and we have a lot

of *Weltschmerz*. However, as of the 1940s and early 1950s we did not
have any *Weltanschauung* or any *Weltschmerz* either. We just had the
Eisenhower era, and the ideology of this period was that technology
was good for everybody and the more advanced technology you had,
the better. However, we suffered from another form of technological
mythology in also believing that tribal and peasant people had better
go through the earlier stages that we had gone through. Under this
heading, you sell them your old school bus, you send them your outdated sewing machines, and you give them the lowest possible level
of your existing technology, so that they can go through the simple
stages that we went through. We have sent a tremendous amount of
our outmoded technology to other peoples—more consumer technology than production technology—so they can learn and make all
the mistakes that we did.

The general assumption was and still is that it would be good for
other people to go through the idiotic convention we endured of
putting an engine in the front of a car because the horse was there;
but the horse was never there for them, so why perpetuate our pieces
of nonsense? Why not design something that fits? There has been a
general unwillingness in the Western industrialized countries that are
"helping" all the rest of the world by exporting their technology to
them to realize that the exportation of technology is occurring in a
new period of history, and a *new* period of technology.

One of the debates that went on in the 1950s was the dispute
over the various kinds of modernization strategies that were used primarily by the western nations. One strategy was offering them the
old technology, saying, "It will take them a long, long time to learn,
and so we had better start them with the simplest possible stuff we
can export. " This involves our obsolete equipment, which we are
eager to sell anyway. Of course, this is what we do with our firearms
all the time now; we send our out-of-date fighter planes and our out-
of-date tanks and our out-of-date guns all over the world fomenting
violence and revolution. We do this as a way of getting rid of outmoded technology, so we can have enough money to build another
gun of a different type.

At the other extreme are the people who said, "Send them the
most advanced technology"—a complete modern steel plant or a
modern textile mill. Then somebody would come back and report
that the equipment was stacked up somew here in the city, that
nobody has ever used it, and that there was nobody who knew how
to use it. Now it is absolutely ridiculous to send this modern technology out where there is nobody to operate it, yet this was the idiotic
thing that we were doing.

There emerged yet another related discussion about how one could evoke from all these peoples with different degrees of relationship to the modern world the kinds of behavior that were appropriate to operating modern equipment such as airplanes. We had a fascinating discussion, I should say in about 1952, at a meeting of the Society for Applied Anthropology in Canada, where an Englishman proposed that the way to make nomads from the Middle East into good pilots was to invent a condensed version of the English public school, cold baths and all. He claimed that the English public school (that is, the English private school) built the right kind of character for this task. You would take tribesmen from somewhere in the Middle East and send them to three months' condensed English public school and thereby give them the right character to operate airlines. This infuriated the Canadians who did not want anything English; so the discussion did not really deal with the issue but with the Canadian rejection of English moralities (I might add in passing that this is about the level that most anthropological discussions reach; we are not as sophisticated about our own culture as we are about other cultures).

No one looking at things in the 1950s was very much concerned with the human aspect of modernization, but merely with the problem of how modern technology was to be introduced everywhere with the least possible damage. Anthropologists, sociologists, and some educators were concerned with reducing the damage, if any, by having as little dislocation as possible. They pondered such problems as what did you do to prevent terrific conflicts between young and old and to minimize disorganization or juvenile delinquency (Mead, 1963a). However, there was very widespread agreement that technology was good, that substituting new forms of power for old forms of power was good and whether you believed you could skip stages or not, you thought it was absolutely necessary to distribute power there. Certain individuals said that countries that have no coal or oil should be sent atomic reactors; they do not take up very much space and an atomic energy plant can quickly be installed.

There were also the suggestions that we could take people with classical educations and let them read gauges. It was very hard to turn them into good mechanics because of their aristocratic intellectual tradition, which forbids the use of one's hands. Thus it was argued that you could take people with a classical Burmese education or an Indian education or a Greek education and turn them into people who could function in an atomic plant even though you could not get them to mend an automobile or a truck. This was another way in which we could short cut stages of development and take advantage at another level of what was already available.

THE GROWING RECOGNITION OF PROBLEMS

By the early 1960s we were beginning to recognize a series of difficulties. We were beginning to analyze the relationships among the developed countries and the underdeveloped countries, and at that point "underdeveloped" became a pejorative term and was changed to the "developing countries." In 1963 the United Nations had a conference on scientific and technological aid to the emerging nations (Mead, 1963b). The general belief still held that technology was completely good and the main problem was discovering the means to export it to the less industrialized countries. Related to this was the concern with raising enough working capital while at the same time arranging for the competing major powers to cooperate in getting them what they needed.

At about this time alert people were beginning to say that we were not going to be able to export our modernized technology to everybody in the world, and not everyone would benefit from it. Instead, the gap between the poor countries and the rich countries was going to increase (Theobold, 1962). At that point the dichotomy between the rich and the poor countries was invented, an idea which is spiritually appealing but very inaccurate because the countries of the world are actually on a continuum (Mead, 1967). The idea was given currency that it was the rich versus the poor; the poor countries were going to get poorer and poorer and poorer and the rich were going to get richer and richer and richer. Furthermore, there was not going to be any way to prevent this, because the poor countries were the ones that were producing raw materials.

We must realize that modernization in Africa or New Guinea or parts of South America was thought to depend upon getting people to grow crops that are commercially valuable in the world's markets. So, you have coffee grown in the mountains of New Guinea or you have schemes to have people grow rubber. These schemes involved taking peoples who had lived on subsistence agriculture and giving them a commercially valuable crop. The crop itself had to be sold in the world market and was absolutely dependent on the state of the market. Analysts like Robert Theobold (1962) pointed out that the minute rubber or coffee or cotton or wool was grown in a way that gave a decent wage to the people who grew it, the developed countries would merely produce it synthetically, and would stop buying their cotton, wool, or rubber. Anthropologists who have studied particular small countries are very conscious of what happens if you take a tribe and start growing coffee, for instance, and the bottom falls out of the coffee market. Anybody who has ever worked in the

Caribbean has seen this happen over and over again. One little island starts selling something, and if it works, every other Caribbean island starts selling it and the market price falls. Everybody is disappointed and disgruntled and miserable and the impetus toward change, which may have been quite genuine at the start, is depressed and destroyed.

"The Green Revolution"

The economists who had been promoting large-scale industrialization realized that this emphasis had resulted in the depopulation of the countrysides in favor of the cities. They began to comprehend that this incredible increase in urbanization was very, very dangerous and that something ought to be done about agriculture, which they had been virtually ignoring in their concentration on industry.

There followed a brief period of great excitement, the Green Revolution, in which everything was going to be solved by miracle rice and miracle wheat. These crops are, without a doubt, miracles of modern technology. In the International Rice Institute in the Philippines they have collected all the forms of rice that have ever been grown anywhere in the world, grown them in experimental seedbeds, and analyzed them genetically. From this they can now produce a seed with a given growing time, a given kind of grain, and a given height of stalk that will resist disease and weather. They can prescribe a grain which will be absolutely appropriate to an area and give a tenfold increase in yield; what we had done in agriculture before tended to give only a ten percent improvement. People are going to worry about their own prejudices, their own social organization, their religious beliefs, and their caste behavior rather than a ten percent improved growth; but nobody is going to oppose a tenfold increase. This has a kind of technological massiveness that simply overwhelms all the reservations that many of us have talked about.

In 1968 there were still people in the Philippines who talked mainly about food habits and the fact that people preferred one kind of rice to another. However, the Philippines were importing rice from everywhere in the world at that time because there was a shortage and they were eating *any* kind of rice. The possibility of a tenfold increase in yield here produced a new wave of optimism. Instead of having rural people rushing into the cities and becoming a burden, we were now going to have a kind of agriculture that would support people in the country for several generations while they got *ready* to absorb all the wonderful new technology.

THE ENVIRONMENTAL CRISIS

What followed was the real recognition of what was happening to the environment and the environmental crisis. When this was heralded by Rachel Carson's *Silent Spring* (1962), the technological and scientific establishment did its best to discredit it and to discredit her. Gradually the terrible damage to the environment began to become visible. We began to realize that we were facing a worldwide ecological crisis, that we did not have inexhaustible supplies of the atmosphere, oceans, and rivers. We found that without recognizing it, we had crossed a line between the old types of technology and the kind of greater food supply and greater amenities and greater possibilities that were the givens in a new era in which we were endangering all the life support systems of the entire planet. Almost overnight the image of technology changed in the minds of a lot of the general public and particularly of students, from being a beneficial thing that was going to bring all peoples into a fuller and better life, into a demon.

We have had, of course, a great many other manifestations of this new kind of "demonology," but it has changed the whole conceptualization of what modernization means. Instead of hailing the Green Revolution we are now recognizing that when we export these beautiful new grains we are exporting with them pesticides and fertilizers and, therefore, exporting pollution. We cannot depend on the Green Revolution after all.

There are additional hazards, although they are somewhat overemphasized. For example, if an entire country plants one kind of seed, a pest could wipe out the whole of that crop. The safety that resides in diversity, in the very diversity provided by small societies, has been analyzed recently in a critique of the attempts to introduce large-scale agricultural schemes in East Africa (Campbell, 1971). Each little farmer in this area knew that he had a little bit of land that would work when there was a drought, and another little bit of land that would work when there was too much rain, so that virtually each individual or household had some security against the adversity of climatic disorders. When you introduce large-scale mono-agriculture, with one seed, you may be exposing entire segments of a country to famine. If we had the whole world to draw on, and if we had a large enough surplus of food and the ships to transport it, we might be able to care for a region that had such a famine. Unfortunately, we do not have this capability, and consequently the new technology is increasing the potential for famine. We have to look everywhere for the significance of such breaks in natural cycles which are the result of the technology that has been developed since

World War II. Ideas about the pros or cons of technology, such as these new biochemical industrial developments, have to be tempered by these newly realized consequences.

It was 1965 when Robert Theobold introduced into the discussions of the World Council of Churches considerations about what was going to happen between the rich and the poor countries due to our emphasis on synthetic products. It was 1971 when Barry Commoner, in a speech to the United Nations non-governmental groups preparing for the Stockholm Conference on the Environment, pointed out that we may have to go back to natural products. He argued that the cost of using cotton is far less than the pollution cost of the energy expended in producing synthetic substitutes (Commoner, 1971). We are now going to have to look realistically at two sets of factors: (1) the extent to which the materials themselves are non-biodegradable, and (2) the energy costs of producing synthetics. Actually the whole shift from the use of wool, cotton, rubber and other natural products to the production of synthetic substitutes on which technological progress of the developed world is presently being postulated may have to be completely reversed.

It took only five years to make this drastic change in understanding what is happening; of course, this view is as onesided in many ways as was the earlier one. Fear about the new kind of seeds, fear of the results of mono-agriculture, fear of the destruction of species that are essential in the various life support systems, fear that we will exhaust the atmosphere and contaminate the oceans before we manage to reverse this kind of behavior, is now gripping a great many of the planners of the world. Even the smallest groups of primitive people are caught in this. Should the Eskimo go back to his harpoon; and, since we cannot manage New York City, should we glorify the ecological balance that was established by handfuls of Indians without the technological means of destroying the buffalo?

At present one of the things that we are hearing about that is playing a considerable role both in some anthropological discussions and a great deal of student enthusiasm, is that the American Indians were great ecologists. The honest truth is that there were not enough Indians in North America to damage the environment very much. The Indians had a level of technology that did not enable them to kill too many animals. The minute they got guns they went after the buffalo with the same or perhaps greater enthusiasm as other peoples had shown. However, at the time when the American Indians lived in very widely dispersed tribes, they did have a symbolic relationship to the environment, which we are going to have to emulate at a more complex level. The Indian who, after he had eaten a fish, put the bones back in the creek and said, "Little brother, go back and be born again so I can eat you again" was symbolically talking about recycling. That is a perfect mythological, religious, poetic statement of recycling in which man recognizes that he is a part of nature and that his life depends upon recognizing that he is part of nature instead of standing apart from it.

The Significance of Diversification

We are developing a feedback into worldwide theories of change of the experience of small groups in a variety of ways. For instance, the recognition that safety lies in diversification is also being currently expressed in consumer movements under the aegis of Ralph Nader and his associates who warn shoppers, "Use the detergent that is least contaminating, but don't all use the same one. We will give you a list of ten detergents that we think are better than the other thirty and will do less damage, but don't everybody in the neighborhood use the same one because if you do you might produce absolutely unknown results!" The recognition that the minute you have something synthetic you have done something so different to the environment and that magnification and amplification endanger the environment gives a completely new value to diversification, to small cultures, to their particular ways of doing things, and to variety in every part of the world.

Variety has now been given a new standing it did not enjoy before. It is an answer to the people who advocated a unified world order, advocating the disappearance of all these idiosyncratic, odd little tribes and parochialisms in favor of uniformity and efficiency. It used to be hard to argue with those people on behalf of diversity. They said standardization would mean people were going to have more to eat, better medical care, longer lives, lower infant mortality, and all that would be good. Today it is not hard at all, and people are turning to diversification as a strength and as a protection. Before, people felt you either preserve the beautiful local native culture, and that was charming and romantic and unhealthful, or you had mass education, mass medical care, and a decreased infant death rate. This is no longer the argument, and diversification is now becoming a refuge.

This can be also illustrated with the question of a world language (Mead and Modley, 1968). We now realize that the only way we can save the little languages of the world so that they make their contribution to the world is to have a secondary world language that is not a language of a major power. If it is a major language, it will spread at the expense of the small languages spoken by the politically power-less peoples. If, on the other hand, we had a secondary language that was of no political importance, everybody could learn to speak it without political implications and all the little languages could sur-vive for poetry and lullabies and all the diverse contributions that they make.

Now it is within this kind of setting that we will here be dis-cussing what happens today in particular instances and particular cases of modernization. Our discussions will to a degree transcend these major pitfalls in understanding. For example, we will not be talking in terms of introducing change into a society by living in the village for three months to find out who the local leader is. It took a lot of anthropological fieldwork to find out who the local leader was, especially in Asian countries where he hides behind a lot of fronts. We would send people in and they would study who the local leader was and how to get the local leader to get the local people to build three miles of road.

That was the only way people thought you were going to get roads built, until we began realizing that you can have a machine that knocks down the trees and lays down the cement behind it as it goes, and then you do not need any local leaders at all. Then the sort of effort and the sort of democratic behavior that came out of it in look-ing for local leaders suddenly became absolutely irrelevant. Conse-quently we had a period where the daydream of the technological planners was that we were going to bulldoze all roads through the whole of Asia and Africa without worrying about the people at all.

Hence we come into the present period with the realization that we had better pay a great deal of attention to the people and to the local sit-uation, because spreading these standardized techniques all over the world contaminates, pollutes, and endangers the environment.

REFERENCES

Campbell, J. 1971. *Culture as a Variable in Directed Agricultural Change in East Africa,* Ph.D. dissertation, Columbia University.

Carson R. 1962. "Silent Spring", serialized in the *New Yorker*, June.

Commoner, B. 1971. "The Hidden Cost of Economic Growth," *CBNS Notes*, 4:3. (Center for the Biology of Natural Systems). St. Louis: Washington University.

Mead, M. 1943. "The Role of Small South Sea Cultures in the Post-War World," *American Anthropologist*, 45:193-196.

314 MARGARET MEAD

_____. 1956. *New Lives for Old: Cultural Transformation–Manus, 1928-1953*. New York: Mentor.

_____. 1963a. "Patterns of Worldwide Cultural Change in the 1960s," *Social Problems of Development and Urbanization*, 8:1-15. (U.S. Papers Prepared for the U.N. Conference on the Application of Science and Technology for the Benefit of Less Developed Areas). Washington: U.S. Government Printing Office

_____. 1963b. "Geneva: Helping the Less Developed Nations–Lessons from the U.N. Conference," *International Science and Technology*, 16:86-87.

_____. 1967. "The Rights of Primitive People: Papua-New Guinea: A Crucial Instance," *Foreign Affairs*, 45:304-308.

_____, and R. Modley. 1968. "Communication Among All People Everywhere," *Natural History*, 77(7):56-63.

Theobold, R. 1962. *Profit Potential in the Developing Countries*. New York: American Management Association.

1974c

WAYS TO DEAL WITH THE CURRENT SOCIAL TRANSFORMATION*

Editor's Commentary

In this article Mead addresses the international community of futurists in the official publication of the World Future Society, which had been established seven years earlier at the dawn of the present Futures Studies movement.

Although Mead does not here explicitly identify herself as a futurist, it is clear that she is at home with, and sympathetic to, futurist ways of looking at the world.

Of particular interest is the sidebar, which seems implicitly to chide futurists (or people she so defines) for having not been "responsible about the next decade, the next quarter century, the next fifty years ...".

* * *

I want to talk about a few of the possible strategies that we can use in the coming few years to enhance our ability to deal with the fact that we know something is happening.

Now I don't think we have any idea how peculiar that is. You know, we say, "This transformation is comparable to the Copernican Revolution," but at the time we were having the Copernican Revolution, nobody knew it. And when the Industrial Revolution was occurring, nobody knew it either. As for the Old Stone Age, I think there's very little chance people know they were in the Old Stone Age. But about two weeks after Hiroshima, people were talking about the Atomic Age, and there was even on the streets of New York about that time, something renamed "The Atomic Laundry." So this is the first time in history that man has been able to label what was happening to him while it was happening, and this is profoundly important, and I think, very worth considering.

At any rate, here we are—we've named ourselves. We know that we are in a transformation period, and we know that this is as important as the Copernican Revolution, the Industrial Revolution, or the

* *The Futurist* (June 1974): 122-123.

period when man stopped being nomadic and became sedentary
(there are various figures of speech, and one's about as good as
another). The principal point is that we know we're here.

We Need to Develop an Extra-somatic Memory

I think one of the outstanding things that we've got to do is to
develop, in George Land's phrase, an extra-somatic memory so that
our tendencies to blur and forget our uncomfortable lessons from the
past can be overcome. (See Grow or Die: A Unifying Principle of
Transformation by George Land. New York: Random House, 1973.) If
we look at man as a creature, one of the things that we find is that he
has a tendency to forget pain. Probably that is very important,
because if we could remember the most painful moments in our lives
and continue to remember them, we probably couldn't survive.

Now when we try to generalize this ordinary human capacity to
forget—this human amnesia—to communities, and look at communities in the past, we find the same thing. They were unable to
remember what had happened to them: they went back and built on
the slope of the volcano or the fault in San Francisco. This capacity in
the past was probably very useful. lots of people lived on islands and
there wasn't any place to go but a volcano. If they were going to survive at all, they had to go back and build there and risk being overcome by lava. Those who were left would have to go back and build
there again.

But this human capacity to forget has ceased to be a valuable characteristic. And we have no reason to believe that we can alter the kind
of human physiology that may be half a million years old. Individual
human beings are going to continue to sort out and blur and forget
the things that are too painful to remember. Therefore, we've got to
build something else; we've got to build an extra-somatic memory of
some sort. And I suggest that one of the principal pieces of research
that we might be doing at present is to figure out what will give us that
kind of continual warning system. We've done a little thinking about
it and our present feeling is that we can define it in two ways:

1. It's got to be something that changes, because any continual
   signal like "Drive slowly" has no effect on people if they see
   it day after day without any alteration.
2. Human beings have to do something in response to it: If
   you merely take in a set of warnings, even though the set of
   warnings change, they will in time have no effect.

So we need to set up some system or sets of systems that will command our attention and demand some responsive activity. One of the things that we have now in New York City is a daily report on the air—whether we can breathe or not. And that has some effect. You listen each day and you don't get totally accustomed to being suffocated, because the report changes, and some days they say you won't be as suffocated.

There are more and more reports on the state of those things in the society that are unsatisfactory, and undoubtedly this will make us more alert to the things that need to be done. It's very useful to know the pollen count, the components of the air, the toxic substances that are now going around the earth, the new radioactivity that is pouring into the atmosphere—the series of things that we're going to have to be alert to if we are going to make necessary changes.

But it isn't much use just to be told that the air is unbreatheable if there is nothing for you to do about it. Possibly if you have to stop, as they say you do in Japan, to get a little oxygen, that may have some effect. Somehow we've got to keep ourselves alert to whether an emergency situation is rising or falling and what kind of activity it demands from us.

We Have an Opportunity to Reduce the Barriers Between Nation States

In the next quarter century, we may have an opportunity which we may not have again. Within this period, we are not yet going to conquer pollution, because we are not going to have the necessary technology to prevent our contaminating the atmosphere, and we may contaminate it so badly, we won't be here.

But if we exercise our ingenuity we probably can, in the next twenty-five years, work out ways of handling our technology so it doesn't endanger the atmosphere any longer. We haven't done it yet and we don't know whether we're going to do it, and in that period when we're not sure how bad the contamination of the atmosphere is, the whole world shares the same dangers.

The whole world has never shared the same dangers before, and it may not continue to share them. It's quite conceivable that in 25 years, we may discover ways of boxing off parts of the world. Our interdependence at the present depends on trade, on certain kinds of technology, on communication, and on a few beliefs, such as the belief in the brotherhood of man, and we might get over that. (We haven't believed in the brotherhood of man very long and we could stop quite rapidly.)

But at present we have a climate of opinion that recognizes that we're all one species, that the world is highly interdependent, and that the air is endangered. That endangered air gives us something to share. Human beings have never been able to share very well. We have have always put up fences; we've always guarded frontiers against other people, and we've always tried to protect what we have against others—and, a good deal of the time, made inroads on what others have. But you can't do any of those things with the air. The air is the one substance that we can't fence off and of which we can't obtain exclusive possession. We can't protect ourselves against other people's contamination. If a toxic substance were introduced into the air in the room, we'd all go down together, and there would be no way in which on person could get an extra bit of air.

So this is an ideal moment in history—a moment that we can possibly seize to build interdependent social institutions that we haven't had before. I don't think we can assume that this opportunity will continue. Many people do. They say, "The world has become interdependent, and it will stay that way." Maybe it won't, but maybe we have a moment in history now where we do share a common danger that we can't fence off, we can't arm against, can't put up barriers to, and therefore, a moment when we may learn to protect ourselves from disaster.

It gives us a chance to deal with a problem that has beset us for a long while, the assumed contrast between what is called patriotism—loving our own country—and internationalism—a sense of the necessity of living in one world and relating to one world. We have a tendency to think of those things as opposed, but when the air is endangered, they are not opposed. The only way that we will have any hope of saving our own loved country is to cut down on the kinds of poison that are going to poison our own people and go right around the world and poison other people, and come back and poison one's own people again. So we may shift from our emphasis on frontiers to an emphasis on the center of the country. People in each country may care as deeply as they can about the center of that country.

> *"I suggested in the mid-1950s that we ought to have a Chair of the Future, like a Chair of the Middle Ages or of Classical Greece, I'm not sure I'm glad I did, because to date I don't think we've had anything like the degree of responsibility that I had envisaged. I had envisaged a group of people who were as responsible about the next decade, the next quarter-century, the next fifty years, as say, a Medievalist would be about the whole of what we know about the Middle Ages, that is, someone who would be responsible for fitting it together as well as he or she could."*

There is also the possibility that we may be able to diminish some of the other existing barriers—too much of a barrier around the nuclear family and too much of a barrier around the nation state, and not enough commitment to the community and to the wider region. We may be able to arrange it so that the more you love your family, the more you love your community, and the more you love the world. That is a possible sequence, whereas we now build a sequence that says: The more you love your family, the more you hate your neighbors, and want to beat them; and the more you care about your nation, the more you denigrate other nations. The sequences are not inevitable, but they have developed rather directly from the condition of territorial expansion and territorial protectiveness. During the next 25 years, we may have a period in which that will not be the case.

We Need to Give Everyone Children to Care About

I'd like to mention what looks to me like the best way of getting people to take a longer look into the future than they're willing to take at present and that is for every person to know small children that he or she cares about. The one way that you cannot avoid thinking about the future, is if you have a two-year-old child in front of you who is growing. When you think about ten years from now that child will be twelve; when you think of twenty, that child will be twenty-two and you begin to wonder: what will that child's children be like? This biological guarantee of foresightedness has carried human beings forward as they forgot the troubles of their past and present in concern for the future. Today we'll first have to get the old people out of the gold ghettos and get them back into the community and give each of them a child to think about.

1975

DISCUSSION [ABOUT HOW ANTHROPOLOGISTS CAN PERFORM BETTER IN APPLIED ROLES]*

Editor's Commentary

This item is a spontaneous speech to fellow anthropologists. Gone is the Meadian "we." In its place is the Meadian "I," telling her colleagues frankly and bluntly that too many of them were wedded to past and provincial habits, and were failing to apply their anthropological knowledge and wisdom effectively to the world's needs for future survival. She unsparingly and even sarcastically urges her fellow anthropologists to raise their sights higher than the level of the tribe or the village—so as to have a better chance of making their discipline truly helpful to governments grappling, at the national and international levels, with the real-world challenge of bringing about a safer and better global future. Her talk is an amalgam of wry hyperbole and trenchant insight, which those who knew her will recognize as representative of her characteristic oral—and oratorical—style at professional meetings.

* * *

I think anthropology is one of the good preparations for becoming a foreign-service officer, but the constraints under which a foreign-service officer acts are quite different from those in academia. Thus, if an anthropologist became a foreign-service officer, he would say that he no longer was an anthropologist. He could stop being a foreign-service officer and become an anthropologist again, but if he tried to become one while he was a foreign-service officer, the Lord help him.

You are asking for applied anthropology, that is, asking anthropology to organize either methods of training or methods of research to be useful to diplomats in technical assistance of other people in international affairs. We only do applied anthropology if somebody is going to apply it. We have to have a consumer. What happened in

* In: *Anthropology and Society* ed. Bela C. Maday (Washington, D.C.: The Anthropological Society of Washington, 1975).

World War II is that we had, in every government agency, people who were prepared to use what those of us who were outside or in another agency were producing. We organized that. We assembled a group of people, prepared them, and sent them to Washington, where they were put into various government agencies. Quite a few of us used to meet every other week to exchange information that otherwise would have been stamped "top secret" and never made available. We had consumers for every kind of information. We had people who wanted to know what would happen if a pilot came down in the middle of New Guinea, and what he should do not to be eaten. There was a group of anthropologists who went to work on this. Kenneth Emory ran a school in Hawaii teaching how to come down in the middle of New Guinea and not be eaten, and it was reasonably simple. We had people who wanted to know what problems were likely to come up if you were going to cooperate with the British in a particular area. There were people who wanted to know what was going on in occupied countries and wanted to know, for example, something about Burma. Later they wanted to know why, after bombing fires were put out in a Burmese town, the Burmese started the fires again.

In World War II, everybody wanted information to be used. It was a curious and unique war in which liberals and conservatives, middle-of-the-roaders and extremists, all believed that the war had to be won. So we did not have the internal tensions that we had in other wars, and we had a fine group of consumers in the State Department, in the OSS, in the OWI, in the armed services.

What we could provide was national-character studies. National-character is a useful concept when you want to know things about the relevant behavior of members of a nation. It is more useful if the number of people you are dealing with is large. It may be more useful if you are dealing with an army than if you are dealing with a shopkeeper in every city. The larger the number of people, the more they are acting in a context that they see as national. When you get down to dealing with an individual leader, like Stalin, it is of some use to know that he was an Assitene—that he came from a section of a Moslem group in Georgia—who had been converted to Christianity. But it is far more useful to know more about Russians responding to Stalin.

One reason that people dislike the study of national character as a pursuit is that it is skeletal. It is like grammar. If I described a language merely in terms of the English grammar that we all share, it would be true, but it would not describe the range of vocabulary or sensitivity or our literary knowledge. National character is like a grammar; it is a rudimentary, skeletal statement of shared kinds of behavior that can be related to shared national institutions. Hence, if you described German national character, it would leave out Goethe, and other individual Germans, and all the uniqueness. So, people say that it is not fair.

When the end of the war came, of course everybody was a little tired and anxious to go home. There was still a fair number of people in Washington who were willing to go on and work in this field. A great deal of the very best work was done right after the war. Then came the Joseph McCarthy era and the Korean War, when everybody inside the government who could have used the new material or insights that anthropologists could have produced went home or got fired. By 1952, there was no one in the government to ask for information of the sort anthropologists would have provided or to use it if it had been provided. We began to have boners of a kind that were not made in World War II. This does not mean that this information was not needed. It was impossible for anthropologists to point out that what was being done was not the brightest thing in the world. For instance, when the Poles celebrated their millennium, it was a big moment in the life of the Poles. Polish culture is one of the most straightforward cultures in the world, and we understand it quite well. We know exactly what to say to Poles that will make them happy. But what did the President of the United States do? He made a speech saying that he was going to give better tariff treatment to other Iron Curtain countries. Not a word of Poland's thousand years of defending Western Christianity, not a word about their heroes, and not a word about the help they gave us in the Revolutionary War. That was the speech that was made, and it could not have pleased the Poles in the least.

During the last fifteen years or so, no scientist has been very enthusiastic about working for the federal government. Even if the government did ask us, we were not sure we were going to tell what we knew. I think the withdrawal of anthropologists—just going and sucking their thumbs in corners or marching in demonstrations—was lamentable. If enough anthropologists had been willing to work on Viet Nam, we might have been able to do something that made some sense. But they had all withdrawn. You could not get them to go into anything. At one point we had seven good jobs in technical assistance begging for anthropologists. Most of them remained unfilled.

One reason was our beastly affluence. People do not behave well in an affluent period; we have seen this in this country. There were so many job openings that all you had to do was to write three articles on the same subject for three different journals and you could become an associate professor. People got fascinated with job-hopping and did not want to stop, and they went in for fashionable sub-jects, things that "paid off careerwise." What paid off better than kin-ship? We had ten years of concentration on kinship, out of which we got exactly nothing.

With the Peace Corps came another development. The adminis-tration who planned the Peace Corps did not need a great deal of pol-icy-level expertise from consultants. They knew that other people spoke foreign languages and that you had to learn them. They knew that other people ate other kinds of food that might upset you. So they took the volunteer in gently, through Hawaii, with some extra rice. They had heard about culture shock, which up to that point had been regarded as valuable, something needed to make one into an anthropologist. The Peace Corps planners believed that culture shock was something awful, which the Peace Corps had to cushion. They knew it was upsetting when you thought that nodding your head meant yes and you went to a society where shaking your head meant yes. So the Peace Corps began using the insights of anthropology. One of the things that we have to think of very seriously is whether we want things to just get around. Will one of our principal contri-butions, that is, to get a level of understanding of cultural differences, be part of the stock-in-trade of any educated person who has gone through college?

Anthropologists were brought into the Peace Corps to teach at a very specific level. Volunteers going to Nigeria were supposed to get a course in Nigerian ethnography, and here we ran up against some-thing that is pretty awful in anthropologists. Most of them had not done any thinking about the wider scene for ten years; they did not think about broader issues; they did not care about diplomacy; they did not know anything beyond their particular point. So what did they do? They gave a course on primitive rites among the Ibo or ini-tiation ceremonies of the Yoruba. And Nigerian students who had come over here to study international affairs picketed the course and protested. Our anthropologists were absolutely myopic and did not take anything into account except nice little bits of ethnology.We saw a lot of that. As anthropologists withdrew from the world scene, they more or less withdrew from anything having to do with govern-ment, and turned their backs on all the work that had been done. They went into deciding how many cross-cousins could dance on the head of a pin. They became parochial. If you were to ask a number of anthropologists today, say, what we could expect from a commission which is going to be chaired by a Pole and is going to have an Alger-ian, a Thai, a French Canadian, and a Tanzanian as members, there are precious few who would tackle the question. Again, just after the

Hungarian Uprising of 1956, when we suddenly had a mass of Hungarians coming over here, and nobody knew anything about Hungary, but a lot of people were going to have Hungarians living in their homes, and the dog was going to start speaking Hungarian, we were in an uneasy situation. If you had been told that you had one week to find out what you had to know about Hungarians before they got here, how many of you would have tackled it? Not very many.

Yet, we did things like this all through the war. One of the things we were suddenly asked by the Children's Bureau was to find out what was necessary to feed Greeks. We had five days to do it. Geoffrey Gorer interviewed Renzo Serano, who was an Italian with a Greek aunt and knew about Greeks. We took the information and built it into a set of hypotheses. Then he spent the weekend with Professor Dorothy Lee at Vassar, and she arranged interviews with some twenty-seven people. Then he and I met again and came back to Washington and sorted things out, and he dictated the memorandum Monday morning. Our basic finding was that there were just two parties in Greece: the people who are against the government and the people who are against the people who are against the government. They are still there, all of them. Now, we just would not tackle such things today, although we know a lot more about doing them. One of the reasons we would not tackle them is that most anthropologists have not tried doing them. You have not tackled things at that level.

There is another point, which is equally important. If you are dealing with international affairs, and especially if you are dealing with your own country's activities, you have to be sure of where you stand in your own culture at every single point, or you are no good at it. In New Guinea, where people had seen only six white men, and disliked five of them (because one was an officer and wanted to tax them, another wanted to stick needles in them, another wanted to recruit them, and somebody else was looking for oil), when anthropologists came along and said, "Tell me about yourselves," the people told them. Anthropologists did not have to have skill in rapport techniques under those circumstances. There are no people in the world who do not like to tell you about themselves, especially when nobody else has ever listened. So a few basic anthropological premises, such as that you respect other people and treat them with respect as human beings, as your equals, went a long way. We could do very nice work and come out alive and come back and write a monograph and be as prejudiced Americans as we were when we went in.

If you are going to be an applied anthropologist, it does not mean you cannot write beautiful things about the potentiality of class stratification among the Abelam. You find out which chief has two pigs and which has one. Then you observe that the man who has two pigs feeds his children better than the other. Then you observe that many have ringworm, and nobody has really proven that ringworm is connected with pigs, but it might be, and you can write a very interesting thesis about this. You do not have to understand a thing about yourself or what your own culture is.

You have to have a broader understanding and perspective when you are applying anthropology and it is affecting the future of people. When you are training a group of foreign-service officers or trying to help a technical assistance program or helping somebody write a constitution for Korea that may get applied in South Viet Nam and then may get applied in an African country, and you do not know where you stand in relation to your own culture, you are in trouble. Most anthropology departments do not concern themselves with our own culture—about who you are or what you are or who your grandfather was. They do not tell you that this is something you really ought to know. They are prepared to give some illustrations of the way Russians or English or Americans think. They are probably prepared to present one of the very few things that has been done in this field in the last fifteen years, such as Dillon's book *Gifts and Nations* (1968). This is based on fieldwork in France, in a high culture. He points out that one of our problems with the French was that we wanted to give them everything and could not think of anything they could give us. That annoyed them. We ended up with France withdrawing from NATO.

Are anthropologists prepared to deal with these large problems, with nation-states? Here we are not dealing with little groups of people, but with millions of people like the Japanese or the Chinese, or small countries, if you want to think about the differences between Singapore and Hong Kong. Doing this means that we will not have that lovely comfortable feeling that I always had because only one other person in the world knew anything about the Arapesh. (Now there is a third one, because Don Tuzin has studied some Arapesh that I did not know existed.) It gives you a great sense of mastery if you know, for example, that only three other people wrote about your little tribe, and they are dead. You can read them and be the sole expert. When we work on a large scale, we have to work with a big team of people. We have to trust other people. We have to accept the fact that we have to have an historian, an economist, a political scientist on the team, and that we can only put a special component into the picture. We are not used to putting components into anything; we are very individualistic. We are used to going out and doing the whole job ourselves, being totally in control of it, and we do not know how to cooperate with others. Yet, if we are going to do this kind of study and answer important questions—such as what is likely to happen in an international meeting that has a Polish chairman, or an English chairman; or an English chairman after a Polish chairman after a Swedish chairman—we have to cooperate with many people to find out.

I noticed that Dr. Fisher did not mention Johnson's book *Negotiating with the Russians* (1951), which is a magnificent study. It resulted from the Columbia University Research in Contemporary Cultures project. We asked Philip Mosley to give us an account of his experience in negotiation with the Russians, which was later developed into a book. All sorts of people who had negotiated with the Russians were asked to discuss their experiences in different contexts. This kind of thing can be produced, but only if anthropologists are willing to pay attention to larger entities. I would not have been able to testify for Senate Committees on International Relations if I had not done all those war years of fieldwork. Conversely, what I had to offer to the national and international field was the result of having done very fine (in the sense of fine-grained) fieldwork on very small groups of people. We can take that kind of training and put it to use on a larger scale if we follow a different course from the one we are following at present. In my course at Columbia, all but a few illustrations have to come out of World War II because hardly anything worthwhile has been done in this field since.

It may be important to realize that none of the anthropologists who worked on those World War II projects were young. Most of us had two, three, or four field trips under our belts when we started. I doubt if this is a field in which people should start. However, anyone who is working on the Tolai or the Bemba should pay attention to the government of New Guinea and the government of Australia. Mostly anthropologists regard district officers as uncongenial people, from whom one has to get away as quickly as possible.

In conclusion, I might add that we are in far greater danger now than we were in World War II. Our chances of survival are far less, but I do not see many anthropologists working on population, on the environment, on the legislation, agreements, and negotiations that are necessary if we are going to have a world that does not blow itself up or choke itself to death.

REFERENCES

Bennett, Raymond, and Joseph S. Johnson. 1951. Negotiating with the Russians. Boston: World Peace Foundation.

Dillon, Wilton S. 1968 Gifts and Nations. The Hague: Mouton.

1977

OUR OPEN-ENDED FUTURE*

Editor's Commentary

This final selection is the typescript of a lecture given, and later personally edited, by Mead. During the 1970s she gave closely similar versions of this lecture scores of times to a variety of public audiences. She gave it so often, as she neared the end of her life, that it stands as striking evidence of her deep concern for the future, and of her determination to communicate her anticipations and visions while she still had breath to give them voice. The lecture is a clear expression of Margaret Mead's dedication to anthropology, humanism, and activism, and hence a fine way to conclude this book.

*   *   *

I use the term "open-ended" to suggest that our future is neither predetermined nor predictable: it is, rather, something which lies within our hands, to be shaped and molded by the choices we make in present time. In order to better understand the process of its unfolding, we try to learn from what has happened in the past.

We are able now to trace the process of evolution from the origins of life on our planet through the successive appearance of mammals, primates, early man (used in the inclusive sense of humankind), and man, to the development of writing and growth of cities. Throughout the history of cosmic, biological, and social evolution, there have been options and turning points; there were always various directions which evolution could have taken, and choices that were made. It is curious, however, that man is always seeking neat, rational explanations of "why" the events of the past happened as they did. "The dinosaurs *had* to disappear,' he says, " because they were too slow." His explanations make it seem inevitable, as though that were the *only* direction evolution could possibly have taken. In the same way, we'd like to believe the appearance of man was inevitable. But was it? However valuable we feel that man is, and as delighted as we are to be

* Typsescript, edited by Dr. Mead.

here now, the fact may be that man did not have to happen at all—
that he just happened to happen!

This is not an easy idea for us to accept, but it is a more realistic
approach to understanding our future than to try to extrapolate what
will be from what exists today. It is an erroneous procedure used frequently, for example, in social statistics. Working from effect back to
a presumed cause, statistics now show that a very large number of
juvenile delinquents come from broken homes; but if we start with
the number of children who come from broken homes and work forward, we find that most of them do not, in fact, become delinquents.
It is when one works backwards that one gets a sense—a false sense—
of predictability and predetermination; it doesn't hold true when
dealing with the future. Therefore, when astronomers tell us that our
sun has some six or seven billion years left to shine, it just means that
life on our planet could *potentially* survive that long; it does not mean
it *will*. Nor does the fact that technology is becoming increasingly
dominant today mean that technology will necessarily rule human
society in the future. Technology, in itself, has no power over us; there
are only human beings who choose to use it in a variety of different
ways. Thus, when we view the future as open-ended, we accept a very
concrete responsibility for how we handle what is happening today.

Just twenty years ago, in the 1950's, we believed that one day
spaceships would be able to move us out to colonize other planets in
our solar system. In this belief, people did not worry about exhaust-
ing our planet's resources and the booming population; they perpetuated a very exploitative economy which is at the root of our most
serious problems today.

We now know, thanks to more recent scientific advances, that we are
all alone in this solar system of ours; there is no place in it for us but this
small and very vulnerable planet we call Earth, and nobody on this earth
but "Homo sap," such as he is. That is all we've got. For the first time in
human history, we are aware of our responsibility to protect the earth
and all life that lives upon it. This awareness has already significantly
altered our vision of future alternatives—just as further knowledge (i.e.,
the discovery of other intelligent civilizations in the galaxy and communication with them) will give us a different perspective on man's place in
the universe and make our current notions of the future obsolete.

GOING BACK TO LOOK AHEAD

A broadening of consciousness has been taking place since the time
the first Sputnik was launched, and awareness of time and space was

expanding in unprecedented ways. Our scientists are projecting life further into the future and further out into our solar system, the galaxy, and the universe. Simultaneously, there is a growing interest on the part of our students in the past, and in something called "inner space." They are exploring ancient philosophies, archeology, the development of early man, life under the sea—and they are acutely interested in what goes on inside their own heads. This is a legitimate quest for enlightenment about human behavior and how it relates to events which occurred in the past, which could occur under other circumstances, and which might occur in the future if we work to make them happen.

How hard we are willing to work for the future depends largely upon our image of what that future will be like. If we take the pessimistic view that human nature is getting progressively worse and the future will be grim, it is tempting to just give up, refuse to bring more children into the world, and to live out our lives consuming all the gasoline we can. If, on the other hand, we feel that it *is* possible to master our present-day problems, we can summon up the dedication and political will necessary to create a better world.

Several options for human society in the future appear plausible. (Obviously, those we mention here are not by any means the only ones—and by tomorrow, they may not even appear plausible any more—but they do raise important questions to be considered.)

One possibility is that if certain tendencies in today's society are carried to extremes, they might lead to the development of a very powerful politico-economical structure within which human beings are decidedly subordinate, existing solely to serve and perpetuate the particular political economic machinery. Human components, however, are annoyingly unpredictable and unreliable. To keep things running smoothly, people would have to be shaped, conditioned, desexed, and "improved" by genetic engineering to insure their proper functioning. Call it *Brave New World*, *1984*, or any other name; it could happen.

A second possibility is that we may let ourselves get carried away with technology in and for itself. Originally, technology was conceived of as expanding our own capacities, just as the microscope and the telescope expanded our abilities to see the very small and the very large, and opened up whole new worlds to man. The computer, used as an extension of the human mind and memory, is a marvelous invention that can produce simultaneous views of a large number of variables and present alternatives of an extraordinary scope. But if we lose our perspective on who is serving whom, the computers can seem to have a life of their own. So, some prophesy that, eventually, we'll be able to build computers that won't need people any more. They can build their own societies, travel into outer space, and kick us off like an obsolete stage in the evolutionary process.

This appeals to certain scientists. They would rather see babies born in test tubes than in a woman's womb and eliminate the differences between men and women which sexual reproduction maintains. They would negate the importance of prenatal life within the mother's body, the relationship between the child and both its parents, the family structure—all the things that shape an embryo into a very human being and from the essential nature of our humanity.

People can get very excited about technology. First we invent a new device which helps the blind to sense the presence of objects and enables them to move around rather well without sight; then pretty soon someone comes up with the bright idea that we don't really need eyes anymore, that eyes are not as good as the devices we can invent. It is very important that we start asking ourselves seriously just how much of this technology we really want; how much of it we need, and why do we intuitively fear it?

There are, of course, different kinds of options open to us as well. We might choose to create a human-oriented society which exists and evolves in harmony with the natural world. This supposes, of course, that we take upon ourselves the responsibility not to spoil, exhaust, contaminate, or destroy our biosphere. It supposes we are willing to recognize our basic nature as one which shares the fundamental properties of life with all other living things. We would have to accept children being born of women and fathered by men; that the young grow up, mature, grow old, and die. We would have to respect such things as part of life, part of the very process that has made it possible for us to come as far as we have come.

We might choose, also, to trust the capacity of the human brain to get us to evolutionary stages far beyond our own. It is, after all, the same human brain with which we got from the Stone Age to the present, with which once human beings could learn to count to five, and then conceived of calculus. Only a few of our most brilliant humans have even tapped a meager ten percent of man's extraordinary brain, so it is not at all unreasonable to believe it is capable of achievements far greater than anything known to us today.

The "human-oriented" society does not in any way imply a rejection of technology. It simply means that technology would be subordinate to human ends and that human needs would be considered primary. It is an option embraced by many young people today who are striving to maintain a relationship with the living world.

SURVIVAL AND SCIENCE

Formerly, our tasks for survival were very clearly defined. Females give their lives to producing children while males gave theirs to supplying food so that some of the offspring would live into the reproductive years. But now there are more than enough of our species on the planet, and our numbers may be destroying the atmosphere, the oceans, and all of life which depends on them. This extraordinary crisis has radically changed the nature of our task; we must now focus on protecting our endangered environment.

A new awareness of the problem has reduced the danger to some extent. Only a short time ago, when the United Nations was preparing the Stockholm Conference on the Environment, at least half the governments of the world did not know what it was about. But by the time the Conference convened in 1972, all those nations were sending representatives who could discuss the problems intelligently. A United Nations-fostered awareness has produced a response among the people of this globe and has given rise to technologies which attempt to deal with the problems.

Awareness notwithstanding, human beings have a tendency to forget. In cases of extreme tragedy over which we have no control, forgetfulness is a blessing; it gives people the strength to go on living and caring. But in cases where we have the knowledge to understand the causes of disaster, to rectify its damages, and to prevent its reoccurrence, forgetfulness is inexcusable. If England's killer fog had occurred 150 years ago, it would have been called an "act of God" and they'd have tried to forget it happened. But in our day, we know enough scientifically to do something about it. In our day, the kind of forgetfulness which allows Los Angeles to build hospitals on a known fault is neither beneficial nor functional; it is criminal. It means that people are neither alert nor responsible. They are neither learning from disaster, nor determining how to avoid it in the future.

The need for alertness and responsibility raises an important question: "On the part of whom?" Is management of our environment something which concerns scientists alone? Is knowledge about such matters beyond the reach of the lay public?

There is a popular, but erroneous, idea that people are either scientists or non-scientists, and that a scientist understands all of science, while a non-scientist does not understand much of anything at all. It is not true. In the first place, many of our scientists are highly specialized in one particular field and they may not know a great deal about what is going on in other scientific fields. Scientists, therefore, are as unfamiliar with many important new developments as any intelligent lay citizen, and the distinction we've created between the two groups is essentially false.

The second mistake that we commonly make is to believe that modern science has become so complex that only a small, select group of "magicians" can possibly understand it. Naturally, it requires years of specialized study and training to practice any given science, but there is no reason why ordinarily intelligent citizens cannot grasp a general synopsis of discoveries, developments, and applications if our scientists are willing to communicate to them in straightforward English.

Not only do we as citizens have a right to know what is going on, but given our current situation, we have a *responsibility* to know. Only when the majority of people understand the severe risks we are running with our present policies will they be able to exert the political and economic pressures necessary for effective action.

Our problems are not essentially technological (we already have the technology to clean up the atmosphere and the oceans and we have the technology to develop clean, safe energy sources); rather, they are problems of political *will*. Their solutions depend upon the willingness—not of scientists alone, but of society as a whole—to spend the necessary time, effort ... and money.

SURVIVAL AND LOVE

Political "will" is a question of motivation. How, we ask ourselves, can people care enough, work hard enough, and sacrifice enough to save their environment? How do we get them to the point where they will commit themselves as completely to the common good as they do to their own well-being and that of their families? Historically, human beings have never behaved very well in this respect except during wartime. When the things they care for the most— their country, their family, their religion, their language, the ashes of their ancestors, and the altars of their gods—have been under direct attack, they have proven themselves capable of sacrifice on every level. But war is dangerous and devastating. Is it the only way to inspire dedicated bravery?

The conditions facing us now are as threatening as any war has ever been. Perhaps, when people become aware of this, they will transcend their shortsighted selfishness. Perhaps they will feel a different order of priorities and rise to the height of their strength, if they could be made to realize that it is a matter of defending everything they love and live for against tragedy and death.

If a person can't love his or her own children, whom are they going to love? How does he or she learn to love anyone? A capacity to love, just like a capacity to do anything else, is a process of expansion. Nobody starts out by loving the entire world (in fact, people who claim they do are usually intolerant and hostile towards the individuals closest to them). But to those who first experience the love of their own families, there can come a realization that no sharp lines exist around the nuclear family, around the community, or even around one's nation, to be loved exclusively. Loyalty to one particular religion or political system need not negate an appreciation and respect for different cultures, religious faiths, languages, and political philosophy. On the contrary, the more we learn about different people of the world, the more we discover how much we are alike. The development of children and family ties are the basis of a very common and universal human experience of love.

In the last one hundred years, there has been much conflict between nationalists (those who believe that love for one's country comes before all else) and internationalists. Today this polarity is beginning to disappear. The environmental crisis is forcing us to see that nationalism and internationalism are actually one and the same thing. Pollution hasn't got the slightest respect for political borders. Any contamination of the waters or the atmosphere in one locality directly affects the viability of others. It has now become very clear that no nation on this planet can save its own without saving the rest of the world and, at the same time, there can be no protection for the world as a whole unless we are alert to what endangers our own land. One depends upon the other, and both depend upon people caring deeply enough to make the sacrifices necessary to preserve it all.

BRIDGING THE PAST AND FUTURE

Certain facts of modern life act as limiting conditions on what we may be able to accomplish, and they will have their effects on the shape of things to come. One such factor is what we commonly call the "generation gap." The term tends to suggest something that has often occurred in the past and will probably exist in the future between parents and children or teachers and students, but actually, what we are experiencing today is somewhat broader than that. It reflects a tremendous difference in thinking and an inability to communicate between young people who grew up after World War II and those who had grown up before.

When the first of this young generation came to college and started thinking seriously, they took a good fresh look at us "older folks," and they were quite legitimately appalled at what they saw. At Columbia University, in California, France, and all around the world, our children felt themselves profoundly dissatisfied, and (having grown up with electricity, where one presses a button for immediate results) they determined to fix it all up that very year.

Older people do not understand the questions and the rebellion of the young. Youngsters do not understand the answers older people give them. They do not understand, for instance, why we need enough bombs to destroy Russian cities ten times over. "What," they keep asking, "are we going to do with the extra nine?"

The people on either side of the gap are coming from different worlds; they have different perceptions of reality. It is similar to the difference between our grandparents who came from Europe and their native-born children who took the New World ways for granted. Our grandparents were immigrants in space, whereas now, people of the older generation feel that they are immigrants in time. We grew up before television, the bomb, computers, and interplanetary missions; before the world became one global community; and before space probes revealed our isolation in the solar system. We still cannot quite believe that man has really stepped upon the moon, and we surely cannot take it all for granted like the young. Our consciousness is still struggling to embrace the expansion of inner and outer universes in which our children and grandchildren skip back and forth so naturally.

But older people cannot be taken lightly. They have almost all the power, money, and quite a bit of know-how; they can wreck the world long before the young assume positions of power and authority. Therefore, it is very important that the young continue to ask the right questions and that the old seek to understand their meaning; it is important that we establish communication across the gap to find some valid answers.

This will not be easy. Traditionally, children have been able to see in adults a model of what they will one day be, and parents could find in their offspring a renewal of what they had once been. This sense of continuity is denied to us today. This particular generation gap is not going to disappear when our youngsters mature and grow old with children of their own. It will be with us for as long as any of those who grew up before World War II remain alive, because the current generation will not ever resemble them.

Alienation between the generations is aggravated further in a society like ours because people do not think and plan two or three generations ahead. We give our children an education and then we turn them loose to carve out a place in the social structure for themselves. The old, banished to ghettos of their own, are shamefully neglected. People, both young and old, are lonely in a way that human beings have never been lonely before. We have lost the sense of connection between our individual selves and the universal flow of life.

That sense of connection has a lot to do with what our future will be like. If we construct a society in which the three generations live together, work together, and interact (this does not mean we need three-generation biological families sharing a household; it merely means building communities in which children are in contact with the end of life and old people see the new beginnings), it would have profound effects upon a sense of social and political responsibility. Old people are not going to care deeply and personally about what is going to happen fifty or sixty years from now unless they can be with some loved, small children who will be living long after they are dead. The young, in contact with the living past, will benefit from a better understanding of the present and a more responsible commitment to the future.

RECOMMENDED READINGS

Bertalanffy, Ludwig von, and Anatol Rapoport, eds. *General Systems: Yearbook of the Society for General Systems Research.*

Brown, Harrison, and others. *Next Hundred Years.* New York: Viking, 1957; reprinted 1963, Compass C 135. New York: Viking.

Commoner, Barry. *The Closing Circle.* New York: Knopf, 1971.

Maruyama, Magoroh. *1970 American Anthropological Association Cultural Futurology Symposium: PreConference Volume.* University of Minnesota, Training Center for Community Programs, 1970. (Mimeographed.)

Mead, Margaret. *Continuities in Cultural Evolution.* New Haven and London: Yale University Press, 1964; reprinted in paperback 1966.

Scientists' Institute for Public Information. *Environment.* (A monthly publication.)

Waddington, Conrad H. *The Ethical Animal.* Chicago: University of Chicago Press, 1961; reprinted 1967

INDEX